MW00658672

משנה

ArtScroll Series®

Rabbi Nosson Scherman / Rabbi Meir Zlotowitz

General Editors

Timeless Lessons for Today from Rabbi Moshe Chaim Luzzatto's

MESILLAS YESHARIM

Published by

Mesorah Publications, ltd

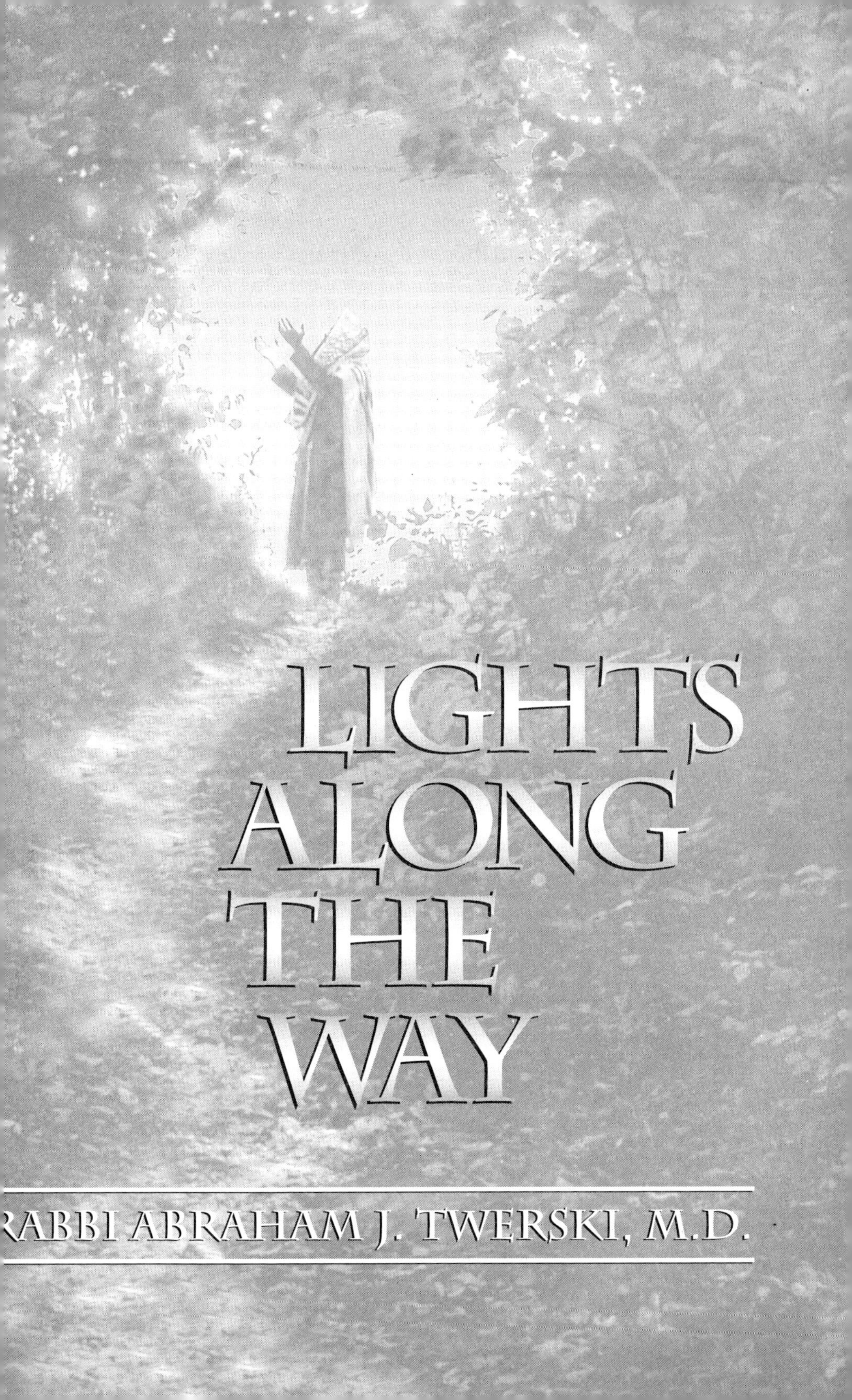

LIGHTS ALONG THE WAY

RABBI ABRAHAM J. TWERSKI, M.D.

FIRST EDITION
First Impression . . . September 1995
Second Impression . . . May 1996

Published and Distributed by
MESORAH PUBLICATIONS, Ltd.
4401 Second Avenue
Brooklyn, New York 11232

Distributed in Europe by
J. LEHMANN HEBREW BOOKSELLERS
20 Cambridge Terrace
Gateshead, Tyne and Wear
England NE8 1RP

Distributed in Israel by
SIFRIATI / A. GITLER – BOOKS
4 Bilu Street
P.O.B. 14075
Tel Aviv 61140

Distributed in Australia & New Zealand by
GOLDS BOOK & GIFT CO.
36 William Street
Balaclava 3183, Vic., Australia

Distributed in South Africa by
KOLLEL BOOKSHOP
22 Muller Street
Yeoville 2198, Johannesburg, South Africa

THE ARTSCROLL SERIES®
LIGHTS ALONG THE WAY

4401 Second Avenue / Brooklyn, N.Y. 11232 / (718) 921-9000

ISBN:
0-89906-338-1 (hard cover)
0-89906-339-X (paperback)

Printed in the United States of America by Noble Book Press Corp.
Bound by Sefercraft Quality Bookbinders, Ltd., Brooklyn, N.Y.

In Loving Memory of My Wife

Devorah Golda

דבורה גאלדא בת הר״ר יעקב ע״ה

ד׳ תמוז תשנ״ה

4 Tammuz 5755

Author's Introduction

In the eighteenth century there was a significant ideological phenomenon in the Torah world. Within one decade two major currents of ethical teachings came into being. The work we are now about to study, *Mesillas Yesharim* was written by Rabbi Moshe Chaim Luzzato (Ramchal) in 1740. In 1734 the Baal Shem Tov began the teachings of chassidus. A century later Rabbi Yisrael of Salant launched the Mussar Movement. All three emphasized the need for refining one's character traits and striving for greater spirituality.

True, there had been several major works prior to this; e.g., *Duties of the Heart* (*Chovos Halevavos*) by Rabbeinu Bachya (circa 1090) and *Gates of Teshuvah* (*Shaarei Teshuvah*) by Rabbeinu Yonah (circa 1220). But the study of character refinement was not incorporated into the yeshivos and taught formally until this later period. Apparently people had been able to derive principles and techniques for the pursuit of spirituality on their own by recourse to the Talmud, the Torah commentaries, and the ethical works. For whatever reason, the need for more formal study was recognized essentially independently by these three Torah leaders.

The institution of change in Jewish lifestyle invariably arouses suspicion and opposition, and this was no exception. The chassidic movement was firmly opposed by some of the Torah establishment, and the attempt to introduce formal study of mussar into yeshivos was also met with much resistance. Time has vindicated these great innovators, and the movements of chassidus and mussar have flourished. These were clearly ideas whose time had come.

The works of Ramchal antedated both chassidus and mussar, and *Path of the Just*, perhaps the most popular of his works, became the primer of mussar. Its greatness and importance can be gauged by a statement by Rabbi Yisrael of Salant, who said, "Volumes like those of the Noda BeYehudah (Rabbi Yechezkel Landau) I can write without limit, but I could not compose even a single page of *Mesillas Yesharim*." If one understands the utter humility and self-effacement of Rabbi Yisrael, and the incomparable and unfathomable genius of the Noda BeYehudah, one can then understand the full meaning of this statement, and the regard with which *Path of the Just* was held.

There are several Talmudic statements that emphasize the primacy of character development. The Midrash states that Torah and mitzvos were given for no other reason than to refine people's character (*Vayikra Rabbah* 13:3). The Creator, with His thorough knowledge of the essence and psychological composition of man, provided the "manufacturer's instruction booklet" for the proper functioning of His product. Only by following the manufacturer's instructions, Torah and mitzvos, can we achieve optimum function.

In my book *Let Us Make Man* (CIS 1987), I dwell on a theme of the Baal Shem Tov, who points out that whereas all creation was carried out by G-d Himself, the expression for creation of man was *naaseh adam, let* ***us*** *make man.* The "us," says the Baal Shem Tov, refers to man and G-d. Only together can the being called man come to fruition.

Let us probe this a bit more deeply. Ramchal points out that with one exception all living things are created in a state of completion, and as they grow the only change they undergo is in size. Some creatures do undergo changes in form, as when the caterpillar becomes a butterfly, but these changes are not the result of any determination on the part of the creature to change itself, but are programmed into its genes. Angels, on the other hand, are totally spiritual beings that undergo no change nor growth whatever.

The human being is the only creature that is incomplete at creation. In addition to physical growth similar to that of other living things, the human being must develop his character and personality. These are not inherent at birth, and although there may be certain traits which are genetic, a person has the capacity to modify his character traits, even to radically transform them.

The definition of man, therefore, is that he is a being that is created incomplete, and must work towards his own perfection. Since this is the being that G-d wanted, it is obvious that man could not have been created complete with a fully developed character and personality, because a being that is complete at birth is either angel or animal, not man. G-d therefore said to man, *"naaseh adam, let* **us** *make man"*; i.e., you and I together. I will give you all the potential, and you are to develop it to its highest degree.

Man reaches his ultimate goal by maximizing his potential for spirituality, and this is done by utilizing the manual and fulfilling the prescribed formula, observance of Torah and mitzvos.

A prerequisite for Torah is *derech eretz*, decent behavior which G-d expected of man even in absence of Torah teachings. The Talmud says, "Had the Torah not been given, man would have been expected to learn proper behavior from observation of nature. He would have learned respect for private property from ants, modesty from cats, and fidelity from pigeons" (*Eruvin* 100b).

One might ask, Is it not possible that without Torah man might have chosen to learn rapaciousness from tigers, promiscuity from dogs, and vanity from peacocks? The answer lies in the statement by King Solomon, that G-d created man with a sense of propriety (*Ecclesiastes* 7:29), and man would have been expected to exercise his innate sense of judgment to emulate desirable characteristics.

This verse from *Ecclesiastes* is germane to this book, since the verse reads that "G-d made man *yashar* (straight, simple, just)" and the title of our work is *Mesillas Yesharim*. Man's work in character development is thus to reach the state of *yashar* which is natural to him.

The concept of *derech eretz* being a prerequisite for Torah is discussed by the chassidic master Rabbi Mendel of Rimanov, who points out that the manna was given to the Israelites in the desert prior to Sinai, and that they were told that each person was to gather a measure of manna for each day, as a test whether they would observe the Torah or not (*Exodus* 16:4). "What is the relationship of the manna to Torah?" asked Rabbi Mendel.

Rabbi Mendel answers that the basic concepts of decent human behavior, respect for the rights of others, and the avoidance of greed and envy are based on a trust that G-d provides each person with his appropriate needs. Greed, envy, and theft, are the results of a person believing unjustifiably that he can gain by such feelings and behavior. If a person recognizes that he would receive only what is to his optimum welfare, there would be no reason to covet or acquire another's belongings. Decent behavior therefore requires a sincere trust in G-d.

This was what the Israelites learned from the manna. Each person received his appropriate share. If one gathered less, he would find his portion increased by itself, and if he gathered more than his due, he would find that the excess disappeared. If someone tried to provide today for tomorrow's needs, he found that anything left over was spoiled. The message was clear: Each day G-d will give you exactly what you need, no more and no less.

When the Israelites discovered that their exact needs were being provided by G-d, they were then able to be free of undesirable character traits, which was a precondition for receiving the Torah. This is why the Talmud says that the Torah is given only to those who eat the manna (*Tanchuma Beshalach* 20). This applies even when we do not have the manna, because we still have the *principles* of the manna: You will get precisely what you need, and there is no reason to infringe upon the rights of others, neither to covet what is theirs nor to take from them.

The goal of this book is thus to point out the path whereby a person can attain the status of *yashar*. As mentioned earlier, being *yashar* is the natural state of man, but whereas animals and angels are created in the completed natural state, man must follow a path that will bring him to the desired state of spiritual perfection. This is the *mesillas yesharim*, the path of the just.

I wish to alert the reader to my tendency to use examples from my work in treatment of alcoholism and drug addiction. In the Scriptures we find numerous instances where the prophet reprimands people for their errant behavior by comparing them to a person who is intoxicated, e.g., "drunk though not with wine; staggering but not with ale" (*Isaiah* 29:9). There are striking similarities between the character defects in the non-alcoholic and the alcoholic, the differences being that in the latter they may be more pronounced and recognizable, hence they may serve as very effective illustrations to demonstrate or explain a particular issue. By the same token, techniques that have been effective in eliminating character defects in the alcoholic may be equally effective in the non-alcoholic. The advantage in using these illustrations is that they are concrete examples taken from actual life situations, hence they may be more impressive than discussing such problems in the abstract. I therefore ask the reader's indulgence to bear with me as I try to make the task of character refinement and achieving spirituality just a bit more lucid if not actually easier.

As an interesting aside, the first edition to *Mesillas Yesharim* was printed in 5500 (1740) in Amsterdam. It had been known for many years that there was a manuscript of the book in the archives of the library in Moscow, but the first access to this manuscript was not achieved until 1991.

The manuscript is in Ramchal's own handwriting, and its form is that of a dialogue between a *chacham* (a wise person) and a *Chassid* (a pious person). In the introduction Ramchal says,

> *There was a man whom G-d had granted a wise and understanding heart, who dedicated himself to investigate and search with wisdom into all that transpires under the heavens. Day and night he was relentless in pursuit of research and analysis into every field of knowledge, to increase his learning and expand his wisdom, whether in the explanation of the Torah and mitzvos or in the study of nature and creation with all of its ramifications and processes. He would set his mind to every difficult subject, saying, "Bring out your forces and let us see their greatness" (Judges 9:29), because his entire ambition was to expand his knowledge and the discoveries of his intellect, whereby his mind could demonstrate the glory of its greatness.*
>
> *One of the various groups of people he would regularly encounter was a group of pious people (Chassidim) who would practice their solitude and piety with sincerity, engaging in recitation of the Psalms and extensive prayer. Each time he saw them he would be stimulated to think, "What do these people do? What is their interest, their intellectual pursuits, and how is it that they appear to be at peace and their minds are tranquil? They do not appear to be upset, they do not appear pressured to know, to investigate, and to understand. The recitation of twenty Psalms a day appears to put their minds at ease, while I agonize to gather wisdom and knowledge, and my desire to discover new information gives me no rest. I find no satisfaction in anything other than intellectual exercises and reaching clear and true principles. I wish I could spend two or three hours with one of these Chassidim to hear from him just what is the knowledge he derives from all his solitude and his constant reading of the books of the pious. I cannot imagine*

what he gets out of them. I never wasted even one hour on these books, and I never had any desire to read them knowing that I will not acquire any knowledge from them. Yet these people study these books from morning to night, as though they had never heard that a person must be just, righteous, and trustworthy, and not be wicked and sinful. I swear, I have an intense desire to listen to one of these Chassidim and find out what it is that satisfies his spirit."

One day the chacham met one of the Chassidim with whom he had been friends in his youth, and this latter person had joined a group of Chassidim and he had not seen him until this day. He was most happy to meet him and said, "Finally, this is a day I have been hoping for." He ran toward him with much joy, and they greeted each other warmly, and he brought him to his home where they rested a bit.

After the introduction, Ramchal proceeds to present a dialogue wherein the *chacham* interrogates the *Chassid,* who clarifies for him the pursuit of spirituality. Whereas the content of this version of *Mesillas Yesharim* is essentially the same as the narrative form, the dialectic does provide a unique flavor which makes this version worthwhile reading even for someone who is thoroughly familiar with the narrative version. Hopefully, the dialectic version will be translated into English thus making it accessible to all.

The sections from Ramchal's *Mesillas Yesharim* are free translations, and not exactly word for word from the text. Furthermore, these are only excerpts and do not represent the full text. The reader is urged to read the complete text of this important work and, as Ramchal recommends in his introduction, to re-read it numerous times.

Rabbi Moshe Chaim Luzzatto

The life of Rabbi Moshe Chaim Luzzatto (Ramchal) was brief, unbelievably productive, and terribly tragic. Ramchal was born in 5467 (1707) and died just short of his fortieth birthday in 5507 (1747). This latter fact is tragic not only because we lost so many years of one of our greatest luminaries, but also because it thwarted one of his greatest desires, as we shall see.

Ramchal was born in Padua, Italy, at that time a major Jewish community. His father was a well-to-do merchant, and apparently provided his brilliant son with instruction in languages as well as Torah. Ramchal was a child prodigy, and his genius was appreciated by the local *rav*, Rabbi Isaiah Bassan, an accomplished Talmudic scholar, who later defended Ramchal against his attackers. Rabbi Bassan writes about Ramchal "... while a very young child, he came to love the Torah with an intense affection, and when he grew into boyhood he was modest, shunning vanity and the foolish impulses of childhood and boyhood. G-d gave him the capacity to listen and to understand, and he became to me like a son." Rabbi Bassan continues to tell how as a young boy Ramchal developed a passion for *kabbalah*.

Ramchal was a literary giant of the first order. He stands beside Rabbi Yehudah HaLevi and Ibn Ezra in his composition of poetry, and he wrote major works on logic. He wrote dramas in which the characters are traits personified, as in *Layesharim Tehillah* where the dramatis personae are Truth, Praise, Passion, Pride, Honesty, etc. By age seventeen he had already authored thousands of pages.

Ramchal followed in the footsteps of King David, composing 150 psalms, corresponding to those in the Scriptures, a brilliant work which, as we will see, brought him much distress. He wrote an introduction to the Talmud, and guides to proper usage of the Hebrew language.

But Ramchal's greatest love was *kabbalah*, and he wrote a major work which he called *The Second Zohar*. Many of his writings in *kabbalah* have been lost, but some have been preserved and are respected as classics, most notably *The One-Hundred-Thirty-Eight Gates of Wisdom*.

Ramchal had a magnetic personality and was an inspiring teacher. At age twenty he taught *kabbalah* to a closely knit group, many of them far senior to him in years. This group accepted him as their unquestioned leader, and they developed a set of bylaws to which they adhered, among them: "Not to treat lightly any rabbinic law, however rigid, or any Jewish custom, but to observe it even more than required, in order to be blameless before the G-d of Israel; to beware of any untruth, so that our lips pronounce nothing but the absolute truth; to complete a review of all the Scriptures, and even the *Mishnah* every month; the merits accrued by their study of Torah would go to the credit of all of Israel rather than to them as individuals." The group studied the *Zohar* intensively, and took an oath not to reveal any of the *kabbalistic* knowledge they acquired without the permission of their teacher (Ramchal).

To understand what transpired to Ramchal we must preface with some historical background. The hope for the ultimate redemption by the Messiah is established by Rambam as one of the thirteen principles of faith that every Jew must accept. We can understand that this hope for redemption was the elixir of life for the Jews who lived under the oppression of the feudal lords and the widespread anti-Semitism in 15th-16th century eastern Europe. Pogroms were frequent, and no Jew could feel secure with his very life, let alone his belongings. In 1648 there were terrible massacres by the Cossacks of Bogdan Chmielnicki, and rivers of Jewish blood flooded the Ukraine.

The despair of the Jews of eastern Europe had reached its nadir, and they were more desperate than ever for Divine redemption. In 1665, a charismatic scholar, well versed in *kabbalah*, and who had attained a substantial following, pronounced himself as the Messiah, promising to fulfill the biblical promise of returning all Jews to their homeland with restoration of the throne of David. This false Messiah, Shabbatai Zevi, with his erudition and personal charm, appealing to people who thirsted for redemption as never before, was able to gather a huge throng of believers, who swore allegiance to him as the Redeemer of Israel. More than just a few notable rabbis of the time were among his followers. Shabbatai Zevi cited *kabbalistic* proofs of his mission, as well as *kabbalistic* predictions that this was indeed to be the year of the ultimate redemption.

This delusion came to a bitter end when Shabbatai Zevi converted to Islam, but not before he had misled thousands of people, some of whom continued to believe in him even after he renounced Judaism! The despair of having their hopes dashed caused much chaos, depression, and confusion among Jews. Many rabbis felt that Shabbatai Zevi had allowed his imagination to soar to psychotic proportions as a result of his delving too deeply into *kabbalah,* and the study of the latter was therefore discouraged.

In a climate such as this, the formation of a secret group to study *kabbalah,* with the declared purpose to hasten the ultimate redemption, and with the glorification of a charismatic young man as their leader, was not looked upon kindly. Matters might have remained rather calm, however, had not one of Ramchal's enthusiastic students written a letter to a friend, in which he described the eminence of his teacher, and in his great admiration for Ramchal he stated that Ramchal is regularly visited by a *maggid,* a heavenly spirit that reveals to him the secrets of the Torah, and that the souls of the Patriarchs come to teach him. This letter fell into the hands of Rabbi Moses Hagiz, a venerated Torah scholar whose father had led the outcry against Shabbatai Zevi, and who was himself vehemently attempting to uproot the remnant of Shabbatai Zevi followers, who were continuing to hail him as the Messiah even after his conversion. Rabbi Hagiz felt that there was too great a danger of repetition of the Shabbatai Zevi debacle, and that a young man who was delving so deeply into the *kabbalah* that he believed he was visited by angels and spirits was likely to think himself the Messiah. (Incidentally, the phenomenon of great Torah authorities being taught by a *maggid* was not unusual. Rabbi Joseph Caro, the compiler of the *Shulchan Aruch,* wrote a book containing the teachings of a *maggid,* and Rabbi Chaim of Volozhin stated that the Gaon of Vilna was visited by a *maggid*.)

Rabbi Hagiz wrote to the rabbis of Venice to take action to subdue this young man's influence. Rabbi Bassan, Ramchal's mentor, defended him vigorously. However, the seeds of suspicion had been planted, and in the next few years Ramchal repeatedly had to defend himself against unjust accusations, such as that he believed that his 150 psalms were superior to those of King David and would replace them after the redemption, and that his *kabbalistic* work, *The Second Zohar,* superseded the original *Zohar.* The established rabbinate ordered Ramchal to turn over his manuscripts to the custody of Rabbi Bassan, and to cease and desist from any further *kabbalistic* writings until he reached forty years of age, and then only if he lived in the Holy Land.

Although Ramchal reluctantly complied with this ordinance, he continued to be suspect, and of course, there is never a dearth of agitators who thrive on creating havoc. One such person was Shlomo Zalman, who reported to the Rabbinate that Ramchal was engaging in Satanic rituals, and that even his mentor, Rabbi Bassan, had discovered Satanic paraphernalia in Ramchal's possession. Although Rabbi Bassan protested that this was a flagrant lie, the harm was done. The Rabbinate issued a *cherem* (excommunication) ordering Ramchal's books to be burned and pronouncing a curse on anyone who studied them.

As a result of financial reversals and also no doubt to escape this hostile environment, the Luzzatto family moved to Amsterdam in 1732. The Jewish community of Amsterdam welcomed the great scholar with open arms, and he finally enjoyed a few years of peace, years during which he wrote *Derech Tevunos,* an Introduction to the Talmud, *Derech Hashem,* a theological-philosophical work, *Daas Tevunos,* a work explaining *kabbalistic* concepts in more commonly used terms, and the epic *Mesillas Yesharim,* the subject of this commentary.

When *Mesillas Yesharim* came into the hands of the Gaon of Vina, he was ecstatic, and stated that there is not a single superfluous word in the entire text. He added that had he lived in Ramchal's lifetime, he would have traveled on foot to learn from him. Rabbi Yisrael of Salant, the father of the Mussar Movement, essentially established *Mesillas Yesharim* as the "book of books" on mussar, and it has remained sacred to all Torah scholars since.

In 1743 Ramchal emigrated to Eretz Yisrael, settling in Acco, and awaited his long-anticipated fortieth birthday. At that time the injunction would expire, and dwelling in the Holy Land, he would be free to once again expounded on *kabbalah.* He was not given this privilege, as he and his family perished in an epidemic when he was just several months shy of his fortieth birthday.

Ramchal is buried in Tevaryah (Tiberias), next to the tomb of Rabbi Akiva. When one visits his grave, one can look down from the height of his burial place to a peaceful Kinneret, the Sea of Galilee. One feels the serenity and security which eluded Ramchal during his brief lifetime.

One may also, on the same day, visit the tomb of Rambam in Tiberias, another giant in Torah and and the unquestioned authority upon which so much of *halachah* is based, but who also experienced excommunication, with his philosophic writings burnt by zealots.

The *Maggid* of Mezeritch said of Ramchal that his life came to a premature end because his generation was not deserving of so great a *tzaddik*. Although he was not appreciated during his lifetime, Ramchal has since been more than vindicated. There is no serious student of Torah who does not study *Mesillas Yesharim*, and like Rambam in the sphere of *halachah*, Ramchal is the teacher par excellence of the ethics of Torah.

LIGHTS ALONG THE WAY

הקדמת הרמח״ל

Ramchal's Introduction

אָמַר הַמְחַבֵּר: הַחִבּוּר הַזֶּה לֹא חִבַּרְתִּיו לְלַמֵּד לִבְנֵי הָאָדָם אֶת אֲשֶׁר לֹא יָדְעוּ, אֶלָּא לְהַזְכִּירָם אֶת הַיָּדוּעַ לָהֶם כְּבָר וּמְפֻרְסָם אֶצְלָם פִּרְסוּם גָּדוֹל. כִּי לֹא תִמְצָא בְּרוֹב דְּבָרַי, אֶלָּא דְּבָרִים שֶׁרוֹב בְּנֵי הָאָדָם יוֹדְעִים אוֹתָם וְלֹא מִסְתַּפְּקִים בָּהֶם כְּלָל, אֶלָּא שֶׁכְּפִי רוֹב פִּרְסוּמָם וּכְנֶגֶד מַה שֶּׁאֲמִיתָּתָם גְּלוּיָה לַכֹּל, כָּךְ הַהֶעְלֵם מֵהֶם מָצוּי מְאֹד וְהַשִּׁכְחָה רַבָּה. עַל כֵּן אֵין הַתּוֹעֶלֶת הַנִּלְקָט מִזֶּה הַסֵּפֶר יוֹצֵא מִן הַקְּרִיאָה בּוֹ פַּעַם אֶחָת, כִּי כְּבָר אֶפְשָׁר שֶׁלֹּא יִמְצָא הַקּוֹרֵא בְּשִׂכְלוֹ חִדּוּשִׁים אַחַר קְרִיאָתוֹ שֶׁלֹּא הָיוּ בוֹ לִפְנֵי קְרִיאָתוֹ, אֶלָּא מְעַט. אֲבָל הַתּוֹעֶלֶת יֵצֵא מִן הַחֲזָרָה עָלָיו וְהַהַתְמָדָה. כִּי יִזָּכְרוּ לוֹ הַדְּבָרִים הָאֵלֶּה הַנִּשְׁכָּחִים מִבְּנֵי הָאָדָם בְּטֶבַע, וְיָשִׂים אֶל לִבּוֹ חוֹבָתוֹ אֲשֶׁר הוּא מִתְעַלֵּם מִמֶּנָּה.

I did not write this book in order to teach people something new of which they had been unaware, but rather to remind them of that which they already knew very well. In most of my words you will not find anything other than observations about which most people have little doubt. However, it is precisely those concepts which are most evident that tend to be overlooked, and ironically, it is common for people to be oblivious to those ideas whose truth is unchallenged. Therefore, since this book contains little new information, there is no advantage in reading it only once, because the reader will not gain any new knowledge. The advantage of this book can result only from repeated readings, because that may remind people of those things that tend to be forgotten, and a person can then set his heart to those obligations which one tends to overlook.

Ramchal calls attention to an all-important psychological principle. It is true that sometimes a person may behave improperly because of ignorance, but more often people do have the knowledge that should deter them from doing wrong, yet, this knowledge does not appear to impact upon their behavior.

The phenomenon of being oblivious to that which one knows is referred to as *denial*. Denial is not the same as lying, because lying is a *conscious* distortion of fact, i.e., the liar knows he is lying, whereas denial is an *unconscious* process, in which a person is totally unaware that he is denying anything, and is certain that he is in possession of the truth.

The dynamics behind denial are clearly stated by the prophet Isaiah, who described this phenomenon several thousand years before Freud. "The heart of this people is fattened, his ears are dull, and his eyes are pasted; lest he understand with his heart, hear with his ears, and see with his eyes, then he would repent and be healed" (*Isaiah* 6:10). The prophet is telling us that a person may refuse to become aware of what is obvious because such awareness would necessitate his making changes in his behavior, and since making changes is uncomfortable, his psychological mechanism allows him to maintain the status quo by rendering him oblivious to some aspects of reality. We are creatures of habit, and changing our ways is fraught with discomfort. To avoid the distress incident to change, our clever unconscious mind prevents our being made aware of those things which would lead to change.

Ramchal proceeds to urge frequent review of his book. One may ask, If denial operates to make one unaware of what one already knows, how is repetition going to help? The answer is that denial can often be overcome by attrition, quite similar to the phenomenon that Rabbi Akiva saw which caused him to turn to Torah when he was already a mature adult. Rabbi Akiva observed that the constant dripping of water had worn away a segment of hard rock and concluded that if solid rock can be impressed by water, certainly he can be impressed by Torah even in his middle years. Similarly, the resistance to awareness can eventually be worn away by repetition.

One can escape the pitfall of denial by thinking, "As a fallible human being, I must have some defects that need correction," and be constantly alert to their detection. Rabbi Levi Yitzchak of Berditchev was once standing at his doorway when a cobbler passed by looking for work. He said to Rabbi Levi Yitzchak, "You must have something that needs fixing, don't you?" Rabbi Levi Yitzchak tearfully turned to his wife and said, "See! Even he can tell."

The last sentence of the author's paragraph cited may well contain the central theme of this book, "A person can then set his heart to those obligations." In Chapter One, Ramchal elaborates on just what is a person's duty in the world, but simply the concept that there *is* a duty should be enough to make a person give serious consideration to his behavior.

All living things tend to seek pleasure and avoid distress. There are times, however, when a person will accept a measure of discomfort in order to achieve a particular goal. A student, for example, will deprive himself of sleep or of various enjoyable activities and spend many hours in study because he wishes to achieve proficiency in a particular field. A businessman or professional person may exert much effort and spend a great deal of time at a task because he seeks a favorable outcome, although he could be enjoying this time in leisure. When we have a goal, sacrifice of pleasure is feasible. If, however, a person has no goal other than pursuit of pleasure, then sacrifice is not likely. It makes no sense to sacrifice pleasure for the sake of having pleasure.

Refining one's character and achieving spirituality may require considerable sacrifice and tolerance of the discomfort of instituting some changes in one's life. This will not occur in a person who has no goal other than pleasure seeking. The entire treatise, therefore, hinges on this single phrase, "To set his heart to the obligations." It is only when one feels a sense of obligation to achieve a goal that one will consider character refinement.

וְתִרְאֶה, אִם תִּתְבּוֹנֵן בַּהֹוֶה בְּרוֹב הָעוֹלָם, כִּי רוֹב אַנְשֵׁי הַשֵּׂכֶל הַמָּהִיר וְהַפִּקְחִים הַחֲרִיפִים יָשִׂימוּ רוֹב הִתְבּוֹנְנָם וְהִסְתַּכְּלוּתָם בְּדַקּוּת הַחָכְמוֹת וְעֹמֶק הָעִיּוּנִים אִישׁ אִישׁ כְּפִי נְטִיַּת שִׂכְלוֹ וְחִשְׁקוֹ הַטִּבְעִי. כִּי יֵשׁ שֶׁיִּטְרְחוּ מְאֹד בְּמֶחְקַר הַבְּרִיאָה וְהַטֶּבַע, וַאֲחֵרִים יִתְּנוּ כָּל עִיּוּנָם לִתְכוּנָה וּלְהַנְדָּסָה, אֲחֵרִים לִמְלָאכוֹת. וַאֲחֵרִים יִכָּנְסוּ יוֹתֵר אֶל הַקֹּדֶשׁ, דְּהַיְנוּ, לִמּוּד הַתּוֹרָה הַקְּדוֹשָׁה. מֵהֶם בְּפִלְפּוּלֵי הַהֲלָכוֹת, מֵהֶם בְּמִדְרָשִׁים, מֵהֶם בְּפִסְקֵי הַדִּינִים. אַךְ

מְעַטִים יִהְיוּ מִן הַמִּין הַזֶּה אֲשֶׁר יִקְבְּעוּ עִיּוּן וְלִמּוּד עַל עִנְיְנֵי שְׁלֵמוּת הָעֲבוֹדָה, עַל הָאַהֲבָה, עַל הַיִּרְאָה, עַל הַדְּבֵקוּת וְעַל כָּל שְׁאָר חֶלְקֵי הַחֲסִידוּת. וְלֹא מִפְּנֵי שֶׁאֵין דְּבָרִים אֵלֶּה עִקָּרִים אֶצְלָם, כִּי אִם תִּשְׁאַל לָהֶם, כָּל אֶחָד יֹאמַר שֶׁזֶּהוּ הָעִקָּר הַגָּדוֹל. וְשֶׁלֹּא יְדֻמֶּה חָכָם, שֶׁיִּהְיֶה חָכָם בֶּאֱמֶת, שֶׁלֹּא יִתְבָּרְרוּ אֶצְלוֹ כָּל הַדְּבָרִים הָאֵלֶּה. אַךְ מַה שֶּׁלֹּא יִרְבּוּ לְעַיֵּן עָלָיו הוּא מִפְּנֵי רוֹב פִּרְסוּם הַדְּבָרִים וּפְשִׁיטוּתָם אֶצְלָם שֶׁלֹּא יֵרָאֶה לָהֶם צֹרֶךְ לְהוֹצִיא בְּעִיּוּנָם זְמַן רָב.

If you will pay attention to what transpires in most of the world, you will find that the majority of intelligent people, who are bright and of sharp mentality, will devote most of their thought and speculation to the intricacies of various sciences and spend their time analyzing various subjects, each person according to his particular inclination and interest. Some will put a great deal of effort into research of creation and the natural sciences. Others will direct their interests to mathematics or engineering, others to the various arts, and yet others will devote time and effort in sacred studies; i.e., learning the holy Torah, which some do by means of discussion of halachah, others with homiletics, others with complex legal decisions. However, relatively few of these people will devote thought and study to perfecting their devotion to G-d; i.e., just what does it mean to love G-d, to fear G-d, to be close to G-d, or to all other aspects of piety. This is not because they do not consider these to be important. On the contrary, everyone agrees that these are indeed of paramount importance, and not one wise person will deny this. Why then do they not devote much time into analysis of these subjects? It is precisely because these subjects are so well known that they do not feel there is any need to spend time analyzing them.

At the time of Ramchal, there were a few texts of mussar which were greatly revered. Scholars no doubt read them in their spare time, but they did not become texts for lectures and courses or even personal study the way that halachic literature did. As we noted, Rabbi Yisrael of Salant's efforts several decades later to make mussar a required subject in yeshivos, to be studied in formal courses, were met with fierce opposition by major educators.

It is related that someone asked Rabbi Yisrael whether the fifteen minutes that he can spare for Torah study every day should be spent learning Talmud or mussar. Rabbi Yisrael said, "Mussar, of course." The man challenged, "Do you mean to say that you consider the study of mussar to supersede Talmud?" "Not at all," said Rabbi Yisrael. "But if you will learn mussar for fifteen minutes, you will discover that you can find three hours for the study of Talmud."

Even those who study Torah diligently should devote time to the study of character refinement and the analysis of where they stand relative to the love and fear of G-d.

The Talmud states that Torah is a double-edged sword. If one is meritorious (*zachah*), it is a powerful force for good; if not (*lo zachah*), it may become a destructive force (Yoma 72b). The Talmudic terms *zachah* and *lo zachah*, meritorious or not meritorious, may also have another interpretation. *Zachah* means "pure," hence *zachah* may mean if a person has purified himself, his Torah will have a positive effect. If he has not purified himself, then the study of Torah can actually have a negative effect, hence it is incumbent upon a person who learns Torah to examine himself carefully. One of the chassidic masters, prior to beginning his study of Talmud would meditate in *teshuvah* and tearfully say, "*Ribono Shel Olam*, Master of the Universe, let me not be one of whom it is said, To the wicked G-d said, why do you speak of My laws . . . for you despised mussar" (*Psalms* 50:16-17). Mussar is thus an essential prerequisite for study of Torah.

וְלֹא יִשָּׁאֵר לִמּוּד הַדְּבָרִים הָאֵלֶּה וּקְרִיאַת הַסְּפָרִים מִזֶּה הַמִּין כִּי אִם אֵצֶל אוֹתָם שֶׁאֵין שִׂכְלָם כָּל־כָּךְ דַּק וְקָרוֹב לִהְיוֹת גַּס, שֶׁאֵלֶּה תִּרְאֶה אוֹתָם שׁוֹקְדִים עַל כָּל זֶה וְלֹא יָזוּזוּ מִמֶּנּוּ, עַד שֶׁלְּפִי הַמִּנְהָג הַנּוֹהֵג בָּעוֹלָם כְּשֶׁתִּרְאֶה אֶחָד מִתְחַסֵּד לֹא תּוּכַל לִמְנֹעַ מִלַּחְשׁוֹד אוֹתוֹ לְגַס הַשֵּׂכֶל.

Consequently (since highly intelligent people spend their time with study of other subjects), the study of perfection of Divine service and the reading of works of this type is generally left to those who are not of keen intelligence, and who may actually be dull, because these are whom you will find immersed in such studies. As a result, it is customary that when one sees a person engaging in pious conduct, one is likely to suspect him of being dull, because otherwise he would be engaged in intellectual pursuits.

Obviously, Ramchal is describing the situation as he saw it in his time, but it is not without its counterpart in today's world.

In many synagogues, between Minchah and Maariv, the rabbi will learn *Ein Yaakov*, which is the non-halachic portion of the Talmud, comprised of ethical content or incidents in the lives of the Talmudic authors, which are lessons in conduct. Attending the rabbi's class are the laity, usually people of limited scholarship. Those who are more erudite will not be found attending the rabbi's class, but rather are sitting by themselves studying more intellectually stimulating matter. Apparently they consider the lessons of *Ein Yaakov* as not for them, but as Ramchal indicates, for those who lack the erudition to study halachah.

This attitude, which prevailed at the time of Ramchal, was also noted by the Baal Shem Tov, who was a contemporary of Ramchal. The Baal Shem Tov went out of his way to court and befriend these unlearned people, whose simple faith and trust in G-d was sincere. Yaavetz, who lived at the time of the Inquisition, writes that when given the choice to accept the Christian faith or be put to death, some scholars rationalized converting, while many of the unlearned folk went to the stake declaring *Shema Yisrael*.

Let me share with you an incident that describes the quality of sincerity to be found in simple folk. Herschel was an immigrant from Russia who had not had the opportunity to become a Torah scholar. He earned his living by peddling rags and collecting scrap metal. When he fell ill, he instructed his son that immediately following his death, he was to open a certain drawer and follow the instructions found within.

In the drawer the son found a bag containing silver dollars with the following explanatory note:

"The silver dollars in this bag are those I received as a result of the mitzvah of *pidyon haben* (redemption of the firstborn son). While I always tried to transact all my business dealings honestly, I cannot be certain that I may not have inadvertently overcharged someone. This money however, is honestly mine without any question, because my father was a Kohen and I am a Kohen, and this money is therefore legitimately mine as G-d has commanded. Therefore, I wish that my shroud and all burial expenses be paid for with this money. I know that I have few merits, but perhaps if I appear before the Heavenly tribunal dressed in garments that were bought with honest money, they will look upon me with compassion."

This is what a simple person thought and felt. Little wonder that the Baal Shem Tov loved his genre.

וְאוּלָם תּוֹלְדוֹת הַמִּנְהָג הַזֶּה רָעוֹת מְאֹד לַחֲכָמִים וּלְבִלְתִּי חֲכָמִים, כִּי גוֹרֵם שֶׁמֵּאֵלֶּה וּמֵאֵלֶּה יֶחְסַר הַחֲסִידוּת הָאֲמִתִּי וְיִהְיֶה יָקָר מְאֹד לִמְצֹא אוֹתוֹ בָּעוֹלָם. כִּי יֶחְסַר מִן הַחֲכָמִים לְמִעוּט עִיּוּנָם בּוֹ וְיֶחְסַר מִן הַבִּלְתִּי חֲכָמִים לְמִעוּט הַשָּׂגָתָם אוֹתוֹ, עַד שֶׁיְּדַמּוּ רוֹב בְּנֵי הָאָדָם שֶׁהַחֲסִידוּת תָּלוּי בַּאֲמִירַת מִזְמוֹרִים הַרְבֵּה וּוִדּוּיִים אֲרֻכִּים מְאֹד, צוֹמוֹת קָשִׁים, וּטְבִילוֹת קֶרַח וָשֶׁלֶג, כֻּלָּם דְּבָרִים אֲשֶׁר אֵין הַשֵּׂכֶל נָח בָּהֶם וְאֵין הַדַּעַת שׁוֹקְטָה.

Both the learned and unlearned people suffer, because neither of them have true piety, and it is very difficult to find a truly pious person. The learned lack true piety because they do not spend enough time investigating it, and the unlearned lack piety because they do not have an accurate concept of it. As a result, most people have a distorted understanding of what piety consists of, assuming it to be limited to recitation of many psalms, long confessions, indulging in severe fasts, and undergoing immersions in snow and ice, all of which are incompatible with sound reason.

While it is true that in the very early mussar writings, fasting and mortification of the flesh are described as acts of penance, Ramchal discourages such practices. The Baal Shem Tov and his disciples followed in his footsteps. Perhaps earlier generations were of a mettle wherein these were proper components of *teshuvah*, but for later generations these were felt to be improper. Inasmuch as these practices were not prescribed by halachah, they were subject to change by later authorities.

A chassidic* master once discovered one of his followers to be fasting frequently. He said to him, "I see you are trying to do a complete job.

---

*Throughout this volume the terms *Chassid* and *Chassidus* (italics u.c. "C") denote a pious person who seeks to attain the ultimate level of piety and saintliness — see chapters 18-21. The terms chassid, chassidic and chassidus (roman l.c. "c") denote a follower of the movement founded by the Baal Shem Tov. One does not necessarily connote the other nor is one mutually exclusive of the other.

First you sinned to ruin your *neshamah*, and now you are fasting to ruin your body as well."

A follower of the Rebbe of Rhizin reported that in order to do penance for his sins he was depriving himself of cooked food all week except for Shabbos. He was wearing nails in his shoes to torment himself, was rolling in the snow to punish himself, and had someone flagellate him to comply with the practice of lashing that the Torah prescribes for certain transgressions.

The Rebbe of Rhizin took the young man to the stable. "See that horse?" he said. "He does not eat cooked food all week, rolls in the snow, has nails in his shoes, and is frequently whipped. Yet he is still a horse."

True *teshuvah* consists of sincere regret for the mistakes one has made, and of achieving a refinement of character that would make it impossible for the same deviant behavior to be repeated. Without sincere regret and character refinement, all self-flagellation is of no use. With them, self-flagellation is unnecessary.

Ramchal appears to assert that even Torah scholars may not derive all that is necessary for proper behavior from their studies. Can there be such a thing as proficiency in Torah without suitable character traits? Listen to what the ethicist, Rabbi Chaim Shmulevitz, has to say:

The Torah relates that when the three angels visited the Patriarch Abraham, "he saw them," then again, "he saw them and ran towards them" (*Genesis* 18:12). Why does the Torah state twice that he saw them?

The Midrash states that Abraham's first sighting was that the Divine Presence was near them, and he therefore realized that they must be great men. Yet, Abraham did not run to greet them until the second sighting, when he saw that they were acting with great respect towards one another, and he then knew that they were just, decent people and ran to greet them.

"Imagine," says Rabbi Shmulevitz, "they were great enough to merit the Divine Presence, yet that did not satisfy Abraham. His criterion was not greatness alone, but whether they were behaving with dignity and respect to one another."

We find a similar concept regarding the disciples of Rabbi Akiva, who were all doubtless very great scholars. Nevertheless, they all perished because they did not act with appropriate respect to one another.

The standards for ethical behavior escalate in proportion to one's Torah scholarship. One of the authors of the Talmud discusses the concept of *chilul Hashem*, desecration of the Name of G-d, one of the most serious transgressions, and he says, "For me, *chilul Hashem* consists of buying meat and not paying the butcher promptly." A Torah scholar is not permitted to provide anyone with even the remotest grounds for questioning his integrity.

This is why Ramchal insists that study of mussar is a necessity for everyone, particularly for Torah scholars.

וְהַחֲסִידוּת הָאֲמִתִּי הַנִּרְצֶה וְהַנֶּחְמָד, רָחוֹק מִצִּיּוּר שִׂכְלֵנוּ, כִּי זֶה דָּבָר פָּשׁוּט, מִלְּתָא דְּלָא רַמְיָא עֲלֵהּ דֶּאֱינָשׁ, לָאו אַדַּעְתֵּהּ. וְאַף־עַל־פִּי שֶׁכְּבָר קְבוּעִים בְּלֵב כָּל הָאָדָם הַיָּשָׁר הַתְחָלוֹתָיו וִיסוֹדוֹתָיו, אִם לֹא יַעֲסוֹק בָּהֶם יִרְאֶה פְּרָטָיו וְלֹא יַכִּירֵם, יַעֲבוֹר עֲלֵיהֶם וְלֹא יַרְגִּישׁ בָּם. רְאֵה כִּי אֵין דִּבְרֵי הַחֲסִידוּת וְעִנְיְנֵי הַיִּרְאָה וְהָאַהֲבָה וְטָהֳרַת הַלֵּב דְּבָרִים מְטֻבָּעִים עַד שֶׁלֹּא יִצְטָרְכוּ אֶמְצָעִים לִקְנוֹתָם, אֶלָּא יִמְצְאוּ אוֹתָם בְּנֵי הָאָדָם בְּעַצְמָם כְּמוֹ שֶׁיִּמְצְאוּ כָּל תְּנוּעוֹתֵיהֶם הַטִּבְעִיּוֹת: כַּשֵּׁנָה וְהַיְקִיצָה, הָרָעָב וְהַשֹּׂבַע, וְכָל שְׁאָר הַתְּנוּעוֹת הַחֲקוּקוֹת בְּטִבְעֵנוּ. אֶלָּא וַדַּאי שֶׁצְּרִיכִים הֵם לְאֶמְצָעִים וְלְתַחְבּוּלוֹת לִקְנוֹת אוֹתָם, וְלֹא יִבָּצְרוּ גַּם כֵּן מַפְסִידִים לָהֶם שֶׁיַּרְחִיקוּם מִן הָאָדָם, וְלֹא יֶחְסְרוּ דְּרָכִים לְהַרְחִיק מַפְסִידֵיהֶם.

The true piety which G-d desires is not easily conceptualized. A person does not devote much thought to something to which he does not feel duty bound. Even though every decent and upright person has the basics and rudiments of piety implanted in his heart, he may not recognize some of the details of piety, and may even transgress them without being aware that he is doing so. The components of piety, such as fear of G-d, love of G-d, and purity of the heart, are not naturally occurring feelings which can be acquired without employing certain techniques. These are not emotions one comes by naturally, as with other states, such as sleep and waking, hunger and satiation, or other physiologic reactions. Rather, the components of piety require various strategies and techniques to acquire them. There is certainly no dearth of deterrents that will impede acquisition of piety, but there are also many ways in which these obstacles can be overcome.

Ramchal continues to strengthen his argument why a concerted study of ethics is essential, and states that unless a person feels a responsibility to carry something out, he is prone to forget it. Ramchal has already alluded to the importance of having a goal in life. The Torah states that part of this responsibility is to "walk in the ways of G-d," and the Talmud explains that walking in the ways of G-d means to emulate the Divine attributes. Unless a person is at all times aware of this responsibility, he may encounter situations where he should apply compassion, forgiveness, and tolerance, which are some of the Divine attributes, yet because he is not consciously thinking about his duties, he may not recognize these opportunities, and may even act with harshness, intolerance, and impatience. This is not because he does not know that he must act otherwise, but rather because he is not cognizant of this at all times, and he may get carried away by his emotions.

The components of piety are not spontaneous reflex reactions. Eating when one is hungry or going to sleep when one is exhausted does not require deliberate effort, because these are spontaneous reactions inherent within one's nature. On the other hand, love of G-d, reverence for G-d, and emulating the Divine attributes are not natural or reflex reactions, and to the contrary, the natural tendencies are often the polar opposite of the desired traits. There are ways in which a person can acquire the necessary spiritual traits, but this requires a conscious, deliberate effort. Therefore, Ramchal concludes, paying close attention and studying the techniques by which one may acquire spirituality are essential.

אִם כֵּן אֵפוֹא אֵיךְ לֹא יִצְטָרֵךְ לְהוֹצִיא זְמַן עַל הָעִיּוּן הַזֶּה לָדַעַת אֲמִתַּת הַדְּבָרִים וְלָדַעַת הַדֶּרֶךְ לִקְנוֹתָם וּלְקַיְּמָם? מֵאַיִן תָּבוֹא הַחָכְמָה הַזֹּאת בְּלֵב הָאָדָם אִם לֹא יְבַקְשֶׁנָּה? וְכֵיוָן שֶׁכְּבָר הִתְאַמֵּת אֵצֶל כָּל חָכָם צֹרֶךְ תְּמִימוּת הָעֲבוֹדָה וְחוֹבַת טָהֳרָתָהּ וּנְקִיּוּתָהּ שֶׁזּוּלַת אֵלֶּה אֵינָהּ נִרְצֵית וַדַּאי כְּלָל, אֶלָּא נִמְאֶסֶת וּמְתֹעֶבֶת, „כִּי כָל־לְבָבוֹת דּוֹרֵשׁ ה׳ וְכָל־יֵצֶר מַחֲשָׁבוֹת (הוּא) מֵבִין" (דברי הימים־א כח, ט) מַה נַּעֲנֶה בְּיוֹם תּוֹכֵחָה, אִם הִתְרַשַּׁלְנוּ מִן הָעִיּוּן הַזֶּה וְהִנַּחְנוּ דָּבָר שֶׁהוּא כָּל כָּךְ מֻטָּל עָלֵינוּ שֶׁהוּא עִקַּר מָה ה׳ אֱלֹהֵינוּ שׁוֹאֵל מֵעִמָּנוּ. הֲיִתָּכֵן שֶׁיִּיגַע וְיַעֲמוֹל שִׂכְלֵנוּ בַּחֲקִירוֹת אֲשֶׁר לֹא נִתְחַיַּבְנוּ בָּם, בְּפִלְפּוּלִים אֲשֶׁר לֹא יֵצֵא לָנוּ שׁוּם פְּרִי מֵהֶם וְדִינִים אֲשֶׁר אֵינָם שַׁיָּכִים לָנוּ, וּמַה שֶּׁחַיָּבִים אָנוּ לְבוֹרְאֵנוּ חוֹבָה רַבָּה נַעַזְבֵהוּ לַהֶרְגֵּל וְנַנִּיחֵהוּ לְמִצְוַת אֲנָשִׁים מְלֻמָּדָה?

How can one possibly justify not devoting adequate time to the study of ethics, to know the truth about these subjects and ways in which desirable traits can be acquired and maintained? Whence will such wisdom come if one does not pursue it? Inasmuch as every intelligent person recognizes the need to perfect himself in Divine service, and that the latter must be pure and free of contaminants for otherwise it is certainly unacceptable to "G-d, Who searches all hearts and understands a person's innermost talents" (I Chronicles 28:9), what will we answer on Judgment Day if we are lax in pursuit of the study of ethics and neglect something which is obligatory and which is the very essence of what G-d asks of us? Is it conceivable that we exhaust our intellect in speculations which are not required of us, in abstract arguments that are fruitless and in laws which have no practical applications, while we neglect our duties toward G-d, relegating them to habit and to mechanical, rote observance?

Ramchal is again critical of people who think they are fulfilling the will of G-d by indulging in abstract discussions of Torah while neglecting the very fundamentals of Torah, i.e., those which lead to spiritual growth.

The Talmud instructs us, "Set aside your own will in deference to the will of G-d" (*Ethics of the Fathers* 2:4). Deference to the will of G-d must be absolute; we must accept His will as He wishes it, not as we think it should be. People may be led to improper acts because of temptation or personal interest, but, says Rabbi Yisrael of Salant, when a person assumes his personal interest to be that which G-d desires, that is the most difficult misconception to overcome. A prime example is the person who rushes to a lecture on mussar, pushing people out of his way and behaving rudely, all in the interest of getting to the mussar lecture on time!

According to the *Zohar*, the sin of the spies sent by Moses, which is the ultimate cause of our suffering in exile for two thousand years, is that they wished to dictate what the Divine will should be. The spies knew that upon entering the Promised Land, the era of miraculous existence would come to an end. People would have to work the fields, devoting time to plowing, planting, harvesting, and processing grain and produce for food. They would have to sew clothes, make shoes, build homes, and dig wells for water. With all these diversions, when would they have time to study Torah? They therefore conspired to sabotage the entry into the Promised Land, reasoning that they would remain in the desert, receiving the manna from Heaven and water from the well of Miriam, protected by the clouds of glory, with their clothing growing along with them, and their shoes never wearing out. They would continue to learn Torah from the great master himself, Moses. Certainly this is more preferable than working the fields with oxen and tending to such mundane matters!

Preferable, to whom? The Divine will was that they were to enter the Promised Land and engage in all the activities required for the maintenance of a society, and while doing so fulfill all the mitzvos involved in normal living. But the spies thought that *they* knew better than G-d. They wished to serve Him in the manner they thought He should be served, thereby rejecting the explicit Divine instructions.

These spies were not ordinary people. They were the leaders of their tribes, men of great stature. If *they* were vulnerable to being misled, perhaps we are no less vulnerable. Rabbi Yisrael of Salant was so right. People sometimes think they are doing what G-d wishes, but in reality, they are pursuing their own interests.

This is the focus of Ramchal's criticism. People may be derelict in the study of the essentials of the Divine wish, the ethical behavior that leads to spirituality, while fancying themselves to be devout.

אִם לֹא נִסְתַּכַּלְנוּ וְלֹא עִיַּנּוּ מַה הִיא הַיִּרְאָה הָאֲמִתִּית וּמַה עֲנָפֶיהָ, אֵיךְ נִקְנֶה אוֹתָהּ וְאֵיךְ נִמָּלֵט מִן הַהֶבֶל הָעוֹלָמִי הַמְשַׁכֵּחַ אוֹתָהּ מִלִּבֵּנוּ? הֲלֹא תִשָּׁכַח וְתֵלֵךְ אַף־עַל־פִּי שֶׁיָּדַעְנוּ חוֹבָתָהּ?

If we do not analyze what true fear of G-d actually means and what are its ramifications, how can we acquire it and how can we escape the forces that make us forgetful of it even though we may know its importance?

The kabbalistic writings state, "There is *yirah* (fear) and again, there is *yirah,*" by which is meant that there are varieties of *yirah,* some very good, some less so.

The concept of *yirah* as fear that G-d will punish someone for transgressing His commandments is not only juvenile and primitive, but also misleading. It conveys the idea that when we sin we hurt G-d, and that He retaliates in anger. But the Scripture states, "If you have sinned, what have you done to Him?" (*Job* 35:6). Every intelligent person should understand that G-d is All perfect, and that by committing sin we harm ourselves, not G-d. What we should fear is that we may be deluded and misled by the *yetzer hara* to do things that are self-destructive. The study of Torah, which provides nourishment for the *neshamah* (soul), and fulfillment of the mitzvos is the only means by which we can bridge the gap between finite man and G-d, and if we are derelict in observance of mitzvos or commit sin, we jeopardize our relationship with G-d. This is what we should fear, and this is the true concept of *yirah*.

When a small child who cannot understand the danger of stepping into traffic runs into the street to retrieve his rubber ball, it may be necessary to spank him in order to discourage him from placing himself at the risk of injury. In this sense we can think of Divine "punishment," as when a person must be disciplined because he lacks the understanding of the true value of Torah and mitzvos. But mature, sensible people should appreciate that the Divine commandments are for our welfare, and the fear of sin should be nothing other than the fear of injuring ourselves, both physically and spiritually. If we do not analyze *yirah* and understand its true meaning, we may remain fixated at a primitive level.

הָאַהֲבָה כְּמוֹ־כֵן, אִם לֹא נִשְׁתַּדֵּל לִקְבּוֹעַ אוֹתָהּ בִּלְבָבֵנוּ בְּכֹחַ כָּל הָאֶמְצָעִים הַמַּגִּיעִים אוֹתָנוּ לָזֶה, אֵיךְ נִמְצָאֶהָ בָּנוּ? מֵאַיִן יָבוֹא הַדְּבֵקוּת וְהַהִתְלַהֲטוּת בְּנַפְשׁוֹתֵינוּ עִמּוֹ יִתְבָּרֵךְ וְעִם תּוֹרָתוֹ, אִם לֹא נִשְׁעֶה אֶל גְּדֻלָּתוֹ וְאֶל רוֹמְמוּתוֹ אֲשֶׁר יוֹלִיד בְּלִבֵּנוּ הַדְּבֵקוּת הַזֶּה?

So also with love of G-d, if we do not make an effort to instill it in our hearts, how will we find it within us? Whence will come the adherence with and the passion of our soul for the Blessed One and with His Torah, if we are not attentive to His greatness and exaltation which could provide us with this communion with Him?

The Tanya states that in every Jew, regardless of how far he may have drifted from Jewishness, there is a nucleus of love for G-d that is concealed in the deepest recesses of the heart.

One of the Torah commentaries explains the vision of the burning thornbush (*Exodus* 3:2-6) with this principle. It is a historical fact that when forced to deny their Jewishness under threat of being put to death, many Jews who had been totally alienated chose to forfeit their lives rather than to convert to another faith. Moses had the prophetic vision of a thornbush, barren of leaves and of fruit, symbolizing a person who is barren of Torah and mitzvos, yet accepting martyrdom with the fiery passion of the greatest *tzaddik*. G-d told him, "I am the G-d of Abraham, Isaac and Jacob"; in other words, within every Jewish soul there is a fragment of Abraham, Isaac, and Jacob, whose lives were totally devoted to G-d. This nucleus may erupt into a passionate love for G-d, when one realizes the vanity of all worldly possessions and pleasures.

If we are not always consciously aware of this intense love for G-d, it is because there are barriers that interfere with this attraction, just as insulation prevents the attraction of a magnet for iron. These barriers are comprised of indulgence in physical desires, which suppress our spiritual aspirations. If we were to realize that at our core we have an intense craving for union with G-d, and that by indulging ourselves we frustrate this natural attraction, we might overcome our temptations and permit our spirituality to issue forth, which would then reveal our inherent love for G-d. But such realization cannot come without proper reflection and meditation.

אֵיךְ תִּטְהַר מַחֲשַׁבְתֵּנוּ אִם לֹא נִשְׁתַּדֵּל לְנַקּוֹתָהּ מִן הַמּוּמִין שֶׁמַּטִּיל בָּהּ הַטֶּבַע הַגּוּפָנִי?

How can our thoughts be pure if we do not make an effort to cleanse them from the defects that are the consequences of our physical nature?

Purity of thought may seem to be an ideal that is beyond the reach of the average person, and can be achieved only by a *tzaddik*. How can we avoid thinking about something that comes to mind? Can we master control of our thought processes?

Ibn Ezra provides an answer to this when he notes, How can the Torah command "You shall not covet?" Is desire under voluntary control? Ibn Ezra explains that a person does not crave anything which is absolutely beyond reachability. Hence, he says, if a person were totally committed to "You shall not kill, you shall not steal, and you shall not commit adultery," the desire for something which is not his would never arise.

A firm resolution to observe all Torah prohibitions would allow for purity of thought.

מִי יְיַשְּׁרֵם וּמִי יְתַקְּנֵם אִם לֹא נָשִׂים לֵב עֲלֵיהֶם וְלֹא נְדַקְדֵּק בַּדָּבָר דִּקְדּוּק גָּדוֹל? הֲלֹא אִם עִיַּנּוּ עַל הַדָּבָר עִיּוּן אֲמִתִּי, הָיִינוּ מוֹצְאִים אוֹתוֹ עַל אֲמִתּוֹ וּמֵיטִיבִים לְעַצְמֵנוּ, וּמְלַמְּדִים אוֹתוֹ לַאֲחֵרִים וּמֵיטִיבִים לָהֶם גַּם־כֵּן.

If we do not attend closely to our character traits which may be in need of correction and being set straight, who will correct them? Truthful analysis of these subjects will benefit us, as well as others to whom we can teach it.

Everyone can benefit from improvement of character traits. There are some traits of which we should totally divest ourselves because they are grossly improper. However, there are also character traits which are commendable, yet even these may need some correction.

An example of this is humility, which the Talmud and all ethicists place at the very top of the list of desirable traits. Yet, when King Saul's humility caused him to yield to the will of the people, thereby disobeying the prophet's instructions, the prophet Samuel sharply rebuked King Saul: "Be it that you are small in your own eyes, I have set you as the leader of Israel" (*I Samuel* 15:17). In other words, even humility can be misplaced, and there are times when one must exert one's leadership and authority rather than be docile and humble.

As with humility, so with other traits. Throughout Torah literature, the qualities of *chesed* and *rachamim* (mercy and compassion) are exalted. Yet the Talmud says that whoever applies mercy in situations which call for strictness will eventually act with cruelty in situations which call for leniency (*Koheles Rabbah* 7:33).

Proper application of character traits requires much thoughtfulness and deliberation, and one cannot rely on reflex reactions even when one's orientation is benign.

הוּא מַה שֶּׁאָמַר שְׁלֹמֹה... "אִם־תְּבַקְשֶׁנָּה כַכָּסֶף וְכַמַּטְמֹנִים תַּחְפְּשֶׂנָּה, אָז תָּבִין יִרְאַת ה׳ וגו׳" אֵינוֹ אוֹמֵר: אָז תָּבִין פִּילוֹסוֹפְיָה, אָז תָּבִין תְּכוּנָה, אָז תָּבִין רְפוּאָה, אָז תָּבִין דִּינִים אָז תָּבִין הֲלָכוֹת אֶלָּא „אָז תָּבִין יִרְאַת ה׳". הֲרֵי לְךָ שֶׁלְּהָבִין הַיִּרְאָה צָרִיךְ לְבַקֵּשׁ אוֹתָהּ כַּכֶּסֶף וּלְחַפֵּשׂ אוֹתָהּ כַּמַּטְמוֹנִים.

This is why Solomon says (Proverbs 2:4-5), "If you will seek it as [one seeks] silver and search for it as for treasure, then you will come to understand the fear of G-d." Note that he does not say, "then you will understand philosophy, or astronomy, or medicine, or laws," but "then you will understand fear of G-d." This indicates that in order to understand fear of G-d, one must "seek it as silver and search for it as for treasure."

The Talmud states, "Everything is in the hands of G-d, except for the fear of G-d" (*Berachos* 33b). In other words, G-d has control over everything, but has left the choice of good and evil to man's free will. When the human being is conceived, there is a Heavenly decree as to whether he will be rich or poor, bright or dull, but it is not decreed whether he will be good or bad. This is a choice which man must make on his own.

It is possible for a person to be endowed with various skills and talents, and the knowledge of various sciences may come easily to him, but fear of G-d is something which man must achieve totally on his own. True, if a person exerts himself in pursuit of truth, G-d will help him in his endeavor, but the person must make the effort.

There are many things in life over which man has little or no control, but whether or not he will fear G-d is completely in his hands. Is it not foolish for a person to spend the greater part of his day pursuing things which are not under his control and neglect the only thing that he is free to achieve by his own efforts?

Rabbi Levi Yitzchak of Berditchev once saw a man hurrying in the street. "Where are you running to?" Rabbi Levi Yitzchak asked. "I am running after my *parnassah* (livelihood)," the man answered. "How do you know your *parnassah* is ahead of you and you are running towards it?" the rabbi asked. "Perhaps it is behind you and you are actually running away from it."

We concentrate most of our efforts in pursuit of *parnassah* which has been predetermined and which is not contingent on how much we exert ourselves. Whether we will or will not find silver and treasure has been Divinely decreed. Yet we do not invest comparable energy in pursuit of spirituality, which is totally dependent on how much effort we expend to achieve it.

The comparison of seeking spirituality to the search for silver and treasure has yet another meaning. One who finds silver or gold is unlikely to be satisfied with his initial gain. To the contrary, he will return to the silver or gold mine to accumulate more and more. This is how one should pursue spiritual growth, because here the goal is truly infinite, and one should never be satisfied with whatever spirituality one has achieved.

אוֹ, הֲנִמְצָא זְמַן לְכָל שְׁאָר חֶלְקֵי הָעִיּוּן וְלָעִיּוּן הַזֶּה לֹא יִהְיֶה זְמַן? לָמָּה לֹא יִקְבַּע אָדָם לְעַצְמוֹ עִתִּים לְפָחוֹת לְהִסְתַּכְּלוּת הַזֶּה אִם מֻכְרָח הוּא בִּשְׁאֵרִית זְמַנּוֹ לִפְנוֹת אֶל עִיּוּנִים אוֹ אֶל עֲסָקִים אֲחֵרִים? וְהִנֵּה הַכָּתוּב אוֹמֵר (איוב כח, כח) „הֵן יִרְאַת אֲדֹנָי הִיא חָכְמָה" . . . כִּי עִיּוּן גָּדוֹל צָרִיךְ עַל־כָּל הַדְּבָרִים הָאֵלֶּה לָדַעַת אוֹתָם בֶּאֱמֶת.

Is it reasonable that we find time to study many other things, but none for analyzing the fear of G-d? Granted that a person is compelled to devote much time to other affairs, but why should he not set aside the minimum daily time for reflection on fear of G-d? The Scripture says, "The fear of G-d is wisdom" (Job 28:28) and obviously, something that is wisdom requires reflection. . . . The fact is that if one is to understand these subjects, much reflection is required.

It is not uncommon for people to have their priorities mixed up. Having established that the observance of Torah and mitzvos is only for our own benefit and that transgressions are to our own detriment, it should follow that our survival instinct should cause us to be alert to those things that are injurious and to cultivate practices that are beneficial to us. To do otherwise is sheer folly.

The drug addict subjects himself to great danger because the drive to satisfy his cravings makes him oblivious to the inherent dangers in drugs, or if he is aware of them, he just ignores them. While we recognize this behavior as foolish, we are less cognizant of the fact that we may be driven by various cravings — money, fame, power — to behave in ways that are self-destructive.

Since fear of G-d, as defined, is in the interest of both physical and spiritual survival, any thinking person would give this subject the highest priority. It has been said that many people squander their health to amass a fortune, only to subsequently squander their fortune in the hope of regaining their health. A bit of rational reflection would protect us from such mistakes.

וּמִי שֶׁיִּתְבּוֹנֵן בָּם יִרְאֶה שֶׁאֵין הַחֲסִידוּת תָּלוּי בְּאוֹתָם הַדְּבָרִים שֶׁיַּחְשְׁבוּ הַמִּתְחַסְּדִים הַטִּפְּשִׁים, אֶלָּא בְּדִבְרֵי שְׁלֵמוּת אֲמִתִּי וְחָכְמָה רַבָּה. הוּא מַה שֶּׁמֹּשֶׁה רַבֵּנוּ, עָלָיו הַשָּׁלוֹם, מְלַמְּדֵנוּ בְּאָמְרוֹ (דברים י, יב): „וְעַתָּה יִשְׂרָאֵל מָה יְיָ אֱלֹהֶיךָ שֹׁאֵל מֵעִמָּךְ, כִּי אִם לְיִרְאָה אֶת יְיָ אֱלֹהֶיךָ לָלֶכֶת בְּכָל דְּרָכָיו וּלְאַהֲבָה אֹתוֹ וְלַעֲבֹד אֶת יְיָ אֱלֹהֶיךָ בְּכָל לְבָבְךָ וּבְכָל נַפְשֶׁךָ, לִשְׁמֹר אֶת מִצְוֹת יְיָ וְאֶת חֻקֹּתָיו וגו׳ ". כָּאן כָּלַל כָּל חֶלְקֵי שְׁלֵמוּת הָעֲבוֹדָה הַנִּרְצֵית לִשְׁמוֹ יִתְבָּרֵךְ, וְהֵם: הַיִּרְאָה, הַהֲלִיכָה בִּדְרָכָיו, הָאַהֲבָה, שְׁלֵמוּת הַלֵּב, וּשְׁמִירַת כָּל הַמִּצְוֹת.

Reflection will reveal that piety is not dependent upon things assumed by foolish people to be saintly behavior, e.g., fasting and self-mortification, but upon true perfection and wisdom. This is what Moses taught us: "And now, Israel, what does the Lord your G-d ask of you, but to fear G-d, to walk in all His ways, and to love Him and to serve G-d with all your heart and all your soul, to observe the mitzvos of G-d and His laws" (Deuteronomy 10:12). Here Moses includes all of the components of Divine service that G-d desires, and these are: fear of G-d, walking in His ways, love of G-d, wholeheartedness, and observance of all the mitzvos.

The words of Moses appear to trivialize his demand: "What is it that G-d asks of you, but to fear G-d," and this is then followed by a menu of rather stringent requirements, including serving G-d with all one's soul, which the Talmud interprets as referring to martyrdom. This is hardly a minor demand.

The fact is that if one understands fear of G-d properly, everything else falls into place. The ultimate goal of one's existence is to achieve a union with G-d. The gap between finite man and infinite man is unbridgeable except via the means that G-d provided: observance of Torah and mitzvos. The "fear" is similar to that of a person who must cross a bridge to reach his desired goal, but there are strong forces, gusts of wind, which threaten to dislodge him from the bridge so that he may be destroyed, let alone never reach his goal. If a person understood this properly, he would concentrate on what it takes to remain firmly on the bridge, to enable him to survive and reach the desired goal. Nothing, but nothing, should take precedence over the prevention of falling off the bridge. Once a person realizes that this is all that life is for, then everything else becomes relatively easy to achieve.

הַיִּרְאָה הִיא יִרְאַת רוֹמְמוּתוֹ יִתְבָּרֵךְ, שֶׁיִּירָא מִלְּפָנָיו כְּמוֹ שֶׁיִּירָא מִלִּפְנֵי מֶלֶךְ גָּדוֹל וְנוֹרָא, וְיֵבוֹשׁ מִגְּדֻלָּתוֹ עַל־כָּל תְּנוּעָה שֶׁהוּא בָּא לְהִתְנוֹעֵעַ, כָּל־שֶׁכֵּן בְּדַבְּרוֹ לְפָנָיו בִּתְפִלָּה אוֹ בְּעָסְקוֹ בְּתוֹרָתוֹ.

Fear of G-d denotes reverence for the majesty of the Blessed One, revering Him as one would a great and mighty king, and a feeling of humility with every action one takes, especially when speaking before Him in prayer, or when studying the Torah.

It is important to note that Ramchal does not refer to *yirah* as "fear of punishment," but rather as a sense of awe, being overwhelmed by the majesty of the Infinite. It is in the same sense that he refers to a person being in a state of humility in the Divine Presence.

In the Hebrew text the term וְיֵבוֹשׁ מִגְּדֻלָּתוֹ, *veyeivosh migdulaso,* is used, which is often translated as "One should be ashamed in consequence of His greatness." This translation makes no sense whatever. In what way should one be "ashamed" by being in the presence of the greatness of G-d?

In English the words "humility" and "humiliation" are derived from the same root, yet humility does not have the negative connotation that humiliation does. In the same way, *veyeivosh* refers to humility rather than to the feeling of shame associated with humiliation.

Many misconceptions have crept in as a result of inaccurate translations of sacred writings from the Hebrew, all the way from the Torah down through the Talmud and later writings. Here we have two examples where inaccurate translations make it appear as though we must live in fear of a punitive G-d and that a person must have a sense of shame. Both are negative concepts. "Fear" and "shame" should be replaced with "reverence" and "humility."

הַהֲלִיכָה בִּדְרָכָיו כּוֹלֵל כָּל עִנְיַן יֹשֶׁר הַמִּדּוֹת וְתִקּוּנָם, וְהוּא מַה שֶּׁבֵּאֲרוּ ז״ל (שבת קל״ג, ב): ,,מַה הוּא רַחוּם אַף אַתָּה רַחוּם וכו׳ ״. וּכְלָל־כָּל־זֶה שֶׁיִּנְהַג הָאָדָם כָּל מִדּוֹתָיו וְכָל מִינֵי פְּעֻלּוֹתָיו עַל־פִּי הַיֹּשֶׁר וְהַמּוּסָר. וְכָלְלוּ חֲכָמֵינוּ ז״ל (אבות ב, א): ,,כָּל שֶׁהִיא תִּפְאֶרֶת לְעוֹשֶׂיהָ וְתִפְאֶרֶת לוֹ מִן הָאָדָם״, דְּהַיְנוּ: כָּל הַהוֹלֵךְ אֶל תַּכְלִית הַהֲטָבָה הָאֲמִתִּית, דְּהַיְנוּ, שֶׁתּוֹלַדְתָּהּ חִזּוּק הַתּוֹרָה וְתִקּוּן אַחֲוַת הַמְּדִינוֹת.

"Walking in His ways" encompasses the propriety of character traits and their correction. This is what our Sages

referred to as, "Just as He is merciful, you shall also be merciful" (Shabbos 133b). The common denominator is that a person should fashion all his character traits and all his actions to conform with what is just and ethical. Our Sages summarize this: "The proper way of life is one that is honorable for its doer and elicits honor from others" (Ethics of the Fathers 2:1), i.e., everything that leads to the goal of that which is truly good, that which will strengthen Torah and establish universal brotherhood.

One of the greatest mitzvos is that of *kiddush Hashem*, sanctifying the Name of G-d. While this term is often used to refer to martyrdom, it can certainly apply to one's daily behavior, how one lives just as well as how one dies.

The Jewish nation was commissioned to be "a kingdom of priests and a holy nation" (*Exodus* 19:6) The behavior of every Jew should reflect this and be of the highest ethical standards. Ramchal stresses this when he says that *all* our character traits and *all* our actions should be just and ethical.

It is wrong to think that one can be Torah observant by choosing which of the mitzvos one wishes to observe and which one may reject. The prohibition against dishonesty and *lashon hara* (slander and gossip) is as binding as that of violation of Shabbos and eating *treifah*.

While observance of Torah will bring honor to a person, it is not intended that the motivation be to receive acclaim from others. Rather, by behaving appropriately according to the rules of Torah, one serves as a living example of the beauty of conducting one's life according to the will of G-d, and thereby one brings glory to the Name of G-d, a true *kiddush Hashem*.

הָאַהֲבָה: שֶׁיִּהְיֶה נִקְבָּע בְּלֶב־הָאָדָם אַהֲבָה אֵלָיו יִתְבָּרֵךְ עַד שֶׁתִּתְעוֹרֵר נַפְשׁוֹ לַעֲשׂוֹת נַחַת רוּחַ לְפָנָיו, כְּמוֹ שֶׁלִּבּוֹ מִתְעוֹרֵר לַעֲשׂוֹת נַחַת רוּחַ לְאָבִיו וּלְאִמּוֹ, וְיִצְטַעֵר אִם חָסֵר זֶה מִצִּדּוֹ אוֹ מֵאֲחֵרִים וִיקַנֵּא עַל זֶה וְיִשְׂמַח שִׂמְחָה רַבָּה בַּעֲשׂוֹתוֹ דָּבָר מִזֶּה.

By love of G-d is meant that there be instilled within a person's heart a love for the Blessed One which will stimulate one to do what is pleasing before Him, just as one's heart is aroused to give pleasure to his father and mother. A person will be distressed if either he or others are lacking in this. He will be zealous for this, and will greatly rejoice when he does anything which is pleasing to G-d.

One of the tests of altruistic love in contrast to self-centered love is that in the former the interest is that the other person be pleased rather than that *I* do the pleasing. One who has an altruistic love for one's father or mother wishes them to be pleased, and is just as happy if someone else does something for them. A self-centered love is, "*I* want to do it for my parents so that they appreciate *me*."

To march with the Torah on Simchas Torah is indeed a tribute to the Torah, but if one's love for Torah is altruistic, why should it make a difference who received the privilege of marching with the Torah in the first *hakafah* (procession)? The insistence of personally receiving the privilege casts some doubt on whom or what one wishes to honor.

The episode of the Korach rebellion (*Numbers* 16) is an example of self-centeredness masquerading under the guise of devotion to G-d. If one is really interested in the Divine will being done, why should it matter who is the High Priest?

Purity of motivation is an important component of spirituality.

שְׁלֵמוּת הַלֵּב הוּא, שֶׁתִּהְיֶה הָעֲבוֹדָה לְפָנָיו יִתְבָּרֵךְ בְּטֹהַר הַכַּוָּנָה דְּהַיְנוּ: לְתַכְלִית עֲבוֹדָתוֹ בִּלְבָד וְלֹא לְשׁוּם פְּנִיָּה אַחֶרֶת. וְנִכְלָל בָּזֶה שֶׁיִּהְיֶה לִבּוֹ שָׁלֵם בָּעֲבוֹדָה וְלֹא כְּפוֹסֵחַ עַל שְׁתֵּי הַסְּעִפִּים אוֹ כְּעוֹשֶׂה מִצְוַת אֲנָשִׁים מְלֻמָּדָה, אֶלָּא שֶׁיִּהְיֶה כָּל לִבּוֹ נָתוּן לָזֶה.

"Wholeheartedness" means that service of the Blessed One be purely motivated, and that the goal be His service alone and nothing else. Included in this, that one's heart be complete in Divine service, is that one's interests not be divided or his observance a matter of rote and habit, but that one's whole heart be dedicated to it.

Personal interest in performing a mitzvah can detract greatly from the virtue manifest in its observance.

Rabbi Chaim Shmulevitz cites the Midrash, that the sin of taking interest on a loan is unique, in that for all other sins which a person may have committed there are angels who intercede and plead for mercy, presenting various arguments on the person's behalf that mitigate his transgression. Not so with the sin of usury, where no plea for mercy is permitted.

Why is this so? Rabbi Shmulevitz explains that one who lends money at interest thinks he is doing a great mitzvah by lending this person money. After all, he is taking less interest than the bank, and perhaps this person might not even qualify for a bank loan. But if he is fulfilling the mitzvah of lending money, it must be done as a *gemilas chesed*, an interest-free loan. By accepting interest he is profiting from what he thinks is a mitzvah, and he is deluding himself into thinking that he is a *tzaddik*. There is no defense for such self-delusion. Performance of a mitzvah should be wholehearted (*Sichos Mussar* 5731:8).

Insofar as wholeheartedness requires full attention and devotion so that our performance is not mechanical or perfunctory, what can we say in our defense? With what degree of *kavannah* (concentration) do we say our prayers?

Rabbi Levi Yitzchak of Berditchev once greeted a person who had just completed the *Amidah* (silent prayer) with a hearty *"Shalom aleichem."* Noting the person's bewilderment, Rabbi Levi Yitzchak said, "During the *Amidah* you were at the marketplace in Kiev, so now I welcome you back home."

שְׁמִירַת כָּל הַמִּצְוֹת, כְּמַשְׁמָעוֹ, דְּהַיְנוּ: שְׁמִירַת כָּל הַמִּצְוֹת כֻּלָּן בְּכָל דִּקְדּוּקֵיהֶן וּתְנָאֵיהֶן.

"Observance of all the mitzvos," as the words imply, refers to observance of the entire body of mitzvos with all of their details and specifications.

In *Deuteronomy* (4:2) Moses commands that we do not add or subtract from the mitzvos of the Torah. If you have a lock whose combination is 6-1-3, it will not open at 6-1-2 nor at 6-1-4. The correct formula for Torah is 6-1-3. Rejecting any part of the Torah is equivalent to rejecting all of Torah.

וְהִנֵּה כָּל אֵלֶּה כְּלָלִים צְרִיכִים פֵּרוּשׁ גָּדוֹל. וּמָצָאתִי לַחֲכָמֵינוּ ז״ל שֶׁכָּלְלוּ הַחֲלָקִים הָאֵלֶּה בְּסֵדֶר וְחִלּוּק אַחֵר יוֹתֵר פְּרָטִי וּמְסֻדָּר לְפִי הַהַדְרָגָה הַמִּצְטָרֶכֶת בָּהֶם לִקְנוֹת אוֹתָם עַל נָכוֹן. וְהוּא מַה שֶׁאָמְרוּ בְּבָרַיְתָא, הוּבְאָה בִּמְקוֹמוֹת שׁוֹנִים בש״ס, וְאֶחָד מֵהֶם בְּפֶרֶק „לִפְנֵי אֵידֵיהֶן" (עבודה זרה כ, ב), זֶה לְשׁוֹנוֹ: „מִכָּאן אָמַר רַבִּי פִּינְחָס בֶּן יָאִיר: תּוֹרָה מְבִיאָה לִידֵי זְהִירוּת, זְהִירוּת מְבִיאָה לִידֵי זְרִיזוּת, זְרִיזוּת מְבִיאָה לִידֵי נְקִיּוּת, נְקִיּוּת מְבִיאָה לִידֵי פְּרִישׁוּת, פְּרִישׁוּת מְבִיאָה לִידֵי טָהֳרָה, טָהֳרָה מְבִיאָה לִידֵי

חֲסִידוּת, חֲסִידוּת מְבִיאָה לִידֵי עֲנָוָה, עֲנָוָה מְבִיאָה לִידֵי יִרְאַת חֵטְא, יִרְאַת חֵטְא מְבִיאָה לִידֵי קְדֻשָּׁה, קְדֻשָּׁה מְבִיאָה לִידֵי רוּחַ הַקֹּדֶשׁ, רוּחַ הַקֹּדֶשׁ מְבִיאָה לִידֵי תְחִיַּת הַמֵּתִים.

All of these principles require a great deal of commentary. Our sages have classified the elements of character refinement in an orderly formula, arranged according to the steps necessary for acquiring them properly. This order is mentioned in various places in the Talmud, one of them in Avodah Zarah 20b, "From this Rabbi Pinchas ben Yair derived: 'Torah leads to watchfulness; and watchfulness leads to diligence; diligence leads to cleanliness; cleanliness leads to abstinence; abstinence leads to purity; purity leads to piety; piety leads to humility; humility leads to fear of wrongdoing; fear of wrongdoing leads to sanctity; sanctity leads to holy spirituality, and holy spirituality leads to resurrection.' "

Ramchal bases his prescription for spiritual and character development on the passage authored by Rabbi Pinchas ben Yair because it provides an orderly, sequential progression of gradations and steps whereby the goal can be realistically achieved and retained. This is an all-important theme. Some components of spirituality are prerequisites for others, and if one leaps ahead of oneself, one may remain with nothing.

The Midrash states that at the miraculous dividing of the waters of the Red Sea the Divine revelation was so great that even the person with the least spirituality had a prophetic vision that surpassed by far the vision of the prophet Ezekiel. We can assume what the intensity of the experience must have been for those at higher spiritual levels. Yet, just three days later, the Israelites rebelled against Moses and wished to return to the enslavement of Egypt. Why had they not been transformed by the intensity of the spiritual experience?

The answer is that they were not prepared for it. Their own spiritual level was inadequate for the prophetic vision to have had an impact upon them and to be so integrated that it would influence their thoughts, emotions, and behavior.

There is no elevator for spirituality. Ramchal emphasizes that it is a step-wise process, and that one must master the antecedent step before going on to the next one. Failure to do so is equivalent to giving a highly sophisticated computer to a child in kindergarten. If one is not prepared for it, its marvelous potential is useless.

We must therefore approach spiritual growth in an orderly fashion, grasping and integrating each level before moving on to the next higher level.

וְהִנֵּה עַל־פִּי הַבָּרַיְתָא הַזֹּאת הִסְכַּמְתִּי לְחַבֵּר חִבּוּרִי זֶה לְלַמֵּד לְעַצְמִי וּלְהַזְכִּיר לַאֲחֵרִים תְּנָאֵי הָעֲבוֹדָה הַשְּׁלֵמָה לְמַדְרְגוֹתֵיהֶם. וַאֲבָאֵר בְּכָל אֶחָד מֵהֶם עִנְיָנָיו וַחֲלָקָיו אוֹ פְּרָטָיו, הַדֶּרֶךְ לִקְנוֹת אוֹתוֹ וּמָה הֵם מַפְסִידָיו, וְהַדֶּרֶךְ לִשָּׁמֵר מֵהֶם. כִּי אֶקְרָא בוֹ אֲנִי וְכָל מִי שֶׁיִּמְצָא בוֹ נַחַת, לְמַעַן נִלְמַד לְיִרְאָה אֶת ה׳ אֱלֹהֵינוּ וְלֹא תִשָּׁכַח מִמֶּנּוּ חוֹבָתֵנוּ לְפָנָיו, וַאֲשֶׁר חָמְרִיּוּת הַטֶּבַע מִשְׁתַּדֵּל לְהָסִיר מִלִּבֵּנוּ – הַקְּרִיאָה וְהַהִסְתַּכְּלוּת יַעֲלֶה עַל זִכְרוֹנֵנוּ וִיעִירֵנוּ אֶל הַמְצֻוֶּה עָלֵינוּ.

I decided to base my work on this passage, in order to teach myself and to remind others of the conditions essential for perfecting the Divine service. For each step, I shall explain its character, its divisions or details, how it is acquired, what may detract from it, and how one can guard himself against such detractions. I will be reading this myself, and all who find it pleasing may do so as well, so that together we can learn to fear G-d, and not forget our obligations to Him. The physical component of our nature tends to discourage spirituality, but the reading and contemplation of this book will return it to our memories and arouse us to do that which we are commanded.

וַה׳ יִהְיֶה בְּכִסְלֵנוּ וְיִשְׁמוֹר רַגְלֵנוּ מִלָּכֶד. וְתִתְקַיֶּם־בָּנוּ בַּקָּשַׁת הַמְשׁוֹרֵר הָאָהוּב לֵאלֹהָיו (תהלים פו, יא): ,,הוֹרֵנִי ה׳ דַּרְכֶּךָ אֲהַלֵּךְ בַּאֲמִתֶּךָ יַחֵד לְבָבִי לְיִרְאָה שְׁמֶךָ״. אָמֵן כֵּן יְהִי רָצוֹן.

May G-d be with our aspirations and protect us from faltering. May there be fulfillment of the prayer of the Psalmist, "Teach me, O G-d, Your ways, so that I can walk in Your truth. Unify my heart to fear Your Name" (Psalms 86:11). Amen, so may it be His will.

The Talmud states, "Correct yourself first and only then you may correct others" (*Bava Metzia* 107b). It is a basic principle of teaching and parenting that one cannot successfully convey to others that which one does not practice oneself. Ramchal therefore states that he, too, needs to follow this prescription for spiritual growth and development, and that he wishes to join with others in striving for spirituality.

Some people who aspire to be teachers and leaders are condescending. They feel that they have already achieved the goal, and that they can impart from their experience and erudition to others. Ramchal makes no such claim. To the contrary, he says that this work is primarily to provide a framework of spiritual growth for himself, but that all those who wish may join together with him.

After all is said and done, a person can only try his best. Success in this venture, as in any others, can come only with the Divine blessing. He therefore closes with, "May it be G-d's will" that we succeed in achieving refinement of our character traits and in spiritual growth.

1

בְּבֵאוּר כְּלָל חוֹבַת הָאָדָם בְּעוֹלָמוֹ

Man's Duty in the World

יְסוֹד הַחֲסִידוּת וְשֹׁרֶשׁ הָעֲבוֹדָה הַתְּמִימָה הוּא שֶׁיִּתְבָּרֵר וְיִתְאַמֵּת אֵצֶל הָאָדָם מַה חוֹבָתוֹ בְּעוֹלָמוֹ וּלְמַה צָרִיךְ שֶׁיָּשִׂים מַבָּטוֹ וּמְגַמָּתוֹ בְּכָל אֲשֶׁר הוּא עָמֵל כָּל יְמֵי חַיָּיו.

Achieving perfection in the service of G-d is dependent on a person's recognition of just what is his duty in the world and the goal towards which he should direct his vision and aspirations in all of his endeavors throughout his lifetime.

King Solomon begins his philosophic work, *Ecclesiastes,* with the statement that "Everything is a nothingness of nothingness," and immediately follows with the question "What remainder is there for a person after all the efforts he exerts under the sun?" If all one's efforts do not produce something that deserves to be considered an ultimate achievement, then all life is nothing but one huge futility. Indeed, Solomon indicates, if one's exertions are directed only toward achievements "under the sun," i.e., of this world, then life is quite pointless. In subsequent chapters, Solomon enumerates and describes all the pleasures a person may have on earth, and states that since these are all transitory, without a substantive "remainder," they are all futile. For life to be meaningful, there must be an ultimate, meaningful goal.

Inasmuch as a meaningful goal is basic and primary, Ramchal states that one cannot begin the journey toward spirituality without a clear concept of that goal.

There is a sharp demarcation between *emunah* (faith) and science, in that science deals primarily with means, whereas *emunah* is concerned with the end, the ultimate goal. Modern engineering can indeed produce a supersonic jet that can get a person to his destination with unprecedented speed, but engineering cannot dictate what that destination should be. Having the finest means of transportation but lacking a destination makes even the most advanced vehicle worthless. Clearly then, one must begin by delineating a goal in life.

וְהִנֵּה מַה שֶּׁהוֹרוּנוּ חֲכָמֵינוּ ז״ל הוּא, שֶׁהָאָדָם לֹא נִבְרָא אֶלָּא לְהִתְעַנֵּג עַל ה׳ וְלֵהָנוֹת מִזִּיו שְׁכִינָתוֹ, שֶׁזֶּהוּ הַתַּעֲנוּג הָאֲמִתִּי וְהָעִדּוּן הַגָּדוֹל מִכָּל הָעִדּוּנִים שֶׁיְּכוֹלִים לְהִמָּצֵא, וּמְקוֹם הָעִדּוּן הַזֶּה בֶּאֱמֶת הוּא הָעוֹלָם הַבָּא, כִּי הוּא הַנִּבְרָא בַּהֲכָנָה הַמִּצְטָרֶכֶת לַדָּבָר הַזֶּה. אַךְ הַדֶּרֶךְ כְּדֵי לְהַגִּיעַ אֶל מְחוֹז חֶפְצֵנוּ זֶה, הוּא זֶה הָעוֹלָם. וְהוּא מַה שֶּׁאָמְרוּ זִכְרוֹנָם לִבְרָכָה, (אבות ד, כא): ,,הָעוֹלָם הַזֶּה דּוֹמֶה לִפְרוֹזְדוֹר בִּפְנֵי הָעוֹלָם הַבָּא״.

Our sages taught us that man was created for the sole purpose of rejoicing in G-d and deriving pleasure from the splendor of His presence. This is the true joy and the greatest pleasure possible. The only place where this may be experienced is the World To Come, which was expressly created to provide for this ultimate pleasure. However, the path whereby we can achieve this desired goal is found in this world. This is why our sages said, "This world is like an antechamber for the World To Come" (Ethics of the Fathers 4:21).

In another work, *The Way of G-d*, Ramchal posits the axiom that G-d created the Universe because "it is the will of One Who is good to do good." Inasmuch as G-d is absolute goodness, and since without a recipient there could be no effusion of this goodness, it was therefore His will to bring the Universe into being so that He could apply this goodness.

The concept of the "will of G-d to do good" is suprarational, since we cannot possibly understand the nature of the Divine will. In human terms, "will" denotes a lack, since after one's will is satisfied, a void has been filled, and one is more pleased than before it was satisfied. This cannot be true of the Divine will, because G-d is All-perfect, has no lack whatever, and there cannot be any change of status in G-d. Hence the term "His simple will" is used in kabballistic works to distinguish it from the will with which man is familiar. Rambam says that the attributes of G-d are one with G-d Himself, and just as man cannot have an understanding of G-d, so man cannot have an understanding of any of G-d's attributes, among which is the Divine will (*Hilchos Teshuvah* 5-5).

The ultimate goal of creation is for man to be in the immanent presence of the splendor of G-d, essentially to become one with G-d, which is the way G-d expresses His goodness. The entire Universe was therefore designed to enable a person to achieve this end.

וְהָאֶמְצָעִים הַמַּגִּיעִים אֶת הָאָדָם לַתַּכְלִית הַזֶּה, הֵם הַמִּצְוֹת אֲשֶׁר צִוָּנוּ עֲלֵיהֶן הָאֵל יִתְבָּרֵךְ שְׁמוֹ. וּמְקוֹם עֲשִׂיַּת הַמִּצְוֹת הוּא רַק הָעוֹלָם הַזֶּה.

The means by which a person can reach this ultimate goal are the mitzvos which G-d commanded us, and the only place for performance of these mitzvos is in this world.

The disparity between finite man and infinite G-d is so vast, that there would be no conceivable way whereby man can unite with G-d. The only way this gap can be bridged is through the method devised by G-d Himself, which consists of observance of the mitzvos. No other technique, regardless how ingenious, can possibly bridge this enormous gap.

The performance of the mitzvos require physical entities and various physical acts. None of the celestial worlds, regardless of their degree of holiness, have the physical ingredients required for fulfillment of mitzvos. Only on this earthly world can mitzvos be fulfilled.

It is said that the Vilna Gaon wept shortly before his death, and explained that he was reluctant to leave a world where for just a few pennies a person can acquire a mitzvah of infinite value. As great as the celestial spheres may be, they are devoid of mitzvos. One of the chassidic masters said, "The Heavenly angels are indeed great and holy, but they cannot give a needy person a single coin for *tzedakah*." This is a distinct and uniquely human privilege.

עַל כֵּן הוּשַׂם הָאָדָם בְּזֶה הָעוֹלָם בַּתְּחִלָּה כְּדֵי שֶׁעַל יְדֵי הָאֶמְצָעִים הָאֵלֶּה הַמִּזְדַּמְּנִים לוֹ כָּאן יוּכַל לְהַגִּיעַ אֶל הַמָּקוֹם אֲשֶׁר הוּכַן לוֹ, שֶׁהוּא הָעוֹלָם הַבָּא, לִרְווֹת שָׁם בַּטּוּב אֲשֶׁר קָנָה לוֹ עַל יְדֵי אֶמְצָעִים אֵלֶּה. וְהוּא מַה שֶּׁאָמְרוּ זִכְרוֹנָם לִבְרָכָה (עירובין כב, א): ,,הַיּוֹם לַעֲשׂוֹתָם וּמָחָר לְקַבֵּל שְׂכָרָם״.

Man was therefore placed first in this world, so that by the means which were provided for him here, he would be able to reach his place in the World To Come, where he will be satiated with the goodness acquired through these means. Our sages referred to this, "Today for performance (of the mitzvos) and tomorrow (in the World To Come) for receiving their reward."

This is a pivotal point of Torah philosophy; i.e., (1) the ultimate goal of existence is to be with G-d in the World To Come, and (2) the only way this can be achieved is through observance of mitzvos.

Some people have postulated that a union with G-d can be achieved by various mental conditions, such as trance states, profound meditation, or mind expansion via hallucinogenic drugs. Ramchal rejects these as well as all other methods that a person may try. The *only* way to achieve union with G-d is via mitzvos.

There is no point in looking for ways to achieve a goal unless one first accepts that goal as desirable. Inasmuch as observance of mitzvos imposes many restrictions and requires denial of many physical gratifications, one's judgment may be so influenced that one may reject a spiritual goal.

The statement (a) "Eat, drink, and be merry *for* (b) tomorrow we die" appears to preach hedonism based on the belief that all there is is this earthly world; i.e., (a) is a consequence of (b), since one's existence is limited, there is no sense in denying oneself physical pleasures. The truth may be just the reverse; i.e., the statement "tomorrow we die" (b) may be a rationalization, a consequence of (a) the wish to gratify all one's desires. Just as a bribe invariably distorts one's judgment (*Deuteronomy* 16:19), so the wish to gratify all his physical cravings may distort one's reasoning, allowing him to conclude whatever he wishes to conclude, thereby rationalizing every aspect of his behavior.

וּכְשֶׁתִּסְתַּכֵּל עוֹד בַּדָּבָר תִּרְאֶה, כִּי הַשְּׁלֵמוּת הָאֲמִתִּי הוּא רַק הַדְּבֵיקוּת בּוֹ יִתְבָּרֵךְ, וְהוּא מַה שֶּׁהָיָה דָוִד הַמֶּלֶךְ אוֹמֵר (תהלים עג, כח): ,,וַאֲנִי קִרְבַת אֱלֹהִים לִי־טוֹב'', וְאוֹמֵר (שם כז, ד): ,,אַחַת שָׁאַלְתִּי מֵאֵת ה' אוֹתָהּ אֲבַקֵּשׁ שִׁבְתִּי בְּבֵית־ה' כָּל־יְמֵי חַיַּי וגו''. כִּי רַק זֶה הוּא הַטּוֹב. וְכָל זוּלַת זֶה שֶׁיַּחְשְׁבוּהוּ בְּנֵי הָאָדָם לְטוֹב, אֵינוֹ אֶלָּא הֶבֶל וְשָׁוְא נִתְעֶה. אָמְנָם לִכְשֶׁיִּזְכֶּה הָאָדָם לַטּוֹבָה הַזֹּאת, רָאוּי שֶׁיַּעֲמוֹל רִאשׁוֹנָה וְיִשְׁתַּדֵּל בִּיגִיעוֹ לִקְנוֹתָהּ, וְהַיְנוּ, שֶׁיִּשְׁתַּדֵּל לִדָּבֵק בּוֹ יִתְבָּרֵךְ בְּכֹחַ מַעֲשִׂים שֶׁתּוֹלַדְתָּם זֶה הָעִנְיָן וְהֵם הֵם הַמִּצְוֹת.

Further analysis (assuming that one can set aside the "bribes" of gratification) will reveal that only union with G-d constitutes true perfection, as King David said, "But as for me, the nearness of G-d is my good" (Psalms 73:28) and "One thing I ask from G-d and that is which I seek: to dwell in the house of G-d all the days of my life" (ibid. 27:4). This alone is the true good, and anything aside from this which people may consider good is nothing but deceptive worthlessness. For a person to obtain the true good it is appropriate that he first labor and persevere in his efforts to acquire it by means of those actions which will achieve this end. These actions are the performance of the mitzvos.

In *The Way of G-d*, Ramchal asks the obvious question. If creation was for the purpose of allowing G-d to express His benevolence, why did He not just create *neshamos* (souls) and put them into the Heavenly realm where they can be in the presence of G-d and partake of the Divine splendor? Why put the *neshamos* into a physical body and create a highly complex universe which the *neshamos* must traverse in order to ultimately be in the Divine presence?

Ramchal responds with the kabballistic observation embodied in the term "bread of humiliation," meaning that when one is given alms, one may indeed satisfy one's appetite, but one feels embarrassed for having partaken of something one did not earn. Anyone who has been a recipient of *tzedakah* will testify to the discomfort and humiliation of feeling himself a parasite. Giving *neshamos* an unearned absolute good would be a contradiction in terms, because a good that is not earned by one's own efforts cannot be an absolute good. Hence it was necessary to place the person in a situation whereby he could earn this good and thereby fully enjoy it.

Ramchal further explains that all goods other than spiritual goods are deceptive. This is in keeping with the teachings of *Ecclesiastes*, and may be easily confirmed by asking people if they are truly happy. People who live under conditions of various kinds of deprivation may think that true happiness can be found among those who have no material deprivation and are free of all economic worries. This misconception is extremely tenacious, and clinical experience confirms the wisdom of generations that happiness is not to be found among those who appear to have all the goods of the world at their command. Ramchal therefore concludes along with King David that the true good is the spiritual good, being at one with G-d. Some of the most severe cases of depression, alcoholism and drug addiction occur in the wealthiest people, who are not in want of any material gratification.

וְהִנֵּה שָׂמוֹ הַקָּדוֹשׁ בָּרוּךְ הוּא לָאָדָם בְּמָקוֹם שֶׁרַבִּים בּוֹ הַמַּרְחִיקִים אוֹתוֹ מִמֶּנּוּ יִתְבָּרֵךְ, וְהֵם הֵם הַתַּאֲווֹת הַחָמְרִיּוֹת אֲשֶׁר אִם יִמָּשֵׁךְ אַחֲרֵיהֶן הִנֵּה הוּא מִתְרַחֵק וְהוֹלֵךְ מִן הַטּוֹב הָאֲמִתִּי, וְנִמְצָא שֶׁהוּא מוּשָׂם בֶּאֱמֶת בְּתוֹךְ הַמִּלְחָמָה הַחֲזָקָה, כִּי כָּל עִנְיָנֵי הָעוֹלָם בֵּין לְטוֹב בֵּין לְמוּטָב הִנֵּה הֵם נִסְיוֹנוֹת לָאָדָם.

G-d put man in a place where there are many factors which can detract a person from Him. These are the physical desires, which, if a person indulges in them, cause him to progressively distance himself from the true good. Thus, man is actually placed in the midst of a raging battle, because everything that he will encounter in the world, whether good or bad, are ordeals for a person.

The theme of "ordeals for a person" is further developed by Ramchal in *The Way of G-d*, where he states that this is a pervasive theme throughout a person's life. *Life is nothing but a series of challenges* of varying types and degrees, which a person must overcome, and which are all tests of his loyalty and devotion to G-d. People of lesser capacity are given relatively minor tests, and people of greater spiritual strength are more stringently tested, all the way to the patriarch Abraham, who was put through ten ordeals, the most trying being the commandment to sacrifice his son Isaac.

The theme of being tested runs through much of Torah literature. In *Deuteronomy* it is predicted that there will be false prophets who will preach against Torah principles and will perform great supernatural miracles as evidence of their authenticity as Divine emissaries. Moses warns us not to heed the words of these false prophets, and as for their miracles, they are nothing but situations whereby G-d wishes to test our devotion and loyalty to Him (*Deuteronomy* 13:2-4).

The Talmud relates a fascinating episode, an intense halachic dispute between Rabbi Eliezer and the other sages, who constituted the vast majority. According to Torah law, the opinion of the majority must be accepted (*Exodus* 23:2). Rabbi Eliezer invoked several miracles to prove his point, and finally appealed to Heaven for a judgment, eliciting a Heavenly voice which proclaimed, "Why do you dispute with Rabbi Eliezer, whose opinion prevails everywhere?" The other sages were adamant, stating that the Torah requires acceptance of the majority opinion, and even a Divine decree cannot alter the authority of Torah (*Bava Metzia* 59b).

Rabbeinu Nissim explains this episode as a Divine test of the mettle of the sages, whether they would adhere to the rule of Torah or be overwhelmed by a miraculous phenomenon.

We humble mortals, so far removed from the greatness of the patriarchs or the sages of the Talmud, are not subjected to such severe tests, but we are tested according to our capacities. Primarily, our tests are whether we will surrender to the ingenious rationalizations which we can devise to justify yielding to our physical desires even when these are forbidden.

The Baal Shem Tov gave a parable of a king who wished to test the loyalty of his subjects, and engaged someone to circulate among the people and incite them to defy his orders. Some foolish people succumbed to the arguments of this agent, whereas the wise reasoned, "Is it possible that a king who is so powerful would tolerate anyone preaching defiance? The fact that this person is permitted to do so can only be because the king has allowed it as a test of our loyalty." If we are wise enough to realize that the *yetzer hara* (evil inclination) is merely a tool of G-d to test our allegiance, turning a deaf ear to his wily arguments is quite simple.

כִּי כָל עִנְיְנֵי הָעוֹלָם בֵּין לְטוֹב בֵּין לְמוּטָב הִנֵּה הֵם נִסְיוֹנוֹת לָאָדָם הֶעָנִי מִצַּד אֶחָד וְהָעשֶׁר מִצַּד אֶחָד כְּעִנְיַן שֶׁאָמַר שְׁלֹמֹה (משלי ל, ט): ,,פֶּן אֶשְׂבַּע וְכִחַשְׁתִּי וְאָמַרְתִּי מִי ה׳ וּפֶן אִוָּרֵשׁ וְגָנַבְתִּי וכו׳ ״. הַשַּׁלְוָה מִצַּד אֶחָד וְהַיִּסּוּרִין מִצַּד אֶחָד, עַד שֶׁנִּמְצֵאת הַמִּלְחָמָה אֵלָיו פָּנִים וְאָחוֹר. וְאִם יִהְיֶה לְבֶן חַיִל וִינַצֵּחַ הַמִּלְחָמָה מִכָּל

הַצְּדָדִין, הוּא יִהְיֶה הָאָדָם הַשָּׁלֵם אֲשֶׁר יִזְכֶּה לִדָּבֵק בְּבוֹרְאוֹ וְיֵצֵא מִן הַפְּרוֹזְדוֹר הַזֶּה וְיִכָּנֵס בַּטְּרַקְלִין לֵאוֹר בְּאוֹר הַחַיִּים. וּכְפִי הַשִּׁעוּר אֲשֶׁר כָּבַשׁ אֶת יִצְרוֹ וְתַאֲווֹתָיו וְנִתְרַחֵק מִן הַמַּרְחִיקִים אוֹתוֹ מֵהַטּוֹב וְנִשְׁתַּדֵּל לִדָּבֵק בּוֹ – כֵּן יַשִּׂיגֵהוּ וְיִשְׂמַח בּוֹ.

A person may be tried by poverty on the one hand and wealth on the other, as Solomon said, "I might become affluent and deny G-d or I might become impoverished and steal."(Proverbs 30:9) A person is thus caught in a battle from the fore and from the rear. If he is victorious on all fronts, he will then be the "complete man," who will succeed in uniting himself with G-d, and when he leaves the antechamber (the earthly world) to enter the palace (the eternal world), he will bask in the light of the Divine splendor. To the extent that one has subdued his evil inclination and desires, avoided those factors which detract from the good, and exerted himself to become united with the good, to that extent will he attain it and rejoice in it.

The Talmud states that on Judgment Day the nations of the world will dispute the right of Israel to its reward, arguing that Israel did not observe the Torah. G-d will then call Nimrod, the king of the Chaldeans, who threw the patriarch Abraham into the fiery furnace when he repudiated idolatry, to testify about Abraham's withstanding this test of his loyalty to G-d. He will call Laban to testify how the patriarch Jacob had served him faithfully even though he repeatedly cheated him. He will call the wife of Potiphar to testify how Joseph had resisted her seduction.

Rabbi Yeruchem Levovitz points out that the essence of this Talmudic passage is that the evil itself will testify how it was overcome by the righteous. Chassidic teachings extend this principle, explaining that nothing could exist in the universe without some nucleus of G-dliness within it; hence even evil must has an attenuated spark of Divinity that enables its existence. When the righteous triumph over evil, they withdraw the spark of Divinity, causing the evil to disintegrate into nothingness, and returning all the alienated sparks of Divinity to their origin. Man's successful survival of the trials with which he is challenged thus results in the eradication of all evil from the world.

It is only natural for a person to desire tranquility, as natural as seeking food when hungry and water when thirsty. Ramchal makes us aware, however, that desirable as it may be, tranquility accomplishes nothing, and struggle is the only constructive aspect of life.

This is stated by the Midrash which Rashi quotes in *Genesis* (37:2), that after suffering persecution from Esau and twenty years of anguish with Laban, the patriarch Jacob wished to live in tranquility, whereupon G-d said, "Tranquility is not for this world. Tranquility is for the World to Come," and Jacob was then subjected to the distress of the disappearance of his beloved son Joseph.

How would Jacob have utilized tranquility? He was not one to pursue idle pastimes. The Torah testifies that Jacob was a perfect person who spent his time in pursuit of the knowledge of G-d. During the fourteen years that he studied at the Academy of Shem he did not have a single full night of sleep. Clearly if Jacob had been free of distractions, he would have devoted himself totally to the pursuit of G-dliness. What was wrong with that?

The answer is found in the verse in *Job* (5:7), *adam l'amal yulad* "Man was created to labor." Our logic may dictate that tranquility is a desirable state, but the Divine wisdom dictates otherwise. When a person is in a state of tranquility, he achieves nothing. His purpose on Earth is to withstand trials. It is important for us to realize that pleasant and desirable as tranquility may be, this should not be the goal we pursue.

Having posited that the world was created for man to achieve a state of spirituality to be able to benefit from the infinite benevolence of G-d, the question remains, for what was everything else in the world created? What is the purpose of everything else in existence? Ramchal continues:

וְאִם תַּעֲמִיק עוֹד בָּעִנְיָן תִּרְאֶה כִּי הָעוֹלָם נִבְרָא לְשִׁמּוּשׁ הָאָדָם. אָמְנָם הִנֵּה הוּא עוֹמֵד בְּשִׁקּוּל גָּדוֹל. כִּי אִם הָאָדָם נִמְשָׁךְ אַחַר הָעוֹלָם וּמִתְרַחֵק מִבּוֹרְאוֹ, הִנֵּה הוּא מִתְקַלְקֵל וּמְקַלְקֵל הָעוֹלָם עִמּוֹ. וְאִם הוּא שׁוֹלֵט בְּעַצְמוֹ וְנִדְבָּק בְּבוֹרְאוֹ וּמִשְׁתַּמֵּשׁ מִן הָעוֹלָם רַק לִהְיוֹת לוֹ לְסִיּוּעַ לַעֲבוֹדַת בּוֹרְאוֹ, הוּא מִתְעַלֶּה וְהָעוֹלָם עַצְמוֹ מִתְעַלֶּה עִמּוֹ. כִּי הִנֵּה עִלּוּי גָּדוֹל הוּא לַבְּרִיּוֹת כֻּלָּם בִּהְיוֹתָם מְשַׁמְּשֵׁי הָאָדָם הַשָּׁלֵם הַמְקֻדָּשׁ בִּקְדֻשָּׁתוֹ יִתְבָּרֵךְ.

The world was created for man's use and man is in the center of a great balance. If man follows earthly pursuits and is drawn away from his Creator, he is impaired, and the rest of the world is impaired along with him. If he becomes master over himself and unites himself with his Creator, using the world only to help him in the service of his Creator, he is elevated and the world is elevated along with him. All creatures are elevated when they serve the "complete man" who is sanctified with the holiness of G-d.

The entire universe takes on meaning when it is used to enable man to achieve the ultimate goal of creation. The universe can be only as meaningful as man is. If man fails to pursue his goal, the entire universe serves no purpose.

Two loiterers were arrested by a police officer, and when they appeared before the magistrate, he asked the first loiterer, "What were you doing when you were arrested?" "Nothing," the man answered. He then turned to the second loiterer, "And what were you doing when you were arrested?" The second loiterer pointed to his friend and said, "I was helping him." It is clear that even the most sophisticated system with a myriad of intermediate functions is meaningless if it produces no end product or serves no ultimate purpose.

Our limited intelligence may not be able to understand the function of many things, how they can possibly be serving man. How is the tiny insect in the tropical rain forest of service to man? How do stars that are billions of light years distant contribute to man's functioning?

The Midrash says that King David in his youth once noticed a spider, and this set him to thinking, Of what possible use is a spider to man? When he later fled from King Saul and hid in a cave, a spider spun a web over the opening of the cave, and upon seeing the spider web, Saul concluded that the cave could not have been recently entered and in this way did not capture David. G-d then said to David, "You should never question the purpose of any of My creations."

This concept of everything in the universe being directed toward man's ultimate goal is far reaching and places an immense responsibility on man. The Talmud states that if a person partakes of the goods of the world without reciting the appropriate *berachah* (blessing), he is essentially stealing from G-d. The goods of the world were meant to be used to enable man to develop himself spiritually. When man fails to do so, he is misappropriating materials that were entrusted to him for a specific purpose, and that is equivalent to "stealing" from G-d.

וּבְעִנְיָן אַבְנֵי הַמָּקוֹם שֶׁלָּקַח יַעֲקֹב וְשָׂם מְרַאֲשׁוֹתָיו אָמְרוּ (חולין צא, ב), „אָמַר רַבִּי יִצְחָק, מְלַמֵּד שֶׁנִּתְקַבְּצוּ כֻּלָּן לְמָקוֹם אֶחָד וְהָיְתָה כָּל אַחַת אוֹמֶרֶת, עָלַי יַנִּיחַ צַדִּיק רֹאשׁוֹ״. וְהִנֵּה עַל הָעִקָּר הַזֶּה הֵעִירוּנוּ זִכְרוֹנָם לִבְרָכָה בְּמִדְרַשׁ קֹהֶלֶת (רבה ז, כח) שֶׁאָמְרוּ, זֶה לְשׁוֹנָם: „רְאֵה אֶת־מַעֲשֵׂה הָאֱלֹהִים וְגו׳ (קהלת ז, יג), בְּשָׁעָה שֶׁבָּרָא הַקָּדוֹשׁ בָּרוּךְ הוּא אֶת אָדָם הָרִאשׁוֹן, נְטָלוֹ וְהֶחֱזִירוֹ עַל כָּל אִילָנֵי גַּן עֵדֶן וְאָמַר לוֹ, רְאֵה מַעֲשַׂי כַּמָּה נָאִים וּמְשֻׁבָּחִים הֵן, וְכָל מַה שֶּׁבָּרָאתִי בִּשְׁבִילְךָ בָּרָאתִי, תֵּן דַּעְתְּךָ שֶׁלֹּא תְקַלְקֵל וְתַחֲרִיב אֶת עוֹלָמִי״.

In relation to the "stones of the place" that Jacob took and put around his head (Genesis 28:11) Rabbi Yitzchak said, "This teaches us that the stones gathered themselves into one spot, each one saying, 'Let the tzaddik place his head upon me' (Chullin 91b). Our sages emphasize this principle when they said, 'See the work of G-d' (Ecclesiastes 7:13). When G-d created Adam, He took him before all the trees of the Garden of Eden and said, 'See how beautiful and praiseworthy all My works are. Everything I have created, was created for your sake. Be cautious that you do not damage and destroy My world' " (Koheles Rabbah 7:28).

Of all creatures, man alone was given free will to choose between doing good or evil. Thus, although there should be a natural attraction of man toward his ultimate goal, the Divine Wisdom set up a counter-force, the *yetzer hara*, to deter man from his goal, so that there would be a true freedom of choice. With the exception of man, everything else in creation should gravitate toward its ultimate goal.

The Talmud says, "Have you ever seen a bird or beast agonize over its *parnassah* (livelihood) the way man does? Now if these creatures, which were created to serve me, are provided with the means of their survival, why do I have to agonize over mine? It is only because I have done wrong and thereby sabotaged my livelihood" (*Kiddushin* 82b).

If man were to live a truly spiritual life in pursuit of his ultimate goal, everything else in creation would be subservient to him and gravitate toward him, seeking its own fulfillment by being of service to man.

This was the status of Adam in the Garden of Eden, when all of nature subordinated itself to him. It was only after Adam sinned by submitting to temptation and turning away from the pursuit of spirituality that nature was no longer subject to serve his needs, and it was then decreed that he would have to wrest his livelihood from the land by the sweat of his brow (*Genesis* 3:19). Yet, to the degree that a person pursues his ultimate goal, to that degree will nature subordinate itself to his needs, as the Talmud points out with the example of the stones that Jacob gathered.

כְּלָלוֹ שֶׁל דָּבָר, הָאָדָם לֹא נִבְרָא בַּעֲבוּר מַצָּבוֹ בָּעוֹלָם הַזֶּה אֶלָּא בַּעֲבוּר מַצָּבוֹ בָּעוֹלָם הַבָּא, אֶלָּא שֶׁמַּצָּבוֹ בָּעוֹלָם הַזֶּה הוּא אֶמְצָעִי לְמַצָּבוֹ בָּעוֹלָם הַבָּא שֶׁהוּא הַתַּכְלִיתִי. עַל כֵּן תִּמְצָא מַאֲמָרֵי חֲכָמֵינוּ ז״ל רַבִּים כֻּלָּם בְּסִגְנוֹן אֶחָד מְדַמִּים הָעוֹלָם הַזֶּה לִמְקוֹם וּזְמַן הַהֲכָנָה וְהָעוֹלָם הַבָּא לִמְקוֹם הַמְּנוּחָה וַאֲכִילַת הַמּוּכָן כְּבָר, וְהוּא מַה שֶּׁאָמְרוּ (אבות ד, כא): „הָעוֹלָם הַזֶּה דּוֹמֶה לִפְרוֹזְדוֹר״, כְּמוֹ שֶׁאָמְרוּ זִכְרוֹנָם לִבְרָכָה: „הַיּוֹם לַעֲשׂוֹתָם וּמָחָר לְקַבֵּל שְׂכָרָם״ (עירובין כב, א).

וְתִרְאֶה בֶּאֱמֶת שֶׁכְּבָר לֹא יוּכַל שׁוּם בַּעַל שֵׂכֶל לְהַאֲמִין שֶׁתַּכְלִית בְּרִיאַת הָאָדָם הוּא לְמַצָּבוֹ בָּעוֹלָם הַזֶּה, כִּי מַה הֵם חַיֵּי הָאָדָם בָּעוֹלָם הַזֶּה? אוֹ מִי הוּא שֶׁשָּׂמֵחַ וְשָׁלֵו מַמָּשׁ בָּעוֹלָם הַזֶּה? „יְמֵי שְׁנוֹתֵינוּ בָּהֶם שִׁבְעִים שָׁנָה וְאִם בִּגְבוּרוֹת שְׁמוֹנִים שָׁנָה וְרָהְבָּם עָמָל וָאָוֶן״ (תהלים צ, י), בְּכַמָּה מִינֵי צַעַר וָחֳלָאִים וּמַכְאוֹבִים וּטְרָדוֹת, וְאַחַר כָּל זֹאת־הַמָּוֶת. אֶחָד מִנִּי אֶלֶף לֹא יִמָּצֵא שֶׁיַּרְבֶּה הָעוֹלָם לוֹ הֲנָחוֹת וְשַׁלְוָה אֲמִתִּית.

To recapitulate, man was not created for his position in this world, but for his position in the World to Come. Being in this world is but a means toward his station in the World to Come, which is the ultimate goal. Our sages describe this world as a place of preparation, and the next world as a place for rest and partaking of what has been prepared. This is also their intent when they say, "This world is like an antechamber," (Ethics of the Fathers 4:21), and "Today (in this world) for the performance (of mitzvos) and tomorrow (in the World to Come) for receiving the reward" (Eruvin 22a).

Truthfully, no intelligent person can believe that the purpose of man's creation could be for his position in this world. For what is a man's life in this world? Who is truly happy and content in this world? "The days of life are seventy years, and if one is very robust, eighty years, and the strongest (of these years) is but travail and inequity"

(Psalms 90:10), with so many different kinds of suffering and disease and pain and burdens! And following all this — death! Not even one in a thousand can be found for whom the world has provided an abundance of gratifications and true peace.

If a person does not believe in G-d and in creation, and assumes the world to be something which "just happened" and that everything in it is the result of undesigned, natural consequences of physical laws, then it is meaningless to talk about a goal and purpose of life. "Goal" and "purpose" of man presuppose a Creator and a design for the universe which make it purposeful.

Unless one were to attribute to the Creator mischief at best or frank cruelty at worst, it is absurd to consider this earthly world as the ultimate purpose of creation and the place where man is to realize his ultimate goal. As Ramchal points out, the proportion of misery to contentment in this world is so overwhelmingly top-heavy on the negative side, that one would have to attribute an inordinate degree of ineptness to the intelligence that designed it, which is totally incompatible with the concept of a Supreme Being. The attributes of wisdom, justice, and benevolence which are understood as being attributes of the Creator do not permit us to accept the earthly world, with the dominance of suffering and distress as the ultimate goal of man. We can come only to one conclusion, that there is another existence where the benevolence of G-d is enjoyed, and that the hardships of existence in this world are but a means to attain the true good in the World to Come.

וְלֹא עוֹד אֶלָּא שֶׁאִם תַּכְלִית בְּרִיאַת הָאָדָם הָיָה לְצֹרֶךְ הָעוֹלָם הַזֶּה, לֹא הָיָה צָרִיךְ מִפְּנֵי זֶה שֶׁתִּנָּפַח בּוֹ נְשָׁמָה כָּל־כָּךְ חֲשׁוּבָה וְעֶלְיוֹנָה שֶׁתִּהְיֶה גְדוֹלָה יוֹתֵר מִן הַמַּלְאָכִים עַצְמָם, כָּל־שֶׁכֵּן שֶׁהִיא אֵינָהּ מוֹצְאָה שׁוּם נַחַת רוּחַ בְּכָל עִנּוּגֵי זֶה הָעוֹלָם. וְהוּא מַה שֶׁלִּמְדוּנוּ זִכְרוֹנָם לִבְרָכָה בְּמִדְרַשׁ קֹהֶלֶת, זוֹ לְשׁוֹנָם (רבה ו, ז): ,,וְגַם הַנֶּפֶשׁ לֹא תִמָּלֵא (קהלת ו, ז), מָשָׁל לְמָה הַדָּבָר דּוֹמֶה, לְעִירוֹנִי שֶׁנָּשָׂא בַּת מְלָכִים אִם יָבִיא לָהּ כָּל מַה שֶּׁבָּעוֹלָם אֵינָם חֲשׁוּבִים לָהּ כְּלוּם שֶׁהִיא בַּת מֶלֶךְ. כָּךְ הַנֶּפֶשׁ, אִלּוּ הֵבֵאתָ לָהּ כָּל מַעֲדַנֵּי עוֹלָם, אֵינָם כְּלוּם לָהּ, לָמָּה? שֶׁהִיא מִן הָעֶלְיוֹנִים״. וְכֵן אָמְרוּ רַבּוֹתֵינוּ זִכְרוֹנָם לִבְרָכָה (אבות ד, כט): ,,עַל כָּרְחֲךָ אַתָּה נוֹצָר וְעַל כָּרְחֲךָ אַתָּה נוֹלָד״. כִּי אֵין הַנְּשָׁמָה אוֹהֶבֶת הָעוֹלָם הַזֶּה

כְּלָל אֶלָּא אַדְּרַבָּא מוֹאֶסֶת בּוֹ. אִם כֵּן וַדַּאי לֹא הָיָה בּוֹרֵא הַבּוֹרֵא יִתְבָּרֵךְ בְּרִיאָה לְתַכְלִית שֶׁהוּא נֶגֶד חָקָּהּ וְנִמְאָס מִמֶּנָּה.

Furthermore, if man had been created solely for the sake of existing in this world, there would have been no need of his being inspired with a soul so exalted as to be greater than that of the heavenly angels; especially since the soul derives absolutely no satisfaction from all of the earthly pleasures. This is what our sages teach us, "and also the soul shall not be satisfied" (Ecclesiastes 6:7). This is analogous to the case of a peasant who married a princess. Even if he brought her all of his worldly possessions, it would mean nothing to her, by virtue of her being accustomed to palatial surroundings, (Koheles Rabbah 6:7). So it is with the soul. Even if it were to be supplied with every pleasure of this world, they would provide nothing for the soul, since it is of a much loftier, spiritual nature. This is why our sages say, "you were created against your will and you were born against your will" (Ethics of the Fathers 4:29), because the soul has no desire to be in this world. Certainly the Creator would not have created for the soul a world that opposes its nature and which it despises.

Whereas Ramchal approaches the absurdity of believing the earthly world to be the ultimate goal of man by virtue of (a) the incompatibility of the spiritual soul with physical pleasures and (b) that for the Divine soul being in this world is an unpleasant ordeal, we can arrive at the same conclusion from another aspect.

Both the colloquial aphorism "ignorance is bliss" and the Scriptural statement that "the wiser one is the more one suffers" (*Ecclesiastes* 1:18) attest to the correlation of increased wisdom with an increase in distress. Cows in a pasture are spared the worries, anxieties, and depression which beset man. Even animals in the wild are far less stressed than intelligent human beings. If the goal of life was to achieve contentment on earth, then bestowing superior intelligence upon man was a grave mistake. Man would have been better off functioning with animal instinct characteristic of lower forms of life.

If someone saw a child dressed in a coat whose sleeves reached the floor and a hat which fell over his eyes, one would immediately conclude that the child had put on his father's clothes. Clothes that are so far beyond his size could not have been designed for him.

If we appreciate the vastness of the human intellect, it is clear that it was not designed primarily to enable man to achieve a maximum of contentment in this world. Something of much lesser capacity and sophistication would have been far better suited for achieving contentment. The ability of the human mind to think abstractly, to philosophize, and to meditate on infinity is an indication that there is much more to man's existence than gratifying one's physical drives. That the human mind could have composed works such as *Ecclesiastes* and the Book of *Job* is the greatest testimony to the spiritual goal of man. Works such as these that analyze the nothingness of the material world and the problem of why the just are subjected to suffering are totally out of place in a world designed for contentment.

It has been said that it requires great fortitude to be a believer. Perhaps so, but it requires even greater fortitude to be a non-believer. True, the belief in G-d leaves one with the conclusion that human suffering makes no sense, but not believing leaves one with the conclusion that nothing makes any sense.

אֶלָּא בְּרִיאָתוֹ שֶׁל הָאָדָם, לְמַצָּבוֹ בָּעוֹלָם הַבָּא הִיא. וְעַל כֵּן נִתְּנָה בּוֹ נְשָׁמָה זֹאת, כִּי לָהּ רָאוּי לַעֲבוֹד וּבָהּ יוּכַל הָאָדָם לְקַבֵּל הַשָּׂכָר בִּמְקוֹמוֹ וּזְמַנּוֹ, שֶׁלֹּא יִהְיֶה דָּבָר נִמְאָס אֶל נִשְׁמָתוֹ בָּעוֹלָם הַזֶּה, אֶלָּא אַדְּרַבָּא נֶאֱהָב וְנֶחְמָד מִמֶּנָּה.

Thus, man was created for his position in the World to Come, and therefore the soul was placed within him, because it is befitting for the soul to serve G-d and through the soul a person may receive his reward in the World to Come. In this way, the soul is not repelled by this world, but to the contrary, the soul can love this world.

Earlier Ramchal stated that the spiritual soul has no tolerance for the world, because worldly pleasures and indulgences are anathema to it. However, since the world is the antechamber, the vehicle whereby one can attain the eternal good, the soul can actually appreciate and desire this world, not for itself, but for what it can lead to.

People who are fanatically fastidious and are repulsed by even a speck of dirt may gladly submit to therapeutic mud packs if the latter portends to relieve the distress of skin diseases or painful joints. They will actually pay to have their body smeared with something that they despise. The anticipation of relief from suffering not only converts and decontaminates the mud, but bestows a positive value on it for its healing qualities.

So it is with the Divine soul, which is repelled by the earthly world and its many physical indulgences. However, inasmuch as the material world is the vehicle whereby the ultimate good of being one with G-d can be achieved, the soul not only tolerates this world, but can actually hold it in high esteem.

Chassidic teaching takes this concept one step further, stating that earthly objects can be changed into spiritual objects and can take on sanctity. Not only does an animal hide become sacred when converted into parchment for a Torah scroll or leather for *tefillin*, but even items which do not achieve an actual state of holiness are elevated when they are incorporated into the pursuit of the ultimate purpose. Thus, the food which provides energy to do mitzvos, and the rest which enables the body to be rejuvenated in order to perform mitzvos, all become spiritual objects and processes. All of life can thus be spiritual.

וְהִנֵּה אַחַר שֶׁיָּדַעְנוּ זֶה, נָבִין מִיָּד חֹמֶר הַמִּצְוֹת אֲשֶׁר עָלֵינוּ וִיקָר הָעֲבוֹדָה אֲשֶׁר בְּיָדֵנוּ, כִּי הִנֵּה אֵלֶּה הֵם הָאֶמְצָעִים הַמְּבִיאִים אוֹתָנוּ אֶל הַשְּׁלֵמוּת הָאֲמִתִּי, אֲשֶׁר בִּלְעָדָם לֹא יֻשַּׂג כְּלָל. וְאוּלָם יָדוּעַ כִּי אֵין הַתַּכְלִית מַגִּיעַ אֶלָּא מִכֹּחַ קִבּוּץ כָּל הָאֶמְצָעִים אֲשֶׁר נִמְצְאוּ וַאֲשֶׁר שִׁמְּשׁוּ לְהַגִּיעוֹ. וּכְפִי כֹּחַ הָאֶמְצָעִים וְשִׁמּוּשָׁם, כֵּן יִהְיֶה הַתַּכְלִית הַנּוֹלָד מֵהֶם.

Once we recognize this, we will readily understand the importance of the mitzvos and the esteem of the Divine service which lies in our hands, since these are the only means which can bring us to true perfection. It should be understood, however, that this goal can be attained only by a consolidation of all the means available for reaching it. How much of the goal one reaches depends on the strength of the means and how they were used.

One might conceptualize the ultimate good as being enclosed and sealed tightly in a safe, to which one can gain access only if one knows the combination and dials it accurately. Thus, the "combination" to achieve the ultimate good of uniting with G-d is comprised of the six-hundred-thirteen mitzvos and their various derivatives. Just as any deviation from the combination of a safe will not permit access to its contents, so will deviation from the Torah preclude unity with G-d.

This analogy is not quite accurate, because in the absence of the correct combination, one can nevertheless access the contents of the safe by forcing the door open with explosives. No such alternate method is available for attaining the ultimate good. The observance of mitzvos is the only method that can unite man with G-d; hence one should accord the mitzvos the utmost importance, since without them the ultimate good is forever unattainable and existence is then without meaning.

מֵעַתָּה וַדַּאי הוּא שֶׁהַדִּקְדּוּק שֶׁיְּדַקְדֵּק עַל עִנְיַן הַמִּצְוֹת וְהָעֲבוֹדָה, מֻכְרָח שֶׁיִּהְיֶה בְּתַכְלִית הַדִּקְדּוּק כַּאֲשֶׁר יְדַקְדְּקוּ שׁוֹקְלֵי הַזָּהָב וְהַפְּנִינִים לְרוֹב יָקְרָם, כִּי תוֹלַדְתָּם נוֹלֶדֶת בַּשְּׁלֵמוּת הָאֲמִתִּי וְהַיְקָר הַנִּצְחִי שֶׁאֵין יְקָר לְמַעְלָה מִמֶּנּוּ.

It is now certain that the precision which one must take in regard to mitzvos and the service of G-d must be extremely exacting, just as those who weigh gold or jewels exercise the utmost precision because of their great value. This is because mitzvos result in the ultimate perfection and eternal wealth, and there is certainly nothing more worthy than that.

The permissible tolerance of error can vary greatly depending on what one is doing and what the consequences of deviation are. For example, a butcher who is assigned to cut slices of steak one and one-half inches thick will be considered to have done an excellent job if he deviates only one or two millimeters either way. On the other hand, an error of even less than a millimeter committed by a surgeon who is operating on a vital organ may result in a patient's death.

Ramchal uses the analogy of a jeweler's scale. In contrast to a grocer's scale which may tolerate a margin of error of several grams, the jeweler's scale must be calibrated so that there not be an error of even a fraction of a carat. The fact that proper performance of mitzvos are the only vehicle whereby a person can reach the very essence of his existence makes it mandatory that one exercise the utmost precision in regard to them. In fact, the eternal character of the consequences of the observance of mitzvos endows them with an importance that far exceeds that of precious jewels.

נמצינו למדים, כי עקר מציאות האדם בעולם הזה הוא רק לקים מצות ולעבוד ולעמוד בנסיון, והנאות העולם אין ראוי שיהיו לו אלא לעזר ולסיוע בלבד לשיהיה לו נחת רוח וישוב דעת למען יוכל לפנות לבו אל העבודה הזאת המטלת עליו. ואמנם ראוי לו שתהיה כל פניתו רק לבורא יתברך, ושלא יהיה לו שום תכלית אחר בכל מעשה שיעשה אם קטן ואם גדול אלא להתקרב אליו יתברך ולשבור כל המחיצות המפסיקות בינו לבין קונו, הן הנה כל עניני החמריות והתלוי בהם עד שימשך אחריו יתברך ממש כברזל אחר אבן השואבת. וכל מה שיוכל לחשוב שהוא אמצעי לקרבה הזאת, ירדוף אחריו ויאחז בו ולא ירפהו, וכל מה שיוכל לחשוב שהוא מניעה לזה, יברח ממנו כברח מן האש.

We may thus conclude that the essence of a man's existence in this world is only to fulfill the mitzvos, to serve G-d, and to withstand trials. Partaking of the pleasures of the world is appropriate only insofar as they aid and assist the person, to provide him with a pleasant disposition and clarity of thought so that he can devote his heart to the service to which he is obligated. However, all his ventures should be directed only toward G-d, and there should be no other purpose in everything he does other than to come close to G-d and to eliminate all the barriers that separate man from his Creator, so that he will be attracted to G-d just as iron is attracted to a magnet. These barriers are the earthly pleasures. Whatever can be a means to enhance this closeness should be pursued and retained. Whatever one thinks will be a deterrent to this closeness should be avoided, just as one flees from fire.

In contrast to earlier ethicists who advocated stringent asceticism as a means to attain spirituality, Ramchal states that even earthly pleasures can be directed towards and incorporated in spirituality. How so? If one provides the body with the nutrition for its optimum function which will in turn enhance one's ability to perform mitzvos, this contributes to the ultimate spiritual goal. The Chafetz Chaim would enter the study hall late at night and order students to go to bed so that they would have adequate rest to allow them to think more clearly the next day. He said that the urge to study into the early hours of the morning may actually be the work of the *yetzer hara*, which wishes to impair a person's understanding of Torah by causing him to exhaust himself through sleep deprivation. Judicious rest, relaxation, and even pastimes can become part of the service of G-d if they are enjoyed for that purpose.

Ramchal cautions us not to deceive ourselves. A person may while away his life in pastimes or in excessive rest, by claiming that he is doing so in order to enhance his strength so that he can better serve G-d. This is no different than someone indulging like a glutton and claiming that he is doing so to be better able to serve G-d. The amount of nutrition that is conducive to good health is known, and excess food is actually detrimental to health and impairs rather than enhances optimum function. A person should be truthful with himself, and not allow himself to be deluded by rationalizations that are intended to justify indulgence in earthly pleasures.

Ramchal adds that proper fulfillment of the mitzvos eliminates the barriers that may obstruct man's union with G-d. The human soul, being part of the Divine essence, craves to be reunited with its source, and there is a natural attraction of the soul to G-d, just as iron filings are attracted to a magnet. A barrier of insulation can obstruct the magnetic pull, and when this insulation is removed, the natural attraction takes place. Similarly, when improper indulgence in physical pleasures, which constitute the barriers between man and G-d, are eliminated, the reunion of the human soul with G-d occurs.

In the introduction, Ramchal emphasized the need to pursue spirituality, bemoaning the fact that many people devote much effort to things that do not enhance spirituality and neglect those things that enable its achievement. In this chapter, Ramchal has defined spirituality as *the union of man with G-d*, pointing out that proper fulfillment of the Divine will is what enables man to achieve this union. Since this goal is the essence of man's existence, he urges active pursuit of those practices that contribute to attainment of this goal, and to assiduously avoid whatever may deter from it. All that remains now is for a person to know what are the practices that lead to the goal, and what kinds of things impede one's reaching that goal. Ramchal now goes on to say:

וְהִנֵּה אַחַר שֶׁיָּדַעְנוּ וְהִתְבָּרֵר אֶצְלֵנוּ אֲמִתַּת הַכְּלַל הַזֶּה, יֶשׁ־לָנוּ לַחֲקֹר עַל פְּרָטָיו לְפִי מַדְרְגוֹתֵיהֶם מִתְּחִלַּת הַדָּבָר וְעַד סוֹפוֹ, כְּמוֹ שֶׁסִּדְּרָם רַבִּי פִּינְחָס בֶּן יָאִיר בְּמַאֲמָר שֶׁלּוֹ שֶׁהֵבֵאנוּ כְּבָר בְּהַקְדָּמָתֵנוּ, וָהֵם: הַזְּהִירוּת, הַזְּרִיזוּת, הַנְּקִיּוּת, הַפְּרִישׁוּת,

הַטָּהֳרָה, הַחֲסִידוּת, הָעֲנָוָה, יִרְאַת הַחֵטְא, וְהַקְּדֻשָּׁה. וְעַתָּה נְבָאֲרֵם אֶחָד אֶחָד בְּסִיַּעְתָּא דִשְׁמַיָּא.

Having recognized the truth of this principle, let us now investigate the details of the ways to achieve spirituality according to their stages from the beginning to the end, as they were arranged by Rabbi Pinchas ben Yair. These stages are: watchfulness, diligence, cleanliness, abstinence, purity, piety, humility, fear of wrongdoing, and sanctity. Let us now, with the help of G-d, explain them one by one.

2

בְּבֵאוּר מִדַּת הַזְּהִירוּת

Clarifying the Trait of Watchfulness

הִנֵּה עִנְיַן הַזְּהִירוּת הוּא שֶׁיִּהְיֶה הָאָדָם נִזְהָר בְּמַעֲשָׂיו וּבְעִנְיָנָיו, כְּלוֹמַר, מִתְבּוֹנֵן וּמְפַקֵּחַ עַל מַעֲשָׂיו וּדְרָכָיו, הֲטוֹבִים הֵם אִם לֹא, לְבִלְתִּי עֲזוֹב נַפְשׁוֹ לְסַכָּנַת הָאֲבַדּוֹן חָס וְחָלִילָה וְלֹא יֵלֵךְ בְּמַהֲלַךְ הֶרְגֵּלוֹ כְּעִוֵּר בָּאֲפֵלָה. וְהִנֵּה זֶה דָּבָר שֶׁהַשֵּׂכֶל יְחַיְּבֵהוּ וַדַּאי. כִּי אַחֲרֵי שֶׁיֵּשׁ לָאָדָם דֵּעָה וְהַשְׂכֵּל לְהַצִּיל אֶת עַצְמוֹ וְלִבְרוֹחַ מֵאֲבַדּוֹן נִשְׁמָתוֹ, אֵיךְ יִתָּכֵן שֶׁיִּרְצֶה לְהַעֲלִים עֵינָיו מֵהַצָּלָתוֹ, אֵין לְךָ פְּחִיתוּת וְהוֹלֵלוּת רַע מִזֶּה וַדַּאי. וְהָעוֹשֶׂה כֵּן הִנֵּה הוּא פָּחוּת מֵהַבְּהֵמוֹת וּמֵהַחַיּוֹת אֲשֶׁר בְּטִבְעָם לִשְׁמוֹר אֶת עַצְמָם וְעַל כֵּן יִבְרְחוּ וְיָנוּסוּ מִכָּל מַה שֶּׁיֵּרָאֶה לָהֶם הֱיוֹתוֹ מַזִּיק לָהֶם. וְהַהוֹלֵךְ בְּעוֹלָמוֹ בְּלִי הִתְבּוֹנְנוּת אִם טוֹבָה דַּרְכּוֹ אוֹ רָעָה, הִנֵּה הוּא כְּסוּמָא הַהוֹלֵךְ עַל שְׂפַת הַנָּהָר אֲשֶׁר סַכָּנָתוֹ וַדַּאי עֲצוּמָה וְרָעָתוֹ קְרוֹבָה מֵהַצָּלָתוֹ. כִּי אוּלָם חֶסְרוֹן הַשְּׁמִירָה מִפְּנֵי הָעִוָּרוֹן הַטִּבְעִי אוֹ מִפְּנֵי הָעִוָּרוֹן הָרְצוֹנִי דְּהַיְינוּ סְתִימַת הָעֵינַיִם בִּבְחִירָה וָחֵפֶץ, אֶחָד הוּא.

Watchfulness means that a person should be cautious in his actions; i.e., to deliberate over his behavior to ascertain whether it is good or not, in order that he does not risk spiritual destruction and so that he does not follow the path of habit as a blind man in darkness. If one has the knowledge and reasoning ability to avoid spiritual destruction, it is inconceivable that he would make himself oblivious to his own salvation. There can be no worse degradation and foolishness than this. Anyone who does so is lower than brute beasts who instinctively protect themselves and flee from anything that appears dangerous to them. Any person who conducts himself without considerations as to whether his way is good or bad, is like a blind person walking at the river's edge whose likelihood of being destroyed is greater than his being saved. There is essentially no difference between physical blindness or a self-induced psychological blindness; i.e., closing one's eyes to reality.

Before considering the methods of Watchfulness, it is only natural to ask, Why should one be watchful? What are the dangers one must avoid?

The answer to this was provided by Moses in *Deuteronomy* 30:15. "Behold, I have set before you life and good on the one hand, and death and evil on the other." This is the basis for Watchfulness. Unless a person understands that evil is identical with death and good is identical with life, there is no point in discussing Watchfulness, or for that matter, any other trait that leads to spirituality.

Although much has been written about the hygienic and other health values of Torah observance, it is quite clear that in equating good and evil with life and death respectively, Moses was referring primarily to spiritual life and spiritual death rather than physical life and death. In the same vein, the Talmud states that "the wicked are referred to as having died even though they are physically alive" (*Berachos* 18b).

It is common practice that the precautions we take to avoid exposing ourselves to danger are commensurate with the magnitude of the risk. Monetarily, we will exercise relatively less caution if what we are investing is money that we can afford to lose. However, if we invest our life savings, we will seek guarantees so that we are not rendered penniless by a turn of events. Physically, we may exercise less caution in exposing ourselves to the sun, where the worst immediate effects that can happen is that excess exposure can result in sunburn, than exposing ourselves to radiation, where an excess can be lethal. How much caution one exercises indicates one's measure of the risk involved. How carefully we guard our spirituality is an indication of how much value we assign to it.

Science classifies man as *homo sapiens*, essentially a "baboon with intellect," and does not provide for the human spirit as comprising an essential part of man. The Torah approach is that man's uniqueness, that which distinguishes him from other living things, is not only his intellect, but his *spirit*, the *neshamah* or Divine soul which G-d instilled within him. Man without this spirit is indeed *homo sapiens*, and while he may be considered biologically human, he is not "man," the being created in the image of G-d. The Talmudic reference to the person who rejects spirituality is that his uniqueness of being "man" has died, although he is biologically alive.

If a person has a true understanding that his very essence as man is dependent on doing right and avoiding wrong, then he will exercise Watchfulness to preserve his spiritual life, just as he is watchful to avoid all threats to his physical survival.

Even within spirituality, the degree of caution one exercises reveals how much importance one attaches to its components. Some people may choose one area of mitzvah observance over another, although this is discouraged by the Talmud. "Be as cautious with what you think is a minor mitzvah as with what you think is a major one, since you have no way of knowing the rewards for various mitzvos" (*Ethics of the Fathers* 2:1).

Rabbi Michoel Ber Weismandel related that he once spent Succos in Yemen. On the day before the festival, a man came into *shul*, and emptied a huge sack of *esrogim* (citrons) onto the table. (In Yemen, *esrogim* are available in abundance.) Each person chose an *esrog* and dropped a few coins into a *pushke* (charity box).

Rabbi Weismandel was taken aback by this. He was accustomed to carefully selecting an *esrog*, and standing among customers who would meticulously examine the *esrog* with a magnifying glass to make sure it was free of the minutest blemish. Acquiring an *esrog* for this precious mitzvah by picking one out of a huge pile seemed to be trivializing the mitzvah.

On the following morning, when one congregant stepped up to the pulpit to serve as *chazzan* (reader) another person came over and pushed him aside, exclaiming "Yesterday he told an untruth. How dare he serve as *chazzan*?" Rabbi Weismandel reflected, "True, we seek to acquire an *esrog* which is free of the minutest blemish. Are we as meticulous in our demands for truth, that a person who represents us before G-d should be without a blemish of falsehood?"

Ideally, we should endeavor that all facets of our lives be without blemish: our *esrog*, our *tefillin*, our *mezuzzah*, our speech, and our behavior as a whole.

Too often we give lip service to spirituality, and are not as concerned about it as a true realization of its importance would warrant. We read in *Ethics of the Fathers* (4:2) that "sin begets sin." This is a statement of fact, an immutable law of nature, that just as the force of gravity attracts an object, so does the force of sin attract another sin. We say this when we recite *Ethics of the Fathers*, but do we really believe it?

A man who completed a course of treatment for alcoholism, as a result of a warning at work that one more drinking episode would result in his being terminated, was very faithful in following all instructions to maintain sobriety. He understood that because he was alcoholic, even one drink could result in an uncontrollable craving and ultimately in a drunken stupor.

After eight months of sobriety, he called in a panic. He had been at a friend's celebration, and had refused any alcoholic drink, but did accept a glass of punch. One sip made him aware that it had been "spiked." He called me in desperation, fearful that this accidental consumption of a small amount of alcohol may set in motion a chain reaction leading to frank drunkenness which would cost him his job and probably his marriage. He was willing to enter the hospital if necessary until the crisis had passed.

Let us suppose that an observant person ate a candy bar which he assumed to be kosher, only to discover that the *hechsher* (rabbinic sanction of *kashrus*) had been withdrawn. He would indeed regret this lapse, and determine that henceforth he would be more watchful and check for a *hechsher* before he eats something. But why doesn't he run to the phone and call the rabbi in a panic like the alcoholic did? "Rabbi," he should say, "I accidentally ate something that was not kosher! Sin leads to sin, and I don't know what this inadvertent sin might bring in its aftermath. What should I do to prevent myself from slipping into frank transgression?"

The difference is that the alcoholic knows for certain that one drink leads to another. He discovered this the hard way, and it is not an abstract concept. We *verbalize* that sin begets sin, but we do not know it the way the alcoholic does. If we were to know this, we would then understand why Watchfulness is important.

Ramchal refers to a person who is not watchful as a "blind person who walks in the darkness." If a person is totally blind, what difference is it whether it is light or dark? The answer is that even though a blind person cannot see where to go, he can be helped and guided by someone who is sighted. But this is only when there is light. In the darkness, neither can he see nor can he get help from others.

A person who neglects being watchful not only fails to exercise his own awareness of danger, but also negates the possibility of receiving proper guidance from people who could help him.

Ramchal emphasizes the danger in allowing behavior to be dictated by habit. Even from the aspect of *homo sapiens*, from a purely intellectual aspect, let alone a spiritual one, every intelligent person should want his behavior to be determined by his intellect. If someone functions by habit, then he has essentially relinquished intellectual control of behavior.

Habitual behavior comes very close to being addictive, often virtually in defiance of intellect. One woman who sought hypnotic treatment to stop smoking was given a post-hypnotic suggestion that cigarettes would taste terrible. She reported that the suggestion was indeed effective, and that cigarettes had a very foul taste, but she had nevertheless continued to smoke two packs a day because she could not break the habit.

There are some things, such as walking, that are automatic actions. We could not possibly function if we had to consciously think about every step we take. But there are more consequential things that we do because we are accustomed to doing them, and we may give them no particular thought. Ramchal points out that this can be hazardous.

The great Talmudist, Rabbi Shlomo Eiger, wrote to his son, "I have noted that you are in the habit of saying 'Sh!' whenever someone in your family talks too loudly. This is a bad habit, because sometimes you may inadvertently say 'Sh' to older people who talk loudly, and that would be disrespectful."

In the famous letter to his son, Ramban writes, "Always pause to think what you are about to say before you speak." How much grief would be avoided if people deliberated on their speech, and gave serious thought to what they were going to say before verbalizing it.

The Talmud states that if a person has committed a forbidden act twice, by the third time he gives it no thought, and assumes it to be permissible (*Yoma* 86b). This is the kind of danger Ramchal ascribes to habit. We may be doing things that are improper, but if we are not aware of this initially, we may simply never think that they are not right.

וְהִנֵּה יִרְמְיָהוּ הָיָה מִתְאוֹנֵן עַל רוֹעַ בְּנֵי דוֹרוֹ מִפְּנֵי הֱיוֹתָם נְגוּעִים בְּנֶגַע הַמִּדָּה הַזֹּאת, שֶׁהָיוּ מַעֲלִימִים עֵינֵיהֶם מִמַּעֲשֵׂיהֶם בְּלִי שֶׁיָּשִׂימוּ לֵב לִרְאוֹת מָה הֵם: הַלְהֵעָשׂוֹת אִם לְהֵעָזֵב? וְאָמַר עֲלֵיהֶם (ירמיהו ח, ו): „אֵין אִישׁ נִחָם עַל רָעָתוֹ לֵאמֹר וגו׳ כֻּלֹּה שָׁב בִּמְרוּצָתָם כְּסוּס שׁוֹטֵף בַּמִּלְחָמָה״. וְהַיְנוּ, שֶׁהָיוּ רוֹדְפִים וְהוֹלְכִים בִּמְרוּצַת הֶרְגֵּלָם וְדַרְכֵיהֶם מִבְּלִי שֶׁיַּנִּיחוּ זְמַן לְעַצְמָם לְדַקְדֵּק עַל הַמַּעֲשִׂים וְהַדְּרָכִים, וְנִמְצָא שֶׁהֵם נוֹפְלִים בְּרָעָה בְּלִי רְאוֹת אוֹתָהּ. וְאוּלָם הִנֵּה זֹאת בֶּאֱמֶת אַחַת מִתַּחְבּוּלוֹת הַיֵּצֶר הָרָע וְעָרְמָתוֹ לְהַכְבִּיד עֲבוֹדָתוֹ בִּתְמִידוּת עַל לִבּוֹת בְּנֵי הָאָדָם עַד שֶׁלֹּא יִשָּׁאֵר לָהֶם רֶוַח לְהִתְבּוֹנֵן וּלְהִסְתַּכֵּל בְּאֵיזֶה דֶּרֶךְ הֵם הוֹלְכִים, כִּי יוֹדֵעַ הוּא שֶׁאִלּוּלֵי הָיוּ שָׂמִים לִבָּם כִּמְעַט קָט עַל דַּרְכֵיהֶם, וַדַּאי שֶׁמִּיָּד הָיוּ מַתְחִילִים לְהִנָּחֵם מִמַּעֲשֵׂיהֶם, וְהָיְתָה הַחֲרָטָה הוֹלֶכֶת וּמִתְגַּבֶּרֶת בָּהֶם עַד שֶׁהָיוּ עוֹזְבִים הַחֵטְא לְגַמְרֵי. וַהֲרֵי זֶה מֵעֵין עֲצַת פַּרְעֹה הָרָשָׁע שֶׁאָמַר (שמות ה, ט): „תִּכְבַּד הָעֲבֹדָה עַל־הָאֲנָשִׁים וגו׳״, שֶׁהָיָה מִתְכַּוֵּן שֶׁלֹּא לְהַנִּיחַ לָהֶם רֶוַח כְּלָל לְבִלְתִּי יִתְּנוּ לֵב אוֹ יָשִׂימוּ עֵצָה נֶגְדּוֹ אֶלָּא הָיָה מִשְׁתַּדֵּל לְהַפְרִיעַ לִבָּם מִכָּל הִתְבּוֹנְנוּת בְּכֹחַ הַתְמָדַת הָעֲבוֹדָה הַבִּלְתִּי מֻפְסֶקֶת.

The prophet Jeremiah complains that the people of his generation were affected with this affliction; i.e., they made themselves oblivious to their actions, and did not pay attention as to whether their actions should be continued or abandoned. He says about these people, "No one regrets his wrongdoing . . . everyone continuing in his course as a horse rushing headlong into battle" (Jeremiah 8:6). In other words, they were operating under the impetus of habit without setting aside any time to evaluate their actions, as a result of which they unwittingly fell into evil. This is one of the common tactics of the yetzer hara, to exert constant pressure on people so that they do not have adequate time to analyze which way they are going. The yetzer hara knows that if they gave even the slightest degree of consideration to them, they would certainly regret their ways, and this regret would continue to progress until they would totally abandon their sinfulness. This is similar to the counsel of the wicked Pharaoh, who said (about the Israelites who requested emancipation), "Increase the labor on these people, etc," whereby his intention was not only to deprive them of any leisure time to avoid their opposing or scheming against him, but also trying to divert their hearts from any consideration and analysis by virtue of persistent, interminable labor.

There are instances when a person may be aroused and shaken loose from habit, and such an instance may be a turning point in one's life. The Talmud tells about the great sage Rabbi Yosi ben Yoezer, who was executed by the Romans. He was led to his execution on a Saturday, riding on a horse with his hands bound behind him. His nephew, Yakum, who had defected to the Romans and had rejected everything Jewish, saw his saintly uncle being led to his execution, and he taunted him, "Look at the horse your Master has provided for you, and look at the horse that my master has given me." Rabbi Yosi calmly replied, "If someone who transgresses the will of G-d is handsomely rewarded, just think of how great the reward is for those who obey His will." Yakum then said, "Is there anyone who was more faithful in obeying G-d's will than you?" To which Rabbi Yosi replied, "If this can happen to those who obey His will, just think what will happen to those who defy His will."

The Talmud states that Rabbi Yosi's words penetrated Yakum like the venom of a snake. He went home, held court on himself, and condemned himself to death for having been so sinful. He then committed suicide utilizing all four methods of execution carried out by the high court. Rabbi Yosi fell into a trance, in which he saw his nephew being escorted into Paradise. "In one brief moment he preceded me to Paradise," he said (*Bereishis Rabbah* 65:18). So many years of sinfulness and defiance of G-d were all reversed in one brief moment when something shocked him out of habitual behavior into *teshuvah*, into realization of the truth.

Alcoholism can be seen as the prototype of destructive habits, and it is noteworthy that an essential feature of recovery is a "spiritual awakening," a phrase that appears in the Twelve Steps of recovery espoused by Alcoholics Anonymous.

The term "spiritual awakening" is an interesting one. We frequently have "awakenings," as when we set the alarm clock for a certain hour. It is not unusual for a person to be awakened by the alarm clock, only to turn it off and go back to sleep. An awakening or an arousal is not enough. We must be prepared to use the moment of awakening to promptly get out of bed, else we will return to sleep and neglect doing all that we should. Similarly, a person may be aroused to spirituality, and something may move him to change his course, but unless he is wise enough to take advantage of it, he may return to his habitual behavior, with the moment of awakening having been wasted.

We are fortunate in having *Shabbos*, a day which is strikingly different from the rest of the week, a day on which the many restrictions of activities provide us with the leisure and the opportunity to think about how we are living and what we are doing with our lives. The Chassidic writings point out that the letters of *Shabbos* also constitute the letters of *tashev*, i.e., of *teshuvah*, and that *Shabbos* is a propitious time for *teshuvah*. This is so because *Shabbos* is a break in our habitual life, and if we take advantage of it, *Shabbos* can give meaning to the entire week.

It is certainly appropriate to enjoy *Shabbos*. Jewish tradition is rich in *Shabbos* delicacies: *challah*, gelfilte fish, roast chicken, chopped liver, *cholent*, and *kugel*. Indeed, it is a mitzvah to partake of tasty foods on *Shabbos*, preparing for the *Shabbos* and according it the courtesy one would give to an honored guest. It is also appropriate to rest and relax on *Shabbos*. However, to allow the entire *Shabbos* to be spent only on physical delights is neglecting the spirit of *Shabbos*. It is a day of *kedushah* (sanctity), on which we should dedicate ourselves to spiritual matters which may not receive our full attention during the work week. Our prayers should be less hurried and recited with greater *kavannah* (concentration). We should read the Torah portion of the week and the commentaries which teach us its applications to our own lives. *Shabbos* can save us from becoming so absorbed with the activities of daily living that we forget why we live.

כֵּן הִיא עֲצַת הַיֵּצֶר־הָרָע מַמָּשׁ עַל בְּנֵי הָאָדָם, כִּי אִישׁ מִלְחָמָה הוּא וּמְלֻמָּד בְּעַרְמִימוּת, וְאִי אֶפְשָׁר לְמַלֵּט מִמֶּנּוּ אֶלָּא בְּחָכְמָה רַבָּה וְהַשְׁקָפָה גְדוֹלָה. הוּא מַה שֶּׁהַנָּבִיא צוֹוֵחַ וְאוֹמֵר (משלי ו, ד): ,,אַל תִּתֵּן שֵׁנָה לְעֵינֶיךָ וּתְנוּמָה לְעַפְעַפֶּיךָ, הִנָּצֵל כִּצְבִי מִיָּד וגו׳׳. וַחֲכָמֵינוּ ז״ל אָמְרוּ (סוטה ה, ב): ,,כָּל הַשָּׂם אָרְחוֹתָיו בָּעוֹלָם־הַזֶּה, זוֹכֶה וְרוֹאֶה בִּישׁוּעָתוֹ שֶׁל הַקָּדוֹשׁ־בָּרוּךְ־הוּא׳׳.

Constant preoccupation is the strategy which the yetzer hara employs against people, because it is a warrior that is adept in cunningness, and it is impossible to escape from it without great wisdom and a comprehensive perspective. This is why the prophet cries out, "Pay attention to your ways" (Haggai 1:7), and Solomon says, "Do not give sleep to your eyes nor slumber to your eyelids. Save yourself as a deer from the hand of the hunter" (Proverbs 6:4). Our sages said, "All those who deliberate on their ways in this world will merit and will see G-d's salvation" (Sotah 5b).

Ramchal's delineation of the *yetzer hara* as a wily foe is an important concept. Let me again refer to the prototype of the recovering alcoholic, as representing someone who must make a major change of course in life. The recovery book for the alcoholic states, "We must remember that our *enemy* is alcohol, cunning, baffling, and powerful." We need only substitute the word *yetzer hara* for alcohol, and we have an important observation: Our enemy is the *yetzer hara*, cunning, baffling, and powerful.

The Talmud and all ethical works portray the *yetzer hara* as the enemy of mankind, lying in wait to destroy man. Indeed, this is first stated in *Genesis* 4:7, "Sin lurks at your doorstep, and you are the object of its desire (i.e., to destroy you").

Awareness of the *yetzer hara* as a cunning enemy, seeking to seduce, entrap, and destroy a person should put one on extreme guard. In Greek mythology, there is the story of Ulysses, who was told about the beautiful, irresistible music of the Sirens, a music so enchanting that sailors who heard it were attracted to it, only to be drawn to their death as their ships were wrecked on the reefs. Ulysses wished to hear the music of the Sirens, yet he knew that to expose himself to this would mean certain death. He therefore stuffed the ears of his crew with beeswax, and had himself securely tied to the mast. He gave his crew orders to row in the direction of the harbor to where the music of the Sirens could no longer be heard, and to continue to row past the harbor. They were not to deviate from these orders, and even if he were to issue any new orders to them or they were to see him gesturing otherwise from his position on the mast, they were to completely ignore him.

The sailors did as they told. Ulysses was firmly tied to the mast, and the sailors were rendered oblivious to all sound by having their ears clogged with beeswax. As they rowed near the harbor, Ulysses, hearing the music of the Sirens, began shouting to the crew to change their course and head for the harbor. "I am your captain!" he screamed. "You must obey my orders," but the crew continued to row on. Ulysses struggled fiercely against the ropes to free himself so that he could get the crew to change course, but he was unable to do so. The crew eventually took the ship beyond the harbor to where the music of the Sirens could no longer be heard, and Ulysses fell away, exhausted by his fierce struggle. It was only then that he realized how close he had come to being destroyed, and that if he had not tied himself to the mast and rendered his crew deaf to the music of the Sirens, they would all have been killed.

These are the kinds of desperate measures we must take to protect ourselves from the seduction of the *yetzer hara*. Inasmuch as we cannot make ourselves deaf to its enticements, we must find the equivalent of binding ourselves to the mast so that we are not lured to destruction. As an enemy, the *yetzer hara* is cunning, baffling, and powerful, constantly seeking new ways to destroy us. This is why the prophet exhorts us to pay attention to our ways, and Solomon warns us to be aware of being trapped.

The actual time spent in behavior that is readily identifiable as mitzvos is rather scant, consisting of the few moments of prayer every day, the grace after meals, Shabbos and the festivals. The major transgressions of yielding to temptation or lust or to forbidden foods are indeed dangerous, but can be avoided with moderate effort. The lion's share of the day is spent in work, in business, and in social interactions. These are areas which we are not likely to immediately relate to Torah and mitzvos, and this is where we must be on constant guard against the cunning of the *yetzer hara*.

How easy it is to relax one's guard and in a rather innocent conversation say something derogatory about another person. This is a grave transgression of *lashon hara*, a sin which the Talmud equates to the cardinal sins of adultery, idolatry, and murder, and which can seriously undermine one's quest for spirituality. How easy it is to stretch the truth, rationalizing why it is permissible to lie under certain circumstances.

It is of interest that whereas all precautionary laws to prevent transgressing a Scriptural prohibition are of rabbinic origin, there is one and only one precautionary measure which is stated in the Scriptures, and that is against lying. The Torah not only states "Do not lie" (*Leviticus* 19:11), but also "*Keep a distance* from falsehood" (*Exodus* 23:7), which means "take the necessary precautions to avoid the need to lie." The Torah clearly assigns the highest priority to truthfulness.

We know what it means not to lie, but what are the precautionary measures one must take? How does one distance oneself from falsehood? The answer is simple. Before doing anything, pause a moment and think, "Is this something I might sometimes have to deny doing?" If so, then do not do it. Doing something which you might subsequently have to deny is approximating yourself to falsehood. Keeping one's distance from falsehood means behaving in such a manner that one will have no need to lie. This is the kind of Watchfulness one must exercise to prevent entrapment by the *yetzer hara*.

וּפָשׁוּט הוּא שֶׁאֲפִלּוּ אִם יְפַקַּח הָאָדָם עַל עַצְמוֹ אֵין בְּכֹחוֹ לִנָּצֵל אִלּוּלֵי הַקָּדוֹשׁ־בָּרוּךְ־הוּא עוֹזְרוֹ, כִּי הַיֵּצֶר־הָרָע תַּקִּיף מְאֹד, וּכְמַאֲמַר הַכָּתוּב (תהילים לז, לב): ,,צוֹפֶה רָשָׁע לַצַּדִּיק וּמְבַקֵּשׁ לַהֲמִיתוֹ, ה׳ לֹא עַזְבֶנּוּ וגו׳׳. אַךְ אִם הָאָדָם מְפַקֵּחַ עַל עַצְמוֹ, אָז הַקָּדוֹשׁ־בָּרוּךְ־הוּא עוֹזְרוֹ וְנִצּוֹל מִן הַיֵּצֶר־הָרָע, אֲבָל אִם אֵינוֹ מְפַקֵּחַ הוּא עַל עַצְמוֹ, וַדַּאי שֶׁהַקָּדוֹשׁ־בָּרוּךְ־הוּא לֹא יְפַקַּח עָלָיו. כִּי אִם הוּא אֵינוֹ חָס, מִי יָחוּס עָלָיו? וְהוּא כְּעִנְיַן מַה שֶׁאָמְרוּ רַבּוֹתֵינוּ זִכְרוֹנָם לִבְרָכָה (ברכות לג, א): ,,כָּל מִי שֶׁאֵין בּוֹ דֵּעָה אָסוּר לְרַחֵם עָלָיו׳׳. וְהוּא מַה שֶׁאָמְרוּ (אבות א, יד): ,,אִם אֵין אֲנִי לִי מִי לִי׳׳.

It is clear that without G-d's help, a person could not save himself even if he took all precautions, because the yetzer hara is extremely powerful, as it is written, "The wicked one (the yetzer hara) watches for the righteous and seeks to kill him; G-d will not abandon him" (Psalms 37:32). If a person does watch himself, then he merits Divine help and can be safe from the evil inclination. However, if a person does not give heed to himself, he cannot expect G-d to supervise him. If a person does not care for himself, who should care for him? This is what our sages meant when they said, "One should not have pity on someone who does not exercise his understanding to care for himself" (Berachos 33a). This is also what they meant when they said, "If I am not for myself, who will be for me?" (Ethics of the Fathers 1:14)

Success in achieving spirituality, as well as in every other endeavor, requires two essential components: (1) man's maximum effort, and (2) Divine assistance. Man's unaided efforts are insufficient, but neither can we throw the entire burden upon G-d and say, "Make me spiritual." When a person does all that is within his capacity to do and prays for Divine assistance, it is then that he will succeed.

This is an example of the delicate dependence/independence balance that is necessary in adjusting to life. Some people are so fiercely independent that they are unable to pray for Divine assistance. The Torah warns us against thinking, "My strength and cunning have brought me success" (*Deuteronomy* 8:17). Our own efforts, great as they may be, can succeed only with Divine assistance. Yet our own effort is essential, as the Talmud says, "In the way that a person chooses to walk, he will be led" (*Makkos* 10b). The responsibility for choosing the way lies with each person.

3

בְּחֶלְקֵי הַזְּהִירוּת

Concerning the Divisions of Watchfulness

הִנֵּה הָרוֹצֶה לְפַקֵּחַ עַל עַצְמוֹ, שְׁתַּיִם הֵנָּה הַהַשְׁקָפוֹת הַצְּרִיכוֹת לוֹ. הָאַחַת, שֶׁיִּתְבּוֹנֵן מַהוּ הַטּוֹב הָאֲמִתִּי שֶׁיִּבְחַר בּוֹ הָאָדָם וְהָרַע הָאֲמִתִּי שֶׁיָּנוּס מִמֶּנּוּ. וְהַשֵּׁנִית, עַל הַמַּעֲשִׂים אֲשֶׁר הוּא עוֹשֶׂה לִרְאוֹת אִם הֵם מִכְּלַל הַטּוֹב אוֹ מִכְּלָל הָרָע.

One who wishes to exercise Watchfulness must consider two things: (1) What is the true good one should choose, and what is the true evil one should avoid; and (2) which actions fall under the category of "good" and which under "evil."

Ramchal had said that faulty behavior results not so much from improper thought as from failure to think at all, allowing oneself to act according to habit without deliberating about one's behavior. He now expands on this, stating that deliberation is comprised of two components: (1) What is it that I wish to do; and (2) what is the method to achieve this.

I once bought an item and paid for it with a one-hundred-dollar bill. The merchant ran the bill through a little apparatus to make certain that it was genuine and not counterfeit. He explained that there were some counterfeit one-hundred-dollar bills in circulation that were such exact copies that it was virtually impossible to distinguish between the two by visual inspection.

We may sometimes believe that what we are doing is right and proper because we have rationalized our behavior, having convinced ourselves that what we wanted to do was indeed correct. There is a difference between "genuine" good and "counterfeit" good, and we would do well to run our behavior through an "apparatus" to distinguish between the two. Such an apparatus consists of another person, who, being free of our personal bias, is capable of rendering an objective evaluation.

וָזֶה, בִּשְׁעַת מַעֲשֶׂה וְשֶׁלֹּא בִשְׁעַת מַעֲשֶׂה. בִּשְׁעַת מַעֲשֶׂה, שֶׁלֹּא יַעֲשֶׂה שׁוּם מַעֲשֶׂה מִבְּלִי שֶׁיִּשְׁקוֹל אוֹתוֹ בְּמֹאזְנֵי זֹאת הַיְדִיעָה. וְשֶׁלֹּא בִשְׁעַת מַעֲשֶׂה, שֶׁיַּעֲלֶה לְפָנָיו זִכְרוֹן כְּלָל מַעֲשָׂיו וְיִשְׁקוֹל אוֹתָם כְּמוֹ־כֵן בְּמֹאזְנֵי הַמִּשְׁקָל הַזֶּה לִרְאוֹת מַה יֵּשׁ בָּם מֵהָרַע לְמַעַן יִדְחֶה אוֹתוֹ, וּמַה מִּן הַטּוֹב לְהַתְמִיד בּוֹ וּלְהִתְחַזֵּק בּוֹ. וְאִם יִמְצָא בָהֶם מִן הָרַע, אָז יִתְבּוֹנֵן וְיַחְקוֹר בְּשִׂכְלוֹ אֵיזֶה תַּחְבּוּלָה יַעֲשֶׂה לָסוּר מִן הָרַע הַהוּא וְלִטָּהֵר מִמֶּנּוּ.

These two considerations (analysis and choice of method) should be applied both before taking action and afterward: Before taking action, so that one does not act without careful deliberation, and after having taken action, to review one's behavior, and see what kinds of things one did that should be repeated and reinforced, and what kinds of things were wrong that should be avoided.

Deliberating on our actions in this manner might appear to be an excessive demand, but let us think as to whether we do not already do so when we are confronted with decisions that are of some importance to us.

Rabbi Levi Yitzchak of Berditchev once visited a small town. In the morning a congregant approached him in shul asking, "Are you perhaps a *shochet* (ritual slaughterer)?" Rabbi Levi Yitzchak said that indeed he was. "How wonderful!" the man said. "You are a G-dsend. I am a butcher, and I have a sickly cow. My regular *shochet* will not be here for two more days, and if the cow dies by then, I will lose a substantial amount of money."

Rabbi Levi Yitzchak said he would perform the ritual slaughter, "But first," he said, "I have a favor to ask. I am travelling around to raise money for my daughter's dowry. Perhaps you could lend me fifty rubles, and I assure you that I will repay you."

"What!" the man exclaimed. "You expect me to lend so large a sum to someone whom I don't even know?"

"Just listen to what you have said," Rabbi Levi Yitzchak said. "You are perfectly willing to trust me as a *shochet*, and if I am not a competent *shochet* you will be feeding *treifah* meat to all your customers. Yet my word is good enough for this, but not good enough to trust me with money. Clearly your spiritual values and your material values are reversed in priority."

All Ramchal asks of us is that we give the same consideration to ethical right and wrong as we do to economic right and wrong. We exercise much prudence when our money is at risk. We should be no less cautious when our spirituality is at risk.

וְדָבָר זֶה הוֹדִיעוּנוּ חֲכָמֵינוּ זִכְרוֹנָם לִבְרָכָה בְּאָמְרָם (עירובין יג, ב): ,,נוֹחַ לוֹ לָאָדָם שֶׁלֹּא נִבְרָא יוֹתֵר מִשֶּׁנִּבְרָא וְעַכְשָׁיו שֶׁנִּבְרָא יְפַשְׁפֵּשׁ בְּמַעֲשָׂיו, וְאִיכָּא דְאָמְרֵי יְמַשְׁמֵשׁ בְּמַעֲשָׂיו'' . . . כִּי הִנֵּה הַפִּשְׁפּוּשׁ בַּמַּעֲשִׂים הוּא לַחֲקוֹר עַל כְּלָל הַמַּעֲשִׂים וּלְהִתְבּוֹנֵן בּוֹ, הֲנִמְצָא בָהֶם מַעֲשִׂים אֲשֶׁר לֹא יֵעָשׂוּ אֲשֶׁר אֵינָם הוֹלְכִים עַל פִּי מִצְוֹת ה׳ וְחֻקָּיו, כִּי כָל אֲשֶׁר יִמָּצֵא מֵאֵלֶּה יְבַעֲרֵם מִן הָעוֹלָם. אַךְ הַמִּשְׁמוּשׁ הוּא הַחֲקִירָה אֲפִלּוּ בַּמַּעֲשִׂים הַטּוֹבִים עַצְמָם, לַחֲקוֹר וְלִרְאוֹת הֲיֵשׁ בְּעִנְיָנָם אֵיזֶה פְּנִיָּה אֲשֶׁר לֹא טוֹבָה אוֹ אֵיזֶה חֵלֶק רָע שֶׁיִּצְטָרֵךְ לַהֲסִירוֹ וּלְבַעֲרוֹ.

Our sages say that "it would have been better if man would not have been created (because he is more prone to vice than to virtue), but inasmuch as he has been created, let him examine his deeds." Another version is, "Let him analyze his deeds." ... To "examine" one's deeds means to search whether one may have committed transgressions which should be eliminated. To "analyze" one's deeds means to see whether the good deeds one has done were performed with the proper attitude and dedication.

Spirituality is more than just avoiding evil, and even more than doing good. It means that one must do good in an optimum way, with pure intention and with the desire that these good deeds exert a salutary effect on one's character.

Two chassidim were discussing the quality of their spirituality, and how they will appear before the tribunal on Judgment Day. "Woe is me," said the first chassid. "I will be found to have committed many grievous sins."

"That is not my fear," said the second chassid. "I will plead that I was simply unable to withstand the enormous pressures of temptation exerted upon me by the *yetzer hara*.

"What I am afraid of," he continued, "is not my sins, but my mitzvos. Why didn't I perform the mitzvos properly? When I prayed and studied Torah, why did my mind wander to extraneous matters? Why did I do some mitzvos as rote? Why did I do some mitzvos in an ostentatious manner, to impress people with my piety?"

Discriminating consumers carefully analyze the quality of an item they wish to purchase. Mitzvos, too, should be of the finest quality, and failure to maximize the performance of a mitzvah is a dereliction.

The chassidic master, the Seer of Lublin, was returning from *tashlich*, the ritual whereby we symbolically dispose of our improper acts by casting them into the water, when he met his disciple, Rabbi Naftali of Ropschitz. "Where are you going?" the master asked. "Down to the river," Rabbi Naftali answered, "to retrieve the sins that the master has discarded." In other words, the spirituality of the Seer was so great that he considered some of the mitzvos he had performed to be defective because they were not of the highest quality, whereas for Rabbi Naftali, the spirituality that the master rejected would have been an achievement. It is much like the clothes discarded by wealthy people, which the poor would consider to be valuable acquisitions.

וְהִנְנִי רוֹאֶה צֹרֶךְ לָאָדָם שֶׁיִּהְיֶה מְדַקְדֵּק וְשׁוֹקֵל דְּרָכָיו דְּבַר יוֹם בְּיוֹמוֹ כַּסּוֹחֲרִים הַגְּדוֹלִים אֲשֶׁר יְפַלְּסוּ תָּמִיד כָּל עִסְקֵיהֶם לְמַעַן לֹא יִתְקַלְקְלוּ . . . וְהוּא מַה שֶּׁאָמְרוּ ז״ל . . . ,,עַל־כֵּן יֹאמְרוּ הַמּוֹשְׁלִים בְּיִצְרָם, בּוֹאוּ וּנְחַשֵּׁב חֶשְׁבּוֹנוֹ שֶׁל עוֹלָם, הֶפְסֵד מִצְוָה כְּנֶגֶד שְׂכָרָהּ וּשְׂכַר עֲבֵרָה כְּנֶגֶד הֶפְסֵדָהּ וכו׳ ״.

A person should therefore regularly do a careful daily accounting, similar to merchants who constantly evaluate their business affairs. Our sages say that those who have become masters over their physical temptations are those who say, "Let us calculate: What is the loss one may incur by performance of a mitzvah in comparison to the reward, and what is the gain of a sin in comparison to the loss it entails?"

Proper guidance on how to live can be given only by people who have an accurate perception of reality. A person's perception is often distorted by his desires. In prohibiting a judge from accepting a bribe, the Torah says that "A bribe will blind the eyes of the wise" (*Deuteronomy* 16:19). The Talmud states that anyone who has accepted a bribe cannot possibly avoid a bias, regardless of how much he tries to be objective.

The distorting effect of a bribe can be so great that it can have an impact even if one is not aware of it. The Rabbi of Apt once sat on a trial in a rabbinical court, and after several days of proceedings, abruptly withdrew from the case without any explanation. The following Friday evening, on putting on his Shabbos *kaftan*, he discovered an envelope with money that had been put there by one of the litigants. The Rabbi then said, "I could not understand what had happened, but in the midst of the proceedings I felt myself constantly leaning toward one of the litigants. When I discovered the bribe, I realized that my judgment had been distorted in his favor, and this had occurred even though I was not aware until much later that he had tried to bribe me." Such is the potency of a bribe, that it can affect a person's judgment even if one is not aware of it.

We are all "bribed" by our desires, hence we are "blinded" to reality, because our perceptions may be distorted. We see things the way we want to see them, even though the desire may be unconscious. Just as the Rabbi of Apt noted that his judgment was affected by a bribe of which he was totally unaware, so can our perception of reality be affected by desires of which we may be unaware.

Parents are often frustrated when they observe their children behaving in a self-defeating manner, making decisions that are detrimental to their own welfare. Recalling their own youth, they can recognize how intense desires can lead one to make unwise decisions, and that even highly intelligent youngsters may be misled by personal drives. Parents try to counsel their children, who so often reject parental advice, only to later regret their decisions. We should realize that even as mature adults we are subject to similar distortions of perception and judgment, and accept guidance from those who are wiser and more experienced.

In the Haggadah *From Bondage to Freedom* (Shaar Press 1995), I pointed out that we are often nothing less than slaves to our internal drives, and just as a slave is not free to do things of his own choosing, neither are we free to make correct choices as long as we are dominated by physical drives. It is only when we break loose from this domination that we are free to make proper choices.

וְהוּא מַה שֶׁאָמְרוּ ז״ל „תָּשֶׁת חֹשֶׁךְ וִיהִי לָיְלָה״ (תהלים קד, כ), זֶה הָעוֹלָם־הַזֶּה שֶׁדּוֹמֶה לַלַּיְלָה״. וְהָבֵן כַּמָּה נִפְלָא הַמַּאֲמָר הָאֲמִתִּי הַזֶּה לְמִי שֶׁמַּעֲמִיק לְהָבִין בּוֹ. כִּי הִנֵּה חֹשֶׁךְ הַלַּיְלָה שְׁנֵי מִינֵי טָעוּיוֹת אֶפְשָׁר לוֹ שֶׁיִּגְרוֹם לְעֵין הָאָדָם: אוֹ יְכַסֶּה אֶת הָעַיִן עַד שֶׁלֹּא יִרְאֶה מַה שֶׁלְּפָנָיו כְּלָל, אוֹ שֶׁיַּטְעֶה אוֹתוֹ עַד שֶׁיֵּרָאֶה לוֹ עַמּוּד כְּאִלּוּ הוּא אָדָם, וְאָדָם כְּאִלּוּ הוּא עַמּוּד . . . הָאַחַת אֵינוֹ מַנִּיחַ לוֹ שֶׁיִּרְאֶה הַמִּכְשׁוֹלוֹת שֶׁבְּדַרְכֵי הָעוֹלָם . . . וְהַטָּעוּת הַשֵּׁנִי וְהוּא קָשֶׁה מִן הָרִאשׁוֹן, הוּא שֶׁמַּטְעֶה רְאִיָּתָם עַד שֶׁרוֹאִים הָרַע כְּאִלּוּ הוּא מַמָּשׁ טוֹב, וְהַטּוֹב כְּאִלּוּ הוּא רָע, וּמִתּוֹךְ כָּךְ מִתְחַזְּקִים וּמַחֲזִיקִים מַעֲשֵׂיהֶם הָרָעִים.

Our sages say, "You make darkness and it is night" (Psalms 104:20), whereby they compare living in this world to being in the darkness of night. This is an excellent metaphor, since darkness can cause two problems in perception. Firstly, one may be unable to see the pitfalls and obstacles in one's way, and secondly, the shadows in the darkness may cause optical illusions, as when one sees a pillar and thinks it to be a person, or vice versa... The first can result in a person falling to his destruction, being unaware of the pitfalls before him... The second is even more serious, because one mistakes good for evil and evil for good, and thereby persists in self-defeating behavior of which one is convinced that it is good and proper.

The reason why Ramchal considers the second error more serious than the first is that if one stumbles in the dark and is injured, he immediately realizes that if he continues on he is likely to be hurt again. He is therefore likely to wait until it gets light before proceeding. The one who thinks he can see what is before him, but actually misperceives reality, may not be as fortunate to be brought to his senses so quickly.

A classic example of the two maladjustments Ramchal describes is the addicted person. We may think of addiction as restricted to habitual use of alcohol and drugs, but the phenomenon of addiction is much broader, including addiction to food, work, gambling, and even to power and acclaim.

Addictive behavior is characterized by *denial*, typically observed in the alcoholic, whose drinking is grossly destructive. While this is obvious to everyone else, the alcoholic may be completely oblivious to its ramifications. A second phenomenon occurs when the addiction results in distortion of thought, feeling, and judgment, which I described in *Addictive Thinking* (Hazelden 1990). An addict is capable of the most complex and even bizarre rationalizations, which he thoroughly believes to be true. Like someone in the dark who mistakes a pillar for a person and shoots at the pillar under the assumption that it is a hostile aggressor, the addict may see enemies where none exist. And just as in darkness one may fail to recognize a hostile foe, assuming him to be a pillar or tree, so in addiction one may not see danger signals, but may think harmful things to be beneficial. Countless people have gone down to ruin and have taken others with them because they were operating in "darkness"; i.e., an inability to apperceive reality correctly as a result of the dominance of their internal drives.

הָא לְמַה זֶּה דּוֹמֶה? לְגַן־הַמְּבוּכָה . . . וּבֵינֵיהֶם שְׁבִילִים רַבִּים נְבוּכִים וּמְעוֹרָבִים, כֻּלָּם דּוֹמִים זֶה לָזֶה וְהַתַּכְלִית בָּם הוּא לְהַגִּיעַ אֶל אַכְסַדְרָה אַחַת שֶׁבְּאֶמְצָעָם. וְאָמְנָם הַשְּׁבִילִים הָאֵלֶּה מֵהֶם יְשָׁרִים וּמַגִּיעִים בֶּאֱמֶת אֶל הָאַכְסַדְרָה, וּמֵהֶם מַשְׁגִּים אֶת הָאָדָם וּמַרְחִיקִים אוֹתוֹ מִמֶּנָּה. וְאָמְנָם הַהוֹלֵךְ בֵּין הַשְּׁבִילִים הוּא לֹא יוּכַל לִרְאוֹת וְלָדַעַת כְּלָל אִם הוּא בַּשְּׁבִיל הָאֲמִתִּי אוֹ בַּכּוֹזֵב, כִּי כֻּלָּם שָׁוִים וְאֵין הֶפְרֵשׁ בֵּינֵיהֶם לָעַיִן הָרוֹאָה אוֹתָם, אִם לֹא שֶׁיֵּדַע הַדֶּרֶךְ בִּבְקִיאוּת וּטְבִיעוּת עַיִן שֶׁכְּבָר נִכְנַס בָּם וְהִגִּיעַ אֶל הַתַּכְלִית שֶׁהוּא הָאַכְסַדְרָה. וְהִנֵּה הָעוֹמֵד כְּבָר עַל הָאַכְסַדְרָה הוּא רוֹאֶה כָּל הַדְּרָכִים לְפָנָיו וּמַבְחִין בֵּין הָאֲמִתִּיִּים וְהַכּוֹזְבִים, וְהוּא יָכוֹל לְהַזְהִיר אֶת הַהוֹלְכִים בָּם, לוֹמַר: זֶה הַדֶּרֶךְ לְכוּ בוֹ! וְהִנֵּה, מִי שֶׁיִּרְצֶה לְהַאֲמִין לוֹ, יַגִּיעַ לַמָּקוֹם הַמְיֻעָד. וּמִי שֶׁלֹּא יִרְצֶה לְהַאֲמִין וְיִרְצֶה לָלֶכֶת אַחַר עֵינָיו, וַדַּאי שֶׁיִּשָּׁאֵר אוֹבֵד וְלֹא יַגִּיעַ אֵלָיו.

Living in this world may be compared to a maze, where there are numerous paths, many of which are confusing and interlacing, and all of which appear similar. The goal is to reach a portico in its midst. Some of the paths indeed lead to the goal, while others are deceptive and lead away from the goal. However, one cannot tell which is which, unless one has successfully mastered the maze and reached the portico. Someone standing on top of the portico has a view of all the paths, which are true and which are deceptive, and he can call to those who enter the maze, "Follow this path," or "Avoid that path." One who heeds this guide will soon arrive at the goal, while one who persists in pursuing his own intellect will blunder and may never arrive at the goal.

My work as a psychiatrist has enabled me to appreciate the accuracy of Ramchal's metaphor. The world is indeed very much like a maze, with more paths leading to dead ends or away from the goal than toward it. There are some people who, by virtue of their experience and knowledge, can point out which paths should be avoided and what kinds of behavior are self-defeating. A wise person will take advantage of this wisdom and experience, and avoid at least some erroneous ways which are pointed out to him. Those who are intoxicated with their own intelligence and refuse guidance are likely to follow paths that lead nowhere.

Of course, the validity of the metaphor is based on the premise that there is a goal to be reached, which Ramchal discussed in Chapter One. There are those who have never chosen a goal, and others who believe that there is no ultimate goal. The latter's only motivation may be to "eat, drink, and be merry, for tomorrow we die." Ironically, even hedonism is deceptive, because so many physical gratifications are but transitory pleasures, whose consequences can be exceedingly painful for a long period of time.

It is characteristic of the pleasure-driven person that he scorns wise direction, doing only that which he believes will give him immediate gratification. It is only when he begins to suffer the consequences of his behavior that he may seek guidance. While it is never too late to correct one's errant ways, much of the harm that has been done to oneself and to others cannot be undone after one has awakened to the truth. A person who has wandered aimlessly through the maze, and after being totally exhausted finally surrenders and heeds the instructions of the guide on the portico may ultimately arrive at the goal, but he may then be old and weary, and may have lost many opportunities while engaged in his futile efforts.

וְאָמְנָם מַה הִיא הָעֵצָה שֶׁהֵם נוֹתְנִים לָנוּ? בּוֹאוּ חֶשְׁבּוֹן, בּוֹאוּ וּנְחַשֵּׁב חֶשְׁבּוֹנוֹ שֶׁל עוֹלָם, כִּי כְּבָר הֵם נִסּוּ וְרָאוּ וְיָדְעוּ שֶׁזֶּה לְבַדּוֹ הוּא הַדֶּרֶךְ הָאֲמִתִּי לְהַגִּיעַ הָאָדָם אֶל הַטּוֹבָה אֲשֶׁר הוּא מְבַקֵּשׁ וְלֹא זוּלַת זֶה.

כְּלָלוֹ שֶׁל דָּבָר: צָרִיךְ הָאָדָם לִהְיוֹת מִתְבּוֹנֵן בְּשִׂכְלוֹ תָּמִיד . . . מַה הוּא הַדֶּרֶךְ הָאֲמִתִּי לְפִי חֹק הַתּוֹרָה שֶׁהָאָדָם צָרִיךְ לֵילֵךְ בּוֹ. וְאַחַר כָּךְ יָבוֹא לְהִתְבּוֹנֵן עַל מַעֲשָׂיו אִם הֵם עַל הַדֶּרֶךְ הַזֶּה אִם לֹא . . . וּכְמוֹ שֶׁהַכָּתוּב אוֹמֵר . . . ,,נַחְפְּשָׂה דְרָכֵינוּ וְנַחְקוֹרָה וְנָשׁוּבָה עַד ה׳ ״.

What is the advice the wise people give? "Come, let us make a careful accounting." They can do so because they have already tried and have found which is the only true path that can lead to the goal.

Let us summarize. A person must constantly consider what is the correct path which Torah designates, and whether his actions keep him on that path. This is what the prophet says, "Let us seek our ways and examine them, and we will return to G-d" (Lamentations 3:40).

In my rehabilitation center, we have a section for adults and one for adolescents. The people in the older group have gone through the myriad miseries of addiction, having themselves suffered greatly and inflicting suffering on others, particularly on those they loved most. The younger group have generally come to our attention as a result of their parents discovering they were using drugs or as a result of running afoul of the law. As a rule, they are too young to have experienced many of the painful consequences of the older group.

The older people often look at the younger ones and say, "I wish someone would have intervened in my life when I was sixteen. I could have avoided two unsuccessful marriages, loss of numerous jobs, and much damage to my body. How lucky these young ones are." One might think that the younger ones would listen to these people who tell them, "Don't be foolish. Don't do what I did. Listen to your counselor. I wish I had been given the opportunity." But alas! Youth is often impetuous, and instead of learning from the mistakes of others, they may say, "It won't happen to me."

In all walks of life there are those who stand on top of the portico and from their vantage point can point to the right path. Those who are wise will listen.

4

בְּבֵאוּר קְנִיַּת הַזְּהִירוּת

How One May Acquire Watchfulness

הִנֵּה מַה שֶּׁמֵּבִיא אֶת הָאָדָם עַל־דֶּרֶךְ־כְּלָל אֶל הַזְּהִירוּת, הוּא לִמּוּד הַתּוֹרָה. וְהוּא מַה שֶּׁאָמַר רַבִּי פִּינְחָס בִּתְחִלַּת הַבָּרָיְתָא: תּוֹרָה מְבִיאָה לִידֵי זְהִירוּת. אָמְנָם עַל־דֶּרֶךְ־פְּרָט, הַמֵּבִיא לָזֶה הוּא הַהִתְבּוֹנְנוּת עַל חֹמֶר הָעֲבוֹדָה אֲשֶׁר חַיָּב בָּהּ הָאָדָם, וְעֹמֶק הַדִּין עָלֶיהָ. וְיֵצֵא לוֹ זֶה, מִן הָעִיּוּן בַּמַּעֲשִׂים הַכְּתוּבִים בְּסִפְרֵי הַקֹּדֶשׁ וּמִן הַלִּמּוּד בְּמַאֲמָרֵי הַחֲכָמִים זִכְרוֹנָם לִבְרָכָה הַמְעוֹרְרִים עַל זֶה.

Generally, what brings a person to Watchfulness is the study of Torah, and this is why Rabbi Pinchas ben Yair began the ten steps by stating, "Torah leads to Watchfulness." In particular, it is the reflection on one's obligation to serve G-d and the severity of judgment which it involves that leads to Watchfulness. The latter is achieved by analysis of the Scriptures and the Talmud.

Having established (in Chapter One) that the purpose and goal of one's existence is to unite with G-d, and that the only way this can be achieved is through observance of the Torah, it follows that anything that threatens to jeopardize achievement of the ultimate goal would be zealously guarded against. Just as someone whose prime goal is to accumulate wealth will be on the alert to protect his investments and belongings, so a person whose goal is to become one with G-d will take great caution to avoid whatever might jeopardize this relationship.

Observance of Torah requires careful analysis of the Scriptures and the rabbinic works. There are various levels of understanding of Torah, and the greater one's understanding, the greater the likelihood of achieving a totally Torah-oriented life.

Great Torah scholars were guided in every facet of their lives by Torah principles. An excellent example of this is an incident involving Rabbi Chaim Ozer Grodzenski, the last rabbi of Vilna, who once received a guest on Succos. Since Rabbi Chaim Ozer was sick with a cold, he was exempt from eating in the *succah*, and he excused himself. His wife served the guest in the *succah*, and the latter was surprised when, in the midst of the meal, Rabbi Chaim Ozer joined him, all bundled up due to his cold. Noting the guest's surprise, Rabbi Chaim Ozer explained. "I did not eat in the *succah* because the *halachah* states that one who is sickly is exempt from this mitzvah. However, there is also a mitzvah of *hachnassas orchim* (hospitality to guests) which requires a host to be company to his guests. In this latter mitzvah, there is no exemption for having a cold. Therefore, although I did not eat in the *succah*, I have come to join you so that you should not be alone."

Here we see how every move was given careful consideration to be in compliance with *halachah*.

וְהִנֵּה יֵשׁ בַּהִתְבּוֹנְנוּת הַזֶּה הֶעָרוֹת בְּהַדְרָגָה לִשְׁלֵמֵי הַדַּעַת, וְלַפְּחוּתִים מֵהֶם, וּלְכָל הֶהָמוֹן כֻּלּוֹ. לִשְׁלֵמֵי הַדַּעַת, תִּהְיֶה לָהֶם הַהֶעָרָה בְּמַה שֶׁיִּתְבָּרֵר לָהֶם כִּי רַק הַשְּׁלֵמוּת הוּא הַדָּבָר הָרָאוּי שֶׁיֵּחָמֵד מֵהֶם וְלֹא זוּלַת זֶה, וְשֶׁאֵין רַע גָּדוֹל מֵחֶסְרוֹן הַשְּׁלֵמוּת וְהַהֶרְחֵק מִמֶּנּוּ. . . . שֶׁיִּתְבָּאֵר זֶה אֶצְלָם וְיִתְבָּאֵר לָהֶם כְּמוֹ כֵן הֱיוֹת הָאֶמְצָעִים אֵלָיו הַמַּעֲשִׂים הַטּוֹבִים וְהַמִּדּוֹת הַטּוֹבוֹת, וַדַּאי הוּא שֶׁלֹּא יִתְרַצּוּ מֵעוֹלָם לְהַמְעִיט בְּאֵלֶּה הָאֶמְצָעִים אוֹ לְהָקֵל בָּהֶם. . . . וְהִנֵּה סוֹף זֹאת הַמַּדְרֵגָה הִיא הַנִּקְרֵאת יִרְאַת חֵטְא, שֶׁהִיא מִן הַמְשֻׁבָּחוֹת שֶׁבַּמַּדְרֵגוֹת, שֶׁיִּהְיֶה הָאָדָם יָרֵא תָּמִיד וְדוֹאֵג פֶּן יִמָּצֵא בְיָדוֹ אֵיזֶה שֶׁמֶץ חֵטְא שֶׁיְּעַכְּבֵהוּ מִן הַשְּׁלֵמוּת אֲשֶׁר הוּא חַיָּב לְהִשְׁתַּדֵּל בַּעֲבוּרוֹ.

There are various levels of understanding (why Watchfulness is necessary). People with profound understanding are motivated by their awareness that the only desirable goal is to perfect themselves, and that there can be nothing worse than that which interferes with their efforts for (achieving) perfection. Inasmuch as virtuous deeds and traits are the means to this end, they will be careful not to be lax in maximizing the actions that will bring them to their desired goal. . . . This is the true meaning of "fear of sin"; i.e., that sin may jeopardize their realizing the desired goal.

It is common experience that the kinds of means one utilizes in any venture depends on the importance of the end he wishes to achieve. For example, a particular medication may be available in a purer form and also in a somewhat less potent form. A person who is seriously concerned about his health will spend the extra money to obtain the former, believing that it will be more effective in curing his disease. The more one is desirous of effective treatment, the more one will go to the expense of obtaining the finest medication available. Similarly, the more serious the disease, the greater will be the caution to avoid anything that might interfere with recovery. While a person will be concerned about his teeth as well as his heart, there is no question that the average person will exert greater caution with care of his heart than with his teeth.

How diligently one performs mitzvos and refines one's character traits is contingent on how much he understands the ultimate goal, and how much he understands the relationship of these mitzvos as the only means to achieve that goal. Investing more time in prayer and Torah study may indeed detract from the time one invests in work, but as with the person who will spend the extra money to obtain the finest quality medicine, so will the person assume the cost of dedicating more time to spiritual endeavors. Those who rush through their prayers and hurry off to work may not have this highest level of understanding to which Ramchal is referring.

It is of interest that the word *chet* (sin) also means "to miss the target," as in archery. This philology reinforces the concept that sin interferes with achieving the ultimate goal. Hence, people of the highest level of understanding are afraid of sin not because they will be punished, but because it defeats their very purpose in life.

אַךְ לַפְּחוּתִים מֵאֵלֶּה, תִּהְיֶה הַהֶעָרָה לְפִי הַבְחָנָתָם, וְהוּא, לְפִי עִנְיַן הַכָּבוֹד אֲשֶׁר הֵם מִתְאַוִּים לוֹ. וָזֶה, כִּי זֶה פָּשׁוּט אֵצֶל כָּל בַּעַל־דָּת, שֶׁאֵין הַמַּדְרֵגוֹת מִתְחַלְּקוֹת בָּעוֹלָם הָאֲמִתִּי שֶׁהוּא הָעוֹלָם הַבָּא, אֶלָּא לְפִי הַמַּעֲשִׂים.

Those of lesser understanding will be motivated (to Watchfulness) because of the reward of honor they anticipate in the World to Come. Inasmuch as they believe that their reward in the eternal world depends on their deeds in this world, they will observe the Torah because they wish to assure themselves of the highest reward, knowing that in the eternal world there is nothing additional they can accomplish.

While reward and punishment are principles of the Jewish faith, they should not be the prime motivating factor for proper behavior. In fact, they are rather juvenile considerations. A small child who cannot grasp the importance of various health measures may have to be motivated by external reward, such as a gold star on his chart for brushing his teeth. To offer such a reward to a mature adult would be insulting.

Yet, people who are not at the highest level of understanding may require this external motivation. While this service of G-d is not of the highest degree, the performance of mitzvos and the study of Torah, even if done with ulterior motives, may elevate one to a higher level. Thus, the less preferable motivation may lead to a enhanced motivation.

While external reward is not considered the ideal motivation, there is one outstanding example: *tzedakah* (charity). Here the desired result is that the poor have their needs provided for, and how this is achieved is secondary. People are therefore encouraged to donate to charity even if their only motivation is because they desire public acknowledgment as benefactors of the poor. Furthermore, the Talmud states that "One who donates to *tzedakah* and prays that by virtue of this mitzvah his child should be healed is a *tzaddik*" (*Pesachim* 8a). Mitzvos that benefit others may be performed for external reward.

וְהִנֵּה יֵשׁ מֵהַפְּתָאִים הַמְבַקְשִׁים רַק לְהָקֵל מֵעֲלֵיהֶם, שֶׁיֹּאמְרוּ: לָמָּה נְיַגֵּעַ עַצְמֵנוּ בְּכָל־כָּךְ חֲסִידוּת וּפְרִישׁוּת, הֲלֹא דַי לָנוּ שֶׁלֹּא נִהְיֶה מֵהָרְשָׁעִים הַנִּדּוֹנִים בַּגֵּיהִנֹּם, אֲנַחְנוּ לֹא נִדְחוֹק עַצְמֵנוּ לִכָּנֵס בְּגַן־עֵדֶן לִפְנַי וְלִפְנִים: אִם לֹא יִהְיֶה לָנוּ חֵלֶק גָּדוֹל, יִהְיֶה לָנוּ חֵלֶק קָטָן, אָנוּ דַי לָנוּ בָּזֶה.

אָמְנָם שְׁאֵלָה אַחַת נִשְׁאַל מֵהֶם: הֲיוּכְלוּ כָּל־כָּךְ עַל נְקַלָּה לִסְבּוֹל בָּעוֹלָם־הַזֶּה הַחוֹלֵף לִרְאוֹת אֶחָד מֵחַבְרֵיהֶם מְכֻבָּד וּמְנֻשָּׂא יוֹתֵר מֵהֶם וּמוֹשֵׁל עֲלֵיהֶם וְכָל־שֶׁכֵּן אֶחָד מֵעַבְדֵיהֶם אוֹ מִן הָעֲנִיִּים הַנִּבְזִים וּשְׁפָלִים בְּעֵינֵיהֶם וְלֹא יִצְטַעֲרוּ וְלֹא יִהְיֶה דָמָם רוֹתֵחַ בְּקִרְבָּם? . . . מֵעַתָּה אִם כָּךְ קָשֶׁה עֲלֵיהֶם לִהְיוֹת שְׁפָלִים מִזּוּלָתָם בְּמַעֲלוֹת הַמְדֻמּוֹת וְהַכּוֹזְבוֹת, שֶׁאֵין הַשִּׁפְלוּת בָּם אֶלָּא לְפָנִים וְלֹא

הַהִנָּשֵׂא אֶלָּא שָׁוְא וָשֶׁקֶר, אֵיךְ יוּכְלוּ לִסְבּוֹל שֶׁיִּרְאוּ עַצְמָם שְׁפָלִים יוֹתֵר מֵאוֹתָם הָאֲנָשִׁים עַצְמָם אֲשֶׁר הֵם עַתָּה שְׁפָלִים מֵהֶם. וְזֶה בִּמְקוֹם הַמַּעֲלָה הָאֲמִתִּית וְהַיְקָר הַנִּצְחִי, שֶׁאַף־עַל־פִּי שֶׁעַכְשָׁו אֵין מַכִּירִים אוֹתוֹ וְאֶת עֶרְכּוֹ, עַל־כֵּן לֹא יָחוּשׁוּ אֵלָיו – אָז בִּזְמַנּוֹ, וַדַּאי שֶׁיַּכִּירוּהוּ לַאֲמִתּוֹ לְצַעֲרָם וּלְבָשְׁתָּם, וַדַּאי שֶׁלֹּא יִהְיֶה לָהֶם זֶה אֶלָּא צַעַר גָּדוֹל וְנִצְחִי. . . . כִּי לֹא יִהְיֶה עוֹד בְּיָדָם לְתַקֵּן אֶת אֲשֶׁר שִׁחֵתוּ.

Some foolish people who wish to ease the burdens of performance may say, "Why exert ourselves with so much piety? So we won't reach the highest levels in Paradise. It is enough that we will avoid Gehinnom. No need to deprive ourselves of worldly pleasures in order to attain a greater share of Paradise. A lesser share will suffice." . . .
Let us ask them, Are you being truthful with yourselves? Are you not envious when other people have more than you, or are in more exalted positions? How would you feel if someone who was subordinate to you would surpass you? And if you are distressed by envy in this world, whose pleasures and honors are all transitory, how distressed will you be in the eternal world, to see others who have achieved higher levels in Paradise, while you not only lag far behind, but can no longer do anything to better your status, and must resign yourself to an inferior status for eternity?

In my discussion of the components of spirituality (*I'd Like to Call for Help, But I Don't Know the Number*, Holt 1995), I listed as one of the factors that distinguishes man from other forms of life the ability to think about the future and the consequences of one's behavior. Doing things for the momentary pleasure or gain, and neglecting to consider the long term consequences of one's actions, is a dereliction of one's very humanity.

People who have a Torah orientation and believe in the eternity of the *neshamah*, and that its status in the World to Come depends on its achievements in this world, are deceiving themselves if they claim they will not be bothered by achieving a lesser status in Paradise. The undeniable fact is that they are distressed when they do not have the conveniences and prestige that others have achieved, particularly when the two set out from the same starting point. The diligent person achieves much, while the indolent person who achieves nothing looks upon his neighbor with much envy.

People who have fretted away the most productive years of life by indulging themselves come to a point of much regret. The pleasures of the past are long forgotten, and they have nothing to show for themselves. They look back upon the wasted past and are angry with themselves for having squandered this most precious resource, their most productive years, while others who used the time more wisely are secure and happy with their accomplishments.

Even this analogy is not adequate, because while a waste of one's younger years is certainly regrettable, there is still something one can salvage in one's later years. Not so with someone who has squandered the years in this world, and who arrives in the World to Come with meager merits. All one can have is regrets and self-recrimination, because there is nothing one can achieve in the World to Come. Everything must be done in the earthly world, and what is not done here cannot be done anywhere else.

The thought "I will be satisfied with less" is nothing but a patent rationalization to justify one's indolence in pursuit of spirituality. For those who claim to be satisfied with less, Ramchal says, "Show me that this is true of you now."

אַךְ הַהֶעָרָה לְכָל-הֶהָמוֹן, הִנֵּה הִיא בְּעִנְיַן הַשָּׂכָר וָעֹנֶשׁ עַצְמָם בִּרְאוֹת עֹמֶק הַדִּין עַד הֵיכָן מַגִּיעַ, אֲשֶׁר בֶּאֱמֶת רָאוּי לְהִזְדַּעְזֵעַ וּלְהִתְחָרֵד תָּמִיד, כִּי מִי יַעֲמֹד בְּיוֹם-הַדִּין וּמִי יִצְדַּק לִפְנֵי בוֹרְאוֹ בַּאֲשֶׁר הַשְׁקָפָתוֹ מְדַקְדֶּקֶת עַל כָּל דָּבָר קָטָן אוֹ גָּדוֹל.

The average person, however, may be motivated only by the promise of reward and punishment for one's actions. This should indeed be a most sobering consideration, because who can ever appear free of sin on Judgment Day, before the Creator who scrutinizes one's every move, small or great.

We have alluded to reward and punishment as being juvenile motivation, and indeed we are taught, "Do not be like servants who serve their master only for compensation" (*Ethics of the Fathers* 1:3). Yet, people who are fully grown and mature in every other way may lack the more advanced levels of understanding, and their behavior may be controlled only because of fear of punishment.

It is important to understand that Divine punishment is not a form of retaliation for having disobeyed G-d. G-d is perfect and is not harmed by a person's misbehavior. There are numerous references in the Scriptures and in the Talmud that the punishment for a transgression lies in the transgression itself. When someone sits in the direct sun too long and sustains a sunburn, it is not that he is being "punished" for his foolish behavior, for disregarding instructions against overexposure to the sun. Rather, it is inherent in the exposure to the sun that he will sustain a painful sunburn. Similarly, G-d designed the world in such a manner that prohibited acts carry a punitive consequence, whether in this world or the World to Come.

Ramchal now goes on to explain that there is no favoritism in the application of reward and punishment, just as one cannot expect that his many merits will protect him from sunburn. To the contrary, just as a person with more sensitive skin will burn more quickly than someone whose skin is less sensitive, so will people of great spirituality suffer the consequences of seemingly minor infractions. A faint stain that would not be noticeable on coarse material may be a marked blemish on fine silk. Ramchal then goes on to show how the greatest of our personages, the patriarchs whose spirituality was unsurpassed, as well as other *tzaddikim*, suffered consequences for behavior that would not have been considered sinful for people of lesser status. Every person must therefore be watchful, and one should not think that because one may have many mitzvos, one's transgressions will be overlooked. A person with a greater level of Torah observance is held to an even higher standard. Every meritorious act carries its reward, and every infraction carries its punishment.

Sometimes I think that all that needs to be done on Judgment Day is to play a video of one's life, from beginning to end. What greater punishment can there be than having to watch some of the foolish things one did? This would be a severe enough punishment if the viewing is private, but what if an audience is invited to watch the replay? If we keep in mind that everything we do, without exception, is being recorded on video for future viewing, we may be much more careful about our behavior.

וְאִם תֹּאמַר, אִם כֵּן, מִדַּת הָרַחֲמִים לָמָּה הִיא עוֹמֶדֶת, כֵּיוָן שֶׁעַל כָּל פָּנִים צָרִיךְ לְדַקְדֵּק בַּדִּין עַל כָּל דָּבָר? הַתְּשׁוּבָה, וַדַּאי, מִדַּת הָרַחֲמִים הִיא קִיּוּמוֹ שֶׁל עוֹלָם, שֶׁלֹּא הָיָה עוֹמֵד זוּלָתוֹ כְּלָל וּכְלָל. וְאַף־עַל־פִּי־כֵן אֵין מִדַּת הַדִּין לוֹקָה.

But (if we are held accountable for everything we do), what is the function of the Divine attribute of mercy? The answer is that the attribute of mercy maintains the world, since the world could not exist without it. Yet, this does not detract from the principle of justice.

The Midrash states that the Divine wisdom knew that mankind could not exist if the consequences of improper behavior were prompt and unmitigated. The Creator therefore included the attribute of mercy in the process of creation, as well as the mechanism of *teshuvah* (repentance and atonement). These now function to permit persons who have sinned to avoid the punitive consequences, if they make proper amends for their behavior.

We may understand this a bit better if we think of the model of "delayed action." A person may do something which would normally result in a distressing consequence. The attribute of mercy functions to suspend this distressing consequence, thus giving the person an opportunity to do *teshuvah.* The latter is a mechanism, instituted by the Divine wisdom, that can actually undo the improper act. If the person fails to do proper *teshuvah,* he will reap the distressing consequences of his sin, whether in this world or in the World to Come.

Teshuvah is a special, Divine gift. In secular law a person who has committed a theft can make restitution, but for sins such as the violation of *Shabbos* or forbidden relationships there is no restitution. *Teshuvah,* which consists primarily of sincere regret for committing the sin and of so altering one's character that this sin would not be repeated, accomplishes "restitution," and the sin can be forgiven. Suspending the consequences of the sin and permitting an opportunity for *teshuvah* are derivatives of the Divine attribute of mercy.

In addition to these "built-in" features, i.e., the punishment inherent in the act and its suspension pending *teshuvah,* there is also *hashgachah,* special Divine attention and intervention by G-d when He deems it fit. Acts of *hashgachah* are often beyond the grasp of human intelligence, and one must accept the Divine judgment by faith. The Talmud states that Moses sought to understand this concept, especially in regard to why the righteous suffer, and G-d told him that this secret cannot be revealed to any living person.

There may thus be distressing occurrences that are Divinely ordained, the reason for which is known only to G-d. These may be specific disciplinary measures, but distress may also occur for a variety of reasons. For example, the Talmud states that there is a concept of "sufferings because of Divine love." Various explanations have been offered for this phenomenon, but it essentially remains a mystery, and an issue of faith.

Divine wisdom may inflict suffering for reasons unknowable to us, but one thing is certain: The Divine judgment is exact, and no suffering exists beyond that which was ordained.

Torah commentaries cite as an example the Midrash which states that when the brothers sold Joseph into slavery, the caravan that took him to Egypt was one that carried fragrant spices (*Genesis* 37:25). The Midrash points out that these caravans usually transported malodorous tar, but that G-d designed it so that Joseph would not be annoyed by the irritating odor of tar.

The commentaries ask, When something so overwhelmingly traumatic as being kidnapped and sold into slavery was happening to Joseph, would it really have made a significant difference to him whether the odors he was exposed to were pleasant or unpleasant? The answer is that this is an indication of the precision of the Divine wisdom. Joseph was being punished for carrying *lashon hara* (slander) about his brothers to Jacob, and for this he was sold into slavery. However, not one iota of discomfort beyond that which was his due was permitted to occur. Hence he was spared the irritation of unpleasant odors.

דְּהַיְנוּ שֶׁבִּהְיוֹת הַשָּׁב מַכִּיר אֶת חֶטְאוֹ וּמוֹדֶה בוֹ וּמִתְבּוֹנֵן עַל רָעָתוֹ וְשָׁב וּמִתְחָרֵט עָלָיו חֲרָטָה גְּמוּרָה דְּמֵעִקָּרָא כַּחֲרָטַת הַנֹּדֵר מַמָּשׁ שֶׁהוּא מִתְנַחֵם לְגַמְרֵי וְהָיָה חָפֵץ וּמִשְׁתּוֹקֵק שֶׁמֵּעוֹלָם לֹא הָיָה נַעֲשֶׂה הַדָּבָר הַהוּא וּמִצְטַעֵר בְּלִבּוֹ צַעַר חָזָק עַל שֶׁכְּבָר נַעֲשָׂה הַדָּבָר וְעוֹזֵב אוֹתוֹ לְהַבָּא וּבוֹרֵחַ מִמֶּנּוּ, הִנֵּה עֲקִירַת הַדָּבָר מֵרְצוֹנוֹ יֵחָשֵׁב לוֹ כַּעֲקִירַת הַנֵּדֶר וּמִתְכַּפֵּר לוֹ . . . וְזֶה חֶסֶד וַדַּאי שֶׁאֵינָהּ מִשּׁוּרַת הַדִּין, אַךְ עַל־כָּל־פָּנִים הִנֵּה הוּא חֶסֶד שֶׁאֵינוֹ מַכְחִישׁ הַדִּין לְגַמְרֵי.

אַךְ שֶׁיְּוָתְרוּ עֲבֵרוֹת בְּלֹא כְלוּם אוֹ שֶׁלֹּא יַשְׁגִּיחַ עֲלֵיהֶם, זֶה הָיָה נֶגֶד הַדִּין לְגַמְרֵי . . . נִמְצָא, שֶׁאֵין לָאָדָם הָרוֹצֶה לִפְקֹחַ עֵינָיו פִּתּוּי שֶׁיּוּכַל לְהִתְפַּתּוֹת בּוֹ לְבִלְתִּי הִזָּהֵר בְּמַעֲשָׂיו תַּכְלִית הַזְּהִירוּת וּלְדַקְדֵּק בָּם תַּכְלִית הַדִּקְדּוּק.

Thus, when a person recognizes his sin, admits it, reflects on the wrong he did, sincerely wishes he had never committed the act, genuinely agonizes over it, and takes steps to prevent its recurrence (all of which constitutes true teshuvah) that sin is then totally erased. . . This is clearly a function of G-d's loving kindness (the attribute of mercy), since absolute justice does not provide for this. But neither does this contradict justice . . .

However, that sins should be overlooked or ignored would be a gross defiance of justice. . . . Hence there is no way that any thinking person can justify not exercising the maximum of Watchfulness.

Ramchal has provided cogent arguments for the need for Watchfulness for persons of all levels of understanding. These are so convincing that one wonders why there would be any dereliction in Watchfulness. Ramchal now proceeds to point out why such dereliction may occur.

5

בְּבֵאוּר מַפְסִידֵי הַזְּהִירוּת וְהַהַרְחָקָה מֵהֶם

The Factors Which Detract from Watchfulness, and Their Avoidance

הִנֵּה מַפְסִידֵי הַמִּדָּה הַזֹּאת וּמַרְחִיקֶיהָ הֵם שְׁלֹשָׁה: הָאֶחָד, הוּא הַטִּפּוּל וְהַטִּרְדָּה הָעוֹלָמִית; הַשֵּׁנִי, הַשְּׂחוֹק וְהַלָּצוֹן; הַשְּׁלִישִׁי, הַחֶבְרָה הָרָעָה; וּנְדַבֵּר בָּהֶם אֶחָד לְאֶחָד.
הִנֵּה הַטִּפּוּל וְהַטִּרְדָּה כְּבָר דִּבַּרְנוּ מֵהֶם לְמַעְלָה, כִּי בִהְיוֹת הָאָדָם טָרוּד בְּעִנְיְנֵי עוֹלָמוֹ, הִנֵּה מַחְשְׁבוֹתָיו אֲסוּרוֹת בְּזִקֵּי הַמַּשָּׂא אֲשֶׁר עֲלֵיהֶם, וְאִי אֶפְשָׁר לָהֶם לָתֵת לֵב אֶל הַמַּעֲשֶׂה. וְהַחֲכָמִים עֲלֵיהֶם הַשָּׁלוֹם, בִּרְאוֹתָם זֶה אָמְרוּ (אבות ד, י): ,,הֱוֵי מְמַעֵט בְּעֵסֶק וַעֲסוֹק בַּתּוֹרָה״. כִּי הִנֵּה הָעֵסֶק מֻכְרָח הוּא לָאָדָם לְצֹרֶךְ פַּרְנָסָתוֹ, אַךְ רִבּוּי הָעֵסֶק אֵינוֹ מֻכְרָח שֶׁיִּהְיֶה כָּל־כָּךְ גָּדוֹל עַד שֶׁלֹּא יַנִּיחַ מָקוֹם אֶל עֲבוֹדָתוֹ,

There are three factors that may detract from Watchfulness: (1) preoccupation and over-involvement with mundane matters; (2) levity and scoffing; and (3) keeping bad company.

Earlier we mentioned that total preoccupation with the daily activities of life precludes giving proper thought to one's deeds. This is why our sages say, "Minimize your occupation and occupy yourself with Torah" (Ethics of the Fathers 4:10). Obviously a person must engage in work or business for a livelihood, but these should not so totally occupy his time as to leave no time for Divine service.

Ramchal is not blind to reality and does not advocate that a person separate himself from the normal pace of life. Working for a livelihood is fully compatible with spirituality, and with avoiding wrongful acts. However, if one becomes so preoccupied with work or business that he does not leave adequate time for meditation and for contemplating about his behavior, he is indeed derelict. If a person has no time to think about his behavior, his actions are literally thoughtless, and Ramchal has already expounded on the pitfalls of acting out of habit rather than out of deliberation.

Preoccupation with economic activities contributes to lack of spirituality in yet another way. The rules of the game of economics differ radically from those of morality. Even if one avoids violation of business ethics, the criteria of good and bad in economics are much different than moral good and bad. In economics, the "bottom line" is decisive: Profit is good, loss is bad. A venture which was entered into after thorough market research, with expert advice and solid financing, yet goes bankrupt, is a "bad" venture. On the other hand, a business that was started in a most reckless manner, with total disregard for sound business principles, yet turned a windfall profit, is a "good" venture, and the entrepreneur is considered a financial wizard.

In matters of a moral nature, good and bad are determined by intent and by how and why one does something, and not by outcome. Thus, if a surgeon were to perform a totally unnecessary operation solely out of avarice to collect a hefty fee, and happened to discover a small cancer whose existence was unsuspected and remove it, thereby saving the patient's life, he is nevertheless an unscrupulous surgeon. On the other hand, if a surgeon is faced with a difficult decision whether to operate or not, and he seeks expert consultation and agonizes over the decision in the desire to do what is best for the patient, he is a "good" surgeon even if the patient does not survive the operation.

The problem is that people who are thoroughly immersed in economics may unwittingly apply the rules of economics to morality, and may come to believe that success is morally good and failure is morally bad. People who have amassed great fortunes may be idolized, even though the methods by which they accomplished these were unethical. On the other hand, parents who have devoted themselves selflessly to raising their children properly, only to have a child become socially deviant, often feel guilty for their actions, as though they had done something wrong.

The failure to set aside time for analyzing one's behavior and the adoption of inappropriate criteria for moral good and bad may lead to a disregard of Watchfulness.

וּכְמַאֲמַר רַבִּי פִּינְחָס: „תּוֹרָה מְבִיאָה לִידֵי זְהִירוּת" . . . וּכְמוֹ שֶׁאָמְרוּ ז"ל (קידושין ל, ב): „בָּרָאתִי יֵצֶר הָרָע בָּרָאתִי לוֹ תּוֹרָה תַּבְלִין". וְהִנֵּה פָּשׁוּט הוּא, שֶׁאִם הַבּוֹרֵא לֹא בָרָא לְמַכָּה זוֹ אֶלָּא רְפוּאָה זוֹ, אִי אֶפְשָׁר בְּשׁוּם פָּנִים שֶׁיִּרָפֵא הָאָדָם מִזֹּאת הַמַּכָּה בִּלְתִּי זֹאת הָרְפוּאָה, וּמִי שֶׁיַּחֲשׁוֹב לְהִנָּצֵל זוּלָתָהּ, אֵינוֹ אֶלָּא טוֹעֶה, וְיִרְאֶה טָעוּתוֹ לְבַסּוֹף בְּשֶׁיָּמוּת בְּחֶטְאוֹ. כִּי הִנֵּה הַיֵּצֶר הָרָע בֶּאֱמֶת חָזָק הוּא בָּאָדָם מְאֹד, וּמִבְּלִי יְדִיעָתוֹ שֶׁל הָאָדָם הוֹלֵךְ הוּא וּמִתְגַּבֵּר בּוֹ וְשׁוֹלֵט עָלָיו.

This is why Rabbi Pinchas ben Yair stated, "Torah leads to Watchfulness." This is in keeping with the Talmudic statement that G-d said, "I created the yetzer hara (the evil inclination) and I created Torah as its antidote" (Kiddushin 30b). Since Torah is the specific antidote to counteract the yetzer hara, it is absurd to think that one can escape the yetzer hara without applying Torah. The yetzer hara is insidious and extremely powerful, and can overwhelm a person without his knowledge. Unless one takes the specific antidote, he may be unaware of the yetzer hara's dominance until it is too late.

In medicine we know that there are conditions that are due to certain deficiencies; e.g., scurvy, which results from a deficiency of Vitamin C. Nothing will cure scurvy other than Vitamin C. One may take megadoses of other vitamins, eat various health foods, and engage in vigorous exercise, but nothing will change until Vitamin C is absorbed in sufficient quantity.

This is how we must understand the specificity of Torah to counteract the *yetzer hara*. No other stratagem can be effective.

The Rebbe of Rhizin had noted a young chassid engaging in the practices of piety which Ramchal discourages, i.e., mortification of the flesh. "Just what is it that you wish to accomplish?" the Rebbe asked.

"I wish to break my bad character traits," the *chassid* answered.

"You will break your neck before you break a single trait," the Rebbe said. "Study Torah diligently and observe the mitzvos properly and your bad traits will disappear."

Torah contains a magic charm, as it were, that can successfully counteract the *yetzer hara*. There is one distinction, however, between the analogy of Vitamin C for scurvy and Torah for the *yetzer hara*, and that is that whereas Vitamin C will cure scurvy regardless of how and why it is taken, Torah must be studied with the intent that it should lead to character refinement. As we have noted, the *yetzer hara* is very wily and may distort even Torah teachings for its purpose.

One of the chassidic masters tried to impress this point on his followers. One time he ran breathlessly up and down the aisles of the house of study, as if in pursuit of someone. After giving much chase, he grasped at the bookshelves, and fell against them, exhausted. To the surprised onlookers he said, "I saw the *yetzer hara* here, and I tried to capture him, but he eluded me. Just as I was about to seize him, he hid himself among the volumes of Torah."

Some people have strange ideas of mitzvos. "That person is a scoundrel. It is a mitzvah to berate him." This is nothing but the counsel of the *yetzer hara*, disguising a grievous sin as a mitzvah. Some people who have some Torah knowledge consider themselves superior to others who are less fortunate and did not have the opportunity to learn, and look down upon them. When Torah is used for vanity, this is the *yetzer hara* at work.

When a person studies Torah and makes a sincere effort to apply its teachings, that Torah can subdue the *yetzer hara*. One can then have true moral values of good and evil, and direct one's behavior toward fulfillment of the Divine will rather than to gratifying one's physical desires.

וְהִנֵּה בִּכְלָל זֶה גַּם כֵּן קְבִיעוּת הָעִתִּים אֶל חֶשְׁבּוֹן הַמַּעֲשֶׂה וְתִקּוּנוֹ כְּמוֹ שֶׁכָּתַבְתִּי לְמַעְלָה. וּמִלְּבַד כָּל זֶה מַה שֶּׁיִּשָּׁאֵר לוֹ פְּנַאי מֵעֲסָקָיו, אִם חָכָם הוּא וַדַּאי שֶׁלֹּא יְאַבְּדֵהוּ, אֶלָּא יֹאחֵז בּוֹ מִיָּד וְלֹא יַרְפֵּהוּ, לַעֲסוֹק בּוֹ בְּעֵסֶק נַפְשׁוֹ וְתִקּוּן עֲבוֹדָתוֹ.

Included in this is setting aside specific time for contemplation of one's actions and on improving one's behavior. Furthermore, the wise person will utilize every free moment for self-improvement and betterment of the Divine service.

Setting aside a specific time for meditation is extremely important. It is only natural for a person to procrastinate, and unless one designates a time for meditation, one may never get around to it. People who feel that jogging is healthy, but realize that they may give other things priority, set aside a specific time for jogging, and this becomes an inviolable part of their schedule. This is what one should do with time for meditation.

Ramchal also suggests putting every free moment to constructive use. There are some people who, having nothing that demands their attention, seek some way to "kill time," little realizing that they are destroying the most precious commodity they possess. The *yetzer hara* thrives on such waste of free time.

A young man approached a chassidic master with a problem. He had inherited a store from his father, but whereas the father did a thriving business, the store was doing very poorly in his hands. The master asked him, "What do you do when there are no customers?"

"I read the newspaper," he said, "or look out the window to see what's going on."

The master said, "There is your answer. When your father had no customers, he would recite *Tehillim* (*Psalms*) or study a portion of the *Mishnah*. To distract him from this, the *yetzer hara* would send him many customers. But you waste your free time, which is exactly what the *yetzer hara* desires, and he therefore discourages people from coming to your store."

אַךְ הַשֵּׁנִי, הִנֵּה הוּא קָשֶׁה מְאֹד, וְהוּא הַשְּׂחוֹק וְהַלָּצוֹן, כִּי מִי שֶׁטּוֹבֵעַ בָּם הוּא כְּמִי שֶׁטּוֹבֵעַ בַּיָּם הַגָּדוֹל שֶׁקָּשֶׁה מְאֹד לְהִמָּלֵט מִמֶּנּוּ. כִּי הִנֵּה הַשְּׂחוֹק הוּא מְאַבֵּד אֶת לֵב הָאָדָם, שֶׁכְּבָר אֵין הַטַּעַם וְהַדֵּעָה מוֹשֶׁלֶת בּוֹ, וַהֲרֵי הוּא כְּשִׁכּוֹר אוֹ שׁוֹטֶה אֲשֶׁר אִי אֶפְשָׁר לָתֵת לָהֶם עָרְמָה אוֹ לְהַנְהִיגָם, כִּי אֵינָם מְקַבְּלִים הַנְהָגָה, . . . לְפִי, שֶׁכְּמוֹ שֶׁכָּל מְצִיאוּת הַזְּהִירוּת תָּלוּי בְּשִׂימַת הַלֵּב עַל הַדָּבָר, כֵּן כָּל עַצְמוֹ שֶׁל הַשְּׂחוֹק אֵינוֹ אֶלָּא מֵסִיר הַלֵּב מִן הַמַּחֲשָׁבוֹת הַיְשָׁרוֹת וְהָעִיּוּנִיּוֹת,

The second factor that deters one from Watchfulness is more severe, and that is scoffing and levity. One who is immersed in these is like someone drowning in the ocean. Scoffing and levity so affect a person's emotions that reasoning and logic are totally ineffective, and one is then like the intoxicated or insane person who is not amenable to being guided. . . . Just as the essence of Watchfulness involves applying one's heart to deliberating over his behavior, the essence of scoffing and levity is to deter one from attentive thinking.

Ramchal is essentially referring to the premise developed in Chapter One, that a person has a duty and a mission in life. If a person accepts this premise, then life is serious business, to be approached with sober thought. If one does not see life as being purposeful and goal directed, then there is nothing to stand in the way of hedonism.

A person's physical drives may be so powerful that he may rationalize to justify his selfish impulses. Paganism was nothing other than a contrived religion whereby a person fashioned the kinds of gods who would decree that which he wished to hear, thereby giving him sanction to gratify all his desires. Another mechanism to achieve the same end is scoffing, dismissing everything as being inconsequential. The scoffer denies the existence of G-d, and cynically disparages all standards of behavior, thereby freeing himself of any discomfort of conscience which would result from violating a moral code. For the scoffer there is no moral code, and Ramchal's analogy to the intoxicated or insane person is valid. The scoffer is obstinate in the face of all logical argument, just as the active alcoholic cannot be deterred from drinking by pointing out to him its ruinous consequences.

וְתִרְאֶה קְשִׁי הַלָּצוֹן וְהַשְׁחָתָתוֹ הָרַבָּה, כִּי כְּמוֹ הַמָּגֵן הַמָּשׁוּחַ בְּשֶׁמֶן אֲשֶׁר יַשְׁמִיט וְיַפִּיל מֵעָלָיו הַחִצִּים וּמַשְׁלִיכָם לָאָרֶץ וְלֹא יַנִּיחַ אוֹתָם שֶׁיַּגִּיעוּ אֶל גּוּף הָאָדָם, כֵּן הַלָּצוֹן בִּפְנֵי הַתּוֹכָחָה וְהַמַּרְדוּת, כִּי בְּלֵיצָנוּת אֶחָד וּבִשְׂחוֹק קָטָן יַפִּיל הָאָדָם מֵעָלָיו רִבּוּי גָּדוֹל מִן הַהִתְעוֹרְרוּת וְהַהִתְפָּעֲלוּת מַה שֶּׁהַלֵּב מִתְעוֹרֵר וּמִתְפָּעֵל מִדֵּי רְאוֹתוֹ אוֹ שָׁמְעוֹ עִנְיָנִים שֶׁיְּעִירוּהוּ אֶל הַחֶשְׁבּוֹן וְהַפִּשְׁפּוּשׁ בַּמַּעֲשִׂים, . . . אַךְ הַלֵּצִים שֶׁאֵינָם מִתְפָּעֲלִים מִן הַתּוֹכָחוֹת מִפְּנֵי כֹּחַ לֵיצָנוּתָם, אֵין לָהֶם תִּקּוּן אֶלָּא הַשְּׁפָטִים.

Just as a shield lubricated with oil will cause all arrows to slide off, so too does scoffing cause all impressions that would normally arouse a person to reflection to fall away. This is not due to a lack of intelligence, but rather to the power of scoffing to obliterate all facets of moral evaluation. . .it is because scoffers are not influenced by exhortation that they cannot be corrected except by painful experiences.

The active alcoholic functions with the mechanism of *denial*, being unable to recognize that alcohol is ruining him. The scoffer is equally in denial, and anything that threatens to break through this denial is dismissed with derision.

There is an anecdote about a farmer who sold a mule, and told the buyer that the animal obeys instructions. When all the buyer's calls failed to move the beast, he complained to the farmer, who then struck the mule a mighty blow with a heavy piece of lumber, saying "Now move!"

"I thought you said the animal obeys instructions," the buyer said.

"Sure," the farmer responded, "but first you have to get his attention."

Just as the alcoholic may not be brought to his senses by anything less than a major crisis, so too with the scoffer. The Book of *Proverbs* is replete with references to the destructive behavior of the *letz* (scoffer), who is resistant to all counsel and efforts by the wise to correct his behavior. As Ramchal points out, this is not a matter of intelligence, since the denial of both the alcoholic and the scoffer can be found in people of the highest intelligence and sophistication.

וְהַמַּפְסִיד הַשְּׁלִישִׁי הוּא הַחֶבְרָה, . . . הִנֵּה אֲנַחְנוּ רוֹאִים פְּעָמִים רַבּוֹת אֲפִילוּ אַחַר שֶׁנִּתְאַמֵּת אֵצֶל הָאָדָם חוֹבַת הָעֲבוֹדַת וְהַזְּהִירוּת בָּהּ, יִתְרַפֶּה מִמֶּנָּה אוֹ יַעֲבוֹר עַל אֵיזֶה דְּבָרִים מִמֶּנָּה כְּדֵי שֶׁלֹּא יִלְעֲגוּ עָלָיו חֲבֵרָיו אוֹ כְּדֵי לְהִתְעָרֵב עִמָּהֶם, . . . וְדָוִד הַמֶּלֶךְ אָמַר (תהילים א, א): ,,אַשְׁרֵי הָאִישׁ אֲשֶׁר לֹא הָלַךְ וגו׳ ״, . . . וְיַחֲשׁוֹב בְּדַעְתּוֹ כִּי לוּלֵי הָיָה לוֹ לְהַרְוִיחַ מָמוֹן הַרְבֵּה, הֶהָיָה מַנִּיחַ מַה שֶּׁהָיָה צָרִיךְ לָזֶה מִפְּנֵי חֲבֵרָיו שֶׁלֹּא יִלְעָגוּ. כָּל־שֶׁכֵּן שֶׁלֹּא יִרְצֶה לְאַבֵּד נִשְׁמָתוֹ מִפְּנֵי לַעַג.

The third deterrent is bad company.... We often find that a person who does understand his duties and the need for Watchfulness may weaken in his resolve in order to avoid being mocked by his peers or to be able to mix freely with them.... This is why King David begins Psalms with "Fortunate is the person who does not associate with the wicked, the sinful, and the scoffers" ... Let a person think, "If I stood to make a huge profit, would I be deterred by people who mock me?" Certainly one should not place his soul at risk because he fears being ridiculed. To the contrary, one should ridicule those who mock him.

How many young people have been lured to self-destruction because of peer pressure, succumbing to deadly drug use and other noxious behaviors because they did not wish to be alienated by their friends! In a less dramatic way, many people flow with the tide, doing whatever their neighbors think is fashionable, because they do not wish to be thought of as non-conformists.

A person should have the strength of his convictions. Granted, he may wish to critically examine his beliefs, but he should nevertheless trust in his own judgment rather than being swept along with the tide. Of course, one should seek the input of the wise in making value judgments. Demagogues thrive on the power of peer pressure, and they can cause an entire population to commit the worst atrocities, all because each individual fears being singled out as a non-conformist.

Sometimes resistance to peer pressure requires a degree of activism. It is told that a man who exhibited a sign "Repent, ye sinners!" was asked whether he really believed his demonstration would cause anyone to change their behavior. "No," he said, "but it will stop me from becoming like them."

The first paragraph of the *Shulchan Aruch* (Code of Jewish Law) states, "A person should not be deterred by those who mock him." One must live according to what he believes to be right and proper.

6

בְּבֵאוּר מִדַּת הַזְּרִיזוּת

Clarifying the Trait of Zerizus

The Hebrew word *Zerizus* is not easily translated. The word "zeal" might be most appropriate, except that it is commonly associated with the word "zealot" and hence carries a flavor of fanaticism and intolerance, whereas *Zerizus* is a totally benign term. *Zerizus* connotes an attitude of devotion, enthusiasm, diligence, agility and fervor, especially in relationship to doing the Divine will, and it indicates an overwhelming willingness and readiness to accomplish this.

Zerizus is perhaps best defined as the attitude the Talmud ascribes to the patriarch Abraham, who was commanded by G-d to offer his beloved son Isaac as a sacrifice. The Torah states that "Abraham arose early in the morning" (*Genesis* 22:3); i.e., that although he was about to lose the child for whom he had prayed and who was given to him at an advanced age, Abraham did not delay in order to enjoy just a few more hours with his son, but rather arose at the crack of dawn, eager to carry out the Divine command. This is what *Zerizus* is all about.

Inasmuch as no single word accurately conveys the meaning of *Zerizus*, I chose to retain the Hebrew, and ask the reader to think of all the positive terms listed above that are contained in this single word.

אַחַר הַזְהִירוּת יָבוֹא הַזְּרִיזוּת, כִּי הַזְּהִירוּת סוֹבֵב עַל הַ,,לֹא תַעֲשֶׂה'' וְהַזְּרִיזוּת עַל הָ,,עֲשֵׂה'', וְהַיְנוּ, ,,סוּר מֵרָע וַעֲשֵׂה טוֹב.''

Zerizus follows "Watchfulness," because whereas Watchfulness relates to avoidance of transgressing prohibitions, Zerizus relates to performance of positive mitzvos. In following the dictum "Avoid evil and do good" (Psalms 34:15), we addressed Watchfulness first.

As a rule, one must first shun evil and then seek to do good. It makes no sense to put on fine clothes before one has cleansed oneself of mud. There is no point in trying to elevate oneself spiritually while one is engaged in behavior that is morally base.

However, one may argue that a positive deed is the best method to extricate oneself from negative behavior, and that a tiny bit of light can banish a great deal of darkness. The verse of *Psalms* cited can also be read as "Avoid evil *by* doing good." Indeed, the Rabbi of Kotzk said that the reason one should not sin is not because it is forbidden, but rather because one should be so occupied doing what one should be doing that one simply has no time to sin. At any rate, even the former interpretation does not mean that one must be completely free of sin before doing mitzvos, but that one should at least be in the process of divesting oneself of objectionable acts, working toward a goal of total observance.

וְזֶה, כִּי כְמוֹ שֶׁצָּרִיךְ פִּקְחוּת גָּדוֹל וְהַשְׁקָפָה רַבָּה לְהִנָּצֵל מִמּוֹקְשֵׁי הַיֵּצֶר וּלְהִמָּלֵט מִן הָרַע שֶׁלֹּא יִשְׁלוֹט בָּנוּ לְהִתְעָרֵב בְּמַעֲשֵׂינוּ, כֵּן צָרִיךְ פִּקְחוּת גָּדוֹל וְהַשְׁקָפָה לֶאֱחֹז בַּמִּצְוֹת וְלִזְכּוֹת בָּהֶם וְלֹא תֹאבַדְנָה מִמֶּנּוּ. כִּי כְמוֹ שֶׁמְּסַבֵּב וּמִשְׁתַּדֵּל הַיֵּצֶר־הָרַע בְּתַחְבּוּלוֹתָיו לְהַפִּיל אֶת הָאָדָם בְּמִכְמוֹרוֹת הַחֵטְא, כֵּן מִשְׁתַּדֵּל לִמְנוֹעַ מִמֶּנּוּ עֲשִׂיַּת הַמִּצְוֹת וּלְאַבְּדָם מִמֶּנּוּ. וְאִם יִתְרַפֶּה וְיִתְעַצֵּל וְלֹא יִתְחַזֵּק לִרְדּוֹף אַחֲרֵיהֶם וְלִתְמוֹךְ בָּם, יִשָּׁאֵר נָעוּר וָרֵק מֵהֶם בְּוַדַּאי.

Just as it requires vast intelligence and a great deal of foresight to avoid entrapment by the yetzer hara into evil, these are equally essential to acquire mitzvos. Just as the yetzer hara plots to snare a person into sin, he similarly tries to prevent him from performance of mitzvos, and if one is weak and indolent in their performance, he may remain devoid of these mitzvos.

The measure of *Zerizus* one has is indicative of one's degree of devotion to G-d. The Talmud states, "Do His will as though it were your own" (*Ethics of the Fathers* 2:4). If a person has a strong desire for something, he may move heaven and earth to get it. He is likely to go after the object of his desire with much zeal, and is not apt to let anything stand in his way. This is how one should behave in doing the Divine will.

It is related that on the night following the close of Passover, Rabbi Levi Yitzchak of Berditchev would sit at the window all night, looking anxiously for the first sign of dawn, at which time he would be permitted to put on the *tefillin*. Having been deprived of this mitzvah for the eight days of the festival, he longed for it like someone who has been separated from his beloved. It is characteristic of Rabbi Levi Yitzchak that after the conclusion of the Yom Kippur fast, while others hurried to satisfy their hunger, Rabbi Levi Yitzchak studied the laws of *Succah* in preparation for the approaching festival. His hunger for the mitzvah surpassed his physical hunger.

Our great Torah personalities were able to embody *Zerizus* because the will of G-d was primary, and their own will was even less than secondary. The Talmud relates that Rabbi Abahu had an interpreter, who explained his sermons in lay language to the public. The interpreter's wife boasted to Rabbi Abahu's wife, "My husband is every bit as learned and as original as yours, and he humbles himself to function as an interpreter because of his intense humility." Rabbi Abahu's wife told her husband about the interpreter's wife's *chutzpah*, and he responded, "What difference does it make who is more brilliant? The end result is that between the two of us, the Divine teachings are conveyed to the populace, and that is all that matters" (*Sotah* 40a). The Divine will is all that counts.

It is only when one's own will predominates that one may lack *Zerizus*. Practicing *Zerizus* may enable a person to subordinate himself and to place his own will before that of G-d.

וְתִרְאֶה כִּי טֶבַע הָאָדָם כָּבֵד מְאוֹד, כִּי עַפְרִיּוּת הַחָמְרִיּוּת גַּס, עַל כֵּן לֹא יַחְפּוֹץ הָאָדָם בְּטֹרַח וּמְלָאכָה. וּמִי שֶׁרוֹצֶה לִזְכּוֹת לַעֲבוֹדַת הַבּוֹרֵא יִתְבָּרֵךְ, צָרִיךְ שֶׁיִּתְגַּבֵּר נֶגֶד טִבְעוֹ עַצְמוֹ וְיִתְגַּבֵּר וְיִזְדָּרֵז, שֶׁאִם הוּא מַנִּיחַ עַצְמוֹ בְּיַד כְּבֵדוּתוֹ, וַדַּאי הוּא שֶׁלֹּא יַצְלִיחַ . . . וּמִקְרָא מָלֵא הוּא (יהושע א, ז): ,,חֲזַק וֶאֱמַץ מְאֹד לִשְׁמֹר לַעֲשׂוֹת כְּכָל־הַתּוֹרָה" . . . וְאָמַר (משלי ו, י): ,,מְעַט שֵׁנוֹת מְעַט

תְּנוּמוֹת מְעַט חִבֻּק יָדַיִם לִשְׁכָּב, וּבָא־כִמְהַלֵּךְ רֵאשֶׁךָ וּמַחְסֹרְךָ כְּאִישׁ מָגֵן". כִּי הִנֵּה הֶעָצֵל, אַף־עַל־פִּי שֶׁאֵינוֹ עוֹשֶׂה רַע בְּקוּם עֲשֵׂה, הִנֵּה הוּא מֵבִיא אֶת הָרָעָה עָלָיו בְּשֵׁב וְאַל תַּעֲשֶׂה שֶׁלּוֹ.

Just as the nature of an object is to remain at rest, so is the nature of a person, as a physical entity, to be at rest and not to exert oneself. One who wishes to merit doing the Divine service must therefore overcome the natural inclination, because if he follows his natural tendencies, he cannot succeed. . . The Torah exhorts us, "Strengthen yourself and be courageous to observe and fulfill the Torah" (Joshua 1:7). . . This is why Solomon repeatedly warns against the evil and the ruin of indolence: "Just a little more sleep, a little more slumber, a little folding of the hands, and your poverty is suddenly upon you" (Proverbs 6:10). Although the indolent person is not actively evil, his passivity is destructive.

If we look upon the human being as a composite of a physical body and a spirit, the role of *Zerizus* in development of spirituality becomes obvious. The natural state of the physical body, like any other object in the world, is that of inertia. Movement requires an expenditure of energy, i.e., overcoming the natural state. Any development of the spirit requires work.

The natural appetites of hunger and thirst cause enough discomfort to overcome the inertia, so that a person will be moved to seek food and water. The discomfort of cold will cause him to clothe himself and seek shelter from the elements. However, in the absence of discomfort, the natural inertia will prevail. If one observes the behavior of a person who has taken heroin, for example, one sees the result of a human who is without discomfort. Heroin removes all drives, and with uninterrupted use of this drug, a person would die of dehydration and starvation, since there is no hunger nor thirst to overcome the inertia.

Inasmuch as a person has spiritual needs, a lack of spirituality will result in some discomfort. However, whereas deprivation of food and water causes specific and even intense sensations of hunger and thirst, deprivation of spiritual nourishment causes a vague sense of discontent. The person feels unhappy but, in contrast to hunger and thirst, does not know just what it is he is lacking. This may be because hunger and thirst occur soon after birth, whereas spiritual needs do not arise until the person is well along in life. Since a person is often unable to identify that what he is lacking is spirituality, he may try to remedy his discontent by other means, whether it be accumulating wealth, alcohol, tranquilizers, drugs, or food. Indeed, that is the way many addictions develop.

וְאָמַר עוֹד לְבָאֵר רָעַת הֶעָצֵל בְּאוּר צִיּוּרִי, מַה שֶׁיִּקְרֶה וְיִוָּלֵד לְעֵינֵינוּ יוֹם יוֹם (שם כד, ל): ,,עַל־שְׂדֵה אִישׁ־עָצֵל עָבַרְתִּי וְעַל־כֶּרֶם אָדָם חֲסַר־לֵב, וְהִנֵּה עָלָה כֻלּוֹ קִמְּשׂוֹנִים כָּסּוּ פָנָיו חֲרֻלִּים וגו׳ . . . וְהִנֵּה מִלְּבַד פְּשׁוּטוֹ אֲשֶׁר הוּא אֲמִתִּי כְּמַשְׁמָעוֹ שֶׁהוּא מַה שֶּׁקּוֹרֶה אֶל שְׂדֵה הֶעָצֵל מַמָּשׁ, הִנֵּה דָּרְשׁוּ בּוֹ חֲכָמִים ז״ל מִדְרָשׁ נָאֶה, זֶה לְשׁוֹנָם (ילקוט שמעוני, משלי תתקס״א): ,,וְהִנֵּה עָלָה כֻלּוֹ קִמְּשׂוֹנִים, שֶׁמְּבַקֵּשׁ פֵּרוּשׁ שֶׁל פָּרָשָׁה וְאֵינוֹ מוֹצֵא. כָּסּוּ פָנָיו וגו׳, מִתּוֹךְ שֶׁלֹּא עָמַל בָּהֶם, הוּא יוֹשֵׁב וּמְטַמֵּא אֶת הַטָּהוֹר וּמְטַהֵר אֶת הַטָּמֵא . . . כִּי רָעַת הֶעָצֵל אֵינָהּ בָּאָה בְּבַת אַחַת, אֶלָּא מְעַט מְעַט . . . הִנֵּה בַּתְּחִלָּה אֵינוֹ אֶלָּא מַחֲסִיר הַטֹּרַח אֲשֶׁר הָיָה רָאוּי לוֹ, וּמִזֶּה נִמְשָׁךְ שֶׁלֹּא יִלְמַד בַּתּוֹרָה כְּכָל הַצֹּרֶךְ. וּמִפְּנֵי חֶסְרוֹן הַלִּמּוּד, כְּשֶׁיָּבוֹא אַחַר־כָּךְ לִלְמוֹד תֶּחְסַר לוֹ הַהֲבָנָה . . . הִנֵּה יְגַלֶּה בָהּ פָּנִים שֶׁלֹּא כַהֲלָכָה, וְיַשְׁחִית הָאֱמֶת וְיַהַפְכָהּ.

Solomon portrays the evil of indolence as follows: "I passed by the field of a lazy man and by the vineyard of a foolish person, and they were overgrown with thorns, covered with weeds, etc." (Proverbs 24:30). . . In addition to its obvious meaning, the sages interpret the overgrowth of thorns and weeds as referring to a distortion of judgment and values. . . The harmful consequences of indolence may not appear suddenly, but develop gradually. . . Lack of diligence in learning leads to deficiency in knowledge and then to faulty thinking. . . ultimately resulting in perversion of truth, so that one sees what is true as false and what is false as true.

Failure to plow, till, water, and weed will result in growth of thorns and weeds rather than fruits and vegetables. While these consequences of indolence are bad enough, it may be even worse if the foolish person thinks these wild growths to be edible foods, and poisons his system by their ingestion.

A person who fails because of indolence may not see his laziness as being the cause, and may attribute his failure to other factors. He may think himself to be dull or lacking in skills, and resign himself to poor achievement. He may place the blame for his failure on others, which may result in severe deterioration of interpersonal relations as he generates anger against those whom he holds responsible for his difficulties. These distortions of judgment, complicated by the persisting indolence, may eventually lead to a disastrous outcome.

וְהִנֵּה אֲנַחְנוּ רוֹאִים בְּעֵינֵינוּ כַּמָּה וְכַמָּה פְּעָמִים שֶׁכְּבָר לִבּוֹ שֶׁל הָאָדָם יוֹדֵעַ חוֹבָתוֹ וְנִתְאַמֵּת אֶצְלוֹ מַה שֶּׁרָאוּי לוֹ לְהַצָּלַת נַפְשׁוֹ וּמַה שֶּׁחוֹבָה עָלָיו מִצַּד בּוֹרְאוֹ, וְאַף־עַל־פִּי־כֵן יַנִּיחֵהוּ, לֹא מֵחֶסְרוֹן הַכָּרַת הַחוֹבָה הַהִיא וְלֹא לְשׁוּם טַעַם אַחֵר, אֶלָּא מִפְּנֵי שֶׁכְּבֵדוּת הָעַצְלָה מִתְגַּבֶּרֶת עָלָיו . . . וְאוּלָם אִם תִּשְׁאַל אֶת פִּי הֶעָצֵל, יָבוֹא לְךָ בְּמַאֲמָרִים רַבִּים מִמַּאַמְרֵי הַחֲכָמִים, וְהַמִּקְרָאוֹת מִן הַכְּתוּבִים, וְהַטְּעָנוֹת מִן הַשֵּׂכֶל, אֲשֶׁר כֻּלָּם יוֹרוּ לוֹ, לְפִי דַעְתּוֹ הַמְשֻׁבֶּשֶׁת, לְהָקֵל עָלָיו וּלְהַנִּיחוֹ בִּמְנוּחַת עַצְלָתוֹ. וְהוּא אֵינֶנּוּ רוֹאֶה שֶׁאֵין הַטְּעָנוֹת הָהֵם וְהַטְּעָמִים הָהֵם נוֹלָדִים לוֹ מִפְּנֵי שִׁקּוּל דַּעְתּוֹ, אֶלָּא מִמְּקוֹר עַצְלָתוֹ הֵם נוֹבְעִים, אֲשֶׁר בִּהְיוֹתָהּ הִיא גּוֹבֶרֶת בּוֹ, מַטָּה דַעְתּוֹ וְשִׂכְלוֹ אֶל הַטְּעָנוֹת הָאֵלֶּה, אֲשֶׁר לֹא יִשְׁמַע לְקוֹל הַחֲכָמִים וְאַנְשֵׁי הַדֵּעָה הַנְּכוֹנָה. הוּא מַה שֶּׁשְּׁלֹמֹה צוֹוֵחַ וְאוֹמֵר (משלי כו, טז): „חָכָם עָצֵל בְּעֵינָיו מִשִּׁבְעָה מְשִׁיבֵי טָעַם״. כִּי הָעַצְלָה אֵינֶנָּה מַנַּחַת לוֹ שֶׁיִּהְיֶה אֲפִילוּ חָשׁ לְדִבְרֵי הַמּוֹכִיחִים אוֹתוֹ, אֶלָּא יַחֲשׁוֹב הַכֹּל לְתוֹעִים וְשׁוֹטִים וְהוּא לְבַדּוֹ חָכָם.

We often see that a person may be aware of his obligations and may know what is incumbent upon him to do in the Divine service, yet neglect it, not because of lack of intelligence, but only because his indolence is dominant. . . He will come up with a myriad of excuses, and even quote Scripture, Talmud, and present logical arguments to support his erroneous thinking. He is incapable of seeing that all these excuses are born of laziness rather than intelligence, and this causes him to turn a deaf ear to constructive criticism. Solomon says, "A lazy person thinks himself wiser than seven sages" (Proverbs 26:16), and indeed he considers everyone else a fool, and only he is wise.

The resistance to take action results in countless rationalizations, with the indolent person convincing himself of their truth. The capacity to rationalize is widespread, and occurs even in people who are not manifestly indolent. The function of rationalization is to permit the individual to maintain the status quo. It is most prominent in the alcoholic, who continues his destructive drinking despite incontrovertible evidence of the harm he is doing to himself and others. A recovered alcoholic, reflecting on his many years of destructive drinking, said, "I never took a drink unless I was convinced that it was the right thing to do at that time."

Rationalization, whether it occurs in the indolent person, in the alcoholic, or in the "normal" individual is invariably disadvantageous. By definition, a rationalization is "giving logical reasons in place of the true reason," and since it is self-deceptive, rationalization is harmful. Deluding oneself cannot but result in adverse consequences. The more logical a rationalization, the more dangerous it is, because it is more likely to be mistaken for the truth. Hence, people of greater intelligence are more likely to be more expert at rationalization. Any psychotherapist will testify that the most sophisticated patients are apt to be the most difficult to treat, because they believe most strongly in their own lies.

וְהִנֵּה תֵּדַע כִּי זֶה כְּלָל גָּדוֹל מְנֻסֶּה בִּמְלֶאכֶת הַפְּרִישׁוּת, שֶׁכָּל קֻלָּא צְרִיכָה בְּדִיקָה. כִּי אַף־עַל־פִּי שֶׁיְּכוֹלָה לִהְיוֹת יְשָׁרָה וּנְכוֹחָה, אָמְנָם, קָרוֹב הַדָּבָר שֶׁתִּהְיֶה מֵעֲצוֹת הַיֵּצֶר וּמִרְמוֹתָיו, עַל כֵּן צָרִיךְ לִבְדּוֹק אַחֲרֶיהָ בַּחֲקִירוֹת וּדְרִישׁוֹת רַבּוֹת.

A principle that experience has proven valid is that any desire which tends to ease one's burdens should be considered suspect. While such decisions may be correct, it is likely that they originate from the yetzer hara, and should be scrutinized most carefully.

The alarm clock rings in the morning, and as the person awakens, he realizes he has an early appointment. He then begins to reflect on the importance of keeping that appointment. Perhaps the whole thing was a mistake, and not really necessary at all. He begins to weigh pros and cons.

Ramchal cautions that the arguments in favor of not keeping the appointment, which would then permit the person to stay in bed longer, are highly suspect of being rationalizations. They are generated by the desire to remain in bed, and if the person convinces himself of their validity, he is likely to later regret his decision when he discovers that his failure to keep the appointment was to his great disadvantage.

A chassid once asked the Rebbe of Rhizin for a guideline to proper conduct. One cannot always have recourse to *Shulchan Aruch* (Code of Jewish Law), nor is it possible for all problems to be addressed in the *Shulchan Aruch*. The Rebbe of Rhizin responded, "Do as a tightrope walker does. The way he maintains his delicate balance is that when he feels himself drawn to one side, he leans a bit toward the other.

"When you feel yourself tempted to do something, lean a bit toward the other side. As you process the pros and cons for any proposed action that would satisfy a desire, give greater credibility to the arguments that are against gratification. Those that are for gratification are likely to be spurious rationalizations.

וְתִרְאֶה שֶׁהַמַּלְאָכִים נִשְׁתַּבְּחוּ בְּמִדָּה הַטּוֹבָה הַזֹּאת . . . וְאוֹמֵר (יחזקאל א, יד): ,,וְהַחַיּוֹת רָצוֹא וָשׁוֹב כְּמַרְאֵה הַבָּזָק". וְהִנֵּה הָאָדָם הוּא אָדָם וְלֹא מַלְאָךְ . . . אַךְ וַדַּאי, שֶׁכָּל מַה שֶּׁיּוּכַל לְהִתְקָרֵב בְּמַדְרֵגָתוֹ אֵלָיו, רָאוּי הוּא שֶׁיִּתְקָרֵב. וְדָוִד הַמֶּלֶךְ הָיָה מְשַׁבֵּחַ עַל חֶלְקוֹ וְאוֹמֵר (תהלים קיט, ס): ,,חַשְׁתִּי וְלֹא הִתְמַהְמָהְתִּי לִשְׁמֹר מִצְוֹתֶיךָ".

The Scriptures describe the heavenly angels as having Zerizus to do the Divine bidding ... acting swiftly "as streaks of lightning" (Ezekiel 1:14). While a person is a human being rather than an angel, ... his aspiration should be to emulate their Zerizus, as King David said, "I was quick and I did not hesitate in observing your mitzvos (Psalms 119:60).

Why the reference to angels? The human being is a composite of (a) a physical body, which is very much akin to that of any brute beast, subject to various physical strivings, and (b) a *neshamah,* a Divine spirit which is very much akin to an angel.

Animals cannot be faulted for following their physical temptations, because that is the nature of an animal. Nor can angels, in truth, be praiseworthy for their unrestrained execution of the Divine bidding, since there is nothing to impede their doing so. It is perhaps a mistake to speak of angels as being spirit*ual*, since all they are is pure spirit. It is the human being whose physical nature generally draws him away from the Divine bidding who may be considered spiritual, when he allows the angelic component of his being rather than the animal component to determine his behavior. The angelic quality of *Zerizus*, when exercised by man, is therefore an important step toward spirituality.

7

בְּבֵאוּר חֶלְקֵי הַזְּרִיזוּת

Components of Zerizus

חֶלְקֵי הַזְּרִיזוּת שְׁנַיִם, אֶחָד קֹדֶם הַתְחָלַת הַמַּעֲשֶׂה וְאֶחָד אַחֲרֵי כֵן. קֹדֶם הַתְחָלַת הַמַּעֲשֶׂה הוּא שֶׁלֹּא יַחֲמִיץ הָאָדָם אֶת הַמִּצְוָה, אֶלָּא בְּהַגִּיעַ זְמַנָּהּ אוֹ בְּהִזְדַּמְּנָהּ לְפָנָיו אוֹ בַּעֲלוֹתָהּ בְּמַחֲשַׁבְתּוֹ, יְמַהֵר יָחִישׁ מַעֲשֵׂהוּ לֶאֱחוֹז בָּהּ וְלַעֲשׂוֹת אוֹתָהּ וְלֹא יַנִּיחַ זְמַן לִזְמַן שֶׁיִּתְרַבֶּה בֵּינְתַּיִם; כִּי אֵין סַכָּנָה כְּסַכָּנָתוֹ, אֲשֶׁר הִנֵּה כָּל רֶגַע שֶׁמִּתְחַדֵּשׁ, יוּכַל לְהִתְחַדֵּשׁ אֵיזֶה עִכּוּב לַמַּעֲשֶׂה הַטּוֹב.

Zerizus can be divided into two components, one prior to taking action; and the second, once the act has been initiated. The first means that one should not postpone a mitzvah, but when the opportunity presents itself or comes to mind, to promptly perform it without delay. Allowing even a brief period to elapse permits opportunities for various kinds of hindrances to occur (and the mitzvah may be delayed indefinitely).

Ramchal's warning should strike a familiar note. How often have we postponed doing something, only to discover that by the time we got around to doing it, the opportunity had passed. In medicine there is a principle of the "golden hour" to surgically close an open wound. After this brief period has passed, the possibility of infectious organisms having taken root is too great, and the wound must be allowed to heal slowly, which may take weeks instead of days, and may result in unsightly scarring. This principle holds true in doing mitzvos as well. One should take advantage of the "golden hour."

The *yetzer hara* is cunning, and can provide many rationalizations, such as "Why do the mitzvah in such haste? If you prepare for it more leisurely, you will be able to perform it in a much better manner." Under the guise of piety, the *yetzer hara* can undermine performance of mitzvos.

The chassidic master Rabbi Nachum of Czernobyl was approached by a man who was in desperate need of money to marry off his daughter, and said he needed 150 rubles. The following day, a wealthy chassid came to Rabbi Nachum with a donation of 150 rubles for *tzedakah*. Rabbi Nachum was overjoyed and sent for the man, with the intention of giving him the money.

While awaiting the man's arrival, Rabbi Nachum began to think that perhaps it was not proper to give this entire, huge sum to this one person. After all, he was besieged daily by poor people who needed help. If he gave the man 75 rubles or say, 100 rubles, that would still be a very respectable sum, and he would have enough left over for other needy people. The man could raise the balance by himself. The more he thought about it, the more it seemed appropriate to divide the money among the many poor.

Rabbi Nachum then thought, "Here I have two differing opinions. Obviously, one emanates from the *yetzer tov* (the good inclination) and the other from the *yetzer hara*. Which is which?" He then concluded that the first impulse was to give the entire sum to the man, and in all likelihood the subsequent considerations were the work of the *yetzer hara*. Furthermore, it is characteristic of the *yetzer tov* to suggest only once, whereas the *yetzer hara* is in the habit of nagging. Inasmuch as the thought to give the whole amount to the man occurred only once, and the idea to spread the money was a recurring one, the latter must be the counsel of the *yetzer hara*.

The slogan "Do it now" applies only to spiritual matters. Physical gratifications, on the contrary, should preferably be delayed to give one the opportunity to reflect whether they are really essential. It is said that when an executive displayed a sign "Do it now!" in the office, his accountant promptly took off with a huge sum of company money.

In addiction we have the prototype of the desire for immediate gratification. The addict gives no consideration whatever to the grave consequences that may result from yielding to his desire. The approaches to spiritual versus physical acts are thus polar opposites.

Spiritual acts should be performed with *Zerizus*, and physical gratifications should be given considerable thought to make sure they are necessary and appropriate.

We may be a bit embarrassed if we scrutinize our own behavior to discover that we often reverse things, and while we may be quite diligent in doing things we like to do, we may be less enthusiastic in doing those things we should do.

וְתִרְאֶה שֶׁהָאָדָם אֲשֶׁר תִּלַהֵט נַפְשׁוֹ בַּעֲבוֹדַת בּוֹרְאוֹ, וַדַּאי שֶׁלֹּא יִתְעַצֵּל בַּעֲשִׂיַּת מִצְוֹתָיו, אֶלָּא תִּהְיֶה תְנוּעָתוֹ כִּתְנוּעַת הָאֵשׁ הַמְּהִירָה, כִּי לֹא יָנוּחַ וְלֹא יִשְׁקוֹט עַד אִם כִּלָּה הַדָּבָר לְהַשְׁלִימוֹ. וְאָמְנָם, הִתְבּוֹנֵן עוֹד, שֶׁכְּמוֹ שֶׁהַזְּרִיזוּת הוּא תּוֹלֶדֶת הַהִתְלַהֲטוּת הַפְּנִימִי, כֵּן מִן הַזְּרִיזוּת יִוָּלֵד הַהִתְלַהֲטוּת. וְהַיְנוּ, כִּי מִי שֶׁמַּרְגִּישׁ עַצְמוֹ בְּמַעֲשֵׂה הַמִּצְוָה, כְּמוֹ שֶׁהוּא מְמַהֵר תְּנוּעָתוֹ הַחִיצוֹנָה כֵּן הִנֵּה הוּא גוֹרֵם שֶׁתִּבְעַר בּוֹ תְנוּעָתוֹ הַפְּנִימִית כְּמוֹ כֵן, וְהַחֵשֶׁק וְהַחֵפֶץ יִתְגַּבֵּר בּוֹ וְיֵלֵךְ. אַךְ אִם יִתְנַהֵג בִּכְבֵדוּת בִּתְנוּעַת אֵבָרָיו, גַּם תְּנוּעַת רוּחוֹ תִּשְׁקַע וְתִכְבֶּה.

A person who has a fervent desire to serve G-d will certainly not be indolent in doing His will, but will move with the rapidity of fire, not resting until he brings a mitzvah to its completion. Furthermore, just as Zerizus is a result of such fervent desire, acting with Zerizus also gives rise to fervor. The external act of a mitzvah, when done with Zerizus, tends to bring about an internal enthusiasm, in sharp contrast to a person who does mitzvos sluggishly, whose enthusiasm soon fades.

Ramchal proceeds on to the second component of *Zerizus*. Some people may be aroused to do a mitzvah, but whereas they begin with enthusiasm, this may wane. For example, after a moving *drashah* (sermon) on the importance of daily study of Torah, the *daf yomi* (daily Talmud) class may be heavily attended, but after several days the number of attendees begins to diminish, until several weeks have elapsed and only the nucleus of faithful regulars remain. Or a particular charitable venture may be initiated, with great interest shown by many people who enthusiastically sign up as volunteers, but as time passes, it is like pulling teeth to get them to participate actively. Ramchal points out that *Zerizus* requires keeping up the momentum.

Ramchal also notes another time-proven phenomenon. Just as fervent desire leads to *Zerizus*, the reverse can also be true: *Zerizus* can lead to fervor.

The Talmud states that a person should engage in mitzvos even if he does not have the proper *kavannah* (intent and concentration), because the *kavannah* will come with the action (*Pesachim* 50b). The reason for this is that *yetzer hara* is obstructionist, and prevents a person from developing a strong desire to do the Divine will, because this would lead to the kind of behavior that the *yetzer hara* opposes. If the person forces himself to do mitzvos even without *kavannah*, the *yetzer hara* will eventually relent. Inasmuch as it sees that it has lost the battle to discourage performance of the mitzvah, it retreats, and the person is now free to do the mitzvah with greater fervor.

The *yetzer hara* opposes spiritual progress, and one of his stratagems is to drain the emotion of performance of mitzvos. Isaiah noted this when he said "The hearts of these people are fattened, their eyes pasted, and their ears clogged, lest they see with their eyes, hear with their ears, feel with their hearts, and repent" (*Isaiah* 6:10). It is noteworthy that Isaiah begins with "their hearts are fattened," i.e., they lack the fervor for the Divine will, and this leads to refusal to see and hear. When it comes to action, he reverses the order, because if one compels oneself to see and hear, this will lead to understanding and feeling. In other words, even if you do not have the enthusiasm for mitzvos, do them anyway with diligence, and the enthusiasm will follow.

וְאָמְנָם כְּבָר יָדַעְתָּ, שֶׁהַנִּרְצֶה יוֹתֵר בַּעֲבוֹדַת הַבּוֹרֵא, יִתְבָּרֵךְ שְׁמוֹ, הוּא חֵפֶץ הַלֵּב וּתְשׁוּקַת הַנְּשָׁמָה. וְהוּא מַה שֶּׁדָּוִד הַמֶּלֶךְ מִתְהַלֵּל בְּחֶלְקוֹ הַטּוֹב וְאוֹמֵר (תהלים מב, ב): ,,כְּאַיָּל תַּעֲרֹג עַל־אֲפִיקֵי־מַיִם כֵּן נַפְשִׁי תַעֲרֹג אֵלֶיךָ אֱלֹהִים . . . וְאוּלָם הָאָדָם אֲשֶׁר אֵין הַחֶמְדָּה הַזֹּאת לוֹהֶטֶת בּוֹ כָּרָאוּי, עֵצָה טוֹבָה הִיא לוֹ שֶׁיִּשְׁדָּרֵז בִּרְצוֹנוֹ, כְּדֵי שֶׁיִּמָּשֵׁךְ מִזֶּה שֶׁתִּוָּלֵד בּוֹ הַחֶמְדָּה, כִּי הַתְּנוּעָה הַחִיצוֹנָה מְעוֹרֶרֶת הַפְּנִימִית.

It is known that what is most desirable in the Divine service is the devotion of the heart, as King David says, "As a hart yearns for water, so does my soul yearn for You" (Psalms 42:2) . . . If one lacks this fervor, it is advisable that he act by force of will, because outer movements awaken inner ones.

The traditional psychotherapeutic approach, which dominated psychology until recent years, was that symptoms were the result of deep-rooted emotional traumas and unresolved conflicts. The theory was that a thorough understanding of these would eliminate the symptoms. Repeated treatment failures led to this psychodynamic approach being increasingly replaced by a behavioristic approach; namely, change behavior first, and the internal problems can then be resolved. Working from the outside in has proven to be much more effective than working from the inside out.

While the goal of doing the Divine will is to have a sincere devotion to G-d, it is a mistake to think that one can be "spiritual at heart" but not in behavior. Experience has proven that behavior is more likely to arouse the spirit than the reverse.

8

בְּדֶרֶךְ קְנִיַּת הַזְּרִיזוּת

Acquiring Zerizus

הִנֵּה הָאֶמְצָעִים אֲשֶׁר נִקְנֶה בָם הַזְּרִיזוּת, הֵם הֵם אוֹתָם אֲשֶׁר נִקְנֶה בָם הַזְּהִירוּת . . . וְאֵין הֶפְרֵשׁ בֵּינֵיהֶם אֶלָּא שֶׁזֶּה בַּעֲשִׂין וְזֶה בַּלָּאוִין . . . מַה שֶּׁיּוּכַל לְהַגְבִּיר הַהִתְעוֹרְרוּת הַזֶּה הוּא הַהִסְתַּכְּלוּת בְּרוֹב הַטּוֹבוֹת, שֶׁהַקָּדוֹשׁ־בָּרוּךְ־הוּא עוֹשֶׂה עִם הָאָדָם . . . הִנֵּה יַרְבֶּה לְהַכִּיר לְעַצְמוֹ חוֹבָה רַבָּה אֶל הָאֵל הַמֵּטִיב לוֹ . . . כִּי הֲרֵי הוֹאִיל וְאֵינוֹ יָכוֹל וַדַּאי לִגְמוֹל לוֹ טוֹבָתוֹ יִתְבָּרֵךְ, לְפָחוֹת יוֹדֶה לִשְׁמוֹ וִיקַיֵּם מִצְוֹתָיו.

The means to acquire Zerizus are essentially the same as those for acquiring Watchfulness. . . Whereas Watchfulness relates to avoidance of prohibited acts, Zerizus relates to stimulation to do mitzvos, but otherwise the two are similar. . . . However, what can reinforce Zerizus is an awareness of the Divine benevolence and the endless kindnesses which G-d does with a person. . . The more one appreciates these, the more one realizes his obligation to do the Divine will.

Our prayers are replete with expressions of gratitude to G-d, and in the *Amidah* (silent prayer) we express our thanks "For the many miracles that are daily with us, and the wonders and kindnesses in every season — evening, morning, and afternoon."

There is a principle in Torah that no evil ever emanates from G-d. His benevolence may be manifest, or may be clothed in what we may experience as distress, i.e., blessings in disguise. It is a test of faith, and requires a profound belief in G-d to withstand some of the stresses in life, both those of a personal nature, and those that affect a multitude, such as severe floods, earthquakes, and the Holocaust.

We must realize that each of us can see only one tiny fragment of the universe, both in time and space. If a person were to look at a single piece of a million-piece jigsaw puzzle, he could not possibly understand what it portrays. Only when it fits in with the million other pieces does the picture appear. Similarly, what one sees in a single life span is but one small piece of an enormous jigsaw puzzle, and only the One who has a comprehensive perspective of eternity in time and infinity in space can understand why things must be as they are.

It is related that during the lifetime of the chassidic master, the Maggid of Mezeritch, the Czarist rulers did not issue any new anti-Semitic decrees, but after his death these were renewed. One of the Maggid's disciples wondered why this was so. Inasmuch as *tzaddikim* in heaven are in even closer proximity to G-d than during their lifetime, how was it that the Maggid was not now interceding on the Jews' behalf?

The Maggid appeared to this disciple in a dream and said, "When I occupied a physical body and with my human intelligence perceived a decree to be evil, I interceded to have it revoked. Now, from my vantage point in heaven, I can see that these decrees are for an ultimate good. I cannot intervene to revoke something which is for the good."

The firm belief in the benevolence of G-d will enable a person to be grateful, and as gratitude increases one's devotion to G-d, the measure of one's *Zerizus* is enhanced.

וְהִנְּךָ רוֹאֶה, שֶׁכְּלַלְתִּי פֹּה בְּדְבָרַי שְׁלֹשֶׁת הַמַּדְרֵגוֹת אֲשֶׁר חִלַּקְתִּים בַּזְּהִירוּת . . . שֶׁלִּשְׁלֵמֵי הַדַּעַת תִּהְיֶה הַהֶעָרָה מִצַּד עֵרֶךְ הַמַּעֲשִׂים וַחֲשִׁיבוּתָם: לַפְּחוּתִים מֵהֶם, מִצַּד הָעוֹלָם הַבָּא וּכְבוֹדוֹ . . . וְלֶהָמוֹן, מִצַּד הָעוֹלָם הַזֶּה וּצְרָכָיו.

The three levels of understanding that were discussed in regard to Watchfulness apply to Zerizus as well . . . Those of greatest understanding will be motivated by a sense of duty and belief in the intrinsic value of mitzvos. Those of lesser understanding will be motivated by the anticipation of reward in the World to Come . . . and those of the third level (the general population) will be motivated by anticipation of reward in this world.

The Talmud states that there is no reward in our earthly existence for fulfillment of mitzvos. The reason given is that reward for even a single mitzvah is so great that there is no vehicle in this world whereby it can be adequately compensated. Yet the Torah repeatedly cites the good that we will reap from observance of mitzvos.

The commentaries explain that inasmuch as optimal fulfillment of mitzvos requires good health and economic security, these will be provided for the Torah-observant person not as reward, but as means to enable him to continue to do the Divine will. Someone who is physically limited cannot study Torah nor fulfill many mitzvos properly, and one who is impoverished cannot fulfill the various mitzvos of *tzedakah*. Hence, although being blessed with earthly rewards is not a compensation for mitzvos, the person who cannot envision other reasons for doing the Divine will may do so in order to merit health and economic success, which he will be given as means to perform the mitzvos.

9

בְּבֵאוּר מַפְסִידֵי הַזְּרִיזוּת וְהַהַרְחָקָה מֵהֶם
Factors that Detract from Zerizus

הִנֵּה מַפְסִידֵי הַזְּרִיזוּת הֵם הֵם מַגְדִּילֵי הָעַצְלָה. וְהַגָּדוֹל שֶׁבְּכֻלָּם, הוּא בַּקָּשַׁת הַמְּנוּחָה הַגּוּפִיִּית וְשִׂנְאַת הַטֹּרַח וְאַהֲבַת הָעִדּוּנִים בְּתַשְׁלוּם כָּל תְּנָאֵיהֶם . . . כִּי הִנֵּה אָדָם כָּזֶה הִנֵּה יִקְשֶׁה עָלָיו לְהַשְׁכִּים לְבָתֵּי־כְנֵסִיּוֹת בַּבֹּקֶר, אוֹ לְקַצֵּר בִּסְעֻדָּתוֹ מִפְּנֵי תְּפִלַּת הַמִּנְחָה בֵּין הָעַרְבַּיִם, אוֹ לָצֵאת לִדְבַר מִצְוָה אִם לֹא יִהְיֶה הָעֵת בָּרוּר, כָּל־שֶׁכֵּן לְמַהֵר עַצְמוֹ לְדִבְרֵי מִצְוָה אוֹ לְתַלְמוּד תּוֹרָה. וּמִי שֶׁמַּרְגִּיל עַצְמוֹ לַמִּנְהָגוֹת הָאֵלֶּה, אֵינֶנּוּ אָדוֹן בְּעַצְמוֹ לַעֲשׂוֹת הֵפֶךְ זֶה כְּשֶׁיִּרְצֶה, כִּי כְּבָר נֶאֱסַר רְצוֹנוֹ בְּמַאֲסַר הַהֶרְגֵּל הַנַּעֲשֶׂה טֶבַע שֵׁנִי.

The primary factor that detracts from Zerizus is the pursuit of physical tranquility, loathing for exertion, and indulgence in pleasure ... Someone who strives for these will find it difficult to arise early for morning services, to cut short his meal before afternoon services, to pursue a mitzvah, or to hasten to study Torah. Someone who gets into these habits is no longer master over himself, because his will has become subject to his habits, which become second nature.

In my Haggadah *From Bondage to Freedom* I cited the case of a recovered drug addict who said to his father at the Passover *seder*, "How can you say you were a slave? You don't know what it means to be a slave, but I do. When I was addicted to drugs, I lost every remnant of freedom. Drugs were my master, and I did everything I had to do for them."

Narcotics are not the only master to which a person may fall subject. Anyone who cannot control his actions has become enslaved. Many people who smoke cigarettes know that they are lethal and would like to stop smoking but are unable to do so, and they have become slaves to cigarettes. A person who cannot control his anger has become a slave to rage. Someone who cannot control eating is likewise enslaved, as is someone whose indolence makes it impossible to act swiftly and properly. Ramchal is right. When a person pursues tranquility and pleasure as a primary goal, he may become enslaved by these, and may not be able to free himself to do the things he knows he should do.

A human being should pride himself on being free. Slavery is abhorrent even when it is not cruel, because it deprives a person of the dignity of being free and making his choices in life. *Zerizus* is thus an indication that one is a free person.

וְאָמְנָם צָרִיךְ שֶׁיֵּדַע הָאָדָם כִּי לֹא לִמְנוּחָה הוּא בָעוֹלָם הַזֶּה, אֶלָּא לְעָמָל וָטֹרַח . . . וְעַל זֶה נֶאֱמַר (איוב ה, ז): „כִּי אָדָם לְעָמָל יוּלָּד". וּכְשֶׁיַּרְגִּיל עַצְמוֹ עַל זֶה הַדֶּרֶךְ, יִמְצָא הָעֲבוֹדָה קַלָּה עָלָיו וַדַּאי.

Man was not created for tranquility, but to struggle and toil . . . as is written in Job (5:7), "Man is born to labor." If one accepts this, he will find the Divine service easy.

The brief quote from *Job* contains the Torah *weltanschauung* (worldview): The purpose of man's existence is to toil. Whereas man is permitted to enjoy rest and partake of worldly pleasures, these are not the purpose of his existence, and he must be able to set these aside when necessary. When a person makes rest and pleasure the goals of his existence, he cannot set them aside, as we have seen.

Even pursuit of the Divine wisdom, which is the most noble aspiration a person can have, is not yet the desired goal. Rashi qualifies this as "laboring in Torah" (*Leviticus* 26:3). Indeed, the Talmud interprets the verse of *Job* cited above to mean that man was born to toil and labor in Torah (*Sanhedrin* 99b).

Western culture has been plagued by an epidemic of drug addiction, which has been particularly severe among young people. A major factor that fuels this epidemic is the primacy of pleasure and tranquility. Young people who are disillusioned and do not feel they have gotten their fair share of these culturally accepted goals use brain-altering chemicals to achieve them, at the risk of grave consequences, even death.

Rejection of the hedonistic goals and accepting the principle that man was born to struggle and toil could prevent the devastation of drug addiction.

עוֹד מִמַּפְסִידֵי הַזְּרִיזוּת הוּא רוֹב הַפַּחַד וְגֹדֶל הַמּוֹרָא מִן הַזְּמָן וְתוֹלְדוֹתָיו, כִּי פַּעַם יִירָא מֵהַקֹּר אוֹ מֵהַחֹם, וּפַעַם מֵהַפְּגָעִים, וּפַעַם מִן הֶחֳלָאִים, וּפַעַם מִן הָרוּחַ, וְכֵן כָּל כַּיּוֹצֵא בַּזֶּה. הוּא הָעִנְיָן שֶׁאָמַר שְׁלֹמֹה עָלָיו הַשָּׁלוֹם (משלי כו, יג): ,,אָמַר עָצֵל שַׁחַל בַּדָּרֶךְ אֲרִי בֵּין הָרְחוֹבוֹת״. וּכְבָר גִּנּוּ חֲכָמִים זִכְרוֹנָם לִבְרָכָה הַמִּדָּה הַזֹּאת וְיִחֲסוּהָ אֶל הַחַטָּאִים, וּמִקְרָא מְסַיְּעָם דִּכְתִיב (ישעיה לג, יד): ,,פָּחֲדוּ בְצִיּוֹן חַטָּאִים״ . . . אֶלָּא עַל זֶה נֶאֱמַר (תהילים לז, ג): ,,בְּטַח בַּה׳ וַעֲשֵׂה־טוֹב״.

Another detraction from Zerizus is excessive fear. One may have an unrealistic fear of the cold, the heat, accidents, disease, the wind, etc. As Solomon said, "The indolent person says, '(How could I go out?) There is a lion out there in the road' " (Proverbs 26:13). Our sages consider such fear to be a character defect, based on Isaiah (33:14), "The sinners in Zion fear." . . . This is why the psalmist says (Psalms 37:3), "Trust in G-d and do good."

The problem of anxiety is at the core of psychological theory. On the one hand there is an entity of legitimate fear which is healthy, because only a fool would recklessly expose himself to danger. At the other end of the spectrum is the phenomenon of panic attacks, where a person is suddenly overwhelmed with feelings of terror, in absence of any stimulus which "evoke" such feelings. These attacks are often of a physiological rather than a psychologic or emotional origin, and are due to an imbalance in the body chemistry which can be corrected with proper medication.

This leaves a wide spectrum of anxiety, wherein there is no physiologic abnormality and no actual threat that should evoke legitimate fear. Solomon states that such an anxiety is often a kind of rationalization, or an adaptation to justify a person's indolence.

Frank indolence is not always the reason for such anxiety. Irrational fears may be more or less unconscious defenses to protect a fragile ego.

In *Life's Too Short* (St. Martins Press 1995) I discussed at some length various behaviors that result from unwarranted feelings of inadequacy.

People who feel this way suffer from a two-fold complex: (1) Because they consider themselves inadequate, they anticipate failure, and (2) because they feel inferior, the prospect of failure is devastating.

No one goes through life with one-hundred-percent success, and failures are always unpleasant. While we do our best to succeed, many factors are beyond our control, and even a carefully planned venture may fail. A person should anticipate success, and be able to take failure in stride.

The person who feels inadequate can do neither. Because of lack of self-confidence, he anticipates he will fail, and because of his feelings of unworthiness, he experiences failure as devastating. To avoid being crushed by his anticipated failure, he does nothing, on the premise that if you do not try, you cannot lose.

The solution to this is as the psalmist says, "Trust in G-d and do good." The concept of trust in G-d refers not only to praying for Divine assistance, but also to trust in the G-dliness within oneself. Every person contains within himself a Divine soul, a nucleus of G-dliness, which should help one realize that (1) he is worthy by virtue of possessing a Divine soul, and (2) he has far greater potential than he had ever dreamt. Neurophysiologists say that we actually utilize only a small fraction of our brain capacity.

A true self-awareness can greatly diminish the baseless fears that paralyze a person, and allow him to function with *Zerizus*.

שֶׁמָּא תֹאמַר הֲרֵי מָצִינוּ שֶׁחִיְּבוּ חֲכָמִים בְּכָל מָקוֹם שֶׁיִּשְׁמוֹר הָאָדָם אֶת עַצְמוֹ שְׁמִירָה מְעֻלָּה וְלֹא יָשִׂים עַצְמוֹ בְסַכָּנָה אֲפִילוּ הוּא צַדִּיק וּבַעַל מַעֲשִׂים . . . יֵשׁ יִרְאָה רְאוּיָה וְיֵשׁ יִרְאָה שׁוֹטָה . . . כִּי הִנֵּה הָאָדוֹן בָּרוּךְ־הוּא עָשָׂה אֶת הָאָדָם בַּעַל שֵׂכֶל נָכוֹן וּסְבָרָא נְכוֹחָה לְשֶׁיִּנְהַג עַצְמוֹ עַל דֶּרֶךְ טוֹב וְיִשָּׁמֵר מִן הַדְּבָרִים הַמַּזִּיקִים אֲשֶׁר נִבְרְאוּ לַעֲנוֹשׁ אֶת הָרְשָׁעִים, וּמִי שֶׁיִּרְצֶה שֶׁלֹּא יִנְהַג עַצְמוֹ בְּדֶרֶךְ הַחָכְמָה וְיַפְקִיר עַצְמוֹ לְסַכָּנוֹת, הִנֵּה אֵין זֶה בִטָּחוֹן, אֶלָּא הוֹלֵלוּת. וְהִנֵּה הוּא חוֹטֵא בְּמַה שֶׁהוּא עוֹשֶׂה נֶגֶד רְצוֹן הַבּוֹרֵא יִתְבָּרֵךְ שְׁמוֹ, שֶׁרוֹצֶה שֶׁיִּשְׁמוֹר הָאָדָם אֶת עַצְמוֹ.

One might quote Talmud that it is incumbent upon a person to avoid exposing oneself to danger and expect Divine protection ... One should realize that there is appropriate fear and irrational fear. Sound judgment should enable a person to avoid actual danger, but if one acts foolishly and exposes himself to danger in the hope that G-d will save him, this is simply recklessness and is actually against the Divine will, which dictates that a person should exercise care.

There are some people who seem to function only by going to extremes, and in contrast to the person who worries himself into inaction, they heed no caution whatever. They may even observe mitzvos recklessly and irresponsibly. For example, there is a mitzvah of *tzedakah,* which is of the highest priority and of inestimable merit, yet the Talmud sets a limit of one-fifth of one's earnings for *tzedakah.* Going beyond that may unfairly deprive one's family of their legitimate needs. Rambam advocates the "mean of virtue" for every trait, rejecting all extremes as inappropriate. Thus, the virtue of courage is neither reckless endangerment at the one extreme nor cowardice on the other. One should dress neither ostentatiously in luxurious garments nor in tattered clothes, and so with all traits.

While hesitating to do anything because of irrational fear is at one end of the extreme, rushing in headstrong and neglecting to heed possible danger is at the other. The prudent and virtuous person is alert to real danger, but does not allow himself to be disabled by groundless fears.

וְהִנְּךָ רוֹאֶה, כִּי רָאוּי לַזְּרִיזוּת לִהְיוֹת בְּמַדְרֵגָה אַחַר הַזְּהִירוּת, כִּי עַל הָרוֹב לֹא יִהְיֶה הָאָדָם זָרִיז אִם לֹא יִהְיֶה זָהִיר בַּתְּחִילָּה. כִּי מִי שֶׁלֹּא יָשִׂים לִבּוֹ לְהִזָּהֵר בְּמַעֲשָׂיו וּלְהִתְבּוֹנֵן בָּעֲבוֹדָה וּמִשְׁפָּטֶיהָ שֶׁזּוֹ הִיא מִדַּת הַזְּהִירוּת, כְּמוֹ שֶׁכָּתַבְתִּי, קָשֶׁה שֶׁיִּלְבַּשׁ אַהֲבָה וְחֶמְדָּה אֵלֶיהָ וְיִזְדָּרֵז בִּתְשׁוּקָה לִפְנֵי בּוֹרְאוֹ כִּי הִנֵּה הוּא עוֹדֶנּוּ טוֹבֵעַ בְּתַאֲווֹת הַגּוּפָנִיּוֹת . . . אָמְנָם אַחַר שֶׁכְּבָר פָּקַח עֵינָיו לִרְאוֹת מַעֲשָׂיו וּלְהִזָּהֵר בָּם וְחָשַׁב חֶשְׁבּוֹן הַמִּצְוֹת וְהָעֲבֵרוֹת, כַּאֲשֶׁר זָכַרְנוּ, נָקֵל הוּא לוֹ שֶׁיָּסוּר מִן הָרַע וְיִשְׁתּוֹקֵק אֶל הַטּוֹב וְיִזְדָּרֵז בּוֹ, וְזֶה פָּשׁוּט.

It is only logical for Zerizus to follow Watchfulness. One can hardly practice Zerizus if one is not watchful. Lack of Watchfulness will cause a person to drift into gratifying all physical temptations, which makes it difficult for one to develop love and yearning for G-d... Once a person has succeeded in watching his behavior and calculating the value of good deeds as opposed to sins, he can more easily avoid evil and develop Zerizus to do good.

The ten steps of Rabbi Pinchas ben Yair are not listed haphazardly, but are arranged in a logical order, with each one being a prerequisite for the next. It is not unusual to see people reach for something that is beyond their grasp. Whereas in the physical sense such action is merely futile, in spiritual matters this can be deceptive.

For example, there is a principle that one should not begin the study of *kabballah* until one is thoroughly versed in the entire Talmud and the *halachah,* and even then preferably not until one has reached the age of forty. Adequate knowledge of the Torah, both written and oral, and a sound maturity of mind are essential in order to properly understand *kabballah.* It is therefore quite absurd that people who may lack even a rudimentary knowledge of Torah try to understand *kabballah.* If premature study of *kabballah* were only futile, this would be of little consequence. Unfortunately, those who are inadequately prepared for the study of *kabballah* can be improperly influenced by their distortion of *kabballah,* and may even be carried away by delusional thinking.

One must have patience in developing spirituality. There is no microwave to speed up the process, and one must laboriously achieve each step before preceding to the next.

10

בְּבֵאוּר מִדַּת הַנְּקִיּוּת

Clarifying the Trait of Nekiyus

We find ourselves again at a loss for an accurate translation, this time for the word *Nekiyus*. While it does indeed mean "cleanness," the latter term connotes a physical state of being, of something washed with soap and free of dirt. The word "immaculateness" is a bit clumsy, and still fails to convey the concept of *Nekiyus*. "Purity" might seem more appropriate, but this term is reserved for a trait that we will discuss later. We have little choice but to use the Hebrew *Nekiyus*, by which Ramchal means a state of mind that is free of the *tendency* to do wrong.

מִדַּת הַנְּקִיּוּת הִיא הֱיוֹת הָאָדָם נָקִי לְגַמְרֵי מִכָּל מִדָּה רָעָה וּמִכָּל חֵטְא. לֹא דַי מִמַּה שֶׁהַחֵטְא בּוֹ מְפֻרְסָם וְגָלוּי, אֶלָּא גַּם־כֵּן מִמַּה שֶׁהַלֵּב נִפְתֶּה בּוֹ לְהוֹרוֹת הֶתֵּר בַּדָּבָר, שֶׁכַּאֲשֶׁר נַחְקוֹר עָלָיו בֶּאֱמֶת נִמְצָא שֶׁלֹּא הָיָה הַהֶתֵּר הַהוּא נִרְאֶה לוֹ, אֶלָּא מִפְּנֵי הֱיוֹת הַלֵּב עֲדַיִן נָגוּעַ קְצָת מִן הַתַּאֲוָה, כִּי לֹא טֹהַר מִמֶּנָּה מִכֹּל וָכֹל, עַל כֵּן תְּמַשְׁכֵהוּ לְהָקֵל לוֹ. אַךְ הָאָדָם אֲשֶׁר טֹהַר מִזֶּה הַנֶּגַע לְגַמְרֵי וְנִקָּה מִכָּל רֹשֶׁם רַע שֶׁמַּשְׁאֶרֶת הַתַּאֲוָה אַחֲרֶיהָ, הִנֵּה רְאִיָּתוֹ תִּהְיֶה בְּרוּרָה לְגַמְרֵי וְהַבְחָנָתוֹ זַכָּה וְלֹא תַטֵּהוּ הַחֶמְדָּה לְשׁוּם דָּבָר.

The trait of Nekiyus refers to a person being completely clean of an attitude that could lead to sin. I.e., not only does this person avoid behavior that is patently sinful, but is also beyond rationalizing his behavior. We know that rationalization occurs when a person has a desire for something forbidden, but leads himself to believe that it is actually permissible. Nekiyus means that one has rid himself of all desires for forbidden acts, so that there cannot be an inadvertent transgression resulting from rationalization.

This step constitutes a quantum leap. The first two steps, Watchfulness and *Zerizus*, deal essentially with behavior, whereas *Nekiyus* deals with a state of mind or emotion, such that one not only avoids improper behavior, but no longer has a temptation for such acts. A person who is watchful to avoid committing a sin may conceivably be able to find technicalities and loopholes that would allow him the gratification he seeks. Or, as Ramchal points out, although he is cautious to avoid what he recognizes as sinful, he may be inadvertently duped into thinking that the particular act is permissible. The human mind is most ingenious in convincing itself of what it wishes to believe. Absolute avoidance of sin can result only when the desire thereto has been eradicated.

But is this realistic? After all, a human being is a biological entity, composed of protoplasm which has physical cravings. Granted that a person can train himself to be master of his behavior and exert control of his actions, but can he indeed eradicate the desire?

The answer to this is, Yes. As a practical example, I have heard many recovered alcoholics state that during their early years of recovery they had to restrain themselves more or less often from yielding to the craving for alcohol, but that at some point the craving miraculously disappeared. Some attribute this to Divine intervention, that G-d removed their craving for this harmful substance.

Elimination of desire can come about even without direct Divine intervention. Ibn Ezra comments on the last of the Ten Commandments, "Thou shalt not covet your neighbor's wife" (or anything that belongs to your neighbor) and asks, How can one be instructed not to covet? Is desire something which is subject to legislation? As we previously noted, Ibn Ezra answers that a person would not have a desire for something which he could never possibly attain (*Exodus* 20:14). Thus, if a person who was greedy for wealth was to learn that on a star that is light years distant there is a mountain of gold and diamonds, he would not give it a second thought. Inasmuch as he has no possible access to this wealth, he does not even desire it. Ibn Ezra contends that if a person was absolutely committed to the earlier commandments, i.e., not to steal, not to kill, and not to commit adultery, in a manner that whatever belonged to his neighbor was absolutely inaccessible to him similar to the diamonds on the distant star, he would have no desire whatever for them. "Thou shalt not covet" is thus both a natural consequence and a reinforcement of the previous commandments.

וְהִנְּךָ רוֹאֶה עַתָּה הַהֶפְרֵשׁ שֶׁבֵּין הַזָּהִיר וְהַנָּקִי . . . וָזֶה, כִּי אַף־עַל־פִּי שֶׁהוּא מִשְׁתַּדֵּל לִכְבּוֹשׁ אֶת יִצְרוֹ וְלִכְפּוֹת אֶת תַּאֲווֹתָיו, לֹא מִפְּנֵי זֶה יְשַׁנֶּה אֶת טִבְעוֹ . . . אָמְנָם, אַחַר שֶׁיִּתְרַגֵּל הָאָדָם הֶרְגֵּל גָּדוֹל בַּזְּהִירוּת הַזֶּה עַד שֶׁיִּנָּקֶה נִקָּיוֹן רִאשׁוֹן מִן הַחֲטָאִים הַמְפֻרְסָמִים וְיַרְגִּיל עַצְמוֹ בָּעֲבוֹדָה . . . הַהֶרְגֵּל הַזֶּה יַרְחִיק אוֹתוֹ מֵעִנְיְנֵי הַחֹמֶר וְיַדְבִּיק דַּעְתּוֹ אֶל הַשְּׁלֵמוּת הַנַּפְשִׁי עַד שֶׁסּוֹף־סוֹף יוּכַל לְהַגִּיעַ אֶל הַנִּקָּיוֹן הַשָּׁלֵם, שֶׁכְּבָר יִכְבֶּה אֵשׁ הַתַּאֲוָה הַגּוּפִית מִלִּבּוֹ בְּהִתְגַּבֵּר בּוֹ הַחֶמְדָּה הָאֱלֹהִית.

The difference between the watchful person and the naki . . . is that although the former tries to subdue his cravings, this does not yet bring about a change in his nature . . . whereas once he has achieved total avoidance of sin and develops an intense love for G-d . . . he begins to separate himself from his physical drives and directs himself towards spiritual perfection, so that he is no longer subject to the seduction of his physical drives.

There appears to be a difference of opinion between Ramchal and Rambam. Rambam says that a person should develop a revulsion toward those Torah prohibitions that are immoral and unethical, but those that are not immoral in character yet are forbidden as *chukim*, i.e., laws that are beyond human understanding, such as the prohibition of mixing meat with milk, admixture of wool and linen, or consumption of non-kosher animals, a person should not say, "I despise them," but rather, "I would desire them, but the Torah has forbidden them" (*The Eight Chapters*, Chapter 6). Ramchal seems to be saying that one's love and devotion to G-d should become so intense that one feels an antipathy toward anything which is opposed to the Divine will. According to Ramchal, one should not even desire non-kosher food.

Ramchal's position is supported by Rabbi Shneur Zalman in Tanya, who describes the "average" person as one who is totally observant of all aspects of Torah, but still must subdue his temptations. However, one who proceeds onto the level of *tzaddik* must eliminate even temptation, undergoing the "change in his nature" that Ramchal describes.

וְהִנֵּה וַדַּאי כִּי מְלָאכָה רַבָּה הִיא לָאָדָם לְהַגִּיעַ אֶל שְׁלֵמוּת הַמִּדָּה הַזֹּאת, כִּי הָעֲבֵרוֹת הַנִּכָּרוֹת וִידוּעוֹת קַלּוֹת הֵם לְהִשָּׁמֵר מֵהֶם, כֵּיוָן שֶׁרָעָתָם גְּלוּיָה. אַךְ הַדִּקְדּוּק הַזֶּה... הַמִּצְטָרֵךְ לַנְּקִיּוּת, הוּא הַקָּשֶׁה יוֹתֵר, כִּי הוֹרָאַת הַהֶתֵּר מְכַסֶּה עַל הַחֵטְא... אָמְרוּ זִכְרוֹנָם לִבְרָכָה (בבא בתרא קסה:א) „רֻבָּם בְּגֶזֶל וּמְעוּטָם בַּעֲרָיוֹת. וְכֻלָּם בַּאֲבַק לְשׁוֹן־הָרָע." כִּי מִפְּנֵי רוֹב דַּקּוּתוֹ כָּל בְּנֵי אָדָם נִכְשָׁלִים בּוֹ בְּמַה שֶּׁאֵין מַכִּירִים אוֹתוֹ... וּבְוַדַּאי שֶׁמִּי שֶׁהִגִּיעַ לְזֹאת הַמִּדָּה כְּבַר הִגִּיעַ לְמַדְרֵגָה גְּדוֹלָה, כִּי בִּפְנֵי מִלְחָמָה חֲזָקָה עָמַד וְנִצַּח.

There is no question that this level (Nekiyus) is difficult to attain. Whereas avoidance of obvious sins is relatively easy, since the evil in them is evident, lesser offenses which can be easily rationalized are more difficult to avoid . . . Indeed, the Talmud states that most people succumb to theft, a minority to illicit relations, but everyone succumbs to a modicum of lashon hara (Bava Basra 165a) because the latter may appear to be so innocent that one is not cautious to guard against it . . . Once a person has achieved Nekiyus, so that he does not rationalize even lesser offenses, he has triumphed in a major internal struggle, and has achieved a high level of spirituality.

In what way are a majority of people guilty of theft? If you return home from the store and discover that the clerk gave you five cents extra in change and you do not return it, you are guilty of theft. If you sell an item and discover that you overcharged the customer, you are guilty of theft, and if you do not know which of the many customers it was, you have no way of making restitution. In this way, most people sooner or later are in wrongful possession of another person's property, which constitutes theft.

According to the Talmud, no one escapes a "touch" of *lashon hara*. For example, the Talmud states that one should not praise a person, because praise is likely to result in a negative comment (*Bava Basra* 164b). How so? Just pay attention when someone says, "Mr. X is such a wonderful, kind, and generous person." Quite frequently, one of the listeners will say, "Yes, but . . ." and go on to mention something uncomplimentary about Mr. X. In this way, the person who praised him was indirectly responsible for the negative comment. An excellent method to avoid *lashon hara* is simply not to speak about another person at all. As one ethicist said, "If you wish to praise, praise G-d. If you wish to find fault, look for your own." Try to avoid talking about others.

Ramchal states that even the watchful person may transgress what he considers trivia, and he quotes the Talmud, "Sins that a person tramples on (because he considers them insignificant) are brought before him at the time of judgment" (*Avodah Zarah* 18a). *Nekiyus*, as absolute cleanness, should be thought of in the sense of surgical sterility. In the latter, eradication of most bacteria is not satisfactory, because even one remaining germ may multiply and cause serious infection. *Nekiyus* requires total cleanness, even of minutiae that are improper, and this can be obtained only when one has eliminated all tendency toward wrongdoing.

11

בְּפִרְטֵי מִדַּת הַנְּקִיּוּת

Details of Nekiyus

Ramchal had indicated that even people who profess to be sincere in observance of Torah may inadvertently transgress Torah as a result of distortion in judgment, which are in turn the result of rationalizing and justifying their actions in order to satisfy a desire. He now continues:

פְּרָטֵי מִדַּת הַנְּקִיּוּת רַבִּים הֵם מְאֹד, וְהִנָּם בְּכָל הַפְּרָטִים שֶׁבְּכָל הַשסה מִצְוֹת לֹא תַעֲשֶׂה . . . וְאוּלָם אַף־עַל־פִּי שֶׁבְּכָל הָעֲבֵרוֹת מִשְׁתַּדֵּל הַיֵּצֶר־הָרַע לְהַחֲטִיא אֶת הָאָדָם, כְּבָר יֵשׁ מֵהֶם שֶׁהַטֶּבַע מְחַמְּדָן יוֹתֵר וּבָהֶן מַרְאֶה לוֹ יוֹתֵר הֶתֵּרִים, אֲשֶׁר עַל כֵּן יִצְטָרֵךְ בָּהֶן יוֹתֵר חִזּוּק לְנַצֵּחַ אֶת יִצְרוֹ וּלְהִנָּקוֹת מִן הַחֵטְא. וְכֵן אָמְרוּ ז״ל (חגיגה יא, ב): „גָּזֵל וַעֲרָיוֹת, נַפְשׁוֹ שֶׁל אָדָם מְחַמַּדְתָּן וּמִתְאַוָּה לָהֶן״. וְהִנֵּה אֲנַחְנוּ רוֹאִים שֶׁאַף־עַל־פִּי שֶׁלֹּא רֹב בְּנֵי הָאָדָם גַּנָּבִים בְּגָלוּי הֵם . . . רֻבָּם טוֹעֲמִים טַעַם גְּנֵבָה בְּמַשָּׂאָם וּמַתָּנָם בְּמַה שֶּׁיּוֹרוּ הֶתֵּר לְעַצְמָם לְהִשְׂתַּכֵּר אִישׁ בְּהֶפְסֵדוֹ שֶׁל חֲבֵרוֹ וְיֹאמְרוּ, לְהַרְוִיחַ שָׁאנֵי.

While there are many numerous details regarding Nekiyus, which apply to the three hundred and sixty-five prohibitions of the Torah . . . there are prohibitions where the yetzer hara makes an extra effort to entrap a person, focusing on those things for which a person may have particularly strong desires; hence it is especially important to develop Nekiyus with these. The Talmud states that theft and illicit behavior are especially strong desires (Chagigah 11:2) . . . While most people would never actually steal, many have a "touch" of theft when they rationalize their actions, saying "This is the way business is done."

It is unfortunate that some people think that the Torah laws of ritual are more important than laws governing civil behavior. While one dare not minimize the importance of ritual law, there is much emphasis in the Talmud on civil law. For example, the Talmud states that the first question that one will be asked on his judgment day is "Did you transact honestly?" (*Shabbos* 31a). Or again, "Sins involving injury to another person are not forgiven by Yom Kippur unless one has made proper amends to the injured party" (*Yoma* 85b). Yet, some people who would never look for loopholes in ritual law and are meticulous in observing the strictest standards of *kashrus* may allow themselves much greater leeway in civil law, and may claim, "This is the accepted way of doing business."

If a person were to violate Torah law by eating pork, this is a serious transgression and there is no way one can minimize the gravity of the sin. Yet, this person has transgressed a single Biblical prohibition, whereas if someone profits from dishonest transactions, Ramchal continues. . .

וְאוּלָם לָאוִים הַרְבֵּה נֶאֶמְרוּ בְּגָזֵל: לֹא תִּגְנֹב, לֹא תִגְזֹל, לֹא תַעֲשֹׁק, לֹא תְכַחֲשׁוּ וְלֹא תְשַׁקְּרוּ אִישׁ בַּעֲמִיתוֹ, לֹא תוֹנוּ אִישׁ אֶת אָחִיו, לֹא תַשִּׂיג גְּבוּל רֵעֲךָ. הֵן כָּל אֵלֶּה חִלּוּקֵי דִינִים שֶׁבְּגָזֵל, כּוֹלְלִים מַעֲשִׂים רַבִּים מִן הַמַּעֲשִׂים הַנַּעֲשִׂים בִּכְלַל הַמַּשָּׂא וְהַמַּתָּן הַמְּדִינִי, וּבְכֻלָּם אִסּוּרִים רַבִּים. כִּי לֹא הַמַּעֲשֶׂה הַנִּכָּר וּמְפֻרְסָם בְּעֹשֶׁק וּבְגָזֵל הוּא לְבַדּוֹ הָאָסוּר, אֶלָּא כָּל שֶׁסּוֹף־סוֹף יַגִּיעַ אֵלָיו וְיִגְרוֹם אוֹתוֹ, כְּבָר הוּא בִּכְלַל הָאִסּוּר.

He may transgress many Biblical prohibitions: Thou shalt not steal; Thou shalt not rob; Thou shalt not cheat; Thou shalt not deny; Thou shalt not lie; Thou shalt not deceive; Thou shalt not encroach on another's property. It is possible that a single dishonest business transaction can result in violation of seven Torah prohibitions. This may not involve frank theft, but anything that results in dishonest acquisition is included in these prohibitions.

Many fortunes have been made by what some people may consider to be "shrewd business acumen," but which were actually deceptive and consisted of taking unfair advantage of others. Lying about bids and offers is not permitted by Torah even if "everybody does it."

The Talmud states that Rabbi Yehudah forbade a merchant to give sweets to children in order to entice them to bring their parents to his store as customers. Other rabbis disagreed with this ruling since each merchant had the option to use the same promotional techniques (*Bava Metzia* 60a), but if they would not be able to do so, improper promotions and deceptive advertising are prohibited. The Torah law does not permit "bait and switch" marketing.

While competition is permitted, unfair competitive practices are prohibited. I recall an instance where a young man opened a shop to purchase paper, rags, and scrap metal from peddlers. This shop was on the same street as an established business, and the young man's father, who was a most unlearned man, told him that there was no way he could impinge upon a preexisting business on the same street. The young man protested that he had already signed a lease and was obligated to pay rent for two years. His father said, "I don't care how much rent you have to pay. If you dare open that shop on the same block I will break your arms and legs." This was the attitude of the simple person, who had absorbed Torah principles of fairness in business. While competition is permitted, unfair competitive practices are prohibited. Whether due to a desire for wealth or a fear of poverty, some people may engage in less than ideal business practices, and there is no dearth of rationalizations people will use. A sincere trust in G-d, that He will provide for one's legitimate needs, would eliminate such infractions.

A unique Torah concept is that of robbing someone's time. The Talmud is very strict about theft of time:

וּכְבָר פָּטְרוּ אֶת הַפּוֹעֲלִים הָעוֹשִׂים אֵצֶל בַּעַל הַבַּיִת מִבִּרְכַּת הַמּוֹצִיא וּמִבְּרָכוֹת אַחֲרוֹנוֹת דְּבִרְכַּת הַמָּזוֹן. וַאֲפִלּוּ בִּקְרִיאַת־שְׁמַע, לֹא חִיְּבוּם לִבָּטֵל מִמְּלַאכְתָּן אֶלָּא בְּפָרָשָׁה רִאשׁוֹנָה בִּלְבָד (ברכות טז, ב) . . . הִנֵּה אַבָּא חִלְקִיָּה, אֲפִלּוּ שָׁלוֹם לֹא הֵשִׁיב לְתַלְמִידֵי חֲכָמִים שֶׁנָּתְנוּ לוֹ שָׁלוֹם, שֶׁלֹּא לִבָּטֵל מִמְּלֶאכֶת רֵעֵהוּ (תענית כג, ב) . . . הַשָּׂכוּר אֵצֶל חֲבֵרוֹ לְאֵיזֶה מְלָאכָה שֶׁתִּהְיֶה, הִנֵּה כָּל שְׁעוֹתָיו מְכוּרוֹת הֵן לוֹ . . . וְכָל מַה שֶּׁיִּקַּח מֵהֶן לַהֲנָאַת עַצְמוֹ בְּאֵיזֶה אֹפֶן שֶׁיִּהְיֶה, אֵינוֹ אֶלָּא גֶּזֶל גָּמוּר . . . וְלֹא עוֹד אֶלָּא שֶׁאֲפִלּוּ אִם עָשָׂה מִצְוָה בִּזְמַן מְלַאכְתּוֹ, לֹא לִצְדָקָה תֵּחָשֵׁב לוֹ, אֶלָּא עֲבֵרָה הִיא בְּיָדוֹ . . . כִּי הֲרֵי גֶּזֶל־חֵפֶץ גָּזֵל, וְגֶזֶל־זְמַן גָּזֵל:

The halachah exempts hired workers from reciting many of the blessings over food and does not permit them to recite more than the first section of the Shema (Berachos 16b) . . . Rabbi Abba Chilkiyah did not even return a greeting to scholars when he was working for someone (Taanis 23b) . . . A hired person has sold his time to his employer, and personal use of any time which does not belong to him is theft . . . One may not even perform mitzvos on an employer's time . . . Just as theft of money is theft, so is theft of time.

A person who is otherwise observant of Torah might not think twice about extending the coffee break beyond the allotted time, or leaving a bit early from work if the boss if not there. Ramchal states that this is really no different than burglarizing his home!

The statement "theft of time is every bit as serious as theft of money" should make us more conscious of our behavior. If we have an appointment and do not take the necessary precautions to be there on time, it is more than just a lack of consideration. As Ramchal points out, this constitutes theft, and as noted it is these "minor" transgressions that we trivialize that will surround us on Judgment Day. Even when paying a social call, we should consider how long our company is pleasurable, and at what point we are imposing. Let us think about the times that our visitors overstayed their welcome, and although we were pleased to see them initially, they tarried beyond our desire for their company, thereby preventing us from attending to our own affairs. Yet, we did not wish to be rude and tell them to leave. It is easy to recognize this when one is the host, but more difficult to do so when one is the guest. Hardly anyone would consider himself as being a *goniff* (thief) when visiting a friend, yet if one intrudes on another person's time to that person's displeasure, this does constitute theft. We would do well to keep our visits brief, and if the choice is between the host wishing we had stayed longer or being frustrated while we stayed too long, the former is by far preferable.

The Chazon Ish once assembled a *minyan* (quorum of ten) in his home for *Minchah* (afternoon service), and one of the people told him that he was due at an appointment shortly. The Chazon Ish sent him on his way, stating that keeping the other person waiting was theft of time, and one cannot pray on stolen time.

In this context it is germane to remind people that a *shul* is a place where people go to pray, and that interfering with their prayers may also be considered a theft of their time. While it is appropriate that children who can benefit from the prayer experience be brought to *shul*, the common practice of bringing tiny tots to *shul* is sharply condemned (*Mishnah Berurah* 98:3). Children who are too young to sit quietly with their parents tend to run around in *shul*, converting it to a playground. This is not only disrespectful, but they also disturb others who wish to pray. If a mother needs a period of rest, it is better that the husband remain home and look after the children than to bring them to *shul*. The argument that tiny tots should be introduced to the *shul* environment so that they feel comfortable there is a poor rationalization. The Chafetz Chaim was every bit as interested in providing *chinuch* (training) for children, yet he is adamant that children who run around in *shul* and disturb worshippers should not be brought. In light of what Ramchal has said, one is not performing a mitzvah by doing something improper.

רְאֵה נָא בְּעִנְיַן הַהוֹנָאָה, כַּמָּה נָקֵל הוּא לָאָדָם לְהִתְפַּתּוֹת וְלִכָּשֵׁל כַּאֲשֶׁר לִכְאוֹרָה יֵרָאֶה לוֹ שֶׁרָאוּי הוּא לְהִשְׁתַּדֵּל לְיַפּוֹת סְחוֹרָתוֹ בְּעֵינֵי הָאֲנָשִׁים . . . ,,אֵין מְפַרְכְּסִין הַכֵּלִים הַיְשָׁנִים'' שֶׁיֵּרָאוּ כַּחֲדָשִׁים; ,,אֵין מְעָרְבִין פֵּרוֹת בְּפֵרוֹת אֲפִילוּ חֲדָשִׁים בַּחֲדָשִׁים'' . . . קָרוּי חֲמִשָּׁה שֵׁמוֹת: עַוָּל, שָׂנאוּי, מְשֻׁקָּץ, חֵרֶם, תּוֹעֵבָה (ספרא יט, לה). עוֹד אָמְרוּ ז״ל (בבא קמא קיט, א): ,,כָּל הַגּוֹזֵל אֶת חֲבֵרוֹ אֲפִילוּ שָׁוֶה פְּרוּטָה, כְּאִלּוּ נוֹטֵל נַפְשׁוֹ מִמֶּנּוּ''.

One must be cautious to avoid deceit. While a merchant is permitted to make his merchandise appear attractive, he must be careful not to deceive . . . It is forbidden to refurbish old objects and sell them as new. It is forbidden to mix produce of several qualities to give the impression that all is top quality (Bava Metzia 60a) . . . The Torah condemns such practices as "wrong, hateful, abominable, despised, and detested (by G-d)." Furthermore, the Talmud states that stealing even a penny from a person is as grievous a sin as taking his life (Bava Kamma 119a).

Ramchal spares nothing in his condemnation of less than fair and honest business practices. Let me cite several anecdotes of our great Torah personalities regarding fairness in fiscal matters.

When the Chafetz Chaim was a child of four, he was playing with his friends when a woman selling apples pushed her cart on the street and several apples fell off. The children, including little Yisrael Meir, gleefully picked up the fallen apples and ran off.

At the age of six, when Yisrael Meir began learning *Chumash* and came across the prohibition against theft, he asked his mother for money to buy a few apples. After he paid for the apples, he put them back on the cart and ran off. The honesty that characterized the life of the Chafetz Chaim was evident at age six.

When Rabbi Yitzchok Blazar (known as Reb Itzele of Petersburg) married off his youngest son to the daughter of an ordinary laborer, he heard talk in the town why he had not sought a more distinguished family. Rabbi Itzele remarked, "Had my son married into a wealthy businessman's family, you would not have had any questions, even though there is a likelihood that wealthy business people may take liberties and cut corners in doing business that are in violation of Torah law. But when I chose a laborer who comes by his meager earnings honestly, that seems to bother you."

In 1835 there was a major dispute between the two large Jewish publishing houses in Europe. Each side solicited support from halachic authorities, and scholarly treatises favoring one side or the other were being exchanged. The great sage Rabbi Yisrael of Salant was bewildered. "Why do we not have as great an interest and exchange of opinions in disputes that involve small amounts of money? Why are scholars only aroused by a major dispute? Have they forgotten that the Talmud states, 'There should be no difference whether the dispute is about a penny or one hundred times one hundred dollars (*Sanhedrin* 8a)'?" Rabbi Yisrael did not hesitate to be critical even of acknowledged authorities when he felt that Torah principles of absolute fairness were suffering.

Over and above the primary fault in transacting dishonestly, which is the unjust acquisition of others' property, such behavior also indicates a lack of trust in G-d. A person who sincerely believes in G-d trusts that G-d will provide for his needs and he will never stoop to questionable methods of acquisition.

The chassidic master, Rabbi Mendel of Rimanov, received a complaint from a merchant who was worried that a competitor would cut into his profits. Rabbi Mendel said, "If you observe a horse drinking from a brook, you will see that he taps with his forepaw while drinking. Do you know why? Because when he sees his reflection in the water, he thinks there is another horse drinking, and because he is worried that the other horse will drain off all the water, he tries to scare him off. Now do you wish to share the mentality of a horse? Whatever is destined for you will not be taken away by anyone else."

חִלּוּק גָּדוֹל יֵשׁ בַּדָּבָר, כִּי כָּל . . . מַה שֶּׁהוּא לְהַרְאוֹת אֶת הַקּוֹנִים אֲמִתַּת טוּב הַחֵפֶץ וְיָפְיוֹ, הִנֵּה הַהִשְׁתַּדְּלוּת הַהוּא טוֹב וְיָשָׁר. אַךְ מַה שֶּׁהוּא לְכַסּוֹת מוּמֵי חֶפְצוֹ, אֵינוֹ אֶלָּא אוֹנָאָה וְאָסוּר . . . לֹא אָמַר מֵעִנְיַן הַמִּדּוֹת . . . וְאָמְרוּ ז״ל בבא בתרא פח, ב): ,,קָשֶׁה עָנְשָׁן שֶׁל מִדּוֹת מֵעָנְשָׁן שֶׁל עֲרָיוֹת וכו׳ ״ . . . כָּל שֶׁכֵּן עֲוֹן הָרִבִּית . . . וְאָמְרוּ ז״ל עַל פָּסוּק ,,בְּנֶשֶׁךְ נָתַן וְתַרְבִּית לָקַח חָיֹה לֹא יִחְיֶה״ (יחזקאל יח, יג), שֶׁאֵינוֹ חַי לִתְחִיַּת הַמֵּתִים (שמות רבה לא, ו).

Honest marketing is permissible, but one may not conceal a defect in the merchandise ... The Torah is also very strict about accurate weights and measures ... and the Talmud states that using dishonest weights is among the most grievous of all sins (Bava Basra 88b) ... The sin of usury is also very grave ... of which the Talmud, concerning the posuk in Ezekiel 18:13, says that one who is guilty of usury will not merit resurrection in the World to Come (Shemos Rabbah 31:6).

[To summarize, just as the desire for acquisition is great, so are the pitfalls it presents. Many people practice piety in other affairs, but may fail to achieve commensurate perfection in despising dishonest gain.]

Alas! People may usurp the right to discriminate among Torah prohibitions.

Rabbi Chaim Soloveitchik of Brisk related that the townspeople asked him if they could participate in a *seudas mitzvah* given by a known thief. He at once sent for the thief. "What would you do if you had the opportunity to burglarize a home on Shabbos?" he asked.

"I would do it," the thief answered.

"And if this necessitated breaking a lock and lighting a candle to see in the dark?"

"Then I would break the lock and light a candle," the thief said.

"Suppose it were the home of a non-Jew and you found *treifah* foods there, such as cartons of pork?"

"I would steal them," the thief said, "and sell them to someone who deals in non-kosher food."

"Why wouldn't you eat them yourself?" Rabbi Chaim asked.

The thief reacted with shock. "Eat pork? How dare you say that! Do you think I am not a Jew?"

Rabbi Chaim then asked, "How can you act with revulsion to one Torah prohibition and totally disregard others?"

The thief said, "I don't understand you, Rabbi. Stealing is my livelihood, but what does that have to do with eating pork? I am still a Jew, am I not?"

Rabbi Chaim pointed out the gross distortion of logic a person may undergo if he feels his livelihood is at risk. Incidentally, he allowed the townspeople to partake in the *seudah.*

וְנְדַבֵּר עַתָּה מִן הָעֲרָיוֹת . . . וְהִנֵּה מִי שֶׁיִּרְצֶה לְהִנָּקוֹת לְגַמְרֵי מִזֶּה הַחֵטְא, גַּם לוֹ תִצְטָרֵךְ מְלָאכָה לֹא מְעֶטֶת . . . וּמִקְרָא מָלֵא הוּא (ויקרא יח, ו): „לֹא תִקְרְבוּ לְגַלּוֹת עֶרְוָה" . . . וְעַל זֶה הַדֶּרֶךְ אָסְרוּ בְּעִנְיַן זֶה שֶׁל הָעֲרָיוֹת כָּל מַה שֶּׁהוּא מִמִּינוֹ שֶׁל הַזְּנוּת, אוֹ הַקָּרוֹב אֵלָיו, יִהְיֶה בְּאֵיזֶה חוּשׁ שֶׁיִּהְיֶה, דְּהַיְנוּ, בֵּין בְּמַעֲשֶׂה, בֵּין בִּרְאִיָּה, בֵּין בְּדִבּוּר, בֵּין בִּשְׁמִיעָה, וַאֲפִלּוּ בְּמַחֲשָׁבָה.

Let us now consider the sin of illicit relations . . . Nekiyus of this sin requires much effort . . . and when the Torah says, "Do not come near any illicit relationship" (Leviticus 18:6), it means that one must take precautionary measures to avoid the consequences of improper intimacy . . .

Any physical contact with a woman with whom relations are forbidden is prohibited. . . even listening to her sing, or engaging in unnecessary conversation. Similarly, obscenity, whether speaking it or listening to it, is forbidden. Even private conversation between husband and wife should be free of obscenity. All one's senses and faculties must be clean of impressions which can arouse lust, including avoiding lustful thinking.

In earlier days, there were those who were critical of the extreme measures dictated by *halachah* as precautions against the sin of lust. The dress code of *tznius* (modesty) was mocked as if it were irrational fundamentalism. Prohibition of all physical contact between men and women was decried as fanaticism.

Today one must be frankly thick headed if one fails to realize that our sages were right. Moral decency has become obsolete, and human behavior has fallen far beneath that of brute beasts in the jungle. The latter do not have perversions. Humanity has invoked constitutional law to protect every vice.

Our sages knew where to draw the line. Anyone valuing his life and health would stay miles away from a radioactive disaster area, and no one would consider such a person to be a fundamentalist or fanatic. The danger to one's spiritual and physical welfare secondary to failure to distance oneself from lust is no less, but as Ramchal has emphasized in the discussion of *Nekiyus*, our capacity to rationalize is endless. One is not tempted toward radioactivity, hence one can appreciate the danger.

When physical temptations are intense, rationalization overrides perception of danger, and people dupe themselves into disaster.

וְהַמַּדְרֵגָה הַשְּׁלִישִׁית אַחַר הַגָּזֵל וְהָעֲרָיוֹת לְעִנְיַן הַחֶמְדָּה, הִנֵּה הוּא אִסּוּר הַמַּאֲכָלוֹת, בֵּין בְּעִנְיַן בָּשָׂר בְּחָלָב אוֹ חֵלֶב וָדָם וְעִנְיַן בִּשּׁוּלֵי גוֹיִם, וְעִנְיַן גִּעוּלֵי גוֹיִם, יֵין נְסִיכָם וּסְתָם יֵינָם . . . וְהוּא מַה־שֶּׁאָמְרוּ גַּם כֵּן (יומא לט, א): ,,וְנִטְמֵתֶם בָּם, אַל תִּקְרֵי וְנִטְמֵתֶם אֶלָּא וְנִטַּמְתֶּם״. שֶׁהָעֲבֵרָה מְטַמְטֶמֶת לִבּוֹ שֶׁל אָדָם, כִּי מְסַלֶּקֶת מִמֶּנּוּ הַדֵּעָה הָאֲמִתִּית וְרוּחַ הַשֵּׂכֶל שֶׁהַקָּדוֹשׁ בָּרוּךְ הוּא נוֹתֵן לַחֲסִידִים . . . וְהִנֵּה מִי שֶׁיֵּשׁ לוֹ מֹחַ בְּקָדְקֳדוֹ, יַחֲשׁוֹב אִסּוּרֵי הַמַּאֲכָל כַּמַּאֲכָלִים הָאַרְסִיִּים אוֹ כְּמַאֲכָל שֶׁנִּתְעָרֵב בּוֹ אֵיזֶה דָּבָר אַרְסִי. כִּי הִנֵּה אִם דָּבָר זֶה יֶאֱרַע, הֲיָקֵל אָדָם עַל־עַצְמוֹ לֶאֱכוֹל מִמֶּנּוּ אִם יִשָּׁאֵר לוֹ בּוֹ אֵיזֶה בֵּית מֵחוּשׁ, וַאֲפִלּוּ חֲשָׁשָׁא קְטַנָּה? וַדַּאי שֶׁלֹּא יָקֵל. וְאִם יָקֵל, לֹא יִהְיֶה נֶחֱשָׁב אֶלָּא לְשׁוֹטֶה גָּמוּר. אַף אִסּוּר הַמַּאֲכָל כְּבָר בֵּאַרְנוּ, שֶׁהוּא אֶרֶס מַמָּשׁ לַלֵּב וְלַנֶּפֶשׁ. אִם־כֵּן מִי אֵפוֹא יִהְיֶה הַמֵּקֵל בִּמְקוֹם חֲשָׁשָׁא שֶׁל אִסּוּר אִם בַּעַל שֵׂכֶל הוּא?

Next to the drives for acquisition and illicit behavior is that of prohibited foods, regardless of what the nature of the prohibition may be, whether unclean animals, milk with meat, blood, forbidden wines, etc. These are forbidden in themselves, or as ingredients in other products ... The Talmud (Yoma 39a) says that prohibited foods have a negative effect on a person's emotions, and serve as a barrier between him and G-d ... Every thinking person, if faced with a food that is poisonous or contains a poisonous ingredient, would certainly not eat it even if the danger were minimal.

Who would then be so foolish as to subject himself to foods that damage one's spirit?

Nutritionists say, "You are what you eat," and although some may take issue with this, there is no question that certain foods may have deleterious effects on some people. It is common knowledge that many people have food intolerances, something which was not medically accepted until relatively recently. Just several decades ago milk was considered the ideal food for all infants and children. Today, many children have been found to have lactose intolerance. Similarly, there are many people who have wheat intolerance. While there is some controversy about the effects of sugar, anecdotal data support the claim that some people have severe emotional reactions to sugar. There should no longer be any skepticism that foods can have an effect on mood and emotions.

The human emotional system is a major sensory system and is probably the principal component in one's psychological makeup. Any distortion in emotional perception is apt to have a marked behavioral impact. Disabling the emotional system so that it does not receive accurate stimuli will have major consequences on how a person thinks, feels, and acts. The Talmudic expression asserts that forbidden foods "numb" the heart, making it insensitive to input.

It is related that Rambam had an interchange with some philosophers, and at one point responded, "From your arguments I can detect that you had just eaten from meat of an unclean animal." I.e., the consumption of the food had altered their thinking in a distinctive manner.

Over and above the errors in judgment that can arise from rationalization, there are other major distorting factors if one does not avoid prohibited foods. In rationalization the thought processes are affected by one's desires, although the data input is correct. Forbidden foods go one step further and alter the person's receptors, so that he begins the thought process with inaccurate data, which are then subject to the distorting influence of the forbidden food on the thought processes themselves, in addition to rationalization. This may result in the most unwise decisions. Ramchal points out that it is the greatest folly to subject oneself to such negative influences.

Yet, in my work with substance abusers, I regularly see this folly in operation. People of the highest level of intelligence consume alcohol, cocaine, hallucinogens, and other drugs which have marked deleterious effects on the mind. One would think that people who prize their intellect would protect it with a ferocity, yet just the opposite is true. They are so impulse driven that they subject their minds to grossly toxic effects of substances because of whatever experience it is that they seek. How much grief and suffering could be eliminated if more people adopted *Nekiyus* as described by Ramchal.

וְנְדַבֵּר עַתָּה עַל הַחֲטָאִים הַמְּצוּיִים הַנּוֹלָדִים מֵחֶבְרַת בְּנֵי הָאָדָם וְקִבּוּצָם, כְּגוֹן הוֹנָאַת דְּבָרִים, הַלְבָּנַת הַפָּנִים, הַכְשָׁלַת הָעִוֵּר בְּעֵצָה, רְכִילוּת, שִׂנְאָה וּנְקִימָה, שְׁבוּעוֹת, דְּבַר־שֶׁקֶר וְחִלּוּל הַשֵּׁם, כִּי מִי יֹאמַר נִקֵּיתִי מֵהֶם, טָהַרְתִּי מֵאַשְׁמָה בָּם, כִּי עַנְפֵיהֶם רַבִּים וְדַקִּים עַד מְאֹד אֲשֶׁר הַהִזָּהֵר בָּם טֹרַח גָּדוֹל.

Let us now turn our attention to "social sins"; i.e., those that arise from interpersonal relations, such as verbal abuse, humiliating someone, giving misleading advice, talebearing, hating, taking revenge, taking oaths, lying, and desecrating the Divine Name. The derivatives of these are very numerous, and who can say "I am clean of being at fault in any of these?" Watchfulness in these areas is so extremely difficult (that it requires Nekiyus to be free of them).

As Ramchal has pointed out, Watchfulness is effective only when one realizes that a particular act is sinful, and then takes precautions to avoid it. Where such awareness is lacking, one may not be on guard. Ramchal's solution to this is *Nekiyus*; i.e., to eradicate the source from which such transgressions may arise.

Ramchal stated that lack of recognition may be due to one's judgment faculties being blinded by "bribes," as the Torah says, "A bribe blinds the eyes even of the wise" (*Deuteronomy* 16:19). The bribes Ramchal refers to are the intense physical drives to which a person is subject, and that in order to gratify these drives a person may rationalize that whatever he wishes to do is permissible. Ramchal listed the desire for wealth, lust, and appetite as the strongest drives that may obscure cognizance of sin.

Ramchal now proceeds to list another group of sins which may not be easily recognizable, and he refers to these as the "sins of interpersonal relations." In the process of social interaction we often react reflexly, without taking time to deliberate about what we are going to say. Ramban in the famous letter to his son warned him to "always think before you speak," and while this is excellent advice, it too often goes unheeded. The problem with this category of sins is not that there is an intense drive for gratification as was the case with the first group, but that one simply does not take time out to think before speaking.

הוֹנָאַת הַדְּבָרִים בִּכְלָלָהּ, הוּא לְדַבֵּר בִּפְנֵי חֲבֵרוֹ לְבַד, שֶׁיֵּבוֹשׁ מִמֶּנּוּ, כָּל־שֶׁכֵּן הָאֲמִירָה בִּפְנֵי רַבִּים דָּבָר שֶׁיֵּבוֹשׁ בּוֹ, אוֹ לַעֲשׂוֹת לוֹ מַעֲשֶׂה שֶׁיִּגְרוֹם לוֹ שֶׁיֵּבוֹשׁ, וְהוּא מַה שֶּׁאָמְרוּ בְּפֶרֶק הַזָּהָב (בבא מציעא נח, ב): ,,אִם הָיָה בַּעַל תְּשׁוּבָה, לֹא יֹאמַר לוֹ, זְכוֹר מַעֲשֶׂיךָ הָרִאשׁוֹנִים וכו׳ ״. אִם הָיוּ חֳלָאִים בָּאִים עָלָיו, לֹא יֹאמַר לוֹ כְּדֶרֶךְ שֶׁאָמְרוּ חֲבֵרָיו לְאִיּוֹב.

Verbal abuse can consist of shaming someone even in private, let alone embarrassing him before others, or doing something which can cause him to feel shame. The Talmud says that one may not say to a baal teshuvah (penitent), "Remember how you used to behave" (Bava Metzia 58b). Nor should anyone tell someone who is suffering that he is being punished for his sins.

Nothing is more untrue than the aphorism "Sticks and stones will break my bones but words will never harm me." In *Proverbs* Solomon frequently refers to the deeply penetrating force of harsh words. A physical injury may heal fairly rapidly, whereas a verbal injury may fester indefinitely.

Shame is a totally destructive feeling, and has no redeeming features. Guilt can be constructive and beneficial, because it is the anticipation of the discomfort of feeling guilty that often prevents us from doing wrong, and the pain of guilt may be the motivating force behind making amends and atoning for our misdeeds.

Shame and guilt are not identical. Guilt is "I have *done* bad," whereas shame is "I *am* bad." No human being should consider himself essentially bad. To the contrary, we are essentially good, and it is our acts that may be bad. We therefore can be totally good by rectifying these acts and avoiding them in the future. However, if one feels that one's very essence is bad, one may be totally discouraged from trying to change one's behavior, since this will not alter the fact that one is bad in essence.

A person who has done *teshuvah* and has regretted improper behavior has made the necessary changes. Reminding him of his previous misdeeds does not contribute to his *teshuvah*, and can only make him feel shame. To cause anyone to have this destructive feeling is a grievous sin.

There is indeed a responsibility to assist a person to do *teshuvah,* but one must be extremely cautious how one goes about doing so. Any reprimand must be done out of true love for the other person, and with great consideration and sensitivity for his feelings. Even in the days of the Talmud one sage stated, "I wonder whether there is anyone who is suited to deliver reprimand" (*Arachin* 16b). What shall we say today?

Humiliating someone publicly is one of the most grievous sins a person can commit. While all transgressions are severe, public humiliation is dealt with most harshly by the Talmud, which states that even if a person has studied much Torah and performed many mitzvos, he forfeits his share in the World to Come if he publicly humiliates someone (unless he makes amends and obtains that person's forgiveness. *Ethics of the Fathers* 3:15). An entire lifetime of Torah and mitzvos may be erased by a single moment of thoughtless speech whereby one embarrasses another person publicly. Scriptures compares the tongue to a sharp arrow (*Jeremiah* 9:7), and one should think of oneself as holding an arrow in the bow with the string drawn taut, where even momentarily slackening one's hold on the arrow may cause a fatal injury.

Just how much value the Torah places on protecting a person's honor and avoiding public embarrassment can be seen from a fascinating Midrash in the introduction to *Eichah* (*Lamentations*). The Midrash relates that when Jerusalem fell to the Babylonians, the Temple destroyed, and the Jews massacred and driven into exile, the patriarchs — Abraham, Isaac, and Jacob — and the great leader Moses pleaded before G-d for mercy for their children, invoking their willingness to sacrifice their lives for G-d, but their pleas went unacknowledged. Then the matriarch Rachael approached G-d saying, "You know how much Jacob wanted to marry me, and when I suspected that my father was going to substitute my sister Leah in my place at the wedding, I gave Jacob a secret signal whereby he could detect the ruse. At the last moment, I realized that if Jacob detected and exposed the ruse, my sister would be publicly embarrassed, and to protect her honor I gave her the secret signals. Dear G-d, I was ready to give up the man I was supposed to wed and for whom I had waited for seven long years, solely to avoid my sister's momentary humiliation. Can you not remember this merit, and have mercy on my children?"

Although G-d had ignored the pleas of the patriarchs and Moses, He responded to Rachael, "I swear that by your virtue, Rachael, your children will be returned to their Land."

The virtues of Abraham, who was willing to offer his beloved son Isaac as a sacrifice, and the willingness of Isaac to offer his life to G-d paled in comparison to the virtue of Rachael who protected her sister from a brief moment of public humiliation.

Telling a person who is suffering that he is being punished for his sins is the height of both insensitivity and arrogance. Who has been taken into the private counsel of G-d to know why he permits a person to suffer? In Torah there is a concept of "Ordeals of Love," and while it may be difficult for us to understand how suffering can be a sign of love and why a righteous person may suffer, this is nevertheless an accepted fact. How dare anyone pour salt on an open wound, and add to a person's misery by blaming him for his suffering! While it is true that suffering should lead a person to examine his own behavior, that is a personal thing, not for anyone else to invoke.

The Baal Shem Tov was intolerant of preachers who were insensitive to people's sufferings and who rebuked them with harsh sermons. "Better turn to G-d and plead for your people, who have suffered so bitterly throughout their existence," he said. The chassidic master, Rabbi Elimelech of Lizensk, prayed daily, "Let me see the merits of people and not their faults."

If you are in the company of a person who is suffering, try to comfort him in any way possible, even if only by being there with him so that he does not feel abandoned. Very often we are at a loss for words, not knowing what to say to someone who has experienced a tragedy. This awkward feeling may even cause us to avoid the person, who is then being deprived of our companionship. Do not feel awkward or stupid because you have nothing to say. Even the wisest people may have little to offer in the way of consoling words. Just be there.

בְּעִנְיַן נְתִינַת הָעֵצָה, שָׁנִינוּ בְּתוֹרַת כֹּהֲנִים (ויקרא יט, יד): ,,וְלִפְנֵי עִוֵּר לֹא תִתֵּן מִכְשֹׁל" . . . אַל תִּתֵּן לוֹ עֵצָה שֶׁאֵינָה הוֹגֶנֶת לוֹ וכו', וְאַל תֹּאמַר לוֹ מְכוֹר שָׂדְךָ וְקַח לְךָ חֲמוֹר, וְאַתָּה עוֹקֵף עָלָיו וְנוֹטְלָהּ מִמֶּנּוּ. שֶׁמָּא תֹאמַר, עֵצָה יָפָה אֲנִי נוֹתֵן לוֹ, הֲרֵי הַדָּבָר מָסוּר לַלֵּב, שֶׁנֶּאֱמַר (שם): ,,וְיָרֵאתָ מֵאֱלֹהֶיךָ".

Insofar as giving advice is concerned, the Torah says, "Do not place a stumbling block before a blind person" (Leviticus 19:14) ... which the Talmud interprets as a prohibition against giving misleading advice. Certainly one should not advise a person to sell his property when one has a desire to buy it. G-d knows that the true reason for this advice is for one's personal gain, and this is why the above verse concludes with, "You should fear G-d."

In the latter example, the motive for giving a person bad advice is evident: using an unscrupulous method for one's personal gain. But such malicious behavior must be rare. Why, then, do we daily confess, "We have given bad advice," as if this was more common? Why would anyone wish to mislead someone?

The answer is that this sin is rarely committed with intent to harm. To the contrary, people may wish to be helpful, but may not realize that the advice they are giving is bad. It is not uncommon for people to share medication with friends. "Here, take this. It worked great for me." Little may they suspect that what the doctor prescribed for them may be harmful to someone else.

There is another not uncommon case of giving misleading advice; that is when people whose advice is sought are not aware of their limitations in providing it. I attended four years of vigorous education in medical school, followed by three years of intensive psychiatric training. Not once in these seven years did I have a single lecture on some of the most common afflictions: spouse abuse, alcoholism, drug addiction, compulsive gambling, compulsive eating, bulimia, and other addictive disorders. In the several decades since I completed my training, not enough has changed in the educational system, with the result that many professionals in various fields whose help is sought are simply not competent to provide it in these conditions, and the advice they give may be misleading and counterproductive.

I have seen the tragic results of well-intended but very misleading advice in such cases. Instead of being helpful, this advice only aggravated the problem and delayed effective treatment. People who are in a position where their advice is sought have an obligation to familiarize themselves thoroughly with the nature of the problems that may be brought before them.

הָרְכִילוּת וּלְשׁוֹן־הָרָע, כְּבָר חֻמְרוֹ נוֹדָע וְגֹדֶל עֲנָפָיו כִּי רַבּוּ מְאֹד . . . אַף־עַל־פִּי שֶׁנִּרְאִים דְּבָרִים קַלִּים וּרְחוֹקִים מִן הָרְכִילוּת, הִנֵּה בֶּאֱמֶת מֵאָבָק שֶׁלּוֹ הֵם.

The gravity of talebearing and lashon hara (gossip or slander) and their derivatives is well known. Even things that may not appear to a person to fall under these categories may indeed be such (hence Watchfulness is not adequate, since they are not readily recognized as sinful).

We have already mentioned that indirect *lashon hara* may occur as a result of singing someone's praises, which may elicit a negative comment, "Yes, but..." Even someone who tries to avoid *lashon hara* and is cautious not to speak negatively about others may not be aware that by praising someone he is indirectly contributing to *lashon hara*.

The Chafetz Chaim dedicated his life's work to combating *lashon hara* and wrote several volumes on the subject. Its pitfalls are many, and one may be unaware that he is transgressing this prohibition.

Each day following the morning prayer it is recommended to recite six remembrances emphasized in Torah. One of these is "Remember what G-d did to Miriam when you were leaving Egypt" (*Deuteronomy* 24:9). The Torah relates that Miriam was critical of Moses for adopting abstinence, and mentioned this to Aaron, whereupon she was punished with leprosy (*Numbers* 12:1-15) Miriam was Moses' older sister, who looked after him when he was placed in the basket on the Nile and arranged for him to be nursed by his mother. Miriam no doubt remained protective of Moses and loved him dearly, and her comments were made only because she felt he was making an excessive demand on himself. She certainly had no intention of speaking derogatorily about Moses, yet her comment was considered *lashon hara*.

Even someone who is watchful not to speak *lashon hara* may not be aware that *listening* to *lashon hara* is equally forbidden. It is likely that both speaking and listening to *lashon hara* may have the same root; i.e., a person may feel better about himself if he thinks he is in some way superior to others, hence he may belittle others or be pleased to hear others doing so because it elevates his own ego. Whereas Watchfulness may not be sufficient to avoid all *lashon hara*, this can be accomplished by *Nekiyus*, by ridding oneself of the need to gain self-esteem by disparaging others.

גַּם הַשִּׂנְאָה וְהַנְּקִימָה קָשֶׁה מְאֹד לְשֶׁיִּמָּלֵט מִמֶּנָּה לֵב הוּתַל אֲשֶׁר לִבְנֵי הָאָדָם, כִּי הָאָדָם מַרְגִּישׁ מְאֹד בְּעֶלְבּוֹנוֹתָיו וּמִצְטַעֵר צַעַר גָּדוֹל, וְהַנְּקָמָה לוֹ מְתוּקָה מִדְּבָשׁ, כִּי הִיא מְנוּחָתוֹ לְבַדָּהּ. עַל כֵּן לְשֶׁיִּהְיֶה בְכֹחוֹ לַעֲזוֹב מַה שֶּׁטִּבְעוֹ מַכְרִיחַ אוֹתוֹ וְיַעֲבוֹר עַל מִדּוֹתָיו, וְלֹא יִשְׂנָא מִי שֶׁהֵעִיר בּוֹ הַשִּׂנְאָה, וְלֹא יִקּוֹם מִמֶּנּוּ בְּהִזְדַּמֵּן לוֹ שֶׁיּוּכַל לְהִנָּקֵם, וְלֹא יִטּוֹר לוֹ . . . וְהוּא קַל רַק לְמַלְאֲכֵי־הַשָּׁרֵת

שֶׁאֵין בֵּינֵיהֶם הַמִּדּוֹת הַלָּלוּ . . . אָמְנָם גְּזֵרַת מֶלֶךְ הִיא, וְהַמִּקְרָאוֹת גְּלוּיִים בָּאֵר הֵיטֵב, אֵינָם צְרִיכִים פֵּרוּשׁ, (ויקרא יט, יז): ,,לֹא־תִשְׂנָא אֶת־אָחִיךָ בִּלְבָבֶךָ״, ,,לֹא־תִקֹּם וְלֹא־תִטֹּר אֶת־בְּנֵי עַמֶּךָ״ (שם, יח). וְעִנְיַן הַנְּקִימָה וְהַנְּטִירָה יָדוּעַ, דְּהַיְנוּ: נְקִימָה, לִמְנֹעַ מֵהֵיטִיב לְמִי שֶׁלֹּא רָצָה לְהֵיטִיב לוֹ אוֹ שֶׁהֵרַע לוֹ כְּבָר. וּנְטִירָה, לְהַזְכִּיר בְּעֵת שֶׁהוּא מֵיטִיב לְמִי שֶׁהֵרַע לוֹ אֵיזֶה זִכָּרוֹן מִן הָרָעָה שֶׁעָשָׂה לוֹ.

Hatred and revenge are also difficult to escape. A person is very sensitive to being insulted, and his only comfort from this anguish may be taking revenge, which is to him sweeter than honey. It requires the utmost strength and courage to overcome the natural tendency to hate the one who offended him and not to hold a grudge against him . . . This may be easy for angels who do not have a nature to hate when offended, but it is extremely difficult for mortals . . . Yet the Divine decree is explicit: "Do not take revenge nor bear a grudge" (Leviticus 19:17-18). Not only is revenge forbidden, but even when doing to a kindness to someone who has injured you, you may not say, "I am more decent than you."

A third category that may escape Watchfulness is where one's ego has been attacked. Although this involves no physical craving such as is found in regard to illicit behavior or greed, an offense to one's ego can elicit intense feelings. Furthermore, here the Torah requires not only controlling one's actions, but even ridding oneself of objectional feelings. This is so great a demand that Ramchal states it might logically be expected only of angels, and not of mere mortals. Yet, G-d does not demand anything of us which is beyond our capacity. If we are told not to bear grudges, it is within our means to divest ourselves of them.

In *Self-Improvement? I'm Jewish!* I pointed out that people recovering from alcoholism have come to realize that harboring resentments is likely to lead them into alcoholic relapse. They therefore look for ways to rid themselves of resentments. One method is to realize that since acting-out one's resentments is forbidden, and it is well within a person's means to restrain one's actions, holding onto a grudge accomplishes nothing in the way of avenging one's honor. The only effect harboring a grudge accomplishes is negative to one's own self, since this can contribute to ulcers, migraine headaches, and high blood pressure. Why should I allow someone who has offended me to cause my deterioration? Or as one person aptly put it, "Harboring resentments is allowing someone whom you don't like to live inside your head rent free." The realization that bearing a grudge is futile at best and self-defeating at worst should help one overcome such feelings.

If you are truly concerned that bearing grudges is indeed self-defeating, you will search for ways to divest yourself of these. A time-proven method is to do a kindness to the person whom you resent. This is for self-preservation rather than for an altruistic motive, and he may not even be aware of what you are doing for him. Positives and negatives tend to neutralize one another, and acts of kindness can reduce and eliminate negative feelings.

There is a beautiful prayer included in the *Shema* recited before retiring:

"I forgive everyone who has angered, provoked, or sinned against me, both physically or emotionally, intentionally or unintentionally, whether by word, action, or thought; and may no person come to any suffering because of me."

If one says this prayer daily with proper *kavannah* (concentration and sincerity), he may divest himself of resentments.

Earlier we had noted that Divine justice is absolute, and that there is no "overlooking" of sins. The Divine mercy did provide a mechanism of *teshuvah*, whereby with sincere regret and resolve not to repeat the act, and with adequate change in one's character to assure that the latter would indeed be true, the sin can be forgiven. To be effective, *teshuvah* must be complete and wholehearted.

There is another mechanism which can provide for forgiveness of sins within the Divine system of absolute justice. G-d acts toward a person according to how that person acts, and it is only just that we should be judged by the same criteria we use in our own lives. Thus, if a person is quick to forgive anyone who has offended him, it is not a violation of the rules of justice that he, too, be quickly forgiven. On the other hand, if one refuses to forgive others, he will be dealt with accordingly, and he, too, will not be forgiven. Again, ridding oneself of resentments is simply a matter of self-survival.

The chassidic master Rabbi Levi Yitzchak of Berditchev was bitterly persecuted by opponents of the chassidic movement. One time, when he was away from home, his adversaries put his wife and children on a dung wagon and expelled them from the town. Rabbi Levi Yitzchak's friends were horrified by this atrocious behavior, and asked Rabbi Wolf of Zhitomir to pray to bring down the wrath of G-d on these scoundrels.

Rabbi Wolf said, "You have come too late. Rabbi Levi Yitzchak is already standing in front of the ark reciting *Tehillim* (*Psalms*) and praying fervently that no harm befall these people."

וְכֵן כָּל כַּיּוֹצֵא בָּזֶה מִמִּינֵי הַחֲרִיצוּת שֶׁבַּיֵּצֶר מַה שֶּׁהוּא מִשְׁתַּדֵּל לְפַתּוֹת אֶת לִבּוֹת בְּנֵי־הָאָדָם. עַל כֵּן בָּאָה הַתּוֹרָה וְכָלְלָה כְּלָל שֶׁהַכֹּל נִכְלָל בּוֹ (שם): ,,וְאָהַבְתָּ לְרֵעֲךָ כָּמוֹךָ".

To counteract all the intrigues of the yetzer hara to incite one toward hatred and bearing grudges, the Torah states, "You shall love your neighbor as yourself" (Leviticus 19:17).

The *Talmud Yerushalmi* states that a person should so identify with his neighbor as to feel that they are one. Hence, if your hand accidentally touched a hot or sharp object and caused you to feel pain, would you strike it to punish it for having caused the hurt? Just as you would not punish any part of your body if it hurt you, so should you not punish any other person (*Nedarim* 9:3).

The overriding importance of loving another person as oneself is seen in Rabbi Akiva's statement, "The all-encompassing rule of the Torah is 'love your neighbor as yourself' " (ibid. 9:4). One of the great ethicists said that if this is the "all-encompassing rule" of Torah, then all details of Torah observance must be derivatives of this rule. Hence, if the performance of any mitzvah does not contribute to increasing the love of one's neighbor, it falls short of being true Torah observance.

אוּלָם הַשְּׁבוּעוֹת, אַף־עַל־פִּי שֶׁמִּן הַסְּתָם כָּל שֶׁאֵינוֹ מִן הַהֶדְיוֹטוֹת נִשְׁמָר מֵהוֹצִיא שֵׁם שָׁמַיִם מִפִּיו לְבַטָּלָה כָּל־שֶׁכֵּן בִּשְׁבוּעָה, יֵשׁ עוֹד אֵיזֶה עֲנָפִים קְטַנִּים שֶׁאַף־עַל־פִּי שֶׁאֵינָם מִן הַחֲמוּרִים יוֹתֵר, עַל־כָּל־פָּנִים רָאוּי לְמִי שֶׁרוֹצֶה לִהְיוֹת נָקִי, לִשָּׁמֵר מֵהֶם, וְהוּא מַה שֶּׁאָמְרוּ (שבועות לו, א): ,,אָמַר רַבִּי אֶלְעָזָר: לָאו שְׁבוּעָה וְהֵן שְׁבוּעָה. אָמַר רָבָא: וְהוּא דְּאָמַר לָאו לָאו תְּרֵי זִמְנֵי, וְהוּא דְּאָמַר הֵן הֵן תְּרֵי זִמְנֵי".

As far as oaths are concerned, although most people do not take the Name of G-d in vain, there are some offshoots of this sin which should be avoided. According to the Talmud, repeated assertions of a statement may be considered an oath (Shevuos 36a).

It is not uncommon to hear people say, "I promise," or "I swear this is true," or "So help me G-d," or a similar statement. Such expressions are indeed oaths. Again, Ramchal is showing us why *Nekiyus* is necessary. Such expressions are so commonplace that even a person who is watchful might transgress the grave sin of violating an oath, simply because one does not recognize that these common terms are oaths.

Sincere Torah-observant people avoid taking an oath even when they are certain it is true. In *Generation to Generation* (CIS 1986) I related a story I heard from my father.

My father told of Rabbi Chajkel, who shared the community leadership with Rabbi Azriel, the *dayan*. (Many communities had a *dayan*, or magistrate, whose function was to be the judge or arbitrator in various disputes or litigations.) The two Rabbis were close friends, and frequently studied Torah together.

One time Rabbi Azriel was in Rabbi Chajkel's study, when a woman came and asked Rabbi Chajkel to hold 500 rubles for her in safekeeping. She was leaving town for a few days, and had no one else to whom she could entrust the money.

Later that day, Rabbi Chajkel tried to locate the money but could not find it. He searched all the drawers and cabinets in his study and went through the pockets of all his garments, but to no avail. The money was gone.

With a heavy heart, Rabbi Chajkel went to Rabbi Azriel's home. He asked him whether he had perhaps noticed what he had done with the money which the woman gave him. Rabbi Azriel said that he had not seen him do anything with the money, and that to the best of his recollection, it had remained on the desk.

Rabbi Chajkel sighed deeply, "The money is gone, Reb Azriel," he said. "I have searched everywhere. You and I were the only two people present. I know this sounds absurd, Reb Azriel, but this money was entrusted to me, and although you are above suspicion, I am obligated by *halachah* (Jewish Law) to request that you take an oath that you did not take it."

Rabbi Azriel was shaken. "Take an oath, Reb Chajkel?" he asked. "I should swear? Can you give me just a bit of time to give this some thought?"

"Of course," Rabbi Chajkel answered and left Rabbi Azriel's study.

That evening Rabbi Azriel came to Rabbi Chajkel. "Here are 275 rubles," he said. "That is all I have."

Rabbi Chajkel was upset. He knew that Rabbi Azriel's earnings were very meager, and that he did not own 275 rubles. What was the meaning of this? He knew that Rabbi Azriel was under great pressure to provide a dowry for his daughter who was soon to marry. Could it be that Rabbi Azriel had been unable to resist the temptation, and that confronted with the possible cancellation of the wedding if he failed to provide a dowry, Rabbi Azriel had weakened and had taken the money? That was absurd! But how else would he explain Rabbi Azriel's having a sum so large as 275 rubles?

"I cannot compromise," Rabbi Chajkel said. "If I do not have the 500 rubles to return to the woman, I must demand that you swear."

"Give me one more day," Rabbi Azriel pleaded.

The following day, Rabbi Azriel returned and gave Rabbi Chajkel an additional 125 rubles. "This is all I have," he said.

Rabbi Chajkel was stern. He was now convinced that Rabbi Azriel had succumbed to the stress of his daughter's wedding needs and had indeed taken the money. Not, G-d forbid, with an intent to steal, but just to borrow it for a few weeks until after the wedding, when he would somehow repay it. For how else would the impoverished Rabbi Azriel have amassed 400 rubles in two days?

"500 rubles, Reb Azriel," said Rabbi Chajkel. "Not one kopek less."

"Here is a promissory note to the woman for 100 rubles," said Rabbi Azriel. "I will pay it within 30 days. More I cannot do."

"Good enough," said Rabbi Chajkel. "I shall prevail upon the woman to accept your note."

The next few days, when Rabbi Chajkel met Rabbi Azriel, he looked away. If he saw him coming from afar, he tried to avoid meeting him. He could not make peace with the thought that his trusted friend had yielded to temptation and had taken something belonging to another.

Friday afternoon, Rabbi Chajkel was preparing his study for the Sabbath. The *Mizrach* plaque (a decorative plaque designating which direction was east, so that anyone praying in that room would know which direction to face toward Jerusalem) was hanging crooked, and as he lifted it to hang it straight, the bundle of 500 rubles fell out! Rabbi Chajkel suddenly recalled that he had hidden the money there. He emitted a loud shriek and fell to the ground in a faint.

Rabbi Chajkel's family, hearing the loud cry, came running and revived him. As he came to, he tore at his beard and wept uncontrollably. "What have I done!" he cried. "I falsely accused a *tzaddik* (a righteous or saintly person) of a terrible crime! How could I ever have done such a thing! I have sinned against an innocent man and against G-d!" Nothing his family could say would console him.

In the midst of his weeping and self-flagellation, Rabbi Chajkel said, "I must go to the *tzaddik*, Reb Azriel. I must ask his forgiveness. He may spit at me and throw me out of his house, the rotten cur that I am! How I have caused him to suffer needlessly!"

Rabbi Chajkel ran to Rabbi Azriel's home. Breathlessly he threw open the door. "Reb Azriel, forgive me!" he cried. "I know I am unworthy of your forgiveness, but as a G-d-fearing person, I ask you to do as Almighty G-d does, and forgive the most despicable sinners when they repent their sins!"

Rabbi Azriel's wife came in. "Reb Chajkel," he said, "why do you shout? Reb Azriel is not in the house. He has left to *shul* already." Rabbi Chajkel ran out and hurried to the *shul*. A small crowd had already gathered for *Minchah* (the afternoon services). He ran to the pulpit and pounded on the pulpit for attention.

"Hear me, good people," he cried. "Hear me, Reb Azriel the *tzaddik*. For 20 years, I have been your Rabbi, but I do not deserve to be your Rabbi. I have sinned against an innocent man. I have falsely accused a *tzaddik* of a grave crime. I am not worthy for the earth to support me." The tears flowed freely down his cheeks. He turned and ran to the ark containing the Torah, threw open its doors, and shouted, "Only you, G-d, can forgive me!"

Rabbi Azriel came up and put his arm around his dear friend. "Calm down, Reb Chajkel," he pleaded. "Please, calm yourself. I would gladly forgive you wholeheartedly if there was something which required forgiveness. But what is there to forgive, Reb Chajkel? You have done nothing wrong."

"Nothing wrong?" asked Rabbi Chajkel. "Nothing wrong to accuse my bosom friend, a true *tzaddik*, of so menial an act? You mock at me, Reb Azriel. Yes, you mock at me. But I deserve it, and much more. Whatever you wish to do to me, Reb Azriel, I accept, to my great shame."

"Heaven forbid that I mock at you, Reb Chajkel," said Rabbi Azriel. "You had no other course. There was no one else in the room but you and me, and when you could not locate the money, you had no choice but to conclude that I took it, and to demand that I swear my innocence.

"When I heard that I must swear," Rabbi Azriel continued, "I shuddered. Never in my life have I taken an oath. I therefore took the 250 rubles that I had borrowed for my daughter's wedding, and sold my wife's jewelry for another 25 rubles.

"When you told me that this was not enough," Rabbi Azriel continued, "I sold my library for 125 rubles. I am so grateful, Reb Chajkel, that you took the promissory note for 100 rubles. I am so grateful, for otherwise I do not know what I would have done. I would have been compelled to swear. To swear, even when you know you are swearing the truth, is awesome. You spared me, Reb Chajkel, by accepting my note. I shall never forget this kindness."

וְהִנֵּה דְּבַר־הַשֶּׁקֶר גַּם הוּא חֳלִי רָע נִתְפַּשֵּׁט מְאֹד בִּבְנֵי־הָאָדָם, וְאוּלָם מַדְרֵגוֹת מַדְרֵגוֹת יֵשׁ בּוֹ.

יֵשׁ בְּנֵי־אָדָם שֶׁאֻמָּנוּתָם מַמָּשׁ הוּא הַשַּׁקְרָנוּת, הֵם הַהוֹלְכִים וּבוֹדִים מִלִּבָּם כְּזָבִים גְּמוּרִים לְמַעַן הַרְבּוֹת שִׂיחָה בֵּין הַבְּרִיּוֹת אוֹ לְהֵחָשֵׁב מִן הַחֲכָמִים וְיוֹדְעֵי דְּבָרִים הַרְבֵּה . . . וְיֵשׁ אֲחֵרִים וְהֵם הַמְכַזְּבִים בְּסִפּוּרֵיהֶם וְדִבְרֵיהֶם . . . וְהֵם־הֵם הַבַּדָּאִים אֲשֶׁר אִי־אֶפְשָׁר לְהַאֲמִין לְדִבְרֵיהֶם . . . וְיֵשׁ עוֹד אֲחֵרִים שֶׁחָלְיָם קַל מֵחָלְיֵי הָרִאשׁוֹנִים, וְהֵם אוֹתָם שֶׁאֵינָם קְבוּעִים כָּל־כָּךְ בַּשֶּׁקֶר, אֶלָּא שֶׁלֹּא יָחוּשׁוּ לְהִתְרַחֵק מִמֶּנּוּ . . . וְאָמְנָם הֶחָכָם הוֹדִיעָנוּ, שֶׁכָּל־זֶה הוּא הֵפֶךְ רְצוֹן הַבּוֹרֵא בָּרוּךְ־הוּא, וְהוּא מַה שֶּׁבָּאָה עָלָיו הָאַזְהָרָה (שמות כג, ז): „מִדְּבַר־שֶׁקֶר תִּרְחָק" . . . לְהָעִיר אוֹתָנוּ עַל הַהֶרְחֵק הַגָּדוֹל וְהַבְּרִיחָה הָרַבָּה שֶׁצָּרִיךְ לִבְרֹחַ מִזֶּה.

Lying, too, is a widespread malady and can occur at various levels.

There are some people who are "professional" liars, concocting falsehoods to try and impress people with their knowledge.

Others may not spin tales, but in relating something factual, so embellish it with lies that this becomes a second nature . . . and one can never believe what they say.

Others are somewhat milder, and although they do not constantly lie, they will not shy away from a lie . . . All of these are contrary to the Divine will . . . Note that in prohibiting lying the Torah states, "Distance yourself from a false word," (Exodus 23:7) . . . which indicates that one should take precautions to prevent lying.

The single faculty that prominently distinguishes man from beast is the capacity to speak. Indeed, the verse in *Genesis* (2:7) that describes creation of man by the installation of the breath of G-d within him is translated by Onkeles as "Man became a speaking spirit." Speech is nothing less than a Divine gift, a manifestation of the breath of G-d. To lie is to debase this precious Divine gift.

Ramchal states that *Nekiyus* is necessary to prevent lying. Watchfulness alone is insufficient because a person may not appreciate how surreptitious lying is, and may therefore not guard against it.

Ramchal gives us several excellent portrayals of liars. There are those whose self-esteem is so low that they seek to impress others with their knowledge of things, and since they may know precious little, they invent things to tell others. He refers to these as "professional" liars. Close to this group are those who may not invent things out of whole cloth, but who dramatically embellish a small nucleus of truth with a plethora of lies. In either case, lying becomes a second nature, and these people may come to believe their own fabrications. Since they are unable to distinguish truth from falsehood, Watchfulness may not be effective, and they must work to extricate the root of their tendency to lie. In those cases where the cause of lying is a need to impress others because of one's feelings of inferiority, an improvement of self-esteem may eliminate this need. I addressed this topic at length in *Life's Too Short*.

Ramchal points out that whereas other Torah prohibitions restrict a specific act, and the preventive measures are of rabbinic origin, the prohibition against lying is a distinct exception, because in this instance Scripture itself requires precautionary measures, as is indicated by the verse "You shall *distance yourself* from a false word" (*Exodus* 23:7). As was pointed out earlier, a simple rule of thumb is to never do anything which you may subsequently have to deny, for to do so is setting the stage for a future lie.

Many people take liberties with lying, rationalizing that "white lies" are permissible. There are no grounds in *halachah* for such exceptions. The only time one is permitted to stretch the truth is in order to restore peace between friends who have drifted apart. The example given by the Talmud is the High Priest Aaron, who tried to reconcile feuding people by telling each one that he knows the other person deeply regrets their feud and is desperate to reconcile, but is too embarrassed to initiate peace by apologizing. When the two subsequently met, with each one believing that the other was seeking to reconcile, they promptly embraced. Such stretching of the truth is the only exception, but otherwise there is no loophole for "white lies."

Parents are upset when their children lie to them. Sometimes children lie because they are afraid that they will be punished if they reveal the truth about something they did. Sometimes they lie to try to impress their parents, and sometimes they lie to escape responsibility. Children's lies are really no different than those of adults, and in all likelihood, children learn to lie by observing adults, very often their own parents. For example, instructing a child to respond to a telephone caller, "Just tell him I'm not home," is setting a pattern for the child to extricate himself from difficult situations by lying.

One of the chassidic masters said that the *yetzer hara* is willing to allow a person total adherence to all of Torah and mitzvos in return for getting him to concede to falsehood. This is like punching a hole in the bottom of a pitcher, because regardless of how much water you pour in, nothing will remain. As was pointed out earlier, rationalization is nothing but lying to oneself, and using logical arguments to convince oneself that false is true. When a person has deceived himself, Watchfulness is of little value, because he may believe he is doing right. It is therefore essential that one advance to *nekiyus* to escape the danger of self-deception.

One must be especially wary that one does not deceive oneself to think that sins are mitzvos. Rabbi Yisrael of Salant pointed out that although there are many personal desires that can cause a person to rationalize, it is nevertheless possible that a person may come to his senses and realize that he is yielding to a temptation. The most dangerous type of rationalization is when a person thinks he is doing a mitzvah, whereas he is actually doing a sin. As we previously noted, Rabbi Yisrael states that it is possible for a person to hurry to a lecture on mussar and in his haste be rude, pushing and shoving people, even elderly people, out of his way, possibly even hurting them, all in the Name of G-d so that he can get a seat up front close to the mussar lecturer. It would be far preferable that he forgo this lecture and not be disrespectful or cause harm to others.

As we have seen, the greatest and most encompassing mitzvah in the Torah is *ahavas Yisroel*, to love one's fellow man. Yet how many people find petty causes for strife and bitterness. There are some who think that because a person does not observe the Torah, there is no obligation to love him; nay, it is a mitzvah to despise him. How utterly foolish and ignorant! One chassidic master prayed, "May I learn to love the greatest *tzaddik* (saint) as much as G-d loves the worst *rasha* (sinner)."

The pitfalls of self-deception are many. We regularly pray that G-d show us the way of truth and deter us from falsehood. In addition to prayer, we should avail ourselves of a Torah mentor, to whom we can confide our thoughts and feelings, and who can be an objective observer to alert us to self-deception.

וַחֲכָמִים זִכְרוֹנָם לִבְרָכָה אָמְרוּ (שבת נה, א): ,,חוֹתָמוֹ שֶׁל הַקָּדוֹשׁ־בָּרוּךְ־הוּא־אֱמֶת״ . . . וּכְבָר אָמְרוּ ז״ל (מכות כד, א): ״וְדוֹבֵר אֱמֶת בִּלְבָבוֹ (תהלים טו, ב) כְּגוֹן רַב סַפְרָא וכו׳ ״. וְהָכֵי הֲוָה עֻבְדָּא דְרַב סַפְרָא: הָיָה לוֹ חֵפֶץ אֶחָד לִמְכּוֹר, וּבָא אָדָם אֶחָד לְפָנָיו בְּשָׁעָה שֶׁהָיָה קוֹרֵא קְרִיאַת־שְׁמַע וְאָמַר לוֹ, תֶּן לִי הַחֵפֶץ בְּכָךְ וְכָךְ דָּמִים וְלֹא עָנָהוּ, מִפְּנֵי שֶׁהָיָה קוֹרֵא קְרִיאַת־שְׁמַע. קָסָבַר זֶה, שֶׁלֹּא הָיָה רוֹצֶה לִתְּנוֹ בַּדָּמִים הַלָּלוּ וְהוֹסִיף וְאָמַר, תְּנֵהוּ לִי בְּכָךְ וְכָךְ יוֹתֵר. לְאַחַר שֶׁסִּיֵּם קְרִיאַת־שְׁמַע אָמַר לוֹ, טוֹל הַחֵפֶץ בַּדָּמִים שֶׁאָמַרְתָּ בָּרִאשׁוֹנָה, שֶׁבְּאוֹתָן דָּמִים הָיָה בְּדַעְתִּי לִתְּנוֹ לָךְ.

The Talmud says, "Truth is the signet of G-d" (Shabbos 55a) ... and cites the example of Rabbi Safra, who was approached by someone while he was meditating on the Shema, and was offered a price for an item he wished to sell. He could not interrupt the Shema to respond, and the purchaser, interpreting his silence as a rejection of his offer, progressively increased the price. When Rabbi Safra completed the Shema, he sold the item at the first price the buyer had offered. "I had consented to that price initially, but I could not communicate this to you" (ibid. Rashi). This is what the psalmist means, "One who speaks the truth in his heart" (Psalms 15:2).

Rabbi Safra could have made a greater profit, since the buyer had willingly made a much larger offer. No one would have known that he had accepted the first offer, and even if they had known, it would be easy to justify the larger amount. After all, nothing like a legal contract was formulated by his undisclosed acceptance. What Rabbi Safra was practicing was *Nekiyus*, training himself to live with the truth in his heart. If we truly believe in our values, we should be ready to sacrifice profit for them.

A chassidic master, commenting on the Talmudic statement, "Truth is the signet of G-d," said that whereas any other signet can be falsified and imitated, truth cannot. Any imitation of truth is not truth. Truth is either absolutely genuine, or it is not truth.

We may take it for granted that we are truthful, but our great Torah personalities knew better. They were aware of how treacherous self-deception can be, and that just as one may mistake fool's gold for genuine gold, one may accept an imitation of truth for truth.

The chassidic master, the Seer of Lublin, sent two emissaries to Tomashav to fetch Reb Mendel, whom he wished to have as a disciple. The emissaries failed to find anyone in Tomashav by the name of Mendel who appeared to be appropriate to become a disciple of the master. They then decided to conceal themselves in the synagogue to see whether there might be someone who was keeping his true identity secret.

Past midnight, they saw a young man quietly enter the deserted synagogue, approach the ark, and tearfully recite the *Tehillim* (*Psalms*). At one point the young man opened the ark, and with a heartrending voice cried, "Master of the Universe, show me at least a hair'sbreadth of truth!" The emissaries then came out of hiding, and found that this young man's name was indeed Mendel. "We are emissaries of the Rebbe of Lublin," they said, "and if you are seeking truth, come with us to Lublin." The young Mendel accompanied them to the Seer, and later became the renowned Rabbi of Kotzk, who championed uncompromised truth.

Few of us pray as fervently for truth the way Rabbi Mendel did, perhaps because we think we already have it. Rabbi Mendel knew better.

In the practice of psychiatry, it is tragic to observe people with mental illness experiencing hallucinations and delusions, seeing and hearing things that are not there and believing things that are false, and behaving as if these were factual. It is no less tragic to observe normal people behave according to faulty ideas, being absolutely convinced that they are valid.

Many people have feelings and concepts about themselves that are false, and base their lives on this erroneous data. In *Let Us Make Man* and *Life's Too Short* I discuss the problem of the negative self-image, where people who have many personality assets see themselves in a negative light, and adjust to life according to this false self-concept. Knowing the truth about oneself is indispensable to a healthy adjustment to life.

עַנְפֵּי חִלּוּל הַשֵּׁם גַּם־כֵּן הֵם רַבִּים וּגְדוֹלִים כִּי הַרְבֵּה צָרִיךְ הָאָדָם לִהְיוֹת חָס עַל כְּבוֹד קוֹנוֹ . . . וְאָמְרוּ ז״ל (יומא פו, א): ,,הֵיכִי דָמֵי חִלּוּל הַשֵּׁם? אָמַר רַב, כְּגוֹן אֲנָא דְשָׁקְלְנָא בִּשְׂרָא וְלָא יָהֵיבְנָא דְמֵי לְאַלְתַּר . . . וְהָעִנְיָן, שֶׁכָּל אָדָם לְפִי מַדְרֵגָתוֹ וּלְפִי מַה שֶּׁהוּא נֶחְשָׁב בְּעֵינֵי הַדּוֹר צָרִיךְ שֶׁיִּתְבּוֹנֵן לְבִלְתִּי עֲשׂוֹת דָּבָר בִּלְתִּי הָגוּן לְאִישׁ כְּמוֹתוֹ, כִּי כְּפִי רַבּוֹת חֲשִׁיבוּתוֹ וְחָכְמָתוֹ כֵּן רָאוּי שֶׁיַּרְבֶּה זְהִירוּתוֹ בְּדִבְרֵי הָעֲבוֹדָה וְדִקְדּוּקוֹ בָּהּ.

Insofar as desecration of the Divine Name is concerned, there are numerous aspects to this, and a person must be most cautious to protect the honor of G-d . . . The Talmud quotes Rav as saying, "If I do not pay the butcher promptly, that constitutes desecration of the Divine Name" (Yoma 86a) . . . In other words, a person's behavior must correspond to his status. The more respected a person is, the more sensitive he must be concerning his actions.

Another reason why Watchfulness may not suffice is that some actions are not forbidden per se, and may indeed be acceptable for some individuals, but may be inappropriate for a person of whom people have a right to expect a higher standard of behavior. Thus, while there is nothing wrong with buying on credit, Rav was concerned that if he did not pay his bill promptly, the merchant might say, "Rabbis are lax in paying their debts," and even though this remark may have no justification, it would cast a shadow on the integrity of Torah scholars.

The Midrash states that the primary function of Torah and mitzvos is to refine a person's character (*Midrash Rabbah, Vayikra* 13:3). This justifies people's expectations that a Torah-devout person will behave in a refined manner. If one does not do so, he is casting aspertions on the value of Torah observance, and this constitutes a *chilul Hashem*, a desecration of the Divine Name.

While being discourteous is inconsiderate, it cannot be classified as a sin. Yet, if a Torah-observant person is discourteous, it is very much a sin of *chilul Hashem*, since people are likely to conclude that Torah observance contributes nothing to character refinement. Hence, behavior which is in itself not sinful and may therefore escape the discipline of Watchfulness must be brought under control by *Nekiyus*.

The Talmud states that when a scholar's behavior is exemplary, people will say, "How fortunate are his parents and teachers who taught him Torah. See how pleasant his behavior is" (*Yoma* 86a). On the other hand, if a scholar does not behave properly, people will say, "Woe to his parents and teachers who taught him Torah. See how corrupt his behavior is." A person who manifests Torah observance must therefore take care that his behavior be a *kiddush Hashem* and not a *chilul Hashem*.

וְהִנֵּה כְּמוֹ שֶׁצָּרִיךְ נְקִיּוּת בְּמַעֲשִׂים כָּךְ צָרִיךְ נְקִיּוּת בַּמִּדּוֹת וְכִמְעַט שֶׁיּוֹתֵר קָשֶׁה הוּא הַנְּקִיּוּת בַּמִּדּוֹת מִמַּה שֶּׁהוּא בְּמַעֲשִׂים, כִּי הַטֶּבַע פּוֹעֵל בַּמִּדּוֹת יוֹתֵר מִמַּה שֶּׁהוּא פּוֹעֵל בְּמַעֲשִׂים, יַעַן הַמֶּזֶג וְהַתְּכוּנָה הֵם אוֹ מְסַיְּעִים אוֹ מִתְנַגְּדִים גְּדוֹלִים לָהֶם, וְכָל מִלְחָמָה שֶׁהִיא נֶגֶד נְטִיַּת הַטֶּבַע, מִלְחָמָה חֲזָקָה הִיא.

Just as it is necessary to achieve Nekiyus in one's actions, it is also essential to develop Nekiyus in one's character traits. Indeed, the latter may be even more difficult to achieve, because the natural tendencies affect one's traits even more than one's actions, and any struggle that opposes natural tendencies is particularly difficult.

In truth, Ramchal has been talking about character traits throughout this chapter. He made it a point that Watchfulness can be effective for those actions that a person recognizes to be wrong, but that there are many others that may escape recognition, and to avoid these *Nekiyus* is necessary. *Nekiyus* consists of eliminating the source from which such actions may arise, and these sources are essentially undesirable traits. The distinction Ramchal is now making, therefore, is between traits that manifest themselves more readily in actions, as compared to "pure" character traits.

People may be off guard insofar as character traits are concerned. It is more difficult to be aware of improper traits than of deeds, and since traits are internal phenomena, a person might not think that they are all that harmful. The fact is, however, that ultimately all behavior is but the end product of their traits. Some people may also take a position of "That's the way I am. I was born this way," and assume that their character is cast in stone and that they are not responsible for their traits. While there is no denying that there are genetic factors that affect traits and that many traits are the result of influences of our early childhood experiences, we are nevertheless not prisoners of genes or upbringing, and we *can* make salutary changes in our character traits.

אָמְנָם, כְּמוֹ שֶׁדִּבַּרְנוּ בַּמִּצְוֹת שֶׁהָיָה הַצּוֹרֶךְ בָּם יוֹתֵר, דְּהַיְנוּ, מִמַּה שֶּׁרְגִילוּת בְּנֵי־הָאָדָם לִכָּשֵׁל, כֵּן נְדַבֵּר בַּמִּדּוֹת הָרָאשִׁיּוֹת בַּאֲרִיכוּת עִיּוּן יוֹתֵר, מִפְּנֵי רְגִילוּתֵנוּ בָּם, וָהֵם: הַגַּאֲוָה, הַכַּעַס, הַקִּנְאָה וְהַתַּאֲוָה, הֵן כָּל אֵלֶּה מִדּוֹת רָעוֹת אֲשֶׁר רָעָתָם נִכֶּרֶת וּמְפֻרְסֶמֶת, אֵין צָרִיךְ לָהּ רְאָיוֹת, כִּי הִנֵּה רָעוֹת הֵנָּה בְּעַצְמָן וְרָעוֹת בְּתוֹלְדוֹתֵיהֶן, כִּי כֻּלָּן חוּץ מִשּׁוּרַת הַשֵּׂכֶל וְהַחָכְמָה.

Just as we focused on those actions where lapses are apt to be most frequent, let us now talk about the principal traits which are more common, which are: vanity, anger, envy, and desire. These are evil per se, and also result in evil actions. All these traits may be refractory to intellect and wisdom.

It is related that the great philosopher, Aristotle, had once been observed behaving in a very undignified manner. When he was asked how he could do so, he replied, "I was not Aristotle then."

The Talmud states that a person does not commit sin unless he has taken leave of his senses (*Sotah* 3a). Assuming that a person is of average intelligence, he should recognize the harmful nature of sin and avoid it just as one avoids fire. For a person to do something which is self-defeating he must either have a perceptual distortion, where he just does not see reality correctly, or a distortion of judgment. Either of these is irrational, and such distortions can occur even in people of great intellect.

We have noted earlier that the *yetzer hara* can delude. The rational judgment process requires an unbiased attitude, and when one is under the influence of strong desires one is essentially bribed. The Torah points out that bribes can distort both the perception and judgment of even the wisest and most pious people; hence Ramchal points out that these negative traits may be resistant to intellect and wisdom.

הִנֵּה כְּלַל עִנְיַן הַגַּאֲוָה הוּא זֶה, שֶׁהָאָדָם מַחֲשִׁיב עַצְמוֹ בְּעַצְמוֹ וּבִלְבָבוֹ יְדַמֶּה כִּי לוֹ נָאוָה תְּהִלָּה. וְאָמְנָם, זֶה יָכוֹל לִמָּשֵׁךְ מִסְּבָרוֹת רַבּוֹת מִתְחַלְּפוֹת, כִּי יֵשׁ מִי שֶׁיַּחֲשִׁיב עַצְמוֹ בַּעַל־שֵׂכֶל, וְיֵשׁ מִי שֶׁיַּחֲשִׁיב עַצְמוֹ נָאֶה, וְיֵשׁ מִי שֶׁיַּחֲשִׁיב עַצְמוֹ נִכְבָּד, וְיֵשׁ שֶׁיַּחֲשִׁיב עַצְמוֹ גָּדוֹל, וְיֵשׁ שֶׁיַּחֲשִׁיב עַצְמוֹ חָכָם . . . אַךְ אַחֲרֵי שֶׁקָּבַע הָאָדָם בְּלִבּוֹ הֱיוֹתוֹ חָשׁוּב וְרָאוּי לִתְהִלָּה, לֹא תִהְיֶה הַתּוֹלָדָה הַיּוֹצֵאת מִן הַמַּחֲשָׁבָה הַזֹּאת אַחַת בִּלְבָד, אֶלָּא תּוֹלָדוֹת רַבּוֹת וּמְשֻׁנּוֹת תֵּצֶאנָה מִמֶּנָּה.

Vanity consists of a person being intoxicated with his own importance, considering himself praiseworthy. One person may deem himself intelligent; another thinks himself to be handsome; another, honorable; another, great; another, wise . . . Any of these feelings can give rise to many untoward results, and it is even possible for conflicting reactions to emanate from the same source.

There is unanimity among ethicists that vanity is the worst of all traits, and may even be the root of many other objectionable traits. Yet it is interesting that in his famous letter to his son, while commenting that vanity is the worst of all traits and that the vain person is a "rebel against the kingdom of G-d," Ramban exhorts his son to begin with control of his anger rather than with overcoming vanity. Ramchal, on the other hand, begins with vanity, and then goes on to discuss anger.

The reason for the different approaches is that while vanity is indeed the worst of all negative traits, it is essentially an abstraction rather than a concrete behavior, whereas rage is a behavior. As we shall see in our discussion of anger, it is rage, or the external expression of anger, whose control Ramban is advocating. Since Ramban's letter is a specific list of instructions to his son, he begins with something concrete that is more readily under one's control, rather than vanity, which is a pure sensation. Ramchal, on the other hand, is discussing the underpinnings of negative behavior, and therefore lists vanity first.

Whereas the Divine presence never abandons a person, even if one has sinned greatly, as the Scripture states, "I dwell among them even in their state of defilement" (*Leviticus* 16:16), the vain person is a notable exception, of whom G-d says, "He and I cannot dwell together" (*Arachin* 15b). As Ramban says in his letter, a person should realize that whatever assets he possesses—wealth, wisdom, etc. — are gifts from G-d and nothing that one has achieved by one's own prowess, hence how can one boast about oneself? Vanity can only exist when a person denies that whatever he has is a Divine gift, and this is why vanity is essentially a denial and a defiance of G-d.

There are important psychological aspects that operate in vanity, and Ramchal's acute psychological acumen is evident in his observation that vanity can result in contradictory reactions. We will turn to this analysis a bit later, but first let us note Ramchal's graphic description of several varieties of vanity.

הִנֵּה יִמָּצֵא גֵּאֶה אֶחָד שֶׁיַּחֲשׁוֹב בְּלִבּוֹ שֶׁכֵּיוָן שֶׁהוּא רָאוּי לִתְהִלָּה וְהוּא מְיֻחָד . . . לֹא יֵלֵךְ אֶלָּא בְנַחַת גָּדוֹל, עֲקֵבוֹ בְּצַד גֻּדָלוֹ, לֹא יֵשֵׁב אֶלָּא אַפַּרְקְדָן . . . לֹא יְדַבֵּר עִם הַכֹּל אֶלָּא עִם נִכְבַּדֵּי הָעָם . . . וְכָל שְׁאָר מַעֲשָׂיו: בִּתְנוּעוֹתָיו, בִּפְעֻלּוֹתָיו, בְּמַאֲכָלוֹ וּבְמִשְׁתָּיו, בְּמַלְבּוּשָׁיו וּבְכָל דְּרָכָיו יִתְנַהֵג בִּכְבֵדוּת גָּדוֹל כְּאִלּוּ כָּל בְּשָׂרוֹ עוֹפֶרֶת.

There is the vain person who acts pompously in order to convey an attitude of dignity. He struts, sits upright, hesitates to speak with anyone other than people of eminence, and his dress, eating habits, and all his movements are as deliberate as though he were made of lead.

וְיִמָּצֵא גֵאֶה אַחֵר שֶׁיַּחֲשׁוֹב שֶׁלְּפִי שֶׁהוּא רָאוּי לִתְהִלָּה וְרַב הַמַּעֲלוֹת, צָרִיךְ שֶׁיִּהְיֶה מַרְגִּיז הָאָרֶץ וְשֶׁהַכֹּל יִרְעֲשׁוּ מִפָּנָיו כִּי לֹא יָאוּת שֶׁיֶּהֶרְסוּ בְּנֵי־הָאָדָם לְדַבֵּר עִמּוֹ וּלְבַקֵּשׁ מִמֶּנּוּ דָּבָר, וְאִם יַעְפִּילוּ לַעֲלוֹת אֵלָיו יְבַהֲלֵם בְּקוֹלוֹ וּבְרוּחַ שְׂפָתָיו יְהֻמֵּם בַּעֲנוֹת לָהֶם עַזּוֹת, וּפָנָיו זוֹעֲפוֹת בְּכָל עֵת וּבְכָל שָׁעָה.
וְיֵשׁ גֵּאֶה אַחֵר שֶׁיַּחֲשׁוֹב בְּלִבּוֹ שֶׁכְּבָר הוּא כָּל־כָּךְ גָדוֹל וּמְכֻבָּד עַד שֶׁאִי אֶפְשָׁר לַכָּבוֹד שֶׁיִּתְפָּרֵשׁ מִמֶּנּוּ וְאֵינוֹ צָרִיךְ לוֹ כְּלָל, וּלְהַרְאוֹת הַדָּבָר הַזֶּה יַעֲשֶׂה מַעֲשִׂים כְּמַעֲשֵׂה הֶעָנָיו וַיַּפְרִיז [נ״א וְיַכְרִיז] עַל מִדּוֹתָיו לְהַרְאוֹת שִׁפְלוּת גָּדוֹל וַעֲנָוָה עַד אֵין חֵקֶר, וְלִבּוֹ מִתְנַשֵּׂא בְקִרְבּוֹ לֵאמֹר: אֲנִי כָּל־כָּךְ רָם וְכָל־כָּךְ נִכְבָּד, שֶׁכְּבָר אֵינִי צָרִיךְ לְכָבוֹד, וְאֵין לִי אֶלָּא לְוַתֵּר עָלָיו, שֶׁכְּבָר רַב הוּא אֶצְלִי . . . וְיִמָּצְאוּ גֵאִים אֲחֵרִים שֶׁתִּשָּׁאֵר גַּאֲוָתָם קְבוּרָה בְלִבָּם, לֹא יוֹצִיאוּהָ אֶל הַמַּעֲשֶׂה, אֲבָל יַחְשְׁבוּ בִלְבָבָם שֶׁכְּבָר הֵם חֲכָמִים גְּדוֹלִים יוֹדְעֵי הַדְּבָרִים לַאֲמִתָּם וְשֶׁלֹּא רַבִּים יַחְכְּמוּ כְּמוֹהֶם, עַל־כֵּן לֹא יָשִׁיתוּ לֵב אֶל דִּבְרֵי זוּלָתָם . . . וְסָפֵק אֵין אֶצְלָם עַל סְבָרָתָם.

Another vain person tries to terrorize others. How dare you have the audacity to approach me! Yet another vain person thinks himself so great and honorable that he has no need to impress anyone, and to the contrary, feigns humility, while in his heart he considers himself exalted. In quest of praise he may actually wish people to praise him for his profound humility! Still another thinks himself so much wiser than anyone else that he pays no attention to whatever others say, having no doubt whatever about the correctness of his own views.

וְעַל כֻּלָּם נֶאֱמַר (משלי טז, ה): ,,תּוֹעֲבַת ה׳ כָּל־גְּבַהּ־לֵב״, וּמִכֻּלָּם צָרִיךְ שֶׁיִּנָּקֶה הָרוֹצֶה בְּמִדַּת הַנְּקִיּוּת וְיֵדַע וְיָבִין כִּי אֵין הַגַּאֲוָה אֶלָּא עִוָּרוֹן מַמָּשׁ אֲשֶׁר אֵין שֵׂכֶל הָאָדָם רוֹאֶה חֶסְרוֹנוֹתָיו וּמַכִּיר פְּחִיתוּתוֹ.

Regardless of the subtype of vanity, it is said of all of these, "The vain at heart are an abomination of G-d" (Proverbs 16:5). Vanity is but a blindness, that the person is unaware of his defects and limitations.

Ramchal was certainly a most astute observer of people, and we can confirm his findings with our own observations. His final point, however, where he states that the vain person is unaware of his defects and limitations, and that this is the source of his vanity, requires some clarification.

In *Let Us Make Man* I distinguished between *anivus* (humility), which is the finest of character traits and is a goal of spirituality, and low self-esteem, which is a destructive feeling. The two may appear similar, in that in each case the person does not hold himself to be special, but this similarity is very deceiving. Humility and low self-esteem are at opposite poles.

Low self-esteem refers to a state where a person misperceives himself, and fails to recognize his personality assets and his self-worth. It is characterized by a feeling of shame, of being unworthy, often without knowing just why one feels that way about himself. Sometimes the person does give reasons for his feelings of unworthiness, but these are rationalizations and fabrications that came after the fact. I.e., the feelings of shame and inferiority came first, and being at a loss to explain them, he then concocted reasons why he feels this way about himself.

Such feelings of shame and inferiority are universally destructive, and they have nothing to do with humility. They are likely to result in despair and in failure to take positive action because one does not believe he can achieve. In *Life's Too Short* I described the many psychological symptoms and maladjustments to life that can occur as a result of unwarranted feelings of shame and inferiority.

Inasmuch as these negative feelings about oneself are not based on reality, they are false, and as such cannot possibly be components of humility. As we have seen, the Torah condemns falsehood in whatever shape it comes, and the kabbalistic writings identify falsehood with Satan himself.

A person must know the truth about himself and recognize his strengths, talents, and worthiness. The great ethicist, Rabbi Leib Chasman, said, "One who denies one's strengths is not humble, but rather a fool," and another prominent ethicist, Rabbi Yeruchem Levovitz, said, "Woe unto a person who is not aware of his defects, and does not know what he must correct. But much worse off is the person who does not know his strengths, who is unaware of the tools he must work with to advance himself spiritually."

Awareness of one's personality endowments should not result in vanity. It is much like someone who wished to have a party to celebrate an event, but lacked the finery to do so. His neighbors lent him their fine linens, silverware, china, and crystal, and he was able to prepare an elegant table for his guests. How foolish he would be to display all the finery and boast of his wealth when none of it was his own! Rather, he should be grateful that he had such kind neighbors who helped him, and he may indeed have a feeling of both pride and gratitude that he has these kinds of friends.

So it is with the person who is bright, attractive, gifted, wealthy, etc. There is no reason to deny these endowments, but one should realize how he came by them. They are gifts of G-d, and he should feel proud and grateful for the Divine bounty, and realize that he has a responsibility to put these gifts to maximum use in the Divine service. Since one can never reach perfection, and the ultimate goal of "adequately" serving G-d is never reached, one should feel humble in how relatively little one has done with what he was given, and how much more one must endeavor to do. Thus, the greater one's awareness of one's excellence, the greater should be one's sense of indebtedness to G-d, one's sense of responsibility, and one's humility.

In the past generation we were blessed with a Torah personage, the Chafetz Chaim, who was a paragon of humility and self-effacement. We are fortunate in having eyewitness accounts of this great sage's humility. His many works have become the authoritative guidelines for halachic daily living, and they reveal his immense Torah scholarship.

Just think, if humility would require a denial of one's assets, then the Chafetz Chaim would have had to consider himself bereft of learning. If so, on what basis did he write the authoritative *Mishnah Brurah*, the halachic work of the century? Clearly the Chafetz Chaim was well aware of his vast knowledge of Torah, yet this did not turn his head to vanity. I am certain that when he finished the last paragraph of his magnum opus he did not say, "There! Now the world will recognize who I am," but rather gave thanks to G-d for giving him the means to expound on Torah, and heaving a great sigh, realized that given the capabilities with which G-d had blessed him, he had not even begun to fulfill his mission.

A person should therefore know factually what is right with him and what is wrong with him. This allows him to put his skills to constructive use and to correct his defects. This is a correct perception of reality, and does not result in vanity. It is truth, and truth is always constructive. When actual defects exist, they can be corrected, and such correction contributes to spiritual advancement.

But a person may also misperceive. For whatever reasons, many people develop feelings of inadequacy and inferiority that are not based on fact, and these constitute the destructive feeling of shame. This feeling can be so painful that a person may turn to desperate measures to escape it, and I described several of these mechanisms in *Life's Too Short*. One of these mechanisms is to try to overcome the feelings of shame and unworthiness by thinking oneself superior to everyone else, and trying to elicit praise from everyone to support and reinforce this defensive feeling of superiority. Since the defects in shame are not reality based, there is nothing one can do to correct them. You cannot correct a non-existing fault. The efforts to do so result in trying to fill a bottomless pit, and if one becomes defensively vain, the process is endless, with the vanity progressively increasing and often resulting in arrogance.

Yet, since the underlying feelings of shame are not eliminated, they may periodically break through the vanity, with manifest expressions of worthlessness and self-depreciation. Thus, Ramchal is right on target when he states that two conflicting, contradictory attitudes may emanate from a single source.

As I pointed out in *Let Us Make Man*, there is a way to gain healthy self-esteem and humility, through adoption of a comprehensive Torah way of life. I elaborated on this both in *Self-Improvement? I'm Jewish!* and in *Life's Too Short*. It is possible to overcome both feelings of unwarranted shame and destructive vanity, but one must recognize one has them, and make the requisite efforts to overcome them.

A few words of introduction are in order before approaching Ramchal's discussion of anger. The Hebrew word *Kaas*, which is generally translated as "anger," can actually refer to several different stages of anger, and it is important that we do not confuse these.

There is an emotion which a person experiences when he is irritated or provoked, which is a feeling of anger toward the offender. The provocation may be a personal insult, whether physical or emotional, or may be a sense of outrage at an injustice done to someone else. This initial reaction of the "feeling" of anger is generally not under voluntary control.

While *Kaas* may be used to refer to this initial feeling of anger, it is also used to refer to the *expression* or *manifestation* of anger, and this can, of course, be of varying degrees. A person may say something relatively mild to express his indignation, or something stronger, or shout, or scream profanities, or lash out physically, breaking things or striking someone. *Kaas* may also refer to the emotion of anger that lingers on after the initial reaction to the provocation. Although the initial reaction of feeling anger may not be under voluntary control, the expression of anger or its retention after the initial reaction are subject to voluntary control.

It is clear that the single word *Kaas* can thus refer to three distinct entities, and if we simply translate *Kaas* as anger we can easily become confused as to which type of anger we are talking about. To avoid confusion, I suggest we use three different terms to designate the three stages of anger. Thus, we will refer to the initial reaction, *the feeling* aroused on provocation as "anger," the *expression* of anger as "rage" (which may be mild or severe), and the *retention* of anger after the initial reaction as "resentment." In this way we will avoid much of the misunderstanding that has resulted in many discussions of the proper management of anger.

In translating the text of Ramchal, we will preserve the Hebrew word *Kaas*, and in our discussions of the text, we will use the terms "anger," "rage," and "resentment" according to the above definitions.

וּנְדַבֵּר עַתָּה מִן הַכַּעַס. הִנֵּה יֵשׁ הָרַגְזָן שֶׁאָמְרוּ עָלָיו, (שבת קה, ב): ,,כָּל הַכּוֹעֵס כְּאִלּוּ עוֹבֵד עֲבוֹדָה זָרָה'', וְהוּא הַנִּכְעָס עַל כָּל דָּבָר שֶׁיַּעֲשׂוּ נֶגֶד רְצוֹנוֹ וּמִתְמַלֵּא חֵמָה עַד שֶׁכְּבָר לִבּוֹ בַּל עִמּוֹ וַעֲצָתוֹ נִבְעָרָה. וְהִנֵּה אִישׁ כָּזֶה כְּדַאי לְהַחֲרִיב עוֹלָם מָלֵא אִם יִהְיֶה יְכֹלֶת בְּיָדוֹ, כִּי אֵין הַשֵּׂכֶל שׁוֹלֵט בּוֹ כְּלָל וְהוּא סָר טַעַם מַמָּשׁ כְּכָל הַחַיּוֹת הַטּוֹרְפוֹת . . . וְהוּא קַל וַדַּאי לַעֲבוֹר כָּל־מִינֵי עֲבֵרוֹת שֶׁבָּעוֹלָם.

Let us now discuss Kaas. Of the furious person, the Talmud says, "One who has Kaas is as if he worships idols" (Shabbos 105b), and this is a person who is aroused to Kaas when displeased, and is capable of destroying an entire world if allowed. He does not exercise rational control, and is like a wild, predatory beast. His wrath can lead to transgressions of all types of sins.

It is clear that Ramchal is referring to what we have called "rage," and particularly a violent, uncontrolled discharge of *Kaas*. He uses terms such as "fury" and "wrath," and says that this person can be indiscriminately destructive. This is obviously not the *Kaas* of the initial, involuntary feeling which we are calling "anger." The initial feeling per se does not destroy anything, and one who feels anger when provoked is in no way similar to a wild beast. The Talmud is indeed specific in stating that someone who breaks things or tears garments in his fury is equivalent to an idolater, and not someone who feels angry when provoked.

וְיֵשׁ כַּעֲסָן רָחוֹק מִזֶּה וְהוּא שֶׁלֹּא עַל כָּל דָּבָר אֲשֶׁר יְבוֹאֵהוּ שֶׁלֹּא כִּרְצוֹנוֹ אִם קָטָן וְאִם גָּדוֹל יִבְעַר אַפּוֹ. אַךְ בְּהַגִּיעוֹ לְהַרְגִּיז, יִרְגַּז וְיִכְעַס כַּעַס גָּדוֹל . . . וְיֵשׁ כַּעֲסָן פָּחוֹת מִזֶּה שֶׁלֹּא יִכְעַס עַל נְקַלָּה, וַאֲפִלּוּ כְּשֶׁיַּגִּיעַ לְכַעַס יִהְיֶה כַּעֲסוֹ כַּעַס קָטָן וְלֹא יָסוּר מִדַּרְכֵי הַשֵּׂכֶל אַךְ עוֹדֶנּוּ יִשְׁמוֹר עֶבְרָתוֹ . . . כִּי אֲפִלּוּ זָהִיר אֵינֶנּוּ עֲדַיִן, כִּי עַד שֶׁהַכַּעַס עוֹשֶׂה בּוֹ רֹשֶׁם, לֹא יָצָא מִכְּלָל כַּעֲסָן.

וְיֵשׁ עוֹד פָּחוּת מִזֶּה וְהוּא שֶׁקָּשֶׁה לִכְעוֹס לֹא לְהַשְׁחִית וְלֹא לְכַלֵּה אֶלָּא כַּעַס מְעַט. וְכַמָּה זַעֲמוֹ? רֶגַע וְלֹא יוֹתֵר, דְּהַיְנוּ, מִשָּׁעָה שֶׁהַכַּעַס מִתְעוֹרֵר בּוֹ בְּטֶבַע עַד שֶׁגַּם הַתְּבוּנָה תִתְעוֹרֵר כְּנֶגְדּוֹ . . . הִנֵּה זֶה חֵלֶק טוֹב וַדַּאי כִּי טֶבַע הָאָדָם מִתְעוֹרֵר לְכַעַס וְאִם הוּא מִתְגַּבֵּר עָלָיו, שֶׁאֲפִלּוּ אוֹתוֹ הַכַּעַס הַקַּל לֹא יַעֲמוֹד בּוֹ זְמַן גָּדוֹל אֶלָּא יַעֲבוֹר וְיֵלֵךְ, וַדַּאי שֶׁרָאוּי לְשֶׁבַח הוּא.

Another person is removed from the type in that he is not as easily provoked, but when his threshold is exceeded, manifests intense Kaas. There is a less severe type who does not lose control over his Kaas, but does retain it; (i.e., holds a grudge). This is less destructive than the others, yet his harboring of a grudge makes him a "person of anger."

There is one even less severe, and that is someone who is not easily provoked, and when he does become angry, it is but momentary. This is certainly praiseworthy, because it is natural for a person to feel anger when provoked, and the

Talmud praises a person who can keep his silence when involved in a strife, and can be master over his natural inclination.

While having a high threshold for feeling anger is certainly advantageous, the loss of control when that threshold is exceeded is still very objectionable, because the furious behavior may still be very destructive. Ramchal then describes the other two varieties we have noted; i.e., one who restrains himself from expression of rage, which is certainly an improvement in that there is no uncontrollable destructive behavior. However, since this person harbors a grudge, he may act out his hostile feelings in a more deliberate manner. The least serious stage of anger is when the initial natural reaction is transitory, and is quickly dismissed.

There are several ways in which one may be able to dismiss anger so that it does not escalate to either rage or resentment. We may think about times that we have angered or provoked others only to later regret it and wish that it had never happened. While we may apologize for our actions, there are times when we do not have the opportunity to apologize, but wish the other person would understand how we feel. We should give the same consideration to someone who angers us. He may regret his actions, even if he has not apologized.

We might also realize that since taking revenge is explicitly forbidden by the Torah, just what will we get from harboring resentments? We cannot act out against the other person, and all we will accomplish by bearing a grudge is letting the resentments fester within us, possibly causing depression, migraine headaches, and high blood pressure. Does it make any sense to harm ourselves because we are angry at someone else? This is why Solomon says, "*Kaas* rests in the bosom of a fool" (*Ecclesiastes* 7:9). It is the utmost folly to retain resentments.

Another consideration that may help to dispel anger can be learned from a story of King David, who fled from his rebellious son, Avshalom. One his enemies, Shimi, accosted David with vehement curses. Avishi, David's general, was about to kill Shimi, when David restrained him, saying, "Perhaps he is simply a tool of G-d Who told him to curse me" (see *II Samuel* 16:5-10). This is something to consider when one has been offended. Perhaps it was the Divine intention for this to happen, and the offender was merely the agent for effecting G-d's will. We should then accept the unpleasantness and bear it in silence.

אָמְנָם, מִדָּתוֹ שֶׁל הִלֵּל הַזָּקֵן עוֹלָה עַל כָּל אֵלֶּה, שֶׁכְּבָר לֹא הָיָה מַקְפִּיד עַל שׁוּם דָּבָר וַאֲפִלּוּ הִתְעוֹרְרוּת שֶׁל כַּעַס לֹא נַעֲשָׂה בּוֹ. זֶה הוּא וַדַּאי הַנָּקִי מִן הַכַּעַס מִכֹּל וָכֹל. וְהִנֵּה אֲפִלּוּ לִדְבַר מִצְוָה הִזְהִירוּנוּ ז"ל שֶׁלֹּא לִכְעוֹס, וַאֲפִלּוּ הָרַב עִם תַּלְמִידוֹ וְהָאָב עִם בְּנוֹ, וְלֹא שֶׁלֹּא יְיַסְּרֵם, אֶלָּא יְיַסְּרֵם וִייַסְּרֵם אַךְ מִבְּלִי כַּעַס, כִּי אִם לְהַדְרִיךְ אוֹתָם בַּדֶּרֶךְ הַיְשָׁרָה, וְהַכַּעַס שֶׁיַּרְאֶה לָהֶם יִהְיֶה כַּעַס הַפָּנִים לֹא כַּעַס הַלֵּב.

The ideal, however, was achieved by the great sage, Hillel, who was beyond being provoked into even the initial feeling of anger. This is Nekiyus in regard to anger.

Kaas is even prohibited when it appears to be directed toward a mitzvah, as when a teacher disciplines a student, or a father disciplines a child. This should not be misunderstood to mean that one should not exert discipline, but rather that we should do so without Kaas, and if necessary, one may act as though one were angry, but there should be no Kaas in one's heart.

Ramchal had defined *Nekiyus* as being the elimination of the source of improper behavior. In regard to anger, *Kaas*, this would mean the elimination of the initial feeling of anger. But since we have established that this feeling is a natural response, how can it be eliminated?

Recently we have learned a great deal from the therapeutic technique of biofeedback. This treatment utilizes an electronic apparatus which registers the skin temperature and muscle tension, and indicates when a person is becoming more relaxed or less relaxed. By undergoing biofeedback treatment, a person can learn how to control physiological reactions that heretofore been considered beyond voluntary control. One can learn to increase or decrease one's heart rate at will, or to dilate and constrict the pupils, and even how to regulate one's brainwaves. Biofeedback has confirmed the chassidic teaching that the mind can indeed exert great control over the body's emotional reactions, although this may require extensive training. Thus, although the natural response to provocation is a feeling of anger, it is possible to train oneself not to have this reaction.

Furthermore, even traits that are "natural" and inherent within a person's physiology, and hence not easily subject to removal by oneself, can be removed by G-d. We pray, "Purify our hearts to serve You," and d to eradicate our evil inclinations, even though the *yetzer* .atural human component. We may thus ask of G-d to remove .e initial response of feeling angry, and this is how Hillel may , achieved his equanimity. Of course, G-d may respond to this .equest by telling us that we must first do our homework, and subdue our angry responses to the fullest extent possible, and only after we have made a maximum effort to bring anger under control, may G-d then eliminate the "natural" feeling of anger.

The Talmud says that the adverse consequences of rage are many. "If one is wise, his wisdom leaves him; if he is a prophet, his prophecy leaves him" (*Pesachim* 66b). Rabbi Chaim Shmulevitz points out that this is a natural consequence of rage, and not a punishment, just as if one puts one's hand into fire, it is not a "punishment" that one gets burned. Hence, even if the rage was legitimate and justifiable, the consequences are the same, just as the burn would occur even if one had good reason for putting one's hand into a flame (*Sichos Mussar* 5733:23). The Ramban says that Moses was denied entrance into the Promised Land because of his rage when the Israelites showed their lack of faith in G-d at the Waters of Strife (*Numbers* 20:7-13).

Rabbi Yisrael of Salant stated that people are frequently provoked to anger by items of relatively little importance, but which, at that precise moment, appear to be significant. If one observes an infant, one will note that if someone takes a brightly colored wooden block away from him, he may become very angry and cry. Obviously, the deprivation of the block of wood is meaningless to a mature mind, but to the juvenile mind it means a great deal. So do we, even as mature adults, sometimes perceive trivia as being of great importance, and we react accordingly with rage.

Rabbi Yisrael points out that if a person were engaged in a major transaction where he stood to profit greatly, he would ignore irritating trivia to which he might otherwise react. Why? Because he is preoccupied with something that is so important that it totally obscures the minor irritations. If a person considered every moment of life as precious, as an opportunity to do mitzvos, he too would not be moved by many minor irritations, which will lose their significance in comparison to the great gain one has when observing the mitzvos.

When the chassidic master, the Tzemach Tzedek, felt he was being provoked to anger, he would study the laws pertaining to the prohibition of idol worship. He reasoned that inasmuch as the Talmud equates rage with idolatry, he needed to shore-up his knowledge of this grievous sin, lest his anger progressed to rage. Rabbi Simcha Zissel of Kelm reacted to feelings of anger by setting aside a special garment, and taking an oath that he would withhold reacting to anger until he first put on this garment. This delaying tactic prevented the progression of anger to rage.

Some misguided psychologists advocate discharging one's anger by shouting or punching things. This is utter nonsense, and serves only to intensify the anger. Whereas it is true that unconscious repression of anger may cause psychological symptoms, this is not true of *suppression*, or conscious self-restraint.

The chassidic master, the *Sfas Emes*, was accompanied to the train station by many of his followers. Before boarding the train he said to them, "Do you know why this single engine can pull so many heavy wagons? It is because it contains the steam within itself." The control of anger can be a powerful constructive force.

הַקִּנְאָה גַם הִיא אֵינָהּ אֶלָּא חֶסְרוֹן יְדִיעָה וְסִכְלוּת, כִּי אֵין הַמְקַנֵּא מַרְוִיחַ כְּלוּם לְעַצְמוֹ וְגַם לֹא מַפְסִיד לְמִי שֶׁהוּא מִתְקַנֵּא בוֹ, וְאֵינוֹ אֶלָּא מַפְסִיד לְעַצְמוֹ . . . וְהוּא מַה שֶּׁאָמַר עָלָיו הֶחָכָם (משלי יד, ל): ,,וּרְקַב עֲצָמוֹת קִנְאָה.״

Envy, too, is the result of ignorance and foolish thinking. The envious person gains nothing, the person whom he envies loses nothing, and the only loser is the person who envies . . . as it is written, "Envy is the decay of the bones" (Proverbs 14:30). Envy may eat away at a person so that he cannot enjoy what he does have. Some people feign an attitude of being happy for others, while internally they seethe with envy. Envy is particularly severe if one sees a competitor being successful. If people would truly believe that they received only what was predestined for them, there would be no envy of what others have.

In *Ethics of the Fathers* we read, "Envy, desire, and the quest for acclaim draw a person out of this world" (4:21). Our sages were prescient in psychosomatics, and over two thousand years ago appreciated that a person could be destroyed by certain emotions, of which they placed envy at the top of the list.

Ramchal was well aware of the particularly lethal nature of envy, and how irrational an emotion it is. Just what is accomplished by envy? It does not result in acquiring the coveted item. Furthermore, the displeasure that someone else has results in a person not being able to enjoy even what he does have.

The totally irrational nature of envy became evident to me when I overheard someone remark about a person who was critically ill, "Look at all the attention he is getting!" How absurd to be envious of someone who is gravely ill!

וְתִרְאֶה כִּי אֲחוֹת הַקִּנְאָה הִיא הַחֶמְדָּה וְהַתַּאֲוָה, הֲלֹא הִיא הַמְיַגַּעַת לֵב הָאָדָם עַד יוֹם מוֹתוֹ, וּכְמַאֲמָרָם ז״ל (קהלת רבה א, לד): ,,אֵין אָדָם מֵת וַחֲצִי תַאֲוָתוֹ בְּיָדוֹ״. וְאָמְנָם, עִקַּר הַתַּאֲוָה פּוֹנָה לִשְׁנֵי רָאשִׁים, הָאֶחָד הוּא הַמָּמוֹן וְהַשֵּׁנִי הוּא הַכָּבוֹד . . . הִנֵּה חֶמְדַּת הַמָּמוֹן הִיא הָאוֹסֶרֶת אוֹתוֹ בְּמַאֲסַר הָעוֹלָם וְנוֹתֶנֶת עֲבוֹתוֹת הֶעָמָל וְהָעֵסֶק עַל זְרוֹעוֹתָיו, כְּעִנְיַן הַכָּתוּב (קהלת ה, ט): ,,אֹהֵב כֶּסֶף לֹא־יִשְׂבַּע כֶּסֶף.״

The sister of envy is desire, which can exhaust a person until the day he dies, as the Talmud says, "A person does not die with half of his desire fulfilled" (Koheles Rabbah 1:34). Desire can be of two types: desire for money and desire for acclaim . . .

Desire for money can enslave a person forever, as Solomon says, "One who loves money will never be satisfied with money" (Ecclesiastes 5:9).

As voracious as physical appetites may be, there is at least a temporary point of satiation. One can only eat so much, and when a saturation point is reached, he stops. For greed and envy there are no end points whatever, even momentary.

I recall, as a child, my mother telling me the story of a poor man who was given a magic purse which contained a silver coin. Each time he took out a coin, it was magically replaced by another coin. After several days he was found dead of starvation, atop a huge mound of silver coins. This is hardly a fantasy, because we often observe money-hungry people driving themselves to a premature death because of their greed. The lust for wealth can be every bit as insatiable as the craving for drugs, and in both cases many people have pursued their desire relentlessly, even when shown that this would cost them their very lives.

In commenting on the verse in *Proverbs* (28:25), "The greedy in spirit stirs up strife, but he who trusts in G-d shall be abundantly satisfied,"

Rabbi Samson Raphael Hirsch says, "As for cure, however, greed has only one remedy: faith in G-d. Only someone who thinks that his and his family's destiny is dependent entirely upon himself and his own abilities can become a victim of unlimited greediness. He believes that every new acquisition will afford him security against penury, and once he has finished providing for his own needs, he amasses for his children and grandchildren into the infinite future. But whoever trusts in G-d, confident that it is only G-d's favor which ensures his future and the future of his family, is easily contented. He merely endeavors to fulfill his duty, even in his search for material possessions, and whatever G-d lets him find, within the framework of the Divine commandments, satisfies him" (From the *Wisdom of Mishle*, Feldheim Publishers, 1976).

Rabbi Bunim of Pshische said, "Oh, just where is that ultimate child who is driving the world insane!" He explained, "I see a person totally absorbed in making money, and when I ask him why he does not devote more time to spiritual pursuits, he tells me that while his own material needs are few, he must work hard to provide for his child.

"When this child achieves maturity, he too immerses himself totally in making money, and when asked why he does not make more time for spiritual pursuits, his answer is the same: His own needs are meager, but he must work long hours to provide for his child. This pattern persists generation after generation. Everyone has enough for himself, but they are exhausting themselves for 'the child.' Where, in Heaven's name, is this child for whom everyone is sacrificing their spirituality? Can we not see that this 'child' is but a myth, a figment of one's imagination?"

Ramchal is so right. Greed and envy are sister traits and, like the Sirens in the story of Ulysses, treacherously lure a person to destruction. These traits must be extricated by *Nekiyus*, and we now have three authorities, Ramchal, Rabbi Mendel of Rimanov, and Rabbi Samson Raphael Hirsch that tell us that the only remedy is faith and trust in Divine providence, that G-d will provide for our needs.

יְתֵרָה עָלֶיהָ חֶמְדַּת הַכָּבוֹד, כִּי כְּבָר הָיָה אֶפְשָׁר שֶׁיִּכְבּוֹשׁ הָאָדָם אֶת יִצְרוֹ עַל הַמָּמוֹן וְעַל שְׁאָר הַהֲנָאוֹת, אַךְ הַכָּבוֹד הוּא הַדּוֹחֵק, כִּי אִי אֶפְשָׁר לוֹ לִסְבּוֹל וְלִרְאוֹת אֶת עַצְמוֹ פָּחוּת מֵחֲבֵרָיו.

The desire for acclaim is even stronger than that of acquiring wealth. Even if a person could subdue his lust for money or various pleasures, the desire to be honored may pressure him, because it may be impossible to tolerate seeing oneself as being of a lesser status than one's peers.

Some people go through extensive training to achieve psychological acumen, and some people are simply endowed, probably from birth, with exquisite psychological insights. On the other hand, some of our great Torah personages received their enormous psychological insights from Torah, as is the case with Ramchal, whose knowledge of human nature is nothing less than astonishing.

In modern vernacular, we would say that there is no drive that is as intense and of as long duration as the preservation of one's ego. We can see this drive in operation in young children, and we can see it in full force at age one hundred, when all other lusts and pleasures have faded. Furthermore, if one reads Ramchal carefully, what he is saying is that although the desire for acquisition of wealth is strong enough in its own right, it is fueled and propelled even further by the ego factor, since having wealth has a social value that elevates one's ego.

Even more than money, the need for *kovod* (honor or acclaim) is insatiable, and the *kovod*-hungry person is supersensitive, taking everything as a slight. He is easily offended, and what others may think is a sign of esteem may actually be interpreted by him as derisive. Thus, if the committee arranging the seating at the banquet tries to show their esteem for him by placing him at table number one, the *kovod*-seeker may take offense because he was not seated at the head table with all the dignitaries.

When the Talmud cites "envy, desire, and acclaim" as the three drives that can shorten a person's life, it describes a mutually reinforcing trilogy. The envious person always desires what others have, and he is deeply offended if it appears to him that others are accorded more honor than he has received.

It is amazing how we can have a logical perception when observing others, yet totally lose it when it pertains to us. When seeing someone else exerting himself to be noticed and to receive honor, we may see how utterly ridiculous such behavior is, yet we may be completely unaware of this when we behave similarly. We may think that others are applauding us, when in truth they are laughing at how we have made fools of ourselves by manipulating our being "honored."

The desire to be applauded and praised, like any other desire, can "bribe" us so that we are blind to the truth. The solution to this is to make ourselves so unmoved by applause and praise that they have no effect on us.

The chassidic master, Rabbi Shmelke of Nikolsburg, once arrived in a town where he was greeted by a huge crowd of his followers and admirers. Before meeting the throng he asked for a few moments of privacy, and was given a small room. One of his followers was curious as to what the rabbi was doing in seclusion, and putting his ear to the door, he heard Rabbi Shmelke say, "Welcome, esteemed rabbi! It is such an honor to have you here," and "Shalom, our great leader! Your presence here is a blessing," and other such statements. Later, this follower admitted eavesdropping, and asked the rabbi for an explanation.

Rabbi Shmelke said, "I knew what my followers were going to say to me, and it is so easy for praise to go to one's head, giving rise to the abominable trait of vanity. Now, when you say such praises to yourself, they sound utterly stupid, and they cause no vanity whatever. I therefore said them to myself first, and realized how silly it all sounded. Then, when my followers said the same things, they had no impact upon me."

Rabbi Shmelke continued, "The Talmud says, 'Let your neighbor's honor be as dear to you as your own' (*Ethics of the Fathers* 2:13). Whereas the manifest meaning is that one should respect another person just as one wishes to be respected, it also can mean, 'Let the honor which you receive from others be as meaningless to you as the honor you give to yourself.' "

Many of our great Torah personages shunned honor, and were actually irritated by the praise and acclaim which fell to their lot as leaders. The Tzemach Tzedek of Lubavitch took his son and successor, the young Shmuel, on a trip to several towns where his followers greeted him with a royal welcome. The young Shmuel wrote home about the trip, and how his father was so highly honored. Upon returning home, the Tzemach Tzedek found the letter, and said to his son, "My blood was spilling like water, and you enjoyed it?"

The Tzemach Tzedek explained that a king once wished to personally observe the living conditions of his subjects, but he knew that his very presence would disrupt their normal behavior. He therefore disguised himself as an ordinary foot soldier and, accompanied by one of his officers, went through the kingdom. When people saw the officer, they politely arose and greeted him respectfully, paying no attention whatever to the soldier with him. The officer was greatly distressed that he was being honored while the disguised king was being ignored. "If only these people knew who is here with me, they would give him his due honor, and pay no attention to me."

The Tzemach Tzedek said, "If a person were aware, as one should always be, of the imminent presence of G-d everywhere, yet, because G-d cannot be seen, they honor a human being, this would cause great pain. Why do these foolish people pay respect to me, not realizing that they are in presence of the King of kings, to Whom all honor is due?"

While *kovod* is certainly alluring, a bit of reflection can deflate its enchanting but dangerous effects.

וְעַל דָּבָר זֶה נִכְשְׁלוּ רַבִּים וְנֶאֶבְדוּ. הִנֵּה יָרָבְעָם בֶּן נְבָט לֹא נִטְרַד . . . אֶלָּא בַּעֲבוּר הַכָּבוֹד (סנהדרין קב, א): . . . קֹרַח (במדבר טז, י) . . . הוּא שֶׁגָּרַם לְפִי דַּעַת חֲכָמֵינוּ ז״ל (זהר על במדבר יג, ג) אֶל הַמְרַגְּלִים שֶׁיּוֹצִיאוּ דִבָּה עַל הָאָרֶץ, וְגָרְמוּ מִיתָה לָהֶם וּלְכָל דּוֹרָם . . . שָׁאוּל . . . (שמואל א יח, ז) . . . יוֹאָב . . . (שמואל ב יט, יד).

The Scriptures and Talmud give many examples of how great people were destroyed because of their quest for kovod. Jerovam, the first king of the Ten Tribes (Sanhedrin 102a); Korach (Numbers 16:10); the spies sent by Moses (Zohar, Numbers 13:3), who caused not only their own death, but that of their entire generation; King Saul (I Samuel 18:7); and Joab (II Samuel 19:14).

Ramchal points out that even people of unquestioned greatness were not immune to the lure of *kovod*, and instead of receiving the praise they sought, it brought about their own destruction. There is simply no immunity, and the truly wise person who is aware of this treacherous lure will take measures to guard himself against it.

The Chafetz Chaim gave yet another reason for rejecting *kovod*. "The Talmud states that the reward for mitzvos is in the eternal world, and not in this earthly existence" (*Kiddushin* 39b). This is because a mitzvah is a spiritual entity, and all the vehicles for reward on this earthly world are of a physical character. Using physical items to reward a spiritual mitzvah is unjust; hence G-d saves the reward for mitzvos to be given in the wholly spiritual world.

"*Kovod*, however, is an intangible, and as such is more akin to something spiritual than something physical. *Kovod* can therefore be an appropriate reward for mitzvos. If one accepts *kovod*, he may be receiving his reward for his mitzvos in this transitory earthly existence, and arrive in the eternal world, empty handed and bereft of mitzvos."

כְּלָלוֹ שֶׁל דָּבָר, הַכָּבוֹד הוּא הַדּוֹחֵק אֶת לֵב הָאָדָם יוֹתֵר מִכָּל הַתְּשׁוּקוֹת וְהַחֲמָדוֹת שֶׁבָּעוֹלָם. וְלוּלֵי זֶה, כְּבָר הָיָה הָאָדָם מִתְרַצֶּה לֶאֱכוֹל מַה שֶּׁיּוּכַל, לִלְבּוֹשׁ מַה שֶּׁיְּכַסֶּה עֶרְוָתוֹ, וְלִשְׁכּוֹן בְּבַיִת שֶׁתַּסְתִּירֵהוּ מִן הַפְּגָעִים וְהָיְתָה פַּרְנָסָתוֹ קַלָּה עָלָיו וְלֹא הָיָה צָרִיךְ לְהִתְיַגֵּעַ לְהַעֲשִׁיר כְּלָל, אֶלָּא שֶׁלְּבִלְתִּי רְאוֹת עַצְמוֹ שָׁפָל וּפָחוּת מֵרֵעָיו מַכְנִיס עַצְמוֹ בְּעָבְיֵי הַקּוֹרָה הַזֹּאת וְאֵין קֵץ לְכָל עֲמָלוֹ . . . כַּמָּה הֵם שֶׁמִּתְעַנִּים בָּרָעָב וְיַשְׁפִּילוּ אֶת עַצְמָם לְהִתְפַּרְנֵס מִן הַצְּדָקָה וְלֹא יִתְעַסְּקוּ בִּמְלָאכָה שֶׁלֹּא תִּהְיֶה מְכֻבֶּדֶת בְּעֵינֵיהֶם מִיִּרְאָתָם פֶּן יִמְעַט כְּבוֹדָם. הֲיֵשׁ לְךָ הוֹלֵלוּת גָּדוֹל מִזֶּה? וְיוֹתֵר יִרְצוּ בְּבַטָּלָה הַמְּבִיאָה לִידֵי שִׁעֲמוּם וְלִידֵי זִמָּה וְלִידֵי גָּזֵל וְלִידֵי כָּל גּוּפֵי עֲבֵרוֹת שֶׁלֹּא לְהַשְׁפִּיל מַעֲלָתָם וּלְהַבְזוֹת כְּבוֹדָם הַמְדֻמֶּה . . . וְאָמְרוּ עוֹד (פסחים קיג, א): ,,פְּשׁוֹט נְבֵילְתָא בְּשׁוּקָא וְלָא תֵּימַר, גַּבְרָא רַבָּא אֲנָא, כַּהֲנָא אֲנָא״.

To summarize, kovod can pressure a person into many earthly pursuits, and if not for kovod, many people might make peace with eating ordinary foods, dressing modestly, and living in quarters adequate to provide shelter. One's efforts at earning a livelihood would then be few and simple, and one would not have to exert himself to acquire wealth. It is only because of the drive not to be thought of as inferior to others that people so exhaust themselves ... How many people deprive themselves of essentials and even accept charity, because they do not wish to stoop to work that is beneath their dignity. It is not beyond some people to even cheat and steal rather than to do honest work which they consider unbefitting them. Yet our sages say, "It is preferable to skin hides in the marketplace rather than to assert one's scholarship and say, 'I deserve to be respected'" (Pesachim 113a).

The greatness of a literary work is that it is not restricted to any period of time. Some classical works are of historical interest only, but have no practical application. Not so with the works such as *Mesillas Yesharim,* which is as relevant today as when Ramchal authored it.

The absurdity of accepting charity and living off the dole rather than doing honest work is not appreciated today anymore than it was hundreds of years ago. True self-respect would result in a person supporting himself rather than being dependent on others. That a person can have such grossly perverted values to consider living off the dole as more honorable than any kind of work is an example of how distorted our thinking can be.

The Talmud says, "Love work, and despise positions of authority" (*Ethics of the Fathers* 1:9). Many of the Talmudic sages, the greatest of the great, earned their livelihood by honest labor: Hillel, a woodchopper; Rabbi Yochanan, a cobbler; Rabbi Joshua, a blacksmith; Abba Chilkiyah, a hired day-worker, to name just a few.

It is tragic that some people have their priorities so utterly mixed up.

כְּלָל הַדְּבָרִים, הַכָּבוֹד הוּא מִן הַמִּכְשׁוֹלוֹת הַיּוֹתֵר גְּדוֹלִים אֲשֶׁר לָאָדָם. וְאִי אֶפְשָׁר לוֹ לִהְיוֹת עֶבֶד נֶאֱמָן לְקוֹנוֹ כָּל זְמַן שֶׁהוּא חָס עַל כְּבוֹד עַצְמוֹ, כִּי עַל־כָּל־פָּנִים יִצְטָרֵךְ לְמַעֵט בִּכְבוֹד שָׁמַיִם מִפְּנֵי סִכְלוּתוֹ . . . וְהַכָּבוֹד הָאֲמִתִּי אֵינוֹ אֶלָּא יְדִיעַת הַתּוֹרָה בֶּאֱמֶת . . . וְזוּלָתָהּ אֵינוֹ אֶלָּא כָּבוֹד מְדֻמֶּה וְכוֹזֵב, הֶבֶל וְאֵין בּוֹ מוֹעִיל. וְרָאוּי הַנָּקִי לְהִנָּקוֹת וּלְהִטָּהֵר מִמֶּנּוּ טָהֳרָה גְמוּרָה, אָז יַצְלִיחַ.

Finally, one cannot be a true servant of G-d as long as one is preoccupied with one's own kovod, because this will invariably lead to diminishing the true kovod one should render to G-d ... True kovod consists of knowing and observing the Torah ... and all else that people consider kovod is but a delusion, a worthless emptiness. One should therefore thoroughly cleanse oneself of pursuit of kovod.

וְהִנֵּה כָּלַלְתִּי עַד הֵנָּה רַבִּים מִפְּרָטֵי הַנְּקִיּוּת. וְזֶה בִּנְיַן אָב לְכָל שְׁאָר הַמִּצְוֹת וְהַמִּדּוֹת כֻּלָּם.

While I cited a number of details of Nekiyus, the wise person will apply these principles to all other mitzvos.

וְהִנֵּה אֵינֶנִּי יָכוֹל לְהַכְחִישׁ שֶׁיֵּשׁ קְצָת טֹרַח לָאָדָם לְהַגִּיעַ אֶל הַנְּקִיּוּת הַזֶּה. אַף־עַל־פִּי־כֵן אוֹמֵר אֲנִי שֶׁאֵין צָרִיךְ כָּל כָּךְ כְּמוֹ שֶׁנִּרְאֶה לִכְאוֹרָה וְהַמַּחֲשָׁבָה בַּדָּבָר הַזֶּה קָשָׁה מִן הַמַּעֲשֶׂה, כִּי כַּאֲשֶׁר יָשִׂים הָאָדָם בְּלִבּוֹ וְיִקְבַּע בִּרְצוֹנוֹ בִּקְבִיעוּת לִהְיוֹת מִבַּעֲלֵי הַמִּדָּה הַטּוֹבָה הַזֹּאת, בִּמְעַט הֶרְגֵּל שֶׁיַּרְגִּיל עַצְמוֹ בָּזֶה, תָּשׁוּב לוֹ קַלָּה הַרְבֵּה יוֹתֵר מִמַּה שֶּׁהָיָה יָכוֹל לַחֲשׁוֹב.

There is no denying that achievement of Nekiyus may call for some effort. Nevertheless, it is not as formidable as it seems, and the contemplation of Nekiyus is more difficult than its actual implementation. If one sets one's mind to achieve this admirable trait, just a bit of practice will make it much easier than one thinks it to be.

In his famous letter to his son, Ramban cites the verse in *Psalms* 93:1, "G-d reigned, adorned with splendor," and states that *kovod* or splendor is a Divine garment, and it is forbidden for a subject to wear the royal robes. To do so is to offend the honor of the king. Ramchal approaches this theme from another aspect. Anyone who is in pursuit of *kovod* may be so dominated by this drive that if a conflict occurs, he will sacrifice the Divine honor in order to attain his own. Anytime one behaves improperly, particularly if one represents Torah observance, this constitutes an insult to the Divine honor, as we have noted in our discussion of *chilul Hashem*. The pitfalls in the relentless pursuit of *kovod* are many.

In the final chapter of the Torah, Moses states that the observance of all the Divine commandments, although it may appear to be a tall order and very demanding, is in fact not difficult at all (*Deuteronomy* 30:11-14). Ramchal echoes this, and points out that while *Nekiyus* may appear to be formidable, it is rather easily achievable. As with so many other things the anticipation is far greater than the actuality.

In his guide to daily living, Rabbi Elimelech of Lizensk states that many habits can be overcome simply by making an effort to do otherwise for thirty consecutive days. It is often a question of overcoming inertia, and many resistances can be worn away with just a bit of concerted and consistent effort. If we only give some thought as to how much we exert ourselves, day in and day out, for goals of questionable value, we may realize that we would do well to make at least some investment in furthering our spirituality.

12

בְּדַרְכֵי קְנִיַּת הַנְּקִיּוּת

Ways in Which to Acquire Nekiyus

הִנֵּה הָאֶמְצָעִי הָאֲמִתִּי לִקְנוֹת הַנְּקִיּוּת, הוּא הַתְמָדַת הַקְּרִיאָה בְּדִבְרֵי חֲכָמִים ז״ל, אִם בְּעִנְיָנֵי הַהֲלָכוֹת וְאִם בְּעִנְיָנֵי הַמּוּסָרִים. כִּי הִנֵּה אַחַר שֶׁכְּבָר הִתְאַמֵּת אֵצֶל הָאָדָם חוֹבַת הַנְּקִיּוּת וְהַצֹּרֶךְ בּוֹ, אַחַר שֶׁכְּבָר הִשִּׂיג הַזְּהִירוּת וְהַזְּרִיזוּת בְּמַה שֶּׁנִּתְעַסֵּק בְּדַרְכֵי קְנִיָּתָם וְהִתְרַחֵק מִמַּפְסִידֵיהֶם, הִנֵּה לֹא יִשָּׁאֲרוּ לוֹ עַתָּה עִכּוּבִים לִקְנוֹת הַנְּקִיּוּת אֶלָּא יְדִיעַת הַדִּקְדּוּקִים אֲשֶׁר בַּמִּצְוֹת, כְּדֵי שֶׁיּוּכַל לְהִזָּהֵר בְּכֻלָּם.

וְעַל כֵּן הִנֵּה צָרִיךְ לוֹ בְּהֶכְרֵחַ יְדִיעַת הַהֲלָכוֹת עַל בֻּרְיָם, לָדַעַת עַנְפֵי הַמִּצְוֹת . . . וְכֵן בְּעִנְיַן הַמִּדּוֹת מֻכְרַחַת לוֹ קְרִיאַת מַאַמְרֵי הַמּוּסָר לַקַּדְמוֹנִים אוֹ לָאַחֲרוֹנִים . . . כִּי בִּהְיוֹת שִׂכְלוֹ נֵעוֹר עַל הַדָּבָר, הוֹלֵךְ וּמַשְׁגִּיחַ הוּא עַל כָּל־הַצְּדָדִין וּמַמְצִיא עִנְיָנִים חֲדָשִׁים מִמְּקוֹר הָאֱמֶת.

The true means to acquire Nekiyus is through regular study of the halachic and ethical works of the sages. Once a person has accepted the need for Nekiyus and has completed the first two steps of Watchfulness and Zerizus, there is nothing that stands in his way to acquiring Nekiyus . . .

All he needs is the necessary information about the mitzvos . . .

This holds equally true for Nekiyus of traits as well as deeds . . . Once his mind is alerted, he will find new concepts from the source of truth.

The Talmud says, "Let a person learn Torah and perform mitzvos even if he does not have the finest motivations, because doing the mitzvos and studying the Torah will bring about the desirable motivation" (*Pesachim* 50b). The logic behind this is that often the resistance to study of Torah and performance of mitzvos stems from the inconveniences and deprivation of gratification that these may cause. It is understandable that a person may not be highly motivated to do things that are unpleasant. However, if one makes a true commitment to observe Torah and mitzvos come what may, and accepts whatever inconveniences and deprivation of gratifications these may cause, proper motivation eventually results. Having decided to observe Torah and mitzvos at any cost, and knowing that these are the Divine will which will bring him into a closer relationship with G-d, the motivation of doing them for the latter reason is certain to develop.

Once the resistances to actions are overcome, all that one needs to develop the purest of motivations is the awareness of their enormous importance, and how fulfilling the Divine will not only comprises the essence of man's existence, but is the ultimate reason for creation. Since G-d is pleased by our observance of His Torah, one can take pleasure in the knowledge that one is bringing pleasure to G-d. Since pleasing G-d is in itself a mitzvah, we now receive: (1) the merit of the mitzvos; (2) the merit of pleasing G-d by doing His will; (3) providing G-d with additional reason to reward one's behavior and to exercise His benevolence; (4) an additional mitzvah of enabling G-d to reward one's actions, which is pleasing to Him. Hence, a self-reinforcing, infinite cycle can develop with performance of each mitzvah. The more a person gains understanding into the Divine will, as is contained in both *halachah* and ethics, the more intensely will he develop the ideal motivation, which is essential for *Nekiyus*.

13

בְּבֵאוּר מִדַּת הַפְּרִישׁוּת

Clarifying the Trait of Abstinence

If the first three traits stood independently, one might well consider that one who has successfully mastered Watchfulness and thereby avoids transgressing any Scriptural or rabbinic ordinance, and who has also mastered *Zerizus*, and is enthusiastic and diligent in performance of all mitzvos, such a person is indeed in full compliance of Torah. If one has proceeded beyond that and has also mastered *Nekiyus* and cleansed oneself of all the sources that could possibly eventuate in laxity of Torah observance, then one has indeed achieved a very high level of spirituality.

But these three traits do not stand alone, and are but the first three of ten steps toward spirituality; hence we may conclude that even after mastering Watchfulness, *Zerizus*, and *Nekiyus*, one has not yet even reached the halfway mark! We should therefore not be surprised by Ramchal's next remark:

הַפְּרִישׁוּת הוּא תְחִלַּת הַחֲסִידוּת. וְתִרְאֶה שֶׁכָּל מַה שֶּׁבֵּאַרְנוּ עַד עַתָּה הוּא מַה שֶּׁמִּצְטָרֵךְ אֶל הָאָדָם לְשֶׁיִּהְיֶה צַדִּיק וּמִכָּאן וּלְהָלְאָה הוּא לְשֶׁיִּהְיֶה חָסִיד.

Abstinence is the beginning of Chassidus. (At this time we will translate Chassidus as "saintliness," and we will elaborate on this later.) All that has been explained up to this point are the basic requirements for being a righteous person, and from here on we will discuss the requirements for saintliness.

Achievement of Watchfulness, *Zerizus*, and *Nekiyus* only qualifies one as a "righteous" person, but one has not even begun to enter the realm of *Chassidus* or saintliness!

It is interesting to note the consensus of many ethical works. Rabbi Shneur Zalman in *Tanya* describes the rather stringent requirements of achieving total self-mastery, which calls for complete dominance of the *yetzer tov* over the *yetzer hara* in thought, word, and deed. Yet, the subtitle of *Tanya* is "*The Book of the Average Person.*" To these ethicists, someone whom we might consider to be an extraordinary *tzaddik* is in fact just an average person, one who is fulfilling the minimum requirements for Torah observance.

Why go on then? It would seem that we would be fortunate enough to even get anywhere near successful achievement of Watchfulness, *Zerizus*, and *Nekiyus*. Is it realistic to expect more of ourselves?

A chassidic master asked one of his followers what his goal in life was, and the latter responded, "To be a good Jew." The master shook his head. "If you aspire to be a great *tzaddik*, perhaps you will ultimately become a good Jew. If all you aspire to is to be a good Jew, you may fall far short of that." In other words, one should aspire for the highest.

We may understand this by comparing spiritual aspirations to economic aspirations. A person who has a goal to become wealthy generally sets his sights on great wealth, hoping to become a multimillionaire, and exerts himself accordingly, looking for various ways in which to make his fortune. There may be factors that prevent his grandiose plans from materializing, and not all of his endeavors may succeed, but he may achieve sufficient success in some of them to become moderately wealthy. However, if his aspirations are only to achieve the goal of an average income, the various factors that may interfere with these plans may cause him to achieve less than the average person.

So it is with spiritual aspirations. There are numerous factors that can interfere with one's strivings for spirituality. If one sets one's goals high and aims for the ultimate, then even if one should fall short of the goal, one achieves at least the average. If one aspires only to the average, then the deterrents may well leave one grossly lacking in basic spirituality.

וְהִנֵּה כְּלַל הַפְּרִישׁוּת הוּא מַה שֶּׁאָמְרוּ ז״ל (יבמות כ, א): ,,קַדֵּשׁ עַצְמְךָ בַּמֻּתָּר לָךְ״ . . . וְהַכַּוָּנָה בָּזֶה לְשֶׁלֹּא יִפְגַּע בָּאִסּוּר עַצְמוֹ וְהָעִנְיָן, שֶׁכָּל דָּבָר שֶׁיּוּכַל לְהִוָּלֵד מִמֶּנּוּ גְּרָמַת רָע . . . לְהַנִּיחַ מִן הַהֶתֵּרִים עַצְמָם שֶׁלֹּא נֶאֶסְרוּ לְכָל יִשְׂרָאֵל וְלִפְרוֹשׁ מֵהֶם כְּדֵי שֶׁיִּהְיֶה מְרֻחָק מִן הָרָע הֶרְחֵק גָּדוֹל.

The concept of abstinence is based on the Talmudic precept, "Sanctify yourself even with that which is permissible." (Yevamos 20a) . . . In other words, not only must one abstain from that which is forbidden, but one should also restrict oneself from certain things that are permissible . . . The reason for this is that partaking of that which is permissible may indirectly cause transgression of a prohibition.

Again, the similarities between Ramchal and Rabbi Shneur Zalman are striking. The latter said, "That which is forbidden, is, of course, prohibited. But much of what is permissible is unnecessary."

Ramban considers "sanctifying oneself in what is permissible" as being not a characteristic of saintliness, but actually a Scriptural requirement, contained within the commandment "You shall be holy" (*Leviticus* 19:2). He points out that a person may be in full technical compliance with all Torah ordinances, yet be vulgar and indulgent.

Perhaps never before in Jewish history was Ramban's teaching as relevant as in modern times. Until fairly recently, people who observed *kashrus* had, as a rule, a rather austere diet. I recall as a child that there were two types of wines available: sweet wine, and wine without sugar, primarily used by people who had to restrict their sugar intake. Kosher wines were not for the connoisseur. How different things are today, with a variety of strictly kosher wines available that can satisfy even the most discriminating palate. The same is true of almost all foods, so that virtually every non-kosher product has a kosher counterpart, under supervision that satisfies even the most observant person. It is indeed possible for someone to be meticulously observant of *kashrus* and yet have at his disposal an abundance of ethnic foods and gourmet delights that enable one to be physically indulgent.

Spiritual achievements and physical delights are at opposite poles. Spirituality requires simplicity, using the goods of the world for survival and optimal function, to enable a person to pursue the ultimate goal in life: service of G-d. A healthy diet which provides adequate nutrition is essential, but titillating the palate with delicacies is not. Thus, if one is seriously interested in the pursuit of spirituality, one should be satisfied with the essentials of life, and forego all unessential excesses and luxuries.

We will recall that in his introduction, Ramchal was extremely critical of what he referred to as gross misconceptions of piety and saintliness, and he discouraged practices of fasting and self-flagellation as being foolish. In this chapter, his advocacy of abstinence would seem to contradict this previous position. Ramchal therefore goes on to explain.

וְאִם תֹּאמַר, מִנַּיִן לָנוּ לִהְיוֹת מוֹסִיפִים וְהוֹלְכִים בָּאִסּוּרִים, וַהֲרֵי חֲכָמֵינוּ ז״ל אָמְרוּ (ירושלמי נדרים ט, א): ,,לֹא דַיְּךָ מַה שֶּׁאָסְרָה תּוֹרָה, שֶׁאַתָּה בָא לֶאֱסוֹר עָלֶיךָ דְּבָרִים אֲחֵרִים?״ וַהֲרֵי מַה שֶּׁרָאוּ חֲכָמֵינוּ ז״ל בְּחָכְמָתָם שֶׁצָּרִיךְ לֶאֱסוֹר וְלַעֲשׂוֹת מִשְׁמֶרֶת כְּבָר עָשׂוּהוּ . . . וְלָמָּה נְחַדֵּשׁ עַתָּה גְּזֵרוֹת אֲשֶׁר לֹא רָאוּ הֵם לִגְזוֹר אוֹתָם? וְעוֹד, שֶׁאֵין גְּבוּל לַדָּבָר הַזֶּה . . . וַחֲכָמֵינוּ ז״ל אָמְרוּ (ירושלמי קדושין ד, יב), שֶׁעָתִיד אָדָם לִתֵּן דִּין לִפְנֵי הַמָּקוֹם עַל כָּל מַה שֶּׁרָאוּ עֵינָיו וְלֹא רָצָה לֶאֱכוֹל מִמֶּנּוּ אַף־עַל־פִּי שֶׁהָיָה מֻתָּר לוֹ וְהָיָה יָכוֹל.

You might ask, What basis is there for adding on restrictions? Our sages remark (in regard to someone who has taken an oath to abstain from wine or meat), "Are the Torah prohibitions not enough for you, that you have added on more?" (Talmud Yerushalmi, Nedarim 9:1). It would seem that our sages provided sufficient protective ordinances . . . so why do you have to improve upon them? Furthermore, what limits are there to self-imposed restrictions? . . . Does not the Talmud state that a person will be held accountable on Judgment Day for not partaking of the goods of the world? (Talmud Yerushalmi, Kiddushin 4:12).

Ramchal addresses the apparent conflict by pointing out that there are differing opinions in the Talmud which at first appear to be in disaccord, and the resolution of these will serve to reconcile his two apparent opposite statements.

In the Torah we find a provision for the vow of the Nazirite, whose oath includes, among other things, total abstention from grapes and wine, and his period of abstinence is followed by a ritual which includes shaving one's head and bringing sacrificial offerings. One opinion considers the Nazirite to be sacred for having taken this restrictive oath, while another considers him to be sinful for unnecessarily denying himself of something which G-d gave man to enjoy.

The reconciliation is found in the account of the High Priest, Shimon the *Tzaddik*, who saw a young man with attractive long hair, flowing over his shoulders in beautiful locks, approaching the Temple for the rituals of a nazirite. "What prompted you to take an oath that would result in shaving your beautiful hair?" he asked.

The young man answered, "One day I noted my reflection in the water, and seeing how handsome I was, I was tempted to sin. I knew the *yetzer hara* was luring me to sin, and I exclaimed, 'I swear to G-d that I will shave my head in His service.' " The high priest kissed him and said, "You are truly a sacred nazirite."

This young man's self-deprivation had a specific purpose. He did not think that by taking this vow he would become a "super *tzaddik*." Rather, he felt himself extremely vulnerable to sin and took a drastic step to avoid being entrapped by the *yetzer hara*.

The Baal Shem Tov supported Ramchal's position of discouraging mortification of the flesh. Self-deprivation carries a risk that the person may feel he has sacrificed so much for G-d that he is indeed a *tzaddik*, and this may result in vanity, which is the worst sin of all. One of the chassidic masters said, "I actually prefer a *rasha* (sinful person) who knows he is a *rasha*, to a *tzaddik* who knows he is a *tzaddik*." Abstinence is thus not without pitfalls.

The *Talmud Yerushalmi* requires a person to partake of the Divine bounty, but to do so with the realization that it is a Divine gift and to be grateful for it. Thus, a person who eats tasty food, and pronounces the *berachah* (blessing) with proper *kavannah* (concentration) and afterwards recites the closing *berachah* with gratitude toward G-d is converting eating into a mitzvah. Unless one has an appropriate reason for denying oneself that which G-d has provided, one should not do so.

וּנְבָאֵר עַתָּה הַפְּרִישׁוּת הַטּוֹב וְנֹאמַר, כִּי הִנֵּה אַחַר שֶׁהִתְבָּאֵר לָנוּ הֱיוֹת כָּל עִנְיָנֵי הָעוֹלָם נִסְיוֹנוֹת לָאָדָם, וּכְמוֹ שֶׁכָּתַבְנוּ כְּבָר לְמַעְלָה וְהוֹכַחְנוּהוּ בִּרְאָיוֹת וְהִתְאַמֵּת לָנוּ גַּם כֵּן רוֹב חֻלְשַׁת הָאָדָם וְקִרְבַת דַּעְתּוֹ אֶל הָרָעוֹת . . . כָּל־שֶׁכֵּן שֶׁבִּהְיוֹת הָאָדָם מַרְגִּיל עַצְמוֹ לִשְׂבֹּעַ מֵאֲכִילָה וּשְׁתִיָּה, הִנֵּה אִם פַּעַם אַחַת יֶחְסַר לוֹ רְגִילוּתוֹ, יִכְאַב לוֹ וְיַרְגִּישׁ מְאֹד וּמִפְּנֵי זֶה נִמְצָא הוּא מַכְנִיס עַצְמוֹ בְּתֹקֶף עֲמַל הַסְּחוֹרָה וִיגִיעַת הַקִּנְיָן לְשֶׁתִּהְיֶה שֻׁלְחָנוֹ עֲרוּכָה כִּרְצוֹנוֹ וּמִשָּׁם נִמְשָׁךְ אֶל הָעָוֶל וְהַגָּזֵל וּמִשָּׁם אֶל הַשְּׁבוּעוֹת וְכָל שְׁאָר הַחֲטָאִים הַבָּאִים אַחַר זֶה.

Abstinence may be praiseworthy. We have noted earlier that many worldly experiences are trials and temptations, and that a person may be very vulnerable to these . . . A person may increase his vulnerability, as for example, if a person becomes so accustomed to good wine and tasty delicacies that he becomes dependent upon them and they become necessities for him instead of dispensable luxuries. Should something happen whereby he could not afford these, he may be driven to do things that are forbidden in order to satisfy his wants.

One might think that Ramchal had extensive experience with treating drug addiction and alcoholism, because he is giving a very graphic description of addiction. If a person develops a dependence on anything—food, alcohol, tobacco, drugs, designer clothes—he may take desperate measures to obtain the objects he craves. Cigarette addicts have been known to walk long distances in a scathing blizzard to get a pack of cigarettes. Narcotic addicts, whose drugs are very costly, may stop at nothing to get their drug, and will write bad checks, cheat, lie, rob, and steal to get money to finance their habit.

It is understandable that people may take desperate measures to get the bare necessities of life, whereas we should be able to dispense with non-essential luxuries. But whether some things are necessities or luxuries is highly relative.

I recall after World War II, when some of the survivors of the Holocaust came to Israel (then Palestine), there were appeals to send clothing and whatever money one could spare for these people who had lost everything. Our congregation undertook a campaign to gather used clothing and ship it to these people, who had escaped the Holocaust with nothing but their lives. We once received a "Thank You" letter from one of the recipients, and it was written on personalized stationery.

I was appalled. Someone who has nothing and is in need of used clothing can afford to have personalized stationery printed! I commented on this to my father, who told me that he recognized the name of this person, who was a member of a very wealthy family in prewar Poland. "You must understand," he said, "that for her, personalized stationery was taken for granted as an essential of life, along with bread and water. It was simply unthinkable not to have your own stationery. She did not consider this a luxury."

If we only think of it, we will realize that this attitude is quite prevalent. Some people may recall that in the late-1940s air-conditioning was a rarity. In fact, on very hot days, some people would go to a theater because these were the only places that had air-conditioning. Only the wealthiest of families could afford this extravagance in their homes. As time went on, air-conditioning became so widespread that it is no longer considered a luxury. No one would criticize a family living on charity for having an air-conditioner. This phenomenon is equally true of many other technological advances. A family subsisting on public funds is not considered to be misusing their allotment because they have a car, a television, or even a microwave oven. At the time of this writing, it would be considered inappropriate if they were to have a cellular phone, but it is only a matter of time before that too will become a necessity rather than a dispensable luxury.

A person who wishes to devote his life to the study of Torah and performance of mitzvos may decide that he does not wish to be distracted by increasing demands for income that would allow him a higher standard of living. We are told that if we have *bitachon*, trust in G-d, then He will provide for us. "He gives bread to all flesh, for His kindness is eternal" (*Psalms* 136:25). The Divine promise is for bread, not for caviar. Hence, one should limit the time devoted to making money to that which is essential for the necessities of life. It is related that the Chafetz Chaim supported himself and his family through a small shop which his wife tended while he studied Torah. She was instructed that as soon as she had earned enough for that day's provisions, she was to close the shop. Living a most austere life, this great sage lived to be almost one hundred, and benefited the world with his great works of *halachah* and *mussar*. The Chafetz Chaim and many of our great Torah personages adhered to the teachings of *Ethics of the Fathers* (6:4): "This is the way to acquire Torah. Eat bread with salt, drink water by the measure, and sleep on the ground." An austere life is conducive to study of Torah.

Just as the alcoholic cannot see that he has become dependent on alcohol and that his dependency can be ruinous, so are many people unaware that they have developed a lifestyle which may be detrimental, whether this is in order to satisfy their desires for greater comfort and pleasure, or to "keep up with the Joneses." In either case, pure intellect does not rule, and our desires influence our thinking so that we rationalize why we must have things that are in fact not essential to our optimal functioning. A bit of honest reflection will reveal the validity of this.

The person who wishes to avoid the pitfall of dependency and the conversion of luxuries to necessities may take the precaution of leading an austere life. He does not think that by doing so he is a great *tzaddik*, and his austerity does not result in vanity. To him, this is a reasonable decision, just as someone would avoid beginning to smoke cigarettes because of the awareness that it will likely become a habit which will dominate him. Like the nazirite praised by the High Priest, this austere life is a protective measure that has a well-defined purpose, and this type of abstinence is commendable.

הַמַּלְבּוּשִׁים וְהַקִּשּׁוּטִים לֹא הִזְהִירָה הַתּוֹרָה עַל יָפְיָם אוֹ עַל תַּבְנִיתָם, אֶלָּא שֶׁלֹּא יִהְיֶה בָּהֶם כִּלְאַיִם וְיִהְיֶה בָּהֶם צִיצִית וְאָז כֻּלָּם מֻתָּרִים. אָמְנָם, מִי לֹא יֵדַע שֶׁמַּלְבִּישַׁת הַפְּאֵר וְהָרִקְמָה תִּמָּשֵׁךְ הַגַּאֲוָה וְגַם הַזְּנוּת יִגְבַּל בָּהּ, מִלְּבַד הַקִּנְאָה וְהַתַּאֲוָה, וְהָעֹשֶׁק הַנִּמְשָׁכִים מִכָּל מַה שֶּׁהוּא יָקָר עַל אָדָם לְהַשִּׂיגוֹ . . . הַטִּיּוּל וְהַדִּיבּוּר אִם אֵינוֹ בִּדְבַר אִסּוּר, וַדַּאי דִּין תּוֹרָה מֻתָּר הוּא, אָמְנָם כַּמָּה בִּטּוּל תּוֹרָה נִמְשָׁךְ מִמֶּנּוּ, כַּמָּה מִן הַלָּשׁוֹן הָרָע, כַּמָּה מִן הַשְּׁקָרִים, כַּמָּה מִן הַלֵּיצָנוּת.

The only Scriptural ordinances in regard to clothes are the prohibition of a mixture of linen and wool and the requirements for tzitzis on a four-cornered garment. However, it is clear that overindulgence in extravagant garments, while not explicitly prohibited, can lead to vanity (the worst of all character traits) as well as to envy and lust. Furthermore, when expensive clothes becomes a necessity, one may exploit others to acquire them . . .

While socializing is in itself permissible, how much neglect of study of Torah, let alone gossip, slander, lies, and levity, may arise from idle conversation.

Ramchal continues to point out that even after achievement of *Nekiyus* has eliminated temptation to sin, danger can lurk in many activities which are in themselves not sinful. For example, there is no need to wear extravagant clothes in order to keep warm, and one may be dressed very appropriately in modest clothes. One often dresses lavishly to impress others, and this behavior is both a symptom of vanity as well as being provocative of envy, both of which are adverse to spirituality. In addition, if costly clothing becomes an essential need, one may transgress Torah laws in order to acquire the means to obtain them.

Nowhere is the need for caution as great as in socializing. All ethical works emphasize the importance of taking an interest in other people, helping them when they are in need, providing moral and emotional support when possible, and engaging in activities to enhance the welfare of the community. All of these require association and communication with other people, and the various *mitzvos* of *gemilus chasadim* (acts of benevolence) are among the greatest Torah virtues.

However, association with others also provides the opportunity for some of the most grievous transgressions, such as *lashon hara* (slander or gossip) which the Talmud considers equivalent to the cardinal sins of idolatry, adultery, and murder. It also provides fertile grounds for telling lies or wasting precious time in idle talk, time which could otherwise be devoted to Torah study. Yet, few people may consider friendly associations as presenting these dangerous pitfalls.

The Chafetz Chaim once spent a Shabbos at an inn, and the host, not knowing the identity of the great sage, seated him among other guests at the inn, some of whom happened to be horse traders who dominated the conversation at the table with shoptalk. Instead of gracing the Shabbos table with the discussion of the weekly portion of the Torah, they talked incessantly about the horses they had bought or sold.

After Shabbos, someone apprised the innkeeper that he had hosted the Chafetz Chaim. The innkeeper apologized profusely to the great sage for the discourtesy of having seated him among people who talked about nothing other than horses all Shabbos long.

The Chafetz Chaim, who had spent a lifetime in a declared state of war on *lashon hara*, smiled and said, "My dear man, there is no need to apologize. Had these people talked about other people, I would have been subjected to overhearing *lashon hara*, which is so grave a sin. But being that they talked only about horses, why that was just wonderful."

I recall, as a child, that our Shabbos table was always graced with many guests. Occasionally, someone might begin to talk about another person, at which time my father would adroitly intervene and turn the conversation toward a neutral topic.

Socialization and communal participation are important, but we must be on the alert that they do not become a breeding grounds for social transgressions.

כְּלָל הַדָּבָר: כֵּיוָן שֶׁכָּל עִנְיְנֵי הָעוֹלָם אֵינָם אֶלָּא סַכָּנוֹת עֲצוּמוֹת אֵיךְ לֹא יְשֻׁבַּח מִי שֶׁיִּרְצֶה לְמַלֵּט מֵהֶם וּמִי שֶׁיַּרְבֶּה לְהַרְחִיק מֵהֶם. זֶהוּ עִנְיַן הַפְּרִישׁוּת הַטּוֹב, שֶׁלֹּא יִקַּח מִן הָעוֹלָם בְּשׁוּם שִׁמּוּשׁ שֶׁהוּא מִשְׁתַּמֵּשׁ מִמֶּנּוּ, אֶלָּא מַה שֶּׁהוּא מֻכְרָח בּוֹ מִפְּנֵי הַצֹּרֶךְ אֲשֶׁר לוֹ בְּטִבְעוֹ אֵלָיו. הוּא מַה שֶּׁהִשְׁתַּבַּח רַבִּי בְּמַאֲמָר שֶׁזָּכַרְתִּי, שֶׁלֹּא נֶהֱנָה מִן הָעוֹלָם הַזֶּה אֲפִילּוּ בְּאֶצְבַּע קְטַנָּה, עִם הֱיוֹתוֹ נְשִׂיא יִשְׂרָאֵל וְשֻׁלְחָנוֹ שֻׁלְחַן מְלָכִים בְּהֶכְרֵחַ לִיקַר נְשִׂיאוּתוֹ.

To summarize: Inasmuch as the dangers of being lured into worldly pleasures are great, we must commend one who seeks to distance himself from these as being praiseworthy. This type of abstinence is commendable and involves partaking of worldly goods only insofar as is necessary for optimum function. The Talmud relates that Rabbi Yehudah HaNasi, even though his official position required that his table be bedecked regally, stated that he personally did not derive enjoyment from even the least of worldly goods.

We must constantly refer back to the first chapter which deals with man's purpose in this world. If our focus is truly on this goal and it occupies a place of primacy in our lives, then we will engage in those activities which will enhance its achievement, and we will avoid being distracted by extraneous desires. For example, if someone were to run a race, his entire being is then occupied with the single aim of reaching the goal line, and if he were to observe a friend in the audience or pass by a vendor of tasty food, he would certainly not stop to converse with the friend or partake of the food, because this would cause him to lose the race. In fact, all his thoughts are directed on how he should pace himself to be the first to arrive at the goal line.

Ramchal posited the Torah concept on the purpose of man's existence in the first chapter, because all the steps of spiritual growth are derivatives of this principle. While there is no denying that there are very pleasurable diversions in life, the person who is truly goal oriented will not allow himself to be distracted by these diversions, pleasant as they may be, anymore than the participant in a race would stop on the way for pleasantries. The degree of abstinence one practices is therefore an indication of one's conviction of the purpose of existence and one's dedication to achieving that purpose.

וְאִם תִּשְׁאַל וְתֹאמַר: אִם כֵּן אֵפוֹא, שֶׁזֶּה דָבָר מִצְטָרֵךְ וּמֻכְרָח, לָמָּה לֹא גָזְרוּ עָלָיו הַחֲכָמִים כְּמוֹ שֶׁגָּזְרוּ עַל הַסְּיָגוֹת וְתַקָּנוֹת שֶׁגָּזְרוּ? הִנֵּה הַתְּשׁוּבָה מְבוֹאֶרֶת וּפְשׁוּטָה, כִּי לֹא גָזְרוּ חֲכָמִים גְּזֵרָה אֶלָּא אִם כֵּן רוֹב הַצִּבּוּר יְכוֹלִים לַעֲמוֹד בָּהּ (בבא קמא עט, ב), וְאֵין רוֹב הַצִּבּוּר יְכוֹלִים לִהְיוֹת חֲסִידִים, אֲבָל דַּי לָהֶם שֶׁיִּהְיוּ צַדִּיקִים. אַךְ הַשְּׂרִידִים אֲשֶׁר בָּעָם הַחֲפֵצִים לִזְכּוֹת לְקִרְבָתוֹ יִתְבָּרֵךְ וּלְזַכּוֹת בִּזְכוּתָם לְכָל שְׁאָר הֶהָמוֹן הַנִּתְלֶה בָם, לָהֶם מַגִּיעַ לְקַיֵּם מִשְׁנַת חֲסִידִים אֲשֶׁר לֹא יָכְלוּ לְקַיֵּם הָאֲחֵרִים . . . הִנֵּה לְפָחוֹת, יְחִידֵי סְגֻלָּה יִמָּצְאוּ אֲשֶׁר יָכִינוּ אֶת עַצְמָם הֲכָנָה גְמוּרָה וְעַל יְדֵי הַמּוּכָנִים יִזְכּוּ גַּם הַבִּלְתִּי מוּכָנִים אֶל אַהֲבָתוֹ יִתְבָּרֵךְ וְהַשְׁרָאַת שְׁכִינָתוֹ.

One may ask, Why did our sages not make abstinence mandatory? The answer is simple. Abstinence is a requirement for Chassidus, and it is not realistic to expect this of everyone. It suffices for the average person to master the requirements of being righteous (i.e., achieving Watchfulness, Zerizus, and Nekiyus), but Chassidus is for those individuals who wish to advance themselves toward a higher spiritual level ... and thereby help elevate the remainder of the populace to a higher level.

Ramchal establishes an important principle here. *The Torah does not demand anything of us that is beyond our means*. This was stated explicitly by Moses in his last words: "The Torah is not up in the sky nor across the sea where it is inaccessible, but very near to you, in your mouths and in your hearts to fulfill it" (*Deuteronomy* 30:11-14). While observance of Torah may sometimes appear to present a challenge, we must realize that it is a challenge that is well within our capacity to master.

The Talmud relates that a heathen who wished to embrace Judaism asked Hillel for a synopsis of the Torah, and the great sage responded, "Do not do to another what you would not wish to be done to you. This is the basis of Torah, and the remainder of the Torah is an expansion of this principle, which you must learn" (*Shabbos* 31a). It is clear that Hillel was referring to the Scriptural verse "Love another person as you do yourself" (*Leviticus* 19:18), which Rabbi Akiva cited as the all-encompassing rule of Torah (*Bereishis Rabbah* 24:7); yet whereas the Torah presents this in an active sense, i.e., love another person as you do yourself, which is interpreted secularly as the Golden Rule of "Do unto others as you would have others do unto you," Hillel interpreted this in a passive sense, i.e., do not do unto others that which you would not want done unto you. Why did Hillel make this interpretation?

It is likely that the heathen, who was accustomed to a lifestyle relatively free of any restrictions on one's behavior, perceived Judaism as being intolerably demanding: three hundred sixty-five Scriptural prohibitions and numerous rabbinic restrictive ordinances which affect virtually every facet of life! This appeared to be a bit much for someone contemplating conversion to Judaism, and perhaps beyond the capability of the average person to accomplish. Hillel therefore explained to him that the Torah does not expect the average individual to love another person as much as he does himself to the extent that he will exert himself as much for others as he would for himself. This might be expected of a *tzaddik*, but not of the average person. What is possible for everyone to achieve is a degree of restraint, i.e., *not* doing anything to another that one would not wish done to oneself. This, too, requires a fair amount of self-mastery, but is nevertheless well within every person's capacity to achieve. Similarly, although the many requirements of Torah might appear to be formidable to an outsider, Hillel informed the heathen that the observance of every Torah precept falls within the capacity of the average person.

Ramchal therefore states that whereas Watchfulness, *Zerizus* and *Nekiyus* are essential components of spirituality that are required of everyone, it is not realistic to expect everyone to advance to the spirituality of *Chassidus*; hence the sages did not make abstinence mandatory for everyone. The select few who wish to advance themselves to a higher level of spirituality, however, must practice abstinence and the subsequent steps.

A second important point raised by Ramchal is that although only a minority of people may actually attain the highest levels of spirituality, those that do so exert a positive influence on the population as a whole. In the presence of a *tzaddik*, one is inspired to emulate him. How fortunate we are to have lived in a generation which has been graced by the presence of Rabbi Yaakov Kaminetzky, whose personality was a rare combination of majesty and humility, and of Rabbi Moshe Feinstein, whose phenomenal mastery of Torah and unquestioned position as the *posek* (halachic authority) of the generation did not result in an iota of vanity, and of the Steipler Gaon, whose slightest move was calculated to be an implementation of *halachah*, and of others of their caliber, whose genuine caring for every single Jew inspired everyone with a feeling of worthiness and sanctity.

But the responsibility of being an inspiration to others is not restricted to the outstanding leaders of our people. Every person should strive to be an inspiration to his children and to his peers. One may not consider oneself as insignificant. Our ethicists tell us that every Jew is represented by a letter in the Torah, and if even a single letter is defective, the entire scroll is considered *posul* (unusable for communal reading). Although our sages did not make it mandatory, every person has the obligation to strive for the highest levels of spirituality.

אַךְ הַפְּרִישׁוּת הָרָע הוּא כְּדֶרֶךְ הַגּוֹיִם הַסְּכָלִים, אֲשֶׁר לֹא דַי שֶׁאֵינָם לוֹקְחִים מִן הָעוֹלָם מַה שֶּׁאֵין לָהֶם הֶכְרֵחַ בּוֹ, אֶלָּא שֶׁכְּבָר יִמְנְעוּ מֵעַצְמָם גַּם אֶת הֶמֻּכְרָח וְיַיַסְּרוּ גוּפָם בְּיִסּוּרִין וּדְבָרִים זָרִים אֲשֶׁר לֹא חָפֵץ בָּהֶם ה׳ כְּלָל, אֶלָּא אַדְּרַבָּא חֲכָמִים אָמְרוּ (תענית כב, ב): ,,אָסוּר לָאָדָם שֶׁיְּסַגֵּף עַצְמוֹ״ . . . וְהִלֵּל . . . וְהָיָה רוֹחֵץ פָּנָיו וְיָדָיו לִכְבוֹד קוֹנוֹ (ויקרא רבה לד, ג).

The undesirable type of abstinence is that practiced by some foolish people, who deprive themselves of even things that are essential for good health, and practice mortification of the flesh, something for which G-d has no desire. The Talmud states that it is forbidden for a person to torture himself (Taanis 22b). Hillel would tell his students that he eats and bathes out of respect and consideration for his person, which was created in the Divine Image (Vayikra Rabbah 34:3).

הֲרֵי לְךָ הַכְּלָל הָאֲמִתִּי, שֶׁכָּל מַה שֶּׁאֵינוֹ מֻכְרָח לָאָדָם בְּעִנְיָנֵי הָעוֹלָם הַזֶּה רָאוּי לוֹ שֶׁיִּפְרוֹשׁ מֵהֶם. וְכָל מַה שֶּׁהוּא מֻכְרָח לוֹ מֵאֵיזֶה טַעַם שֶׁיִּהְיֶה, כֵּיוָן שֶׁהוּא מֻכְרָח לוֹ, אִם הוּא פּוֹרֵשׁ מִמֶּנּוּ הֲרֵי זֶה חוֹטֵא. הִנֵּה זֶה כְּלָל נֶאֱמָן, אַךְ מִשְׁפַּט הַפְּרָטִים עַל פִּי הַכְּלָל הַזֶּה אֵינוֹ מָסוּר אֶלָּא אֶל שִׁקּוּל הַדַּעַת וּלְפִי שִׂכְלוֹ יְהֻלַּל אִישׁ.

The general rule is therefore that a person should abstain from nonessentials, but not deprive himself of that which is truly necessary. The application of this general principle to individual cases is a matter of individual judgment, and a person will be praised according to his understanding.

Although Ramchal reiterates his criticism of those who consider self-mortification as a method to acquire *Chassidus*, he does leave the door ajar to accommodate exceptions, and this is why he states that application of the general rule to individual cases requires careful judgment.

The Baal Shem Tov was an outspoken opponent of self-imposed fasting, yet it is known that he personally fasted frequently. When asked about this apparent contradiction, one of his disciples explained that when the Baal Shem Tov left his home for solitude and meditation in the woods, he would take food along, but when he returned home at night the food was untouched because he had simply forgotten to eat. In other words, he was so profoundly absorbed in meditation that he had not felt the need for food. This kind of fasting is permissible, in contrast to one who feels he is starving and considers himself saintly for making so great a sacrifice for G-d.

Rabbi Naftali of Ropschitz had no use for people who considered themselves to be *tzaddikim* because they tormented themselves. Once one of the *chassidim* brushed by a person who Rabbi Naftali felt was guilty of such a self-delusion, and Rabbi Naftali said, "Please have respect for that man. Why, he fasts every Monday and Thursday," whereupon the man turned around and said, "What do you mean every Monday and Thursday? I fast from one Shabbos to the next!" This is why one of the chassidic masters said that it is better to act as if one were fasting even if one was thereby deceiving others, rather than to actually fast and deceive oneself into thinking that one was therefore a *tzaddik*.

There may be isolated instances where it is appropriate to do acts of penance that are self-flagellating in nature, but one should do so only under the guidance of a recognized spiritual mentor. Many of the chassidic writings recommend that instead of fasting and making oneself hungry, one should increase one's *tzedakah* (charity) so that the poor do not go hungry. This is certainly wise advice.

14

בְּחֶלְקֵי הַפְּרִישׁוּת

Components of Abstinence

חֶלְקֵי הַפְּרִישׁוּת הָרָאשִׁיִּים שְׁלֹשָׁה. כִּי הִנֵּה יֵשׁ פְּרִישׁוּת בַּהֲנָאוֹת, פְּרִישׁוּת בַּדִּינִים, פְּרִישׁוּת בַּמִּנְהָגִים . . . וְהַפְּרִישׁוּת בַּדִּינִים הוּא לְהַחֲמִיר בָּהֶם תָּמִיד, לָחוּשׁ אֲפִילוּ לְדִבְרֵי יָחִיד בְּמַחֲלֹקֶת אִם טַעֲמוֹ נִרְאֶה אֲפִלּוּ שֶׁאֵין הֲלָכָה כְּמוֹתוֹ וּבִתְנַאי שֶׁלֹּא יִהְיֶה חֻמְרוֹ קֻלּוֹ, וּלְהַחֲמִיר בִּסְפֵקוֹת אֲפִילוּ בַּמָּקוֹם שֶׁאֶפְשָׁר לְהָקֵל בָּהֶם.

There are three principal aspects of Abstinence: Abstinence with regard to pleasures, which we have just discussed, Abstinence with regard to laws, and Abstinence with regard to conduct . . .

Abstinence with regard to laws refers to abstaining from things which have been ruled permissible, if any doubt as to their permissibility has been expressed. Even though the halachah has been established that something is permissible, if there is an opinion to the contrary, a person striving for Chassidus should avoid the more convenient alternative.

This requires some clarification. In the Talmud we find many discussions involving different opinions, some asserting certain things are permissible, others asserting they are not. Throughout the ages *halachah* has been established according to various later authorities, and the *Shulchan Aruch* (Code of Law) is the basic and essentially final *halachic* text. The *Shulchan Aruch* composed by Rabbi Joseph

Caro was accepted by the *Sephardic* Jews, whereas *Ashkenazic* Jews have accepted the amended version by Rabbi Moshe Isserles.

There was a period of about a thousand years between the time of the Talmud and that of Rabbi Moshe Isserles. Some *halachic* authorities feel that inasmuch as Rabbi Moshe Isserles had an exhaustive knowledge of all his predecessors' opinions, his rulings took these into consideration. Hence, they say, there is no reason to be any more stringent than Rabbi Isserles' rulings require, and even *Chassidus* does not require such Abstinence. Deferring to the more stringent opinion would apply only to those laws not ruled upon by Rabbi Moshe Isserles.

The reason why *Chassidus* requires Abstinence on issues where there have been divergent opinions can be understood if we consider how we act when there are different opinions concerning health issues. If a new product were to appear on the market — a food whose processing raised some controversy — the Food and Drug Administration may pronounce it to be safe, while several scientists may state that they are not sure of its safety. If the food is desirable, most people will assume it to be safe, and probably only a minority will avoid it. If the question, however, concerns the safety of a medication to be used during pregnancy, and there is a minority opinion that it may cause serious birth defects, it is likely that there will be much greater hesitation to its use. Why? Because the gravity of birth defects is so serious that people wish to avoid even the slightest risk.

The more a person is aware of the sensitivity of the *neshamah* and its being affected by something which is not *halachically* permissible, the greater is the extent that one will go to avoid even the slightest doubt. For this reason, people who strive for *Chassidus*, seeking perfection in spirituality, will abstain from something even if it has been declared *halachically* permissible, if there is any divergent opinion.

וְהַפְּרִישׁוּת בְּמִנְהָגִים הִיא הִתְבּוֹדְדוּת וְהַהִבָּדֵל מִן הַחֶבְרָה הַמְּדִינִית לְפַנּוֹת לִבּוֹ אֶל הָעֲבוֹדָה וְהַהִתְבּוֹנְנוּת בָּהּ כָּרָאוּי וּבִתְנַאי שֶׁלֹּא יִטֶּה גַם בָּזֶה אֶל הַקָּצֶה הָאַחֵר . . . אֶלָּא יִתְחַבֵּר הָאָדָם עִם הַטּוֹבִים זְמַן מַה שֶּׁמִּצְטָרֵךְ לוֹ לְלִמּוּדוֹ אוֹ לְפַרְנָסָתוֹ וְיִתְבּוֹדֵד אַחַר־כָּךְ לְהִדָּבֵק בֵּאלֹהָיו

Abstinence in conduct refers to secluding oneself from society in order to be able to devote oneself more fully to the Divine service and meditation. One should not go to an extreme of isolation, because one should relate to people . . .

However, one should seek association with upright people as is necessary for one's studies and livelihood, and thereafter one may seclude himself for the purpose of communing with G-d.

Ramchal discourages a monastic lifestyle, and urges that a person participate in improvement of the community as well as in earning a livelihood. However, one should avoid associating with people who may exert a negative influence on one's spirituality.

We hear a great deal about "peer pressure," and some people defend their behavior by saying that they do not wish to stand out as nonconformists. We must be extremely wary of such arguments, because they are often nothing but rationalizations. We can generally choose our associates and friends, and if we feel pressure, it may be because we have gravitated toward the wrong peer group. It is also possible to follow one's own course, which may vary with one's environment, without standing out as a nonconformist. However, in those situations where one's moral principles are at risk, one should not hesitate to adhere to what is right and proper, even if this should differ sharply with one's environs.

15

בְּדַרְכֵי קְנִיַּת הַפְּרִישׁוּת

Acquiring Abstinence

הִנֵּה הַדֶּרֶךְ הַמֻּבְחָר לִקְנוֹת אֶת הַפְּרִישׁוּת הוּא שֶׁיִּסְתַּכֵּל הָאָדָם בִּגְרִיעוּת תַּעֲנוּגוֹת הָעוֹלָם הַזֶּה וּפְחִיתוּתָם מִצַּד עַצְמָם וְהָרָעוֹת הַגְּדוֹלוֹת שֶׁקְּרוֹבוֹת לְהִוָּלֵד מֵהֶם. כִּי הִנֵּה מַה שֶּׁמַּטֶּה הַטֶּבַע אֶל הַתַּעֲנוּגוֹת הָאֵלֶּה עַד שֶׁיִּצְטָרֵךְ כָּל־כָּךְ כֹּחַ וְתַחְבֻּלוֹת לְהַפְּרִישׁוֹ מֵהֶם הוּא פִּתּוּי הָעֵינַיִם הַנִּפְתִּים בְּמַרְאֵה הַדְּבָרִים אֲשֶׁר הוּא טוֹב וְעָרֵב לִכְאוֹרָה . . . אֲבָל כְּשֶׁיִּתְבָּרֵר אֶל הָאָדָם הֱיוֹת הַטּוֹב הַהוּא כּוֹזֵב לְגַמְרֵי מְדֻמֶּה וּבְלִי שׁוּם הַתְמָדָה נְכוֹנָה, וְהָרַע בּוֹ אֲמִתִּי אוֹ קָרוֹב לְהִוָּלֵד מִמֶּנּוּ בֶּאֱמֶת, וַדַּאי שֶׁיִּמְאַס בּוֹ וְלֹא יִרְצֵהוּ כְּלָל;

The best way to acquire Abstinence is to reflect on the insignificance of worldly pleasures and the harm to which they may give rise. What inclines one's nature to these pleasures is the seduction of the senses that makes things seem so good and pleasant ... But if one could only realize that these are superficial appearances which are deceptive, that the good is illusory and at best transitory, and that the harm they are likely to bring in their wake is real and permanent, he is apt to reject these.

Oh, if only *sechel* (intelligence) would prevail! How different human behavior would be!

We watch an infant reach for something that he thinks is pleasant because it is colorful, and he may cry bitterly until he gets it, only to throw it away after a few moments. A small child may wail for ice cream before dinner, and a mother who is totally exhausted from the day's ordeals may throw in the towel and give in to the child, who then does not eat his supper, depriving himself of the essential nutrients for optimum growth. We readily recognize such behavior as juvenile, yet intelligent, mature adults often behave no differently.

Let's begin with an extreme example, the person who has a craving for cocaine, and goes for its euphoriant properties, rendering himself totally oblivious to its dangerous and even lethal effects, his Ph.D. and even Phi Beta Kappa Key notwithstanding. A less extreme and more common example is the learned scholar who puffs away at cigarettes, ignoring what every schoolchild knows, and placing his heart, lungs, and very life at risk for the momentary pleasure of smoking. An even more common example is a person who indulges in foods that are tasty, much to the detriment of his health, increasing his already excessive weight or aggravating his diabetes or high blood pressure. Application of *sechel* would prevent such self-destructive behavior, but even mature, erudite adults, some of whom may consider themselves to be spiritual, behave in so foolish a manner.

The only conclusion one can come to is that seduction of the senses is overpowering, often totally disarming one's intelligence. Ramchal therefore emphasizes that we must energize and reinforce the *sechel* and implement it, in order to recognize the illusory nature of what appears to be pleasant, and to act according to a truly mature understanding of what is the real good.

כָּל־שֶׁכֵּן אִם יָשִׂים אֶל לִבּוֹ הֶחֳלָאִים הָרַבִּים שֶׁיְּכוֹלִים לָבוֹא עָלָיו מֵחֲמַת אֲכִילָתוֹ, וּלְפָחוֹת הַכֹּבֶד שֶׁמַּגִּיעֵהוּ אַחַר הָאֲכִילָה . . . שֶׁלֹּא יָאוּת לְשׂוּם בַּעַל שֵׂכֶל לָשׂוּם עַצְמוֹ בַּסַּכָּנוֹת הָרָעוֹת עַל רֶוַח הַטּוֹב הַמּוּעָט הַהוּא. וְזֶה פָּשׁוּט. וּכְשֶׁיַּרְגִּיל אֶת עַצְמוֹ וְיַתְמִיד בְּעִיּוּנוֹ עַל הָאֱמֶת הַזֹּאת, הִנֵּה מְעַט מְעַט יֵצֵא הָפְשִׁי מִמַּאֲסַר הַסִּכְלוּת אֲשֶׁר חֹשֶׁךְ הַחֹמֶר אוֹסֵר אוֹתוֹ בּוֹ וְלֹא יִתְפַּתֶּה מִפִּתּוּיֵי הַהֲנָאוֹת הַכּוֹזְבוֹת כְּלָל . . . וּכְעִנְיָן זֶה אָמַר שְׁלֹמֹה (קהלת ז, ב): ,,טוֹב לָלֶכֶת אֶל־בֵּית־אֵבֶל מִלֶּכֶת אֶל־בֵּית מִשְׁתֶּה.״

All worldly pleasures are similar to the desire for tasty foods, in that they give but momentary gratification, only to often cause distressing illness ... No thinking person would exchange a momentary pleasure for long-lasting distress. All one needs to do is reflect on this, and eventually one would escape from the trap of foolish thinking ... It is for this reason that Solomon says, "It is better to go to the house of a mourner than to a house of feasting" (Ecclesiastes 7:2).

Think back for a few moments. How many times have you had delicious meals or tasty pastries and condiments? What pleasure do you have from those now? In fact, how much pleasure did you have from them two hours after eating? On the other hand, think of having given *tzedakah* to a needy family, or having provided some help to a person in distress. Even though you may have done this years ago, there is still a good feeling that prevails. Is it not clear that performance of mitzvos results in a good feeling of lasting duration, whereas physical pleasures are gone within moments? This is true even when the pleasures one enjoys are neutral, but so many things people do for pleasure may have undesirable results, as those we have just noted. The contrast is therefore more striking: Engage in mitzvos, and you will get a good feeling of long duration, but if you indulge in earthly pleasures, you may later regret the distresses they cause. Just as a rule of thumb, the wise person will maximize performance of mitzvos and minimize indulgence in earthly pleasures.

It is indeed pleasant to attend a feast: food, drink, singing, and merrymaking. While all this is enjoyable, one does not generally leave a feast enriched with methods for attaining a more spiritual life, and after a short period of time even the memory of it has dissipated. There is, of course, a *seudas mitzvah*, a feast which celebrates performance of a mitzvah, at which there is discussion of Torah concepts, which enlighten one on better ways of living. At the house of the mourner, however, one is confronted with the mortality of man, and as one focuses on the relative brevity of the human sojourn on earth, one is more likely to leave with increased thought to man's permanent existence, i.e., the eternal life of the *neshamah*. It is also customary in the house of the mourner to recite Psalm 49, where the futility of investing oneself in earthly goals is impressively described. So while a visit to a house of feasting is more enjoyable, a visit to a house of mourning is more beneficial.

וּמִמַּה שֶׁצָּרִיךְ לִזָּהֵר בִּקְנִיַּת הַפְּרִישׁוּת הוּא, שֶׁלֹּא יִרְצֶה הָאָדָם לְדַלֵּג וְלִקְפּוֹץ אֶל הַקָּצֶה הָאַחֲרוֹן שֶׁבּוֹ רֶגַע אֶחָד, כִּי זֶה וַדַּאי לֹא יַעֲלֶה בְּיָדוֹ, אֶלָּא יִהְיֶה פּוֹרֵשׁ וְהוֹלֵךְ מְעַט מְעַט, הַיּוֹם יִקְנֶה קְצָת מִמֶּנּוּ וּמָחָר יוֹסִיף עָלָיו מְעַט יוֹתֵר, עַד שֶׁיִּתְרַגֵּל בּוֹ לְגַמְרֵי, כִּי יָשׁוּב לוֹ כְּמוֹ טֶבַע מַמָּשׁ.

One must be careful that one does not go to sudden extremes in Abstinence, because this usually does not succeed. Rather, one should proceed very gradually in Abstinence, bit by bit, adjusting to it so that it becomes a second nature.

In our rehabilitation center, where we advocate the recovery program of Alcoholic Anonymous, there is a sign that says, "The elevator to recovery is broken. Please use the Twelve Steps."

Many people who decide on a lifestyle change wish to undergo an instant transformation. Ramchal correctly points out that such radical changes do not succeed. A human being adapts to things gradually, and rapid changes are not readily tolerated. It is amazing that people are persistently unable to get this message, as is evident in those who wish to lose weight, and go from one "magic" diet to another, losing thirty pounds within weeks, and then regaining that amount (or more). They continually persevere in this pattern, each time expecting that "this time will be different." Experience has proven that sustained weight control depends on a change in lifestyle which must come gradually, rather than any sudden magic fashion.

A radical change to Abstinence is not only poorly tolerated and may result in a rebound reaction, but is also likely to become the extreme form of Abstinence which Ramchal has said is undesirable. A very gradual relinquishing of things that are nonessential will allow for an adjustment that is both well tolerated and also consistent with preservation of a healthy diet, productive interpersonal relationships, and constructive community participation.

16

בְּבֵאוּר מִדַּת הַטָּהֳרָה
The Trait of Purity

Each time we learn of another step of Rabbi Pinchas ben Yair as elaborated upon by Ramchal, we may think that one who has mastered that step has indeed reached the height of spirituality. Certainly someone who has mastered Watchfulness, *Zerizus* and *Neykius*, and then gone on to Abstinence — where he no longer partakes of any goods of the world except insofar as is necessary for survival — is the supreme *tzaddik*. What else could one do to be even more spiritual?

But since we have not yet exhausted all the steps of Rabbi Pinchas ben Yair, it is obvious that there is still more one can do. It is a very sobering thought for those of us who are still struggling with Watchfulness and, particularly if we think that by carefully avoiding all prohibited behavior we are *tzaddikim*, to realize how far we are from the height of spirituality.

How much can be asked of a person? How much more can a person do than what Rabbi Pinchas ben Yair has already proposed in the first four levels of spirituality? Let us note what the Talmud says.

The Torah says, "You shall be holy, because I, your G-d, am holy" (*Leviticus* 19:2), on which the Midrash comments, "You may think that you may be as holy as I, therefore the Torah says, My holiness is superior to yours" (*Vayikra Rabbah* 24:9). Rabbi Chaim Shmulevitz asks, How could anyone be so foolish as to even remotely consider the possibility that mortal man could be as holy as Almighty G-d? This is so absurd a thought that it is not even worth mentioning. Rabbi Shmulevitz points out that the authors of the Talmud had a far greater grasp of the infinity of G-d than we do, and if they suggest that "You may think that you may be as holy as I," it is because they also had a greater grasp of the enormous potential of man. Inasmuch as the essence of man is his *neshamah,* which is an integral part of G-d Himself, then man might conceivably think that he could be as holy as G-d. The only impediment to this accomplishment is that the *neshamah* resides within a body whose needs and drives are nonspiritual, but if a person could succeed in essentially negating his physical self and living only the life of the *neshamah,* he might attain the holiness of G-d himself. It was therefore necessary for the Torah to specify that although man can emulate G-d in many ways and indeed reach an extremely lofty level of holiness, he can never equal the holiness of G-d.

How little we know of ourselves! Every one of us has the capacity to make our physical body nothing other than a temporary repository for the *neshamah,* and a vehicle whereby the *neshamah* can carry out the Divine wish. We can put the many desires of the physical body beyond consideration. The body is not here primarily to be satisfied, but rather to be maintained in order that it can function as an agent for the *neshamah.* This is the spirituality of which Rabbi Pinchas ben Yair speaks, and Ramchal now goes on to explain why there is something more to be achieved, even beyond Abstinence.

הַטָּהֳרָה הִיא תִּקּוּן הַלֵּב וְהַמַּחֲשָׁבוֹת . . . וְעִנְיָנָהּ שֶׁלֹּא יַנִּיחַ הָאָדָם מָקוֹם לַיֵּצֶר בְּמַעֲשָׂיו, אֶלָּא יִהְיוּ כָּל מַעֲשָׂיו עַל צַד הַחָכְמָה וְהַיִּרְאָה וְלֹא עַל צַד הַחֵטְא וְהַתַּאֲוָה. וְזֶה אֲפִלּוּ בַּמַּעֲשִׂים הַגּוּפְנִיִּים וְהַחָמְרִיִּים, שֶׁאֲפִלּוּ אַחֲרֵי הִתְנַהֲגוֹ בִּפְרִישׁוּת, דְּהַיְנוּ, שֶׁלֹּא יִקַּח מִן הָעוֹלָם אֶלָּא הַהֶכְרֵחִי, עֲדַיִן יִצְטָרֵךְ לְטַהֵר לְבָבוֹ וּמַחֲשַׁבְתּוֹ שֶׁגַּם בְּאוֹתוֹ הַמְעַט אֲשֶׁר הוּא לוֹקֵחַ לֹא יְכַוֵּן אֶל הַהֲנָאָה וְהַתַּאֲוָה כְּלָל, אֶלָּא תִהְיֶה כַּוָּנָתוֹ אֶל הַטּוֹב הַיּוֹצֵא מִן הַמַּעֲשֶׂה הַהוּא עַל צַד הַחָכְמָה וְהָעֲבוֹדָה . . . וְעַל דֶּרֶךְ זֶה אָמַר שְׁלֹמֹה (משלי ג, ו): „בְּכָל דְּרָכֶיךָ דָעֵהוּ."

Purity refers to perfection of one's heart and thoughts, which means that one should not allow any room for gratification of physical desires in his actions, but that all one's deeds should be performed with intelligence and with reverence for G-d. In other words, after achieving Abstinence from non-essentials, even the essentials for survival should be used only for maintaining oneself (in order to do the Divine will) rather than for any pleasure contained therein. This is what Solomon meant, "In all your ways, know Him" (Proverbs 3:6).

Ramchal's *chassid* has already mastered Abstinence and partakes of no excesses or luxuries. His food is simple, and his clothes are modest.

But even eating simple food can be enjoyable. Food that contains no salt or is otherwise tasteless may be virtually inedible, hence some gustatory pleasure is necessary to be able to give proper nutrition. Furthermore, it is the sight, smell, and taste of food that initiates the system's secretion of digestive juices, without which food could not be absorbed. There seems to be no escape from enjoying food, even for a *chassid*. The Talmud states, "Make G-d's will your will" (*Ethics of the Fathers* 2:4). When partaking of anything physical, the reason for doing so should be only to fulfill the Divine will, and self-gratification should not enter the picture. This is what Ramchal understood Solomon to mean, "In *all* your ways, know G-d."

One of the chassidic masters stated that eating was abhorrent to him, because he shared this behavior with brute beasts. The Midrash states that when Adam ate of the forbidden fruit and was cursed "The land shall produce thorns and weeds, and you shall eat the vegetation of the land" (*Genesis* 3:18), Adam began to weep. "I and my animal will be eating from the same trough," he said. Once Adam had succumbed to temptation and eaten the forbidden fruit he realized how deeply he had fallen spiritually, and that now his consumption of food was like that of a brute beast. The *kabbalistic* writings speak of the necessity for mankind to rectify the sin of Adam, and in light of what Ramchal is explaining now, we can understand this to mean that ideally man should elevate himself to a level of spirituality where even those actions which are essential for survival are done without any intent to enjoy any pleasant experience inherent in them, but only because it was Divinely decreed that this is what man must do in order to survive.

It is told of the *tzaddik*, Rabbi Chaim of Sanz, that he would study Torah until the early hours of the morning, then retire to bed, telling his *gabbai* (aide) to prepare coffee for him when he awakens. The *gabbai* promptly set to work preparing the coffee, and by the time this was done he heard the *tzaddik* reciting *Modeh Ani* (the prayer upon awakening). The *tzaddik* would then reprimand himself, "What is it with you, Chaim, that you sleep away your life!" His attitude was that just as G-d does not sleep, the *neshamah,* which is a part of G-d, needs no sleep either. Sleep is therefore a concession to the physical part of man, or if you will, man's animal component, and the *tzaddik* considered it beneath the dignity of spiritual man to participate in animal behavior.

Ramchal teaches that for the *chassid,* the truly spiritual person, all physical behavior should be seen as concessions to existence, which should be performed grudgingly rather than embraced in any way.

It may be well to remind ourselves at this point that the name of Ramchal's text is *Mesillas Yesharim,* the path of those who wish to be *yashar*, which means straight, without any deviation. Ramchal has explained that the factors that cause deviation from the straight path are any physical desires to which a person is prone; hence the ideal *yashar* can be achieved only when all the factors which may cause such deviation have been eliminated. This accounts for the need for Abstinence and Purity as defined by Ramchal.

וְאָמְנָם, צָרִיךְ שֶׁתֵּדַע, שֶׁכְּמוֹ שֶׁשַּׁיָּךְ טָהֳרַת הַמַּחֲשָׁבָה בַּמַּעֲשִׂים הַגּוּפְנִיִּים . . . כֵּן שַׁיָּךְ טָהֳרַת הַמַּחֲשָׁבָה בַּמַּעֲשִׂים הַטּוֹבִים . . . הָרַע מִכֻּלָּם הוּא שֶׁאֵינֶנּוּ עוֹבֵד לְשֵׁם עֲבוֹדָה כְּלָל, אֶלָּא לְרַמּוֹת בְּנֵי הָאָדָם וּלְהַרְוִיחַ כָּבוֹד אוֹ מָמוֹן. וְזֶהוּ שֶׁאָמְרוּ בוֹ (ירושלמי ברכות א, ז): ,,נוֹחַ לוֹ שֶׁנֶּהֶפְכָה שִׁלְיָתוֹ עַל פָּנָיו'' . . . אַחֵר שֶׁל שֶׁלֹּא לִשְׁמָהּ, שֶׁהוּא הָעֲבוֹדָה עַל מְנַת לְקַבֵּל פְּרָס, וְעָלָיו אָמְרוּ (פסחים נ, ב): ,,לְעוֹלָם יַעֲסוֹק אָדָם בְּתוֹרָה וּבְמִצְוֹת וַאֲפִלּוּ שֶׁלֹּא לִשְׁמָהּ, שֶׁמִּתּוֹךְ שֶׁלֹּא לִשְׁמָהּ בָּא לִשְׁמָהּ''. אַךְ . . . עֲדַיִן . . . רָחוֹק הוּא מִשְּׁלֵמוּתוֹ . . . שֶׁלִּפְעָמִים הָאָדָם הוֹלֵךְ וְעוֹשֶׂה מִצְוָה לִשְׁמָהּ מַמָּשׁ, שֶׁכָּךְ גָּזַר אָבִינוּ שֶׁבַּשָּׁמַיִם, אָמְנָם לֹא יֶחְדַּל מִלְּשַׁתֵּף עִמָּהּ אֵיזֶה פְּנִיָּה אַחֶרֶת, אוֹ שֶׁיְּשַׁבְּחוּהוּ בְּנֵי הָאָדָם . . . וְלִפְעָמִים . . . בִּשְׂמֹחַ לִבּוֹ עַל הַשֶּׁבַח יַרְבֶּה לְדַקְדֵּק יוֹתֵר.

We should bear in mind that just as there should be purity of thought (motivation) in behavior that relates to bodily needs ... there should also be purity of thought in observance of Torah and mitzvos ... If one studies Torah in order to deceive people, or to thereby gain personal honor, this is condemned by the Talmud (Talmud Yerushalmi Berachos 1:2) ... Study of Torah for the sake of Divine reward is commendable only because it may lead to a higher motivation (Pesachim 50b), but is not yet the ideal ... Sometimes a person may do a mitzvah with pure intent; however, when he finds himself being praised for it, he may then take greater pains in its performance than he would otherwise. (This is an intrusion on purity of intent.)

Rabbi Shneur Zalman once complained to Rabbi Levi Yitzchak of Berditchev that he felt his service of G-d was flawed, and that he was doing things for selfish interests, for his own glorification.

Rabbi Levi Yitzchak tried to comfort him. "Don't be too harsh on yourself," he said. "We are told we are to emulate G-d, and we say in the first *berachah* at a *chuppah* (wedding) that G-d created everything for His own glory."

"Yes," Rabbi Shneur Zalman responded, "but for His own glory was for the glory of G-d, whereas I am doing things for my personal glory."

We can rest assured that neither of these great *tzaddikim* were flawed with what we would consider personal interests, but they were so meticulous in self-scrutiny that the least suggestion of any personal interest was unacceptable to them, as they strove for total devotion in the Divine service. Their chassidic writings are replete with the demand for "*bitul*," or total self-effacement in the service of G-d.

There are numerous accounts from the time of the Talmud onward of Torah scholars who expounded on Torah publicly and later did penance for having felt pride in their brilliant expositions. Would that we would be guilty of "sins" such as these!

Why were *tzaddikim* so self-critical for fear that they might have experienced pleasure in their study of Torah? It is because of a statement by Hillel that "One who takes the crown for his personal use will be removed from the world" (*Ethics of the Fathers* 1:13). The Torah is considered the crown of G-d, and for a subject to use the king's crown for himself in any way constitutes a capital offense.

Our great *tzaddikim* wished to study Torah solely to fulfill the Divine wish, and were often greatly troubled that they took personal pleasure in it. It is related that a *chassid* complained to Rabbi Menachem of Lubavitch (the Tzemach Tzedek) that he had no desire for studying Torah. The Tzemach Tzedek began to weep. "Woe is to me," he said, "what can I do? I do have a desire to study Torah." This chassidic master was concerned that he was motivated by the great joy he experienced in the study of Torah, which for him was not the proper motivation.

וְאָמְנָם אַף־עַל־פִּי שֶׁאִסּוּר כָּזֶה בָּטֵל בְּמִעוּטוֹ, עַל־כָּל־פָּנִים, הַמַּעֲשֶׂה שֶׁתִּתְעָרֵב כָּזֶה בְּתוֹכוֹ טָהוֹר לְגַמְרֵי אֵינֶנּוּ . . . וְאֵינֶנִּי אוֹמֵר שֶׁמַּה שֶּׁהוּא זוּלַת זֶה יִהְיֶה נִדְחֶה לְגַמְרֵי . . . אָמְנָם, עַל הָעֲבוֹדָה הַתְּמִימָה אֲנִי מְדַבֵּר הָרְאוּיָה לְכָל אוֹהֲבֵי ה׳ בֶּאֱמֶת, שֶׁלֹּא יִקָּרֵא בְּזֶה הַשֵּׁם אֶלָּא הָעֲבוֹדָה הַטְּהוֹרָה לְגַמְרֵי, שֶׁלֹּא תִהְיֶה הַפְּנִיָּה בָּהּ אֶלָּא לַשֵּׁם יִתְבָּרֵךְ וְלֹא לְזוּלָתוֹ. וְכָל מַה שֶּׁיִּתְרַחֵק מִן הַמַּדְרֵגָה הַזֹּאת, כְּפִי הַרְבּוֹת רִחוּקוֹ כֵּן יִרְבֶּה הַחִסָּרוֹן בָּהּ.

Even though the defects in purity and motivation may be very minute, any Divine service in which there is the slightest personal interest cannot be said to be perfect ... While G-d certainly does not turn away even imperfect prayers, those who have a true love of G-d will seek to make their serving Him pure in the absolute.

Ramchal's point can be easily understood by an analogy to a diamond. While a diamond with a slight imperfection can still be of great value, it does not compare to one which is completely free of even the slightest defect.

It is related that one year there was a dearth of *esrogim* (citrons) and the Gaon of Vilna was greatly distressed that he would not have the opportunity to perform this once-a-year mitzvah of the four species on *Sukkos*. He asked his disciples to be on the lookout for an *esrog* and to pay whatever price was asked.

One student spied a person with the four species, and discovered this was a merchant who was passing through Vilna on his way home for the festival. The merchant refused to part with the *esrog* for any amount of money, and the student then pleaded with him to remain in Vilna for *Sukkos* to share his *esrog* with the Gaon. In desperation, he promised the man that the great reward that the Gaon would accrue from this mitzvah would be credited to his account. This was a bargain which the man could not refuse.

The Gaon, upon hearing that the reward for the mitzvah had been given away, was overjoyed. "Each time I do a mitzvah, I try to put its reward out of my mind. I want to do the mitzvah because it is G-d's will, rather than for its reward, yet the latter haunts me. Now that I know that the reward for this mitzvah will not be mine, I can truly perform the mitzvah for its own sake."

Although the analogy to diamonds is valid, there is more reason for concern about a tiny defect in the Divine service than in a diamond. The latter is static, and does not propagate, whereas a defect of personal interest in a mitzvah, especially if it is in the nature of pride and vanity, may be far reaching. Vanity and pride — in contrast to carbon spots in diamonds — are not static, but tend to feed on themselves, and may grow to serious proportions.

In the prayers for Rosh Hashanah and Yom Kippur there is a description of the awesome scene when the Heavenly Tribunal sits in judgment on all living things.

"Angels pass swiftly by, trembling with awe." Why, asked one commentary, do the angels hurry by, and why do they tremble?

He answered that when a person performs a mitzvah, he thereby creates a benign angel, that will represent his merits before the Heavenly Tribunal. Perfect performance of a mitzvah will produce a perfectly formed angel. Mitzvos performed with less than perfection will give rise to an angel with deformities. It is only natural for someone to wish to have his deformities go unnoticed. Therefore, since so many angels are the result of less-than-perfect mitzvos, they hurry by the Tribunal swiftly and tremble with the fear that their deformities may nevertheless be noticed.

כִּי מִי שֶׁלֹּא נִתְדַּבֵּק עִמּוֹ יִתְבָּרֵךְ בְּאַהֲבָה אֲמִתִּית, צֵרוּף הָעֲבוֹדָה הַזֹּאת תִּהְיֶה לוֹ לְטֹרַח וּלְמַשָּׂא גָּדוֹל, כִּי יֹאמַר, מִי יוּכַל לַעֲמוֹד בָּזֶה, וַאֲנַחְנוּ בְּנֵי חֹמֶר יְלוּדֵי אִשָּׁה אִי־אֶפְשָׁר לְהַגִּיעַ אֶל הַזִּקּוּק וְהַצֵּרוּף הַזֶּה. אָמְנָם אוֹהֲבֵי ה׳ וַחֲפֵצֵי עֲבוֹדָתוֹ, הִנֵּה שָׂמֵחַ לִבָּם לְהַרְאוֹת אֱמוּנַת אַהֲבָתָם לְפָנָיו יִתְבָּרֵךְ וּלְהִתְעַצֵּם בִּצְרוּפָהּ וְטָהֳרָתָהּ . . . וְהִנֵּה בֶּאֱמֶת זֶהוּ הַמִּבְחָן שֶׁבּוֹ נִבְחָנִים וְנִבְדָּלִים עוֹבְדֵי ה׳ עַצְמָם בְּמַדְרֵגָתָם, כִּי מִי שֶׁיּוֹדֵעַ לְטַהֵר לִבּוֹ יוֹתֵר, הוּא הַמִּתְקָרֵב יוֹתֵר וְהָאָהוּב יוֹתֵר אֶצְלוֹ יִתְבָּרֵךְ.

One who does not cleave to G-d with true love, or who finds such purification of his service of G-d to be tedious and burdensome, may say, How can a mere mortal aspire to such purity? However, those who truly love G-d and desire to serve Him rejoice in showing Him their faithful love for Him and strengthen themselves in purifying it. In fact, the lengths to which one wishes to go to purify his service to G-d is an indication of the extent of his love for G-d.

It is not unusual for people to consider something to be beyond their reach, and at times the reasons they give may indeed seem plausible.

The fact is, however, that there are many things that are within a person's reach, and his considering them otherwise is nothing but a rationalization. The aphorism "Where there is a will there is a way" may indeed have some exceptions, but is nevertheless a truism.

A person who craves a particular food may extend himself somewhat in order to get it, but if this would require an exhausting effort, he might well forgo it. Not so with a cocaine addict who craves cocaine, for whom there is no effort that is too demanding. He will beg, borrow, and often steal in order to get the money for his drug, and will walk barefoot in the snow if necessary to reach his supplier. In the latter case the craving knows no bounds.

"My soul thirsts for You, my flesh pines for You, like one in the desert without water" (*Psalms* 63:2), and "As the hart yearns for water, so does my soul yearn for You, O G-d" (ibid. 42:2). In *Song of Songs* (5:6), Solomon depicts the desire of closeness to G-d as similar to the intense longing for one's beloved. It is told that Rabbi Shneur Zalman was once found at the open Ark pleading in prayer, "I don't want Your *Olam Haba* (World to Come), and I don't want Your *Gan Eden* (Paradise). I want only You."

We must again return to the first chapter, where Ramchal states that the ultimate goal of human existence is to unite with and become absorbed in G-d, even though such a complete union would mean that one ceases to exist as an entity. The *neshamah* being absorbed in G-d, its original source, is the ultimate in self-effacement. Ramchal also explained that all mundane desires comprise the detractions from this unity and identity, hence the first several steps deal with eliminating these barriers, and the more one appreciates that these barriers impede attainment of the ultimate goal of identifying with G-d, the more one can achieve Purity.

הֵם הֵמָּה הָרִאשׁוֹנִים אֲשֶׁר בָּאָרֶץ הֵמָּה . . . ,,רַחֲמָנָא לִבָּא בָּעִי״ . . . וְהִנֵּה הַלֵּב הוּא הַמֶּלֶךְ לְכָל חֶלְקֵי הַגּוּף וְנוֹהֵג בָּם, וְאִם הוּא אֵינוֹ מֵבִיא עַצְמוֹ אֶל עֲבוֹדָתוֹ יִתְבָּרֵךְ, אֵין עֲבוֹדַת שְׁאָר הָאֵבָרִים כְּלוּם, כִּי אֶל אֲשֶׁר יִהְיֶה שָׁמָּה רוּחַ הַלֵּב לָלֶכֶת יֵלֵכוּ. וּמִקְרָא כָּתוּב בְּפֵרוּשׁ (משלי כג, כו): ,,תְּנָה בְנִי לִבְּךָ לִי.״

It is this kind of purity that characterized the patriarchs . . . G-d desires the devotion of the heart . . . Inasmuch as the heart is the king and mover of all other parts of the body, if one's heart is not devoted to G-d, the service of all other organs becomes meaningless. This is why Solomon says, "My son, give your heart to Me" (Proverbs 23:26).

The Talmud states that the patriarchs, Abraham, Isaac, and Jacob, observed all the mitzvos of the Torah even though it had not yet been given to man (*Yoma* 28b). We may ask, If the Torah had not been revealed yet, how did they know what the mitzvos were in order to fulfill them?

Rabbi Levi Yitzchak of Berditchev explains that there are natural cravings within a person that are not learned or acquired, such as hunger, thirst, or weariness. We know to eat when hungry, to drink when thirsty, and to rest when weary, even though we were not taught these responses. Similarly, there are cravings which the *neshamah* has, which are to do that which G-d desires, and this craving is as natural for the *neshamah* as hunger is for the body. There are some diseases which can interfere with a person's appetite, so that one does not feel hungry. Proper treatment of these diseases will allow the natural feeling of hunger to return.

This is equally true of the *neshamah*, which, being part of G-d Himself, is attracted to doing the Divine will, and the *neshamah* wishes to do so even if this will were not revealed. The reason we do not all experience this innate craving for mitzvos is because of the barriers erected by the *yetzer hara*, which drive us to physical gratifications, and thus obscure the natural cravings of the *neshamah*. The patriarchs were so completely devoted to the Divine will that they eliminated all their own personal interests, and this permitted the *neshamah* to function in such a manner that it guided the body to do the mitzvos.

You will recall that we had earlier quoted Solomon's statement that G-d made man *yashar* (straight), and that man deviated from being *yashar* because of his many calculations (*Ecclesiastes* 7:29); i.e., rationalizations, which serve to justify the gratification of various physical desires. We can now understand why the Talmud refers to the patriarchs as *yesharim* (*Avodah Zarah* 25a) because they had eliminated the detractions that cause a person to deviate from being *yashar*. We can also see that the trait of Purity, as described by Ramchal, can return a person to the pristine state of being *yashar*, and why the trait of Purity is therefore an important component of *Mesillas Yesharim*.

17

בְּדַרְכֵי קְנִיַּת הַטָּהֳרָה

The Acquisition of Purity

הִנֵּה הַדֶּרֶךְ לְהַשִּׂיג הַמִּדָּה הַזֹּאת קַל הוּא לְמִי שֶׁכְּבָר הִשְׁתַּדֵּל וְהִשִּׂיג הַמִּדּוֹת הַשְּׁנוּיוֹת עַד הֵנָּה. כִּי הִנֵּה כְּשֶׁיַּחֲשׁוֹב וְיִתְבּוֹנֵן עַל פְּחִיתוּת תַּעֲנוּגֵי הָעוֹלָם וְטוֹבוֹתָיו, כְּמוֹ שֶׁכָּתַבְתִּי לְמַעְלָה, יִמְאַס בָּהֶם וְלֹא יַחְשְׁבֵם אֶלָּא לְרָעוֹת . . . וַדַּאי שֶׁיֵּקַל לוֹ לְהִבָּדֵל מֵהֶם וְלַהֲסִירָם מִלִּבּוֹ . . . בְּשׁוּם מַעֲשֶׂה מִן הַמַּעֲשִׂים, אֶלָּא יִהְיֶה בַּמַּעֲשִׂים הַחָמְרִיִּים כְּאָנוּס, לֹא זוּלַת.

One who has already endeavored and acquired the preceding traits (i.e., Watchfulness, Zerizus, Nekiyus, and Abstinence) will find acquisition of Purity to be quite easy. For when a person reflects on the inferior nature of worldly pleasures, he will regard them as hindrances ... and will withdraw from them ... Any participation in earthly activities will then be performed only because one is compelled to do so (in order to survive).

Purity is an attitude, and as we have noted earlier, attitudes are more likely to follow action than the reverse. Early in my psychiatric career I adhered to the teachings of the psychodynamic schools, trying to help patients arrive at an understanding of the origins of their symptoms, which was supposed to result in their improvement. Too often the understanding had little or no impact on the patient's symptoms, and I then began urging and supporting the patient to modify his behavior, and indeed found that not only did this result in symptom relief, but also greatly facilitated an understanding of the origin of the symptoms where this was felt to be helpful.

Ramchal has indeed advocated meditation and reflection, but these can be productive only after a person has made the necessary behavioral changes according to the traits that precede Purity. Indulgence in physical pleasures and providing gratification for the bodily drives which are essentially animalistic drives, are indeed beneath the dignity of someone who takes pride in being a spiritual being, who should aspire to be more like angels than like beasts. But as reasonable as this is, the truth of this cannot be grasped or appreciated by someone who is actively indulgent. It is virtually impossible to convince a practicing alcoholic of the evils of alcohol while he is drinking his beer, and it is similarly virtually impossible to expect explanation of the dangers of obesity to make an impact on someone who is busily devouring tasty, rich pastries. Only after the person has begun at least a temporary abstinence from these pleasures is there a chance of reasoning with them. Similarly, meditation and reflection on the inferior nature of earthly pleasures cannot achieve anything as long as the person is not abstaining from them.

כִּי הִנֵּה לְטַהֵר מַחֲשַׁבְתּוֹ בְּמַעֲשֵׂי גוּפְנִיּוּתוֹ, הַדֶּרֶךְ הוּא לְהַתְמִיד הִסְתַּכְּלוּתוֹ עַל פְּחִיתוּת הָעוֹלָם וְתַעֲנוּגָיו, כְּמוֹ שֶׁכָּתַבְתִּי; וּלְטַהֵר מַחֲשַׁבְתּוֹ בְּמַעֲשֵׂי עֲבוֹדָתוֹ, יַרְבֶּה הִתְבּוֹנְנוּתוֹ עַל תַּרְמִית הַכָּבוֹד וּכְזָבָיו וְיַרְגִּיל עַצְמוֹ לִבְרֹחַ מִמֶּנּוּ, אָז יִנָּקֶה בְּעֵת עֲבוֹדָתוֹ מִפְּנוֹת אֶל הַשֶּׁבַח וְאֶל הַתְּהִלָּה אֲשֶׁר יְהַלְלוּהוּ בְּנֵי הָאָדָם וְתִהְיֶה מַחֲשַׁבְתּוֹ פּוֹנָה בְּיִחוּד אֶל אֲדוֹנֵנוּ אֲשֶׁר הוּא . . . כָּל טוּבֵנוּ וּשְׁלֵמוּתֵנוּ.

To achieve purity in earthly activities, one must therefore appreciate their inferior nature. But one must also achieve purity in the service of G-d, and this can be accomplished by reflecting on the falseness and deceitfulness of pride. One can then cleanse oneself from the pursuit of praise and devote oneself solely to G-d, Who is the ultimate goal and ultimate perfection.

If we will be frank with ourselves, we will discover that we are often motivated by the desire to be praised. Even when doing mitzvos for the sake of doing mitzvos, it is rare that our performance is not contaminated by at least a smidgen of vanity. The *yetzer hara* sees to it that when we do a mitzvah in the presence of others, it is done with just a bit more fervor than if we do it privately. While performance of mitzvos is always commendable, it is not of the highest quality when even a small amount of vanity is present.

Our *tzaddikim* fought a constant battle to eliminate the participation of the *yetzer hara* in performance of mitzvos. When Rabbi Levi Yitzchak of Berditchev was a newlywed, his father-in-law, Reb Shmuel Peretz, a prominent and well-to-do scholar, was proud to have acquired so illustrious a Torah scholar for his daughter, and wished to display him to the townsfolk. He therefore had Rabbi Levi Yitzchak lead the congregation in *"Ata Horesa,"* the opening prayer of the *Simchas Torah* services. How surprised Reb Shmuel Peretz was to see Rabbi Levi Yitzchak put on the *tallis*, pause, and remove it, then put it on again, only to remove it once again. After several such sequences, Rabbi Levi Yitzchak suddenly cried out, "If you are a scholar and a *chassid*, then you lead the congregation in *'Ata Horesa,'* " and he left the pulpit, to the great embarrassment of his father-in-law.

Rabbi Levi Yitzchak later explained, "Just as I put on my *tallis*, I noted someone at my side, saying 'Wait a minute, I too wish to put on the *tallis*.'

"Who are you?" I asked.

"I am your *yetzer hara*, and I wish to chant *'Ata Horesa'* together with you," he said.

"But I was given this privilege because I am a Torah scholar," I said.

"I, too, am a Torah scholar," the *yetzer hara* answered. "When you studied in *yeshivah*, I was with you all the time."

"But I am a *chassid*, and have the merit of having performed so many mitzvos that I deserve to recite *'Ata Horesa,'* " I said.

"Never mind," the *yetzer hara* answered. "I was always with you when you performed mitzvos. I, too, am a *chassid*."

"Finally," Rabbi Levi Yitzchak continued, "I became so frustrated that I said to the *yetzer hara*, 'If you are such a Torah scholar and a *chassid* and have so many mitzvos, then you may chant *"Ata Horesa"* by yourself,' and I left the pulpit."

This quaint anecdote reveals how demanding our *tzaddikim* were to rid themselves of impure motivation, and were rigorous in pursuit of purity in the service of G-d, devoid of any involvement of the *yetzer hara*.

This anecdote also illustrates Ramchal's observation on the spurious nature of the *yetzer hara*. By saying to the *yetzer hara*, "If you are such a scholar and *chassid*, then you chant *'Ata Horesa'* " — something which is of course impossible — Rabbi Levi Yitzchak was pointing out that the *yetzer hara* is really a nonentity, having no independent existence. The *yetzer hara* cannot do anything on his own, only through the medium of man. It is therefore a weak rationalization to say "The *yetzer hara* made me do it," since the *yetzer hara* is unable to do anything unless one gives him the means to do so. If one conceptualizes the *yetzer hara* as being nothing other than an illusion, one can free oneself of its influence.

וּמִן הַמַּעֲשִׂים הַמַּדְרִיכִים אֶת הָאָדָם לָבוֹא לִידֵי מִדָּה זוֹ, הוּא הַהַזְמָנָה לְדִבְרֵי הָעֲבוֹדָה וְהַמִּצְוֹת, וְהַיְנוּ, שֶׁלֹּא יִכָּנֵס בְּקִיּוּם הַמִּצְוָה בְּפֶתַע פִּתְאֹם שֶׁאֵין דַּעְתּוֹ עֲדַיִן מְיֻשֶּׁבֶת עָלָיו וִיכוֹלָה לְהִתְבּוֹנֵן בְּמַה שֶׁהוּא עוֹשֶׂה, אֶלָּא יַזְמִין עַצְמוֹ לַדָּבָר וְיָכִין לִבּוֹ בְּמִתּוּן עַד שֶׁיִּכָּנֵס בְּהִתְבּוֹנְנוּת וְאָז יִתְבּוֹנֵן מַה הוּא הוֹלֵךְ לַעֲשׂוֹת וְלִפְנֵי מִי הוּא הוֹלֵךְ לַעֲשׂוֹת, שֶׁהֲרֵי בְּהִכָּנְסוֹ בָּעִיּוּן הַזֶּה, קַל הוּא שֶׁיַּשְׁלִיךְ מֵעָלָיו הַפְּנִיּוֹת הַחִיצוֹנִיּוֹת וְיִקְבַּע בְּלִבּוֹ הַכַּוָּנָה הָאֲמִתִּית הָרְצוּיָה. וְתִרְאֶה שֶׁהַחֲסִידִים הָרִאשׁוֹנִים הָיוּ שׁוֹהִים שָׁעָה אַחַת קֹדֶם תְּפִלָּתָם וְאַחַר־כָּךְ מִתְפַּלְּלִים (ברכות ל, ב).

One of the means which can help a person achieve purity is preparing oneself properly for performance of a mitzvah, rather than to do it with an abruptness. If one reflects why he is doing the mitzvah, Whose bidding it is, and before Whom one is serving, it is easy to divest oneself of personal interests. The Talmud states that the saintly people of yore would meditate for an entire hour to prepare themselves for prayer.

As the anecdote of Rabbi Levi Yitzchak demonstrates, proper reflection will expose the falsity of the *yetzer hara*, and will show vanity to be totally bereft of any value. In many congregations there is a sign with a quotation from the last will of Rabbi Eliezer, "Know before Whom you are standing." One who gives serious thought to what prayer is all about may more easily rid oneself of ulterior motives.

In many *siddurim* (prayer books) there is a beautiful prayer, composed by Rabbi Elimelech of Lizensk, known as "The Prayer Before Praying." Just as one should seek Divine assistance in doing all mitzvos properly, one should also do so in regard to prayer; hence it is perfectly logical to pray for the ability to pray properly.

Some of the *chassidic* masters were known to delay praying even beyond the limits prescribed by the *Shulchan Aruch*, which aroused sharp criticism from *misnagdim* (opponents to the *chassidic* movement). The son of the great scholar, Rabbi Shlomo Eiger, who was an avowed *misnaged*, defected to the *chassidic* movement, becoming a follower of the Rebbe of Kotzk. Before returning home he asked the Rebbe, "What am I to tell my father if he asks with what right you pray beyond the time allotted by the *Shulchan Aruch*?"

The Rebbe responded, "Tell him that the Rambam rules that if one hires a worker to chop wood, and the worker spends time sharpening his ax, he must pay for the time spent preparing the tools for the assigned task, because that is an integral part of the job."

This liberty could only be taken by those, who, upon arising at dawn, devoted all their time prior to prayer in preparation for prayer. Delay for any other reason cannot be condoned.

Inasmuch as preparation serves in order to eliminate ulterior motives in performance of mitzvos, it follows that the mitzvah of *tzedakah* requires no preparation, because this is the one mitzvah where personal interest is not considered a contaminant. The purpose of *tzedakah* is so that the poor will not go hungry and unclothed, and as long as that is accomplished, the motivation is of little significance. One should not meditate nor engage in reflection when the opportunity to give *tzedakah* arises, but rather respond swiftly so that the poor can have their needs met promptly.

וְהִנֵּה מַפְסִידֵי הַמִּדָּה, הֵם חֶסְרוֹן הַהִתְבּוֹנְנוּת עַל הָעִנְיָנִים שֶׁזָּכַרְנוּ, דְּהַיְנוּ: סִכְלוּת פְּחִיתוּת הַתַּעֲנוּגִים, רְדִיפַת הַכָּבוֹד, וּמִעוּט הַהֲכָנָה לָעֲבוֹדָה. כִּי הַשְּׁנַיִם הָרִאשׁוֹנִים הֵם מְפַתִּים אֶת הַמַּחֲשָׁבָה . . . וּכְבָר נִקְרְאוּ הַמַּחֲשָׁבוֹת הַחִיצוֹנִיּוֹת ,,זְנוּת הַלֵּב,'' דִּכְתִיב (במדבר טו, לט): ,,וְלֹא תָתוּרוּ אַחֲרֵי לְבַבְכֶם וְאַחֲרֵי עֵינֵיכֶם אֲשֶׁר אַתֶּם זֹנִים אַחֲרֵיהֶם'' . . . וּמִעוּט הַהֲכָנָה גּוֹרֵם לַסִּכְלוּת הַטִּבְעִי הַבָּא מִצַּד הַחֹמֶר שֶׁלֹּא יְגֹרַשׁ מִתּוֹכוֹ, וַהֲרֵי הוּא מַבְאִישׁ אֶת הָעֲבוֹדָה בְּסִרְחוֹנוֹ.

The deterrents to attainment of purity are a result of not paying adequate attention to the above points: i.e., (1) lack of understanding the inferior quality of earthly pleasures; (2) pursuit of glory; (3) inadequate preparation for the Divine service. The first two seduce a person to indulgence . . . and the Scripture refers to this as "adultery of the heart"

(Numbers 15:39) . . . Failure to prepare oneself adequately for the Divine service permits intrusion of personal interests into the Divine service, which contaminate the latter.

Total devotion to the service of G-d, which should be the ultimate goal of one's life, will obviously be defective if any other motivation exists. Total devotion means just that, a singularity of purpose which does not allow entrance to any other motivation, regardless of the nature of the latter.

There have been various advocates of "compartmentalization," e.g., "Give onto G-d what is G-d's and unto Caesar what is Caesar's." Judaism does not condone such a dualism. Everything must be unto G-d, even the most mundane of activities. There are those who advocated, "Be a Jew in your home, but indistinguishable in the street," a misguided and malignant attitude which has resulted in mass assimilation and the defection of countless Jews from the faith of their fathers.

As already mentioned, Judaism is akin to a hermetic system. It is of no value if a hermetic system is 99.9% sealed. The minutest opening destroys the vacuum just as would a major break.

During the time of the Temple in Jerusalem, people ate of the offerings brought upon the Altar, and this was considered part of the mitzvah. In absence of the Altar, the Talmud states that a person's table assumes the function of the Altar in the Temple. I.e., it is not enough that one eats kosher food; eating must be a mitzvah, to provide one with the necessary nutrients so that one can properly fulfill one's mission on earth.

Ramchal also cites pursuit of glory as one of the barriers to purity. We have already elaborated on this elsewhere, but it is of such importance and it may be so surreptitious, that it warrants reemphasis.

It is possible for a person to observe all the earlier traits up to and including Abstinence, and even engage in fasting and other self-deprivations, yet the service of G-d can be grossly flawed because he considers himself a *tzaddik*, given how much he has "sacrificed" for G-d. He may think that because he has concealed his study of Torah, his intense prayer, and self-mortification from the awareness of others, he has therefore achieved humility. He is not aware that considering himself a *tzaddik* is the antithesis of humility.

The *chassidic* master, Rabbi Elimelech of Lizensk, said, "I totally disregard people who tell me I am a *tzaddik*, for what do they know? Only I know the truth about myself. If the prophet Elijah were to tell me

I am a *tzaddik*, I would not believe him either. If the Almighty Himself were to tell me I am *tzaddik*, what could I do? He is absolute truth, and I would have to believe Him. However, I would be obligated to believe Him only for that very brief moment, and the very next moment I would know the truth about myself, how terribly far I am from being a *tzaddik*."

The prophet says, " 'If a man conceals himself in a most secret place, will I not see him?' says G-d" (*Jeremiah* 23:24). The Baal Shem Tov said that this verse also allows itself to be read as, "If a man conceals himself in such a way that his service to G-d is a secret to all, and therefore thinks himself to be an "I," i.e., he believes in his own sanctity, then "I will not countenance him," says G-d. Nothing is so repulsive to G-d as a vain person, even if that vanity is based on one's great piety.

Ramchal now goes on to the next step. Once Purity has been achieved, one can move on to *Chassidus*.

18

בְּבֵאוּר מִדַּת הַחֲסִידוּת

The Trait of Chassidus

Once again we are at a loss for an acceptable translation, this time of the word "*Chassidus*." It is often translated as "saintliness" or "piety," but these words have connotations which represent popular misunderstandings of *Chassidus*, as Ramchal will point out. Using the terms "saintliness" or "piety" may therefore be somewhat misleading. As with *Zerizus* and *Nekiyus*, we will retain the Hebrew "*Chassidus*," which Ramchal now defines.

מִדַּת הַחֲסִידוּת צְרִיכָה הִיא בֶּאֱמֶת לְבֵאוּר גָּדוֹל, כִּי מִנְהָגִים רַבִּים וּדְרָכִים רַבִּים עוֹבְרִים בֵּין רַבִּים מִבְּנֵי הָאָדָם בְּשֵׁם חֲסִידוּת וְאֵינָם אֶלָּא גָּלְמֵי חֲסִידוּת בְּלִי תֹאַר וּבְלִי צוּרָה וּבְלִי תִקּוּן. וְנִמְשָׁךְ זֶה מֵחֶסְרוֹן הָעִיּוּן וְהַהַשְׂכָּלָה הָאֲמִתִּית אֲשֶׁר לְבַעֲלֵי הַמִּדּוֹת הָהֵם, כִּי לֹא טָרְחוּ וְלֹא נִתְיַגְּעוּ לָדַעַת אֶת דֶּרֶךְ ה׳ בִּידִיעָה בְרוּרָה וִישָׁרָה, אֶלָּא הִתְחַסְּדוּ וְהָלְכוּ בְּמַה שֶּׁנִּזְדַּמֵּן לָהֶם לְפִי הַסְּבָרָה הָרִאשׁוֹנָה וְלֹא הֶעֱמִיקוּ בַּדְּבָרִים וְלֹא שָׁקְלוּ אוֹתָם בְּמֹאזְנֵי הַחָכְמָה. וְהִנֵּה אֵלֶּה הִבְאִישׁוּ אֶת רֵיחַ הַחֲסִידוּת בְּעֵינֵי הֲמוֹן הָאֲנָשִׁים וּמִן הַמַּשְׂכִּילִים עִמָּהֶם, בַּאֲשֶׁר כְּבָר יַחְשְׁבוּ שֶׁהַחֲסִידוּת תָּלוּי בְּדִבְרֵי

הֶבֶל אוֹ דְבָרִים נֶגֶד הַשֵּׂכֶל וְהַדֵּעָה הַנְּכוֹנָה, וְיַאֲמִינוּ הֱיוֹת כָּל הַחֲסִידוּת תָּלוּי רַק בַּאֲמִירַת בַּקָּשׁוֹת רַבּוֹת וּוִדּוּיִים גְּדוֹלִים וּבִבְכִיּוֹת וְהִשְׁתַּחֲוָיוֹת גְּדוֹלוֹת וּבְסִגּוּפִים הַזָּרִים שֶׁיְּמִית בָּהֶם הָאָדָם אֶת עַצְמוֹ, כִּטְבִילַת הַקֶּרַח וְהַשֶּׁלֶג וְכַיּוֹצֵא בַּדְּבָרִים הָאֵלֶּה. וְהִנֵּה לֹא יֵדְעוּ כִּי אַף־עַל־פִּי שֶׁקְּצַת דְּבָרִים אֵלֶּה צְרִיכִים לְבַעֲלֵי תְשׁוּבָה וּקְצָתָם רְאוּיִים לַפְּרוּשִׁים, הִנֵּה לֹא עַל אֵלֶּה נוֹסָד הַחֲסִידוּת כְּלָל, כִּי אִם הַטּוֹב שֶׁבַּמִּנְהָגִים הָאֵלֶּה הוּא רָאוּי לְהִתְלַוּוֹת אֶל הַחֲסִידוּת.

The trait of Chassidus requires a thorough explanation, because many practices fall under the rubric of Chassidus, which are nothing but artificial Chassidus, without shape, form, or fashion. This is due to a lack of understanding by those who claim to practice Chassidus, who try to achieve it according to their superficial understanding of it, without weighing it in the scales of wisdom. This has given Chassidus a bad taste, causing people to think that Chassidus consists of illogical behavior, such as recitation of many supplications, lengthy confessions, wailings and bowings, and self-mortification. Chassidus is not at all based on these.

Ramchal is essentially repeating what he said in his introduction, that there are many misconceptions about *Chassidus*. While there may be isolated cases where self-mortification is appropriate, this by no means constitutes *Chassidus*. Ramchal is very critical of those who practice this type of *Chassidus*, since it give *Chassidus* a bad reputation.

It should be noted that the term *Chassidus*, as used here, is not related to the movement initiated by the Baal Shem Tov. The latter movement did not become popular until after Ramchal's death. The term "*chassid*," which connotes a highly spiritual person of exemplary character, is found in the Talmud, and the appellation of "*chassid*" was given to outstanding individuals throughout the ages; e.g. Rabbi Yehudah HaChassid, who lived in the thirteenth century. The term *Chassidus* should therefore not be confused with the philosophy of the *chassidic* movement. Ironically, the Gaon of Vilna, who was an outspoken foe of the *chassidic* movement, is one of those who merited the title "the *chassid*."

וּנְבָאֵר עַתָּה עִנְיָן זֶה עַל הַסֵּדֶר: הִנֵּה שֹׁרֶשׁ הַחֲסִידוּת הוּא מַה שֶּׁאָמְרוּ ז"ל (ברכות יז, א): „אַשְׁרֵי אָדָם שֶׁעֲמָלוֹ בַּתּוֹרָה וְעוֹשֶׂה נַחַת רוּחַ לְיוֹצְרוֹ." וְהָעִנְיָן הוּא כִּי הִנֵּה הַמִּצְוֹת הַמֻּטָּלוֹת עַל כָּל יִשְׂרָאֵל כְּבָר יְדוּעוֹת הֵן וְחוֹבָתָן יְדוּעָה עַד הֵיכָן הִיא מַגַּעַת. אָמְנָם מִי שֶׁאוֹהֵב אֶת הַבּוֹרֵא יִתְבָּרַךְ שְׁמוֹ אַהֲבָה אֲמִתִּית, לֹא יִשְׁתַּדֵּל וִיכַוֵּן לִפְטוֹר עַצְמוֹ בְּמַה שֶּׁכְּבָר מְפֻרְסָם מִן הַחוֹבָה אֲשֶׁר עַל כָּל יִשְׂרָאֵל בִּכְלָל, אֶלָּא יִקְרֶה לוֹ כְּמוֹ שֶׁיִּקְרֶה אֶל בֵּן אוֹהֵב אָבִיו, שֶׁאִלּוּ יְגַלֶּה אָבִיו אֶת דַּעְתּוֹ גִּלּוּי מְעַט שֶׁהוּא חָפֵץ בְּדָבָר מִן הַדְּבָרִים, כְּבָר יַרְבֶּה הַבֵּן בַּדָּבָר הַהוּא וּבַמַּעֲשֶׂה הַהוּא כָּל מַה שֶּׁיּוּכַל. וְאַף־עַל־פִּי שֶׁלֹּא אֲמָרוֹ אָבִיו אֶלָּא פַּעַם אַחַת וּבַחֲצִי דִבּוּר, הִנֵּה דַּי לְאוֹתוֹ הַבֵּן לְהָבִין הֵיכָן דַּעְתּוֹ שֶׁל אָבִיו נוֹטָה לַעֲשׂוֹת לוֹ גַּם אֶת אֲשֶׁר לֹא אָמַר לוֹ בְּפֵרוּשׁ.

The root of Chassidus is contained in the Talmudic passage "Fortunate is he who toils in Torah and gives pleasure to his Creator" (Berachos 17a). Whereas there are mitzvos that are obligatory, and their duty is known to all, a person who truly loves G-d will not be satisfied merely by discharging his obligations. Rather, he will be like a son who loves his father, and if the father in any way indicates what he would like, even by a subtle hint, that would suffice for the son to understand what would please the father, and he will hurry to do this, without waiting to be explicitly instructed to do so.

Earlier we discussed the great spirituality of the patriarchs, whose devotion to G-d was so absolute that they were attracted to doing what was later revealed in the Torah as being the mitzvos, the explicit Divine commandments. Whereas such perfection may not be within our reach, we are instructed in *Ethics of the Fathers* (2:4), "Make His will your will." In addition to the mitzvos, which are the expressed will of G-d, there are other indications, which Ramchal refers to as "subtle hints," as to what pleases G-d. Although these are not incumbent on everyone as are the mitzvos, a person who has an intense love for G-d will strive to do whatever he believes will give G-d pleasure.

One of the richest sources of "subtle hints" is the repository of the stories of the lives of *tzaddikim*. The Talmud states that the narration of the servants of the patriarchs is given greater emphasis in the Torah than the scholarly conclusions of their offspring (*Bereishis Rabbah* 60:11). This is because the narration of the servants provides a description of the behavior of the patriarchs and the latter serves as an indication of the Divine will.

This principle holds true throughout the ages. In fact, all behavior should be modeled after the *tzaddikim* closest to our own time rather than those of yore. We are so far removed from the earlier *tzaddikim* that we cannot properly emulate them. Rabbi Chaim Shmulevitz derives this principle from the Talmud: Model yourself after the *tzaddik* closest to your own generation (*Sichos Mussar* 5732:10).

Another example of *Chassidus* is doing a mitzvah in the finest manner possible. A mitzvah may be duly fulfilled by meeting the minimum requirements, and one who acts because he is duty bound may indeed do so. One who acts out of intense love for G-d, however, will throw himself heart and soul into the mitzvah. For example, a covering for the Torah Scroll can be made of simple material which would suffice. One who loves Torah and wishes to beautify it will make an attractive covering out of fine material, and adorn it with beautiful decorative embroidery. This is true of all other mitzvos as well.

Much emphasis is placed on celebrating performance of mitzvos with joy rather than just fulfilling one's obligation. It is for this reason that we celebrate a *bris* (circumcision), a *pidyon haben* (redemption of the first-born son), or completion of a volume of the Talmud with a festive meal.

One of the chassidic masters said that when the angel Gabriel praises Israel before G-d for their performance of the Divine mitzvos, Satan counters by citing the sins which Jews commit. Gabriel responds, "Granted that they sometimes sin, but it is only because they cannot withstand the temptation Satan places before them. However, have you ever seen anyone celebrate a sin with a festive meal? It is only mitzvos that are celebrated in this way. This shows where their hearts lie."

וְהִנֵּה דָּבָר זֶה אֲנַחְנוּ רוֹאִים אוֹתוֹ בְּעֵינֵינוּ שֶׁיִּוָּלֵד בְּכָל עֵת וּבְכָל שָׁעָה בֵּין כָּל אוֹהֵב וָרֵעַ, בֵּין אִישׁ לְאִשְׁתּוֹ, בֵּין אָב וּבְנוֹ, כְּלָלוֹ שֶׁל דָּבָר – בֵּין כָּל מִי שֶׁהָאַהֲבָה בֵּינֵיהֶם עַזָּה בֶּאֱמֶת, שֶׁלֹּא יֹאמַר: לֹא נִצְטַוֵּיתִי יוֹתֵר, דַּי לִי בְּמַה שֶּׁנִּצְטַוֵּיתִי בְּפֵרוּשׁ, אֶלָּא מִמַּה שֶּׁנִּצְטַוָּה יָדוּן עַל דַּעַת הַמְצַוֶּה וְיִשְׁתַּדֵּל לַעֲשׂוֹת לוֹ מַה שֶּׁיּוּכַל לָדוּן שֶׁיִּהְיֶה לוֹ לְנַחַת. וְהִנֵּה כַּמִּקְרֶה הַזֶּה יִקְרֶה לְמִי שֶׁאוֹהֵב אֶת בּוֹרְאוֹ גַּם כֵּן אַהֲבָה נֶאֱמֶנֶת, כִּי גַּם הוּא מִסּוּג הָאוֹהֲבִים וְתִהְיֶינָה לוֹ הַמִּצְוֹת אֲשֶׁר צֻוּוּיָם גָּלוּי וּמְפֻרְסָם לְגִלּוּי דַּעַת לְבָד, לָדַעַת שֶׁאֶל הָעִנְיָן הַהוּא נוֹטֶה רְצוֹנוֹ וְחֶפְצוֹ יִתְבָּרֵךְ שְׁמוֹ.

We frequently see this attitude toward a person whom one loves, whether husband and wife, or parent and child. Wherever there is an intense love one does not say, "I have fulfilled my obligations," but rather endeavors to give pleasure to those one loves. So it is with one who loves G-d, who does not merely try to discharge his obligation with fulfillment of the mandatory mitzvos, but knowing what it is that gives pleasure to G-d, will do whatever he can to achieve that goal.

There is a mitzvah of *hachnassas orchim*, hospitality to wayfarers. The obligation to perform this mitzvah occurs when a traveler knocks on your door and asks for food or lodging. There is no obligation to go through the town looking for wayfarers. The patriarch Abraham, however, did just that. The Midrash states that there were signposts along the various roads directing travelers to Abraham's home, and furthermore there were doors on four sides of the house so that a weary wayfarer could have prompt and easy entry. When the patriarch was weak following his circumcision, G-d brought out the sun in its full strength to discourage travelers, so that Abraham could rest. However, the patriarch sat outside his home looking for wayfarers to whom he could extend his hospitality, and when G-d saw that his distress in not having guests was so intense, G-d sent three angels in the form of humans so that Abraham could enjoy the mitzvah of *hachnassas orchim*.

Obligations can be discharged grudgingly as when one pays taxes, or with love, as when one pays the expenses of one's household. In either case, one is performing a duty. The husband who loves his wife and the father who loves his children will go beyond this, thinking of ways whereby he can bring them pleasure and cheer. He might bring home flowers, or a little gift he knows his wife will enjoy. Upon seeing something he knows the children will take pleasure in, he may bring it for them. Even after a hard day's work, he will assist his wife with care of the children and the dinner dishes, knowing that she may have had an exhausting day at work or taking care of the home. These are not obligatory on a person, but come out of love, out of the desire to give whatever pleasure one can to those one loves.

This, then, is what constitutes *Chassidus*. Fasting and self-mutilation do not give pleasure to G-d, and are reserved as acts of penance for certain transgressions. True *Chassidus* is seeking to do that which is pleasing to G-d, above and beyond the mandatory mitzvos. We are told that it is His will that we emulate His attributes to be merciful, kind, forgiving, and truthful. The more intense one's love for G-d, the more one will exert oneself to do His will, and please Him.

נִמְצָא כְּלַל הַחֲסִידוּת, הַרְחָבַת קִיּוּם כָּל הַמִּצְוֹת בְּכָל הַצְּדָדִים וְהַתְּנָאִים שֶׁרָאוּי וְשֶׁאֶפְשָׁר. וְהִנְּךָ רוֹאֶה, שֶׁהַחֲסִידוּת מִמִּין הַפְּרִישׁוּת, אֶלָּא שֶׁהַפְּרִישׁוּת בַּלָּאוִין וְהַחֲסִידוּת בַּעֲשִׂין, וּשְׁנֵיהֶם עִנְיָן אֶחָד, שֶׁהוּא לְהוֹסִיף עַל הַמְּפוֹרָשׁ מַה שֶּׁנּוּכַל לָדוּן לְפִי הַמִּצְוָה הַמְּפוֹרֶשֶׁת שֶׁיִּהְיֶה נַחַת רוּחַ לְפָנָיו יִתְבָּרֵךְ.

It is obvious that Chassidus and Abstinence are similar, and that in each case a person goes beyond what is explicitly required of him. They differ only in that Abstinence is an extra effort in avoidance of prohibitive acts, whereas Chassidus is an extra effort in performance of mitzvos.

In his discussion of Abstinence, Ramchal did not mention the similarity to *Chassidus*, but from his discussion of *Chassidus*, we can also gain another perspective on Abstinence. I.e., that a person will refrain from doing something that he knows would be displeasing to G-d, even if this is not in any way explicitly prohibited, either by Scriptural or rabbinic law.

19

בְּבֵאוּר חֶלְקֵי הַחֲסִידוּת
Divisions of Chassidus

חֶלְקֵי הַחֲסִידוּת הָרָאשִׁיִּים, שְׁלֹשָׁה: הָרִאשׁוֹן, בְּמַּעֲשֶׂה. הַשֵּׁנִי, בְּאֹפֶן הָעֲשִׂיָּה. הַשְּׁלִישִׁי, בְּכַוָּנָה. הַחֵלֶק הָרִאשׁוֹן בְּמַּעֲשֶׂה, אַף הוּא יִתְחַלֵּק לִשְׁנֵי חֲלָקִים. הָאֶחָד בְּמַה שֶּׁבֵּין אָדָם לַמָּקוֹם, וְהַשֵּׁנִי בְּמַה שֶּׁבֵּין אָדָם לַחֲבֵרוֹ.
הַחֵלֶק הָרִאשׁוֹן שֶׁבָּרִאשׁוֹן הוּא בְּמַּעֲשֶׂה שֶׁבֵּין אָדָם לַמָּקוֹם, וְעִנְיָנוֹ, קִיּוּם כָּל הַמִּצְוֹת בְּכָל הַדִּקְדּוּקִים שֶׁבָּהֶם עַד מְקוֹם שֶׁיַּד הָאָדָם מַגַּעַת . . . כִּי אַף־עַל־פִּי שֶׁגּוּף הַמִּצְוָה נִשְׁלָם זוּלָתָם וּכְבָר יָצָא בָּזֶה יְדֵי חוֹבָתוֹ . . . אַךְ חֲסִידִים אֵין לָהֶם אֶלָּא לְהַרְבּוֹת בְּהַשְׁלָמָתָם.

There are three divisions of Chassidus: the deed itself, how it is performed, and with what kavannah (intention). The deed itself can be further subdivided into that between man and G-d, and that between man and his fellow man.

As regards the deed between man and G-d, this refers to the fulfillment of mitzvos with all their finer details ... Although the mitzvah may be fulfilled without meticulous details ... the Chassid will wish to do so in a manner that includes the finest details.

We may better understand the quality of a mitzvah through an analogy from today's lifestyle. Every person has an innate desire to maintain his well-being. Nowadays, each cereal box and almost all other packaged food have a listing of the minimum daily requirements that connote the bare necessities one needs to function. But these minimum requirements fall far short of the desired levels for proper nutrition. Therefore most people try to vary their diets by making generous use of the four recommended food groups and thus provide themselves with sound healthy diet.

Some individuals are not satisfied with achieving these levels which effect proper nutrition and opt for even higher standards, by following a diet free of excess fat, white flour, sugar and/or milk products. They choose instead to use only organically grown fruits and vegetables, high-fiber foods and megadoses of vitamins. Even though they can function at satisfactory levels with a "normal" regimen they choose to enhance their capabilities with the use of "extras."

This is equally true of many mitzvos. *Esrog* is a good example. Superficial blemishes caused in the natural growing process do not disqualify an *esrog*, nor is an *esrog* disqualified if it grew without a *pitam*. But an absolutely unblemished *esrog* with a *pitam* is *preferred*, though not required, and many people go to great lengths to find such a "beauty."

For the average person a "minimum requirement" mitzvah may suffice. The *Chassid* wishes his mitzvah to be enhanced with extras.

הַחֵלֶק הַשֵּׁנִי שֶׁבָּרִאשׁוֹן הוּא בְּמַה שֶּׁבֵּין אָדָם לַחֲבֵרוֹ, וְעִנְיָנוֹ, גֹּדֶל הַהֲטָבָה שֶׁיִּהְיֶה הָאָדָם לְעוֹלָם מֵטִיב לַבְּרִיּוֹת וְלֹא מֵרֵעַ לָהֶם . . . בַּגּוּף, שֶׁיִּהְיֶה מִשְׁתַּדֵּל לַעֲזוֹר כָּל אָדָם בְּמַה שֶּׁיּוּכַל וְיָקֵל מַשָּׂאָם מֵעֲלֵיהֶם . . . וְאִם מַגִּיעַ לַחֲבֵרוֹ אֵיזֶה נֵזֶק בְּגוּפוֹ וְהוּא יוּכַל לִמְנוֹעַ אוֹתוֹ אוֹ לַהֲסִירוֹ, יִטְרַח כְּדֵי לַעֲשׂוֹתוֹ.

Insofar as acts between man and his fellow man are concerned, Chassidus requires constant benevolence toward others, avoiding any harm to body, soul, or possessions . . .

"Body" means that one should endeavor to lighten another person's burden in whatever way possible . . . and if one can prevent or remove anything that is damaging to another, he should exert himself to do so.

The mitzvah of *gemilus chasodim*, acts of benevolence, is one that is without limitation. One should do the utmost to be of personal assistance to others in whatever way possible.

The Talmud relates that Elijah told several sages that there were two people in the marketplace who are assured of a place in *Gan Eden*

(Paradise). The sages were curious as to what great mitzvos these people had done to merit so great a reward. They confronted them, asking, "Tell us what you do here." The men replied, "We are comedians. There are some people here who are saddened and are disagreeable. When we see someone who appears dejected, we try to amuse him and bring him cheer, so that he makes peace with everyone" (*Taanis* 22a).

Visiting the sick, comforting the bereaved, bringing joy to a *chassan* and *kallah* (groom and bride) are some examples of easing another's burden, relieving his distress, and increasing his happiness.

The Torah concept of *gemilus chasodim* is particularly pertinent in this day and age, when people are often reluctant to become personally involved in alleviating other people's burdens, and discharge their care for their fellow man via an agency. Hence we have agencies that minister to the elderly, to the disabled, and to neglected children. These agencies are funded by taxes or by charitable contributions, and whereas people will give of their money, they may not give so readily of themselves. As a result of a lack of personal involvement, the needs of many of those who could benefit from assistance are unmet, but no one knows of it. Everyone assumes that the agency responsible for providing the service is doing its job adequately. Little do they realize that these agencies are often underfunded and understaffed, and that they cannot provide more than a mere fraction of the needed services.

In addition, even if a person is unable to relieve the actual burden of one in need it is always possible to empathize, sympathize, and share one's difficulties. The Torah states that when Moses was a prince in the palace of Pharaoh, he "went out amongst his brethren and saw their travail" (*Exodus* 2:11). The Midrash states that he went amongst the slaves and lent his shoulder to help them with their heavy loads. The actual hands-on help to a few of the many thousands of slaves may have been insignificant, but the awareness that he was participating in their distress was felt by all.

Rabbi Yeruchem Levovitz explains that Moses' participation in the labor of the enslaved Israelites was more than a gesture to lift their spirits. He states that when one merely *sees* another's plight, even though one's emotions are aroused, the empathy with the suffering is incomplete. Moses felt that he could not genuinely empathize with his brethren unless he personally felt the heavy weight on his shoulders and his back breaking under the burden. In *Ethics of the Fathers* (6:6) the Talmud states that sharing another person's burden is one of the requisites for acquiring Torah, and Rabbi Yeruchem points out that this trait of caring and sharing goes beyond the mitzvah of loving one's neighbor, since it is a prerequisite for acquisition of Torah.

This aspect of helping another is lacking when *gemilus chasodim* is delegated to an agency. Thus, the *Chassid* is not satisfied with discharging his obligations via an agent. He takes a personal interest and gives of his own time and energy to provide for those in need, identifying with and genuinely sharing in others' distress.

בַּמָּמוֹן, לְסַיְּעוֹ בַּאֲשֶׁר תַּשִּׂיג יָדוֹ וְלִמְנוֹעַ מִמֶּנּוּ הַנְּזָקִין בְּכָל מַה שֶּׁיּוּכַל, וְכָל־שֶׁכֵּן שֶׁיַּרְחִיק הוּא כָּל מִינֵי נְזָקִין שֶׁיְּכוֹלִים לָבוֹא מֵחֲמָתוֹ, בֵּין לְיָחִיד בֵּין לְרַבִּים. וַאֲפִלּוּ שֶׁעַתָּה מִיָּד אֵין הֶזֵּקָם מָצוּי, כֵּיוָן שֶׁיָּכוֹל לָבוֹא לִידֵי כָּךְ, יְסִירֵם וְיַעֲבִירֵם. וְאָמְרוּ ז״ל (אבות ב, יב): ,,יְהִי מָמוֹן חֲבֵרְךָ חָבִיב עָלֶיךָ כְּשֶׁלָּךְ.״

Insofar as possessions are concerned, Chassidus requires providing assistance to ensure that no harm befell another's belongings, and certainly to avoid being the cause of any harm himself, even if the effect would be remote. This applies both to individual and public property. The Talmud says, "Let your fellow man's belongings be as dear to you as your own" (Ethics of the Fathers 2:12).

Ramchal requires respect for public property, and states that it, too, is subject to the Talmudic dictum, "Let your neighbor's property be as dear to you as your own." A *Chassid* does not litter, does not throw things out of the car window, and is careful that his trash is properly contained so that it does not pollute the neighborhood. A person would not wish his home to be cluttered, and one should treat the public property as though it were his own.

The Talmud tells of a man who was clearing his garden and was throwing rocks into the street. A *Chassid* passed by and remarked, "Why do you take rocks from a property that does not belong to you and throw it into your own property?" The man laughed at the *Chassid's* apparently senseless remark.

Awhile later, the man lost all his money and had to sell his house. Walking along the street, he stumbled over one of the rocks he had thrown out of his garden. "How wise that *Chassid* was," he said. "My own property is something I can lose, whereas the public property is always mine" (*Bava Kamma* 50b).

"Let your fellow man's belongings be as dear to you as your own" requires some explanation. We may sometimes take liberties with our own possessions, treating them roughly, particularly if they are not very valuable. This does not give us a license to handle our neighbors possessions carelessly. We must understand the Talmud to mean that we should care for the least of our neighbors' belongings as much as we would for our most precious valuables.

Just how sensitive and considerate one must be not to impinge on another person can be seen from the story of Rabbi Yisrael of Salant, who once visited Warsaw. When word spread that the great sage was in town, throngs gathered at the synagogue for *Minchah* (afternoon prayer). How astonished everyone was that Rabbi Yisrael completed his prayers very quickly, which was a distinct departure from his usual lengthy prayer. Rabbi Yisrael explained, "Many people have closed their stores and shops to greet me. Extending my prayer would have caused them to wait longer and would have taken them away from their work and earnings. I cannot pray at someone else's expense."

When the Chafetz Chaim wrote one of his books, he contracted with a yeshiva student to copy the manuscript for publication, and set a price per page of twenty lines each. In reviewing the copy, the Chafetz Chaim found a number of pages with twenty-two lines. He hurried to the student's home and insisted on calculating how much additional money he owed for the extra lines.

Prior to selling his books, the Chafetz Chaim would meticulously examine each one to make sure that there were no missing pages or other defects in the printing. Some people today have copies of his books with corrections in his own handwriting. It is known that the Chafetz Chaim never wasted a single moment, and used every available second for Torah study. For him to spend so much time leafing through each single book he sold indicates that he considered the avoidance of possibly inadvertently selling defective merchandise to override even the study of Torah.

בַּנֶּפֶשׁ, שֶׁיִּשְׁתַּדֵּל לַעֲשׂוֹת לַחֲבֵרוֹ כָּל קוֹרַת־רוּחַ שֶׁיֵּשׁ בְּיָדוֹ . . . וְכָל־שֶׁכֵּן שֶׁלֹּא יְצַעֲרֶנּוּ בְּשׁוּם מִינֵי צַעַר כְּלָל . . . וּבִכְלָל זֶה רְדִיפַת הַשָּׁלוֹם שֶׁהוּא הַהֲטָבָה הַכְּלָלִית בֵּין כָּל אָדָם לַחֲבֵרוֹ.

Insofar as spirit is concerned, a Chassid will strive to do whatever he can to give pleasure to another person . . . and will certainly avoid causing him any kind of distress . . . This endeavor also includes pursuit of peace, which is the furtherance of good between man and his fellow man.

C*hassidus* requires being most considerate of other people. So much so, that if one knows what will please another person, and it is reasonable to provide him with his wish, the *Chassid* will do so. There are some people who thrive on being honored and recognized, and the *Chassid* will do his best to show the desired respect, even to someone who may be beneath him. The Talmud states that Rabbi Yochanan ben Zakkai was always first to greet others, not waiting for them to greet him first (*Berachos* 18a). Just as a person will try to bring pleasure to his loved ones, so will a *Chassid* have this attitude toward everyone.

The chassidic master, Rabbi David of Lelov, once said, "How can people possibly think of me as a *tzaddik*, when I feel more love for my own children than for other children?" Perhaps we cannot aspire to this level of *Chassidus*, but it does provide us with a concept of what *Chassidus* is all about.

Not every person achieves the levels of learning and spirituality to know what is the true good. As mentioned, some people crave being honored, whereas a more thoughtful person understands the foolishness of such vanity. "Nevertheless," said the Rabbi of Kotzk, "to provide a fool with his foolish pleasures is also a mitzvah." An infant may wail bitterly because it wants a brightly colored block of wood, and although this is a trivial object to an adult, to the child it is all important, and the parent will gladly give him the object of his desire, unless, of course, it has sharp edges or is otherwise dangerous. So it is with adults, who may have desires that to the more enlightened person are juvenile. As long as they are not harmful in any way, the *Chassid* will seek to provide that pleasure.

It goes without saying that a *Chassid* will assiduously avoid offending anyone, and will do everything possible to protect a person's dignity. It is related that Rabbi Akiva Eiger had a guest at the *seder* who accidentally spilled his cup of wine on the table. Instantaneously, Rabbi Akiva Eiger shook the table with his knee, causing other cups to spill, to make it appear that the guest had not been clumsy, and that the spillage was due to the shaky table.

The significance of the above anecdote can be fully appreciated only if one realizes that had Rabbi Akiva Eiger been tardy in shaking the table by even a few seconds, it would have been of no use, since by then the guest's clumsiness would have been evident. The *kuntz* (novelty) was that his response was instantaneous, meaning that he was constantly on the alert to protect other people's dignity and did not have to pause even momentarily to figure out what to do. This is *Chassidus* at its finest.

Ramchal cites numerous examples from the Talmud as to the *Chassidus* of the sages, such as Rabbi Nechunya who attributed his longevity to, "I never derived honor at another person's expense, and a grudge against another person never accompanied me to bed." Rabbi Elazar said, "I observed the sanctity of the synagogue, never using it as a shortcut to my destination, and I never held myself superior to others." Rabbi Zeira said, "I never raised my voice at home, I never walked four cubits without Torah or *tefillin*, and I never took pleasure in someone else's failure" (*Megillah* 27-28).

When Rabbi Nechunya entered the house of study, he would pray, "Protect me from making mistakes that might cause my comrades to ridicule me, lest they be punished for doing so." Rabbi Nechunya was not concerned that he might be humiliated, but that he did not wish to provide grounds that might cause others to sin.

וְהִנֵּה גְּמִילוּת־חֲסָדִים הוּא עִקָּר גָּדוֹל לֶחָסִיד, כִּי חֲסִידוּת עַצְמוֹ נִגְזָר מֵחֶסֶד. וְאָמְרוּ ז״ל (אבות א, ב): „עַל שְׁלֹשָׁה דְּבָרִים הָעוֹלָם עוֹמֵד," וְאֶחָד מֵהֶם גְּמִילוּת־חֲסָדִים . . . וְאָמְרוּ עוֹד (ראה יבמות עט, א): „דָּרַשׁ רָבָא, כָּל מִי שֶׁיֵּשׁ בּוֹ שָׁלֹשׁ מִדּוֹת הַלָּלוּ בְּיָדוּעַ שֶׁהוּא מִזַּרְעוֹ שֶׁל אַבְרָהָם אָבִינוּ: רַחֲמָן, וּבַיְשָׁן, וְגוֹמֵל חֲסָדִים" . . . „בִּשְׁלֹשָׁה דְבָרִים גְּדוֹלָה גְּמִילוּת־חֲסָדִים מִן הַצְּדָקָה: שֶׁהַצְּדָקָה בְּמָמוֹנוֹ, וּגְמִילוּת־חֲסָדִים בְּגוּפוֹ . . . וְאָמְרוּ עוֹד (שבת קנא, ב): „וְנָתַן לְךָ רַחֲמִים וְרִחַמְךָ . . . וְזֶה פָּשׁוּט, כִּי הַקָּדוֹשׁ־בָּרוּךְ־הוּא מוֹדֵד מִדָּה כְּנֶגֶד מִדָּה. וּמִי שֶׁמְּרַחֵם וְעוֹשֶׂה חֶסֶד עִם הַבְּרִיּוֹת, גַּם הוּא בְּדִינוֹ יְרַחֲמוּהוּ וְיִמְחֲלוּ לוֹ עֲוֹנוֹתָיו בְּחֶסֶד, שֶׁהֲרֵי מְחִילָה זוֹ דִּין הוּא, כֵּיוָן שֶׁהִיא מִדָּה כְּנֶגֶד מִדָּתוֹ . . . וּמִי שֶׁאֵינוֹ רוֹצֶה לְהַעֲבִיר עַל מִדּוֹתָיו אוֹ אֵינוֹ רוֹצֶה לִגְמוֹל חֶסֶד, הִנֵּה הַדִּין נוֹתֵן שֶׁגַּם עִמּוֹ לֹא יַעֲשׂוּ אֶלָּא שׁוּרַת הַדִּין. רְאֵה עַתָּה, מִי הוּא זֶה וְאֵיזֶה הוּא שֶׁיּוּכַל לַעֲמוֹד אִם הַקָּדוֹשׁ־בָּרוּךְ־הוּא עוֹשֶׂה עִמּוֹ שׁוּרַת הַדִּין . . . אָמְנָם הָעוֹשֶׂה חֶסֶד, יְקַבֵּל חֶסֶד. וּבְכָל מַה שֶּׁיַּרְבֶּה לַעֲשׂוֹת כָּךְ יַרְבֶּה לְקַבֵּל.

For the Chassid, gemilus chasadim (acts of kindness) is all important. After all, the world Chassid is derived from the word chesed (kindness), and the Talmud considers gemilus chasadim to be a pillar of the universe (Ethics of the

Fathers 1:2)... Furthermore, Rava says that a descendant of Abraham can be identified by three traits: mercy, modesty, and gemilus chasadim (Yevamos 79a. Hence the latter is the essence of Judaism)... Gemilus chasadim is superior even to tzedakah, because the latter is accomplished with one's possessions, whereas gemilus chasadim is enacted with one's self...

The Talmud says that if one is merciful to others, G-d is merciful to him (Shabbos 151b)... G-d acts toward a person correspondingly as the person acts toward others. Hence, one who forgives is himself forgiven... If one insists on exacting stern justice, G-d will demand stern justice of him.

Inasmuch as no person is without sin, how can one possibly avoid a harsh judgment?... Only by gemilus chasadim, whereby he will merit a similar Divine attitude toward him.

Ramchal reinforces his earlier criticism of popular misconceptions of *Chassidus*. Since the etymology of "*Chassidus*" is based on the word "*chesed*," there is no way to consider fasting, lengthy confessions, and self-mortification as constituting *Chassidus*, since these are not acts of kindness and are of no benefit to others. The true *Chassid* champions *chesed* in every possible way. Ramchal goes so far as to say that if one is derelict in *gemilus chasodim*, it raises questions as to his Jewish authenticity as a descendant of Abraham.

Ramchal provides an additional motivation for *Chassidus*. Inasmuch as no human being can be totally free of sin, how can one expect a favorable judgment before the all-knowing Divine Tribunal? His answer is similar to the Baal Shem Tov's interpretation of the verse in *Psalms* (121:5) "G-d is your shadow," which means that just as a person's shadow follows every move he makes, so does G-d react in accord with how a person behaves to others. With those who are stern and strict to others, G-d is stern and strict. To those who are merciful and forgiving, G-d is merciful and forgiving. Practice of *Chassidus* can thus elicit Divine forgiveness that might otherwise not be forthcoming.

וּבִכְלָל הָעִנְיָן הַזֶּה שֶׁלֹּא לְצַעֵר לְשׁוּם בְּרִיָּה אֲפִלּוּ בַּעֲלֵי־חַיִּים, וּלְרַחֵם וְלָחוּס עֲלֵיהֶם . . . וּכְבָר יֵשׁ שֶׁסּוֹבְרִים צַעַר בַּעֲלֵי־חַיִּים דְּאוֹרָיְתָא (שבת קכח, ב): וְעַל־כָּל־פָּנִים, דְּרַבָּנָן.

Included in Chassidus is that one should not inflict pain on any living thing, including animals, but be kind and protective of them . . . Causing pain to animals is forbidden, whether by Scripture or rabbinic law.

The Talmud relates that Rabbi Yehudah HaNasi, who redacted the *Mishnah*, was punished for failure to be kind to an animal. A calf which was being led to slaughter ran off and hid under the Rabbi's cloak. The Rabbi turned the calf over to the butcher, saying to it, "Go, for this is the purpose for which you were created." A Divine edict was therefore issued, "Because you had no mercy on an animal, no mercy will be shown to you," and Rabbi Yehudah was subjected to a prolonged, painful illness.

One day the housekeeper was about to sweep away a nest of tiny animals, and Rabbi Yehudah stopped her, allowing the young to remain in the nest. A Divine edict was then heard, "Because you are considerate of animals, you will be shown mercy," and Rabbi Yehudah's illness left him (*Bava Metzia* 85a).

Whereas plants are not capable of feeling pain, a *Chassid* respects these as well, and does not abuse them. Reb Shraga Feivel Mendlowitz was walking with some of his students, and one of them tore off a leaf from a tree. The rabbi said, "There are four levels of existence: the inanimate, the vegetative, the live, and the human. Each one should be raised to a higher level, so that the inanimate earth nurtures the vegetation, which is eaten by the animal, which provides food and labor for man, who can dedicate his life to G-d. Using vegetation in this way is an elevation, but tearing a leaf off a tree for no constructive purpose at all is demoting the vegetative to the inanimate. This is not the direction in which a person should be heading."

הַחֵלֶק הַשֵּׁנִי מִן הַחֲסִידוּת הוּא בְּאֹפֶן הָעֲשִׂיָּה. וְהִנֵּה גַּם־זֶה נִכְלָל בִּשְׁנֵי עִנְיָנִים. אָמְנָם תַּחְתֵּיהֶם נִכְלָלִים פְּרָטִים רַבִּים. וּשְׁנַיִם הָרָאשִׁיִּים הֵם הַיִּרְאָה וְהָאַהֲבָה . . . בִּכְלָל הַיִּרְאָה יֵשׁ: הַהַכְנָעָה מִלְּפָנָיו יִתְבָּרֵךְ, הַבֹּשֶׁת בִּקְרֹב אֶל עֲבוֹדָתוֹ, וְהַכָּבוֹד הַנַּעֲשֶׂה אֶל מִצְוֹתָיו . . . הַשִּׂמְחָה, הַדְּבֵקוּת וְהַקִּנְאָה . . . הִנֵּה עִקַּר הַיִּרְאָה הִיא יִרְאַת הָרוֹמְמוּת, שֶׁצָּרִיךְ הָאָדָם לַחֲשׁוֹב בְּעוֹדוֹ מִתְפַּלֵּל אוֹ עוֹשֶׂה מִצְוָה כִּי לִפְנֵי מֶלֶךְ־מַלְכֵי־הַמְּלָכִים הוּא מִתְפַּלֵּל אוֹ עוֹשֶׂה הַמַּעֲשֶׂה הַהוּא.

The second division of Chassidus concerns the manner of performance. There are two chief areas: yirah or reverence for G-d, and ahavah, love of G-d, which subsume many particulars ... Reverence refers to humbling himself before G-d, humility in approaching his service, and the honor accorded to mitzvos ... Included in love of G-d are joy, communion, and appropriate zeal ...

The chief aspect of yirah is reverence for the majesty of G-d of which a person must be mindful when praying or performing a mitzvah; i.e., that he is doing so in presence of the King of kings.

It should be noted that whereas earlier Ramchal cited the varieties of *yirah*, such as referring to fear of punishment or fear of G-d, here he refers only to the "lofty" *yirah*, or the sense of awe and reverence consequent to contemplation of the majesty of G-d. The other varieties of *yirah* are not mentioned here because Ramchal is now discussing the *yirah* of *Chassidus*, of one who has mastered the preceding traits and is now at a stage of sincere devotion to G-d, wishing to do only that which he believes will please G-d. This individual is far beyond the juvenile concept of fear of punishment.

Contemplating about G-d can be quite a challenge to the human mind. All our intellectual faculties deal with finite and measurable entities, and our experience does not provide us with any reference point for something that has no beginning, no end, and is immeasurable. We may be overwhelmed by astronomical numbers, as when we talk about a star being a billion light years away, with light traveling at one hundred eighty-six thousand miles per second, and while such an enormous figure is virtually unimaginable, it is nevertheless a measurement, and if one has a large enough blackboard, one could write out the actual number of miles. Concerning infinity, however, there is simply no grasping it at all. Even the astronomical number cited is insignificant in relation to infinity. Thus, we really seem to have no means of contemplating about G-d. In fact, since the human mind knows only finite concepts, it has been said that whatever we *can* think about G-d is *not* true of Him. If we can conceive of something, it must be finite, and nothing that is finite is true of G-d.

Our traditional theologians therefore state that we can only contemplate about the *works* of G-d and about those traits that are apparent to us or have been made known to us through prophetic revelation, but we cannot have any knowledge about G-d Himself. Try as we might, we are limited to human concepts and human terms, even when we speak about G-d as being All-knowing, All-powerful, and Omnipresent. But even with these limitations on our thinking, we can stand in utter awe of a Being so great that He defies any conceptualization, and that this Supreme Being wishes to relate to us, to hear our prayers, and to receive our service. Contemplation of this should result in a profound sense of reverence and self-effacement before G-d.

וְהִנֵּה שְׁלֹשָׁה דְבָרִים צָרִיךְ שֶׁיִסְתַּכֵּל הָאָדָם וְיִתְבּוֹנֵן הֵיטֵב כְּדֵי שֶׁיַּגִּיעַ אֶל זֹאת הַיִּרְאָה. הָאֶחָד, שֶׁהוּא עוֹמֵד מַמָּשׁ לִפְנֵי הַבּוֹרֵא יִתְבָּרַךְ־שְׁמוֹ וְנוֹשֵׂא וְנוֹתֵן עִמּוֹ אַף־עַל־פִּי שֶׁאֵין עֵינוֹ שֶׁל אָדָם רוֹאָהוּ . . . אָמְנָם מִי שֶׁהוּא בַּעַל שֵׂכֶל נָכוֹן, בִּמְעַט הִתְבּוֹנְנוּת וְשִׂימַת לֵב יוּכַל לִקְבּוֹעַ בְּלִבּוֹ אֲמִתַּת הַדָּבָר אֵיךְ הוּא בָּא וְנוֹשֵׂא וְנוֹתֵן מַמָּשׁ עִמּוֹ יִתְבָּרֵךְ, וּלְפָנָיו הוּא מִתְחַנֵּן, וּמֵאִתּוֹ הוּא מְבַקֵּשׁ, וְהוּא יִתְבָּרֵךְ שְׁמוֹ מַאֲזִין לוֹ . . . וְאַחַר שֶׁיִּקְבַּע זֶה בְּדַעְתּוֹ, צָרִיךְ שֶׁיִּתְבּוֹנֵן עַל רוֹמְמוּתוֹ יִתְבָּרֵךְ אֲשֶׁר הוּא מְרוֹמָם וְנִשְׂגָּב עַל כָּל בְּרָכָה וּתְהִלָּה עַל כָּל מִינֵי שְׁלֵמוּת שֶׁתּוּכַל מַחֲשַׁבְתֵּנוּ לְדַמּוֹת וּלְהָבִין. וְעוֹד צָרִיךְ שֶׁיִּתְבּוֹנֵן עַל שִׁפְלוּת הָאָדָם וּפְחִיתוּתוֹ לְפִי חָמְרִיּוּתוֹ וְגַסּוּתוֹ, כָּל־שֶׁכֵּן לְפִי הַחֲטָאִים שֶׁחָטָא מֵעוֹדוֹ, כִּי עַל־כָּל־אֵלֶּה, אִי־אֶפְשָׁר שֶׁלֹּא יֶחֱרַד לִבּוֹ וְלֹא יִרְעַשׁ בְּעוֹדוֹ מְדַבֵּר דְּבָרָיו לְפָנָיו יִתְבָּרֵךְ וּמַזְכִּיר בִּשְׁמוֹ וּמִשְׁתַּדֵּל לְהֵרָצוֹת לוֹ, הוּא מָה שֶׁאָמַר הַכָּתוּב (תהלים ב, יא): ,,עִבְדוּ אֶת־ה׳ בְּיִרְאָה וְגִילוּ בִּרְעָדָה״.

To arrive at yirah one should be mindful of three things: (1) that one is in the imminent presence of G-d and is communicating with Him . . . Even though He is not visible or subject to any sense perception, a person of sound intelligence, with due contemplation, can establish the validity of this, and know that G-d is listening to him . . . (2) once he knows he is standing before G-d he should reflect on His majesty that He is above and beyond anything which the human mind can imagine; and (3) the inferior status of mortal man, who is contaminated with sin. This should cause one to tremble with awe, yet be joyous in the privilege of communicating with G-d, as it is written, "Serve G-d with reverence, and rejoice when there is trembling" (Psalms 2:11).

Primitive people, unable to deal with an abstract concept of G-d, created various icons and idols to facilitate their communication with their deity. The Torah repeatedly emphasizes, "You saw no image (at Sinai)" and again "no image was seen, only a voice" (*Deuteronomy* 4:15,18), and most explicitly prohibits any attempt to concretize G-d in any way. The Torah expects the Jew to rise to a higher level of intelligence and believe in G-d as an abstraction. The phenomenon of the revelation at Sinai, witnessed by two million people, and transmitted from generation to generation, should serve to reinforce our faith in G-d.

One of the fundamental principles of Judaism is Divine providence; i.e., G-d takes an interest in the affairs of man, and of each individual person. One might ask, Given mortal man's inferior status and the unfathomable greatness of G-d, why would He be concerned about a mere human being?

There are two answers to this question. Firstly, the Talmud states that wherever we find a reference to the greatness of G-d in Torah, there we also find His profound humility (*Megillah* 31a). It is thus not extraordinary that the ultimate Greatness is concerned with something so minute. Secondly, we must understand that relative to infinity, there is no difference between the significance of man, the significance of the heavenly angels, the significance of a galaxy, or for that matter the significance of the entire universe. In dealing with a finite object, even something as immense as the ocean, we can say that a single drop is completely insignificant, whereas several trillion gallons of water are of some substance. Relative to infinity, however, there is no difference whether the object is microscopic or of vast proportions. Both are equally insignificant in relationship to infinity. Therefore, either G-d has an interest in nothing, or He has an interest in everything. Large and small lose their meaning relative to the infinite. It is for this reason that man should feel that the infinite G-d does hear his prayers and is concerned about the behavior of every person.

Ramchal states that the attitude in prayer should be one of awe, together with joy, and quotes the verse from *Psalms* 2:11 "Rejoice when there is trembling." One might ask, Are these two emotions not mutually exclusive? How can one be joyous while trembling?

We may understand this with an anecdote of the *chassid* who presented a petition to Rabbi Shneur Zalman, in which he listed all his needs and asked the Rabbi for a blessing. The Rabbi studied the petition a bit, then said, "You seem to have given much attention to what you need, but have you given equal attention to why you are needed?" The *chassid* was stunned with this reprimand and trembled, but the implicit assertion "You are needed," i.e., you *are* significant and you have a purpose, was edifying and a cause for great joy.

וְהִנֵּה דִּבַּרְנוּ עַד עַתָּה מִן הַהַכְנָעָה וּמִן הַבּשֶׁת. וּנְדַבֵּר עַתָּה מֵעִנְיַן הַכָּבוֹד. הִנֵּה כְּבוֹד הַמִּצְוָה וִיקָרָהּ כְּבָר הִזְהִירוּנוּ עָלָיו חֲכָמִים ז״ל וְאָמְרוּ (שבת קלג, י): ,,זֶה אֵלִי וְאַנְוֵהוּ'' (שמות טו, ב) ,,הִתְנָאֶה לְפָנָיו בַּמִּצְוֹת: צִיצִית נָאֶה, תְּפִילִין נָאֶה, סֵפֶר תּוֹרָה נָאֶה, לוּלָב נָאֶה וכו׳. וְכֵן אָמְרוּ (בבא קמא ט, ב): ,,הִדּוּר מִצְוָה עַד שְׁלִישׁ, עַד כָּאן מִשֶּׁלּוֹ, מִכָּאן וָאֵילַךְ מִשֶּׁל הַקָּדוֹשׁ־בָּרוּךְ־הוּא'' . . . וּלְהוֹצִיא מִמִּי שֶׁלְּהָקֵל עַל עַצְמוֹ יֹאמַר, אֵין הַכָּבוֹד אֶלָּא לִבְנֵי אָדָם הַמִּתְפַּתִּים בַּהֲבָלִים אֵלֶּה, אַךְ הַקָּדוֹשׁ־בָּרוּךְ־הוּא אֵינוֹ חוֹשֵׁשׁ לָזֶה כִּי הוּא מְרוֹמָם מִדְּבָרִים הָאֵלֶּה וְנִשְׂגָּב מֵהֶם, וְכֵיוָן שֶׁהַמִּצְוָה נַעֲשֵׂית לַאֲמִתָּהּ, דַּי בָּזֶה. אָמְנָם הָאֱמֶת הוּא, שֶׁהָאָדוֹן בָּרוּךְ־הוּא נִקְרָא אֵל־הַכָּבוֹד וְאָנוּ חַיָּבִים לְכַבְּדוֹ אַף־עַל־פִּי שֶׁאֵינוֹ צָרִיךְ לִכְבוֹדֵנוּ.

Let us now talk about the respect accorded to mitzvos. The Talmud states that the verse "This is my G-d and I will beautify Him" (Exodus 15:2) means that we should make performance of mitzvos attractive: a beautiful tallis, a beautiful Torah Scroll, etc. (Shabbos 133b). Indeed, we are to go to some expense to do mitzvos in a more beautiful manner . . .

There are those who try to extricate themselves from this and say, "G-d does not need all these trimmings. It suffices if we just get the mitzvah done." Let us understand that we are to honor G-d even though He is not in need of it.

Ramchal continues to quote Scriptures and Talmud on the theme of beautifying mitzvos. While it is true that G-d is not in need of our homage, how we do a mitzvah reflects our attitude toward G-d and how much we appreciate our being able to serve Him.

Let us suppose that you had the opportunity to have a dignitary — e.g. the governor of your state — as your dinner guest at home. Do you serve the same menu that you do to the family, or do you try and prepare something special? Do you not bring out your finest linen tablecloths and napkins, finest dishes and silverware, and take great effort to serve the meal in as elegant a manner as possible? Why is all this necessary? The same nourishment can be derived if the food is served on plain dishes without the fancy napkins and dinnerware. The decorative flowers on the table add nothing to nutrition. Why are they there? It is obvious that you go to all the effort of providing all the trimmings and serving the food attractively because your guest is a highly honored, very special person and all the extra trimmings are meant to show your regard for him. Similarly, when you give a gift to a person, you invariably have it wrapped in fancy paper and tied with a brightly colored ribbon. The trimmings do not add to the substance of the gift, yet you may pay extra for gift wrapping in order to make the gift more pleasing. If that is the attitude you have toward a human being, should your attitude toward G-d be any less? We should perform mitzvos in a way that makes them most presentable, not because G-d needs this, but because it shows how dear the mitzvos are to us, and how much we value the privilege of fulfilling G-d's will.

Ramchal quotes the prophet's criticism of those who show greater respect for human dignitaries than for G-d (*Malachi* 1:8). Unfortunately, we are often guilty of this. If we were invited to an audience with a head of a state, we would sit in silence and with due respect, and it would never occur to us to carry on a conversation with our neighbors. Yet in *shul* we are so lacking in decorum, and the noisiness of conversation may reach a decibel level that drowns out the reader. Our Torah leaders throughout the ages have sharply condemned this lack of respect in the synagogue which is an affront to the Divine presence, yet this practice persists. It is high time we took to heart the words we recite upon entering the *shul*: "It is with Your bountiful mercy that I enter Your home, and I bow toward Your holy Ark with reverence" (*Psalms* 69:14). By behaving with proper decorum in the synagogue, we have an opportunity to beautify the mitzvah of prayer at no extra expense.

וְסֵדֶר הַעֲלָאַת בִּכּוּרִים יִהְיֶה לָנוּ לְעֵינַיִם לִרְאוֹת מַה הוּא הַדּוֹרָן שֶׁל מִצְוֹת, שֶׁכָּךְ שָׁנִינוּ (בכורים ג, ג): ,,הַשּׁוֹר הוֹלֵךְ לִפְנֵיהֶם וְקַרְנָיו מְצֻפּוֹת זָהָב וַעֲטֶרֶת שֶׁל זַיִת בְּרֹאשׁוֹ וכו׳ ״. עוֹד שָׁם (מ״ח): ,,הָעֲשִׁירִים מְבִיאִים בִּכּוּרֵיהֶם בִּפְלָתוֹת שֶׁל זָהָב, וְהָעֲנִיִּים בְּסַלֵּי נְצָרִים וכו׳ ״. עוֹד שָׁם (מ״י): ,,שָׁלֹשׁ מִדּוֹת בַּבִּכּוּרִים: בִּכּוּרִים, תּוֹסֶפֶת בִּכּוּרִים, וְעִטּוּר בִּכּוּרִים וכו׳ ״. הֲרֵי לָנוּ בְּהֶדְיָא, כַּמָּה רָאוּי לָנוּ לְהוֹסִיף עַל גּוּפָהּ שֶׁל מִצְוָה כְּדֵי לְהַדְּרָהּ, וּמִכָּאן נִלְמוֹד לְכָל שְׁאָר מִצְוֹת שֶׁבַּתּוֹרָה.

The ritual of the offering of bikkurim (the first-ripened fruits) provides an insight into beautifying mitzvos. The oxen used in the procession had their horns covered with gold, with crowns of olive branches on their heads; the fruits were brought in gold vessels or in beautifully woven reed baskets, and the containers of fruit were lavishly decorated (Bikkurim 3:3). This should serve as an example of beautifying mitzvos.

The reason why Ramchal chose the mitzvah of *bikkurim* as an example lies in the fact that it is so important that the Torah refers to *Shavuos* as the "festival of *bikkurim*" rather than being the day the Torah was given at Sinai. The significance of *bikkurim* lies in its being an expression of profound gratitude to G-d for all He has given us. The offering of *bikkurim* is accompanied by a recitation of our history, our humble origins, the enslavement in Egypt, the Divine deliverance, and finally the entrance into the Promised Land.

Judaism places much emphasis on gratitude. The first words on arising in the morning are *modeh ani*, "I thank You." Our *berachos* (blessings) and prayers are largely expressions of gratitude. Some people seem to have difficulty in expressing gratitude, perhaps because they do not wish to feel beholden to their benefactor. Spirituality requires overcoming such reluctance, and being thankful for favors received. *Bikkurim* is also an avowal of our realization that all we have comes from G-d, and is not the result of our own strengths.

It follows that the person who has trust in G-d and recognizes Him as the provider, and is sincerely grateful for all that G-d has given him, will be the one whose appreciation will result in his wishing to beautify his performance of mitzvos, and express his devotion and gratitude toward G-d by fulfilling the mitzvos in the most attractive manner.

וְהִנֵּה בִּכְלָל זֶה יֵשׁ כִּבּוּד הַשַּׁבָּתוֹת וְיָמִים טוֹבִים . . . אַךְ הַכְּלָל הוּא שֶׁכָּל מַעֲשֶׂה שֶׁבּוֹ נִרְאֶה חֲשִׁיבוּת לַשַּׁבָּת, צְרִיכִים אָנוּ לַעֲשׂוֹתוֹ . . . וְתִרְאֶה שֶׁזּוֹאת הִיא הַיִּרְאָה הָאֲמִתִּית שֶׁהִיא יִרְאַת הָרוֹמְמוּת שֶׁזָּכַרְנוּ.

Shabbos and the festivals should be similarly honored ... Whatever we can do to show how important Shabbos is, should be done. The Talmud cites various examples of the sages who personally helped to prepare for Shabbos ... This is an indication of the true yirah, a reverence for the Majesty of G-d, which is reflected in the manner in which we honor His sacred days.

Shabbos occupies an especially important place in Judaism, so much so that the Talmud says that if one observes *Shabbos* properly, it is equivalent to observing the entire Torah (*Talmud Yerushalmi, Berachos* 1:8).

Shabbos is more than just a day of physical rest. The latter would be merely a recharging of one's batteries, which would essentially make *Shabbos* subservient to the workweek. In Judaism it is just the reverse. The workweek is subservient to *Shabbos*, and indeed, each morning we say in prayer, "Today is the first day toward *Shabbos*; today is the second day toward *Shabbos*, etc."

In *kabbalistic* writings *Shabbos* is referred to as "The day of the *neshamah*." The Jew believes that the essence of life is the soul, and that the body is but the vehicle through which the soul operates. Similarly, the purpose of creation is for the seventh day, and the six weekdays are there so that we can amass the provisions with which to celebrate the *Shabbos*.

Shabbos should therefore be a day of reflection, meditation, prayer, and Torah study. Yes, we have traditional *Shabbos* delicacies, but rather than being an indulgence, this is one way to honor the *Shabbos*, with festive meals. We may visit friends, but the visits should be to strengthen the friendship and to discover what we can do to be of help to our friends. *Shabbos* is the day when parents review the week's Torah study with their children, and the latter can see that their parents are sincerely interested in their mastery of Torah. And as we say in the beautiful *Lecho Dodi* hymn, *Shabbos* is a loving relationship between Israel and the *Shabbos* Queen.

Friday night we welcome the heavenly angels into our homes, and they bring us the Divine blessing. We sing the song "A Woman of Valor," a tribute to the Jewish wife and mother. We recite the *kiddush*, our testimony to the work of creation, "For in six days G-d created the heavens and the earth, and on the seventh day He rested" (*Exodus* 20:11). We live in a world that was purposely created for reasons known only to the Divine wisdom, and in that purposeful world, every person has a purpose for existing. We are not accidental outcomes of a random interplay of unguided forces which happened to result in organic matter, which then somehow became a living cell, and then evolved throughout eons of time to produce the human being. In an accidental world man cannot have a purpose, and one may then resign oneself to hedonism. In the created world, man has a mission, an obligation, and a responsibility.

Shabbos thus gives worth and value to life. Is this not adequate reason why we should honor the *Shabbos* in whatever way possible? Yes, we should wear our finest clothes and we should set our tables elegantly, but even more important is to honor the spirit of *Shabbos*: "Let your speech on *Shabbos* be different than your speech of the workweek" (*Shabbos* 113b). If we sufficiently elevate ourselves spiritually on *Shabbos*, then even if we do descend during the workweek we will nevertheless take some of the *Shabbos* spirit with us, and as we approach the following *Shabbos* on a higher level, we advance even further in spirituality.

It is of interest that in the days of the Talmud, the word of a person who was not credible all during the week was accepted on *Shabbos*, because his reverence for the sanctity of *Shabbos* will prevent him from lying (*Talmud Yerushalmi*, Demai 4:1). *Shabbos* has the capacity to bring out the finest in everyone.

The Talmud quotes G-d as saying, "I have a special gift for Israel in My treasure house, and its name is *Shabbos*" (*Shabbos* 10a). Let us accord *Shabbos* its due honor as a precious gift to us from G-d, a gift that even G-d valued above all others.

וּבִכְלָל הַיִּרְאָה עוֹד כְּבוֹד הַתּוֹרָה וְלוֹמְדֶיהָ . . . ,,הָיָה הוֹלֵךְ מִמָּקוֹם לְמָקוֹם לֹא יַנִּיחֶנּוּ בְּשַׂק וְיַנִּיחֶנּוּ עַל הַחֲמוֹר וְיִרְכַּב עָלָיו אֶלָּא מַנִּיחוֹ בְּחֵיקוֹ וכו׳ ״ . . . וְאָסְרוּ (מגילה כז, א) לְהַנִּיחַ נְבִיאִים וּכְתוּבִים עַל גַּבֵּי חֻמָּשִׁים . . . וְהֶחָסִיד יֶשׁ-לוֹ לִלְמוֹד מֵאֵלֶּה וּלְהוֹסִיף עֲלֵיהֶם כָּהֵנָּה וְכָהֵנָּה לִכְבוֹד שֵׁם ה׳ אֱלֹהָיו.

Included in yirah is respect for the Torah and those who study it. One must show reverence when transporting a Torah Scroll (There are laws pertaining to propriety of stacking Torah volumes), and the Talmud forbids placing Books of Prophets on top of the Pentateuch ... From this a Chassid can derive how to honor the works that contain the Divine word.

We all show reverence for the Torah by rising when it is removed from the Ark. Unfortunately, this reverence is too often shortlived, because once the reader begins reading the Torah, many congregants carry on conversations, and it is not unusual for a reader to pause until silence is restored. Chattering while the Divine word is being read obviously shows a lack of respect for Torah.

Ramchal says that a *Chassid* will derive additional teachings from the regulations requiring proper handling of Torah works, citing that one may not place a Book of the Prophets upon the Pentateuch. What we may derive from this is an important principle of Judaism: respect for and deference to a greater authority.

The Pentateuch is Divine Torah, and the Books of the Prophets are Divine Torah, yet there are levels in sanctity, and we indicate this by always placing the Pentateuch above other books of Torah. Many people extend this to not placing a volume of the Talmud atop the Books of Prophets for the same reason.

Although all works of Torah are sacred and must be treated with utmost respect, we must recognize the levels of sanctity. The Pentateuch is supreme, and no prophet, even with Divine revelation, can alter a single word of it. Nor can the sages of the Talmud go against the word of the prophets. This principle has been extended throughout the ages, so that after completion of the Talmud, no Torah scholar may interpret a *halachah* in disagreement with the Talmud. Furthermore, the scholars of a later area (*acharonim*) may not dispute the *halachic* position of earlier scholars (*rishonim*), although they may favor one *rishon* over another. Regardless of how erudite a person may be, and regardless of his genius, one must defer to prior generations of authorities in *halachah*.

This is not only a *halachic* requirement, but also represents a *weltanschauung* (worldview). For a secular world that ascribes to evolution, man is constantly growing wiser and more sophisticated. Modern man is a vast improvement over Cro-Magnon, and it does not take much to extend this to mean that all children are wiser than their parents. We have witnessed the complete social breakdown and anarchy that has resulted from this refusal to defer to authority, and considering one's mind to be the final judge of everything.

When one sees another Torah volume lying atop the Pentateuch and removes it, one is making a statement of deference to a greater authority. Each ensuing generation is a bit further from those who witnessed the revelation at Sinai. True, we may have computers and mind-boggling scientific advances, but these have not given us greater wisdom. We certainly can get from one place to another faster than our ancestors did, but their destinations in life were superior to ours.

Reverence for Torah shown by recognizing the levels of sanctity should remind us of the fact that the understanding of Torah which previous generations had is beyond our reach. We can only build on their works, not dismantle them.

וּבְעִנְיַן לוֹמְדֵי תוֹרָה, הִנֵּה מִקְרָא כָּתוּב (ויקרא יט, לב): ,,מִפְּנֵי שֵׂיבָה תָּקוּם וְהָדַרְתָּ פְּנֵי זָקֵן", וּמִנָּהּ יַלְפִינָן לְכָל מִינֵי כִּבּוּד שֶׁאֶפְשָׁר לַעֲשׂוֹת לָהֶם שֶׁרָאוּי וַדַּאי לְחָסִיד שֶׁיַּעֲשֵׂהוּ . . . מִי הָאִישׁ הֶחָפֵץ לַעֲשׂוֹת נַחַת־רוּחַ לְיוֹצְרוֹ, הִנֵּה בְּדֶרֶךְ זֶה יֵלֵךְ וְיוֹסִיף לֶקַח בְּתַחְבּוּלוֹתָיו וְלַעֲשׂוֹת הַיָּשָׁר לְפָנָיו יִתְבָּרֵךְ.

In regard to respecting Torah scholars, the Scripture says, "Rise before the elderly and honor the face of the learned" (Leviticus 9:32). This serves as a premise for the Chassid to give honor to Torah scholars in whatever way possible ... Since we know this to be the Divine will, one who wishes to please G-d will extend himself to do what is proper before Him.

Let me share some personal experiences with you. While I have attended yeshivah and I do have *semichah* (ordination as a rabbi), and I did hold a pulpit for a number of years, most of my professional life has been spent as a psychiatrist, and I have M.D. after my name. Some people seem to think that a chassidic rabbi who is also a psychiatrist is rather unusual, a phenomenon worth looking at. I believe this is why I am often invited to address various groups and events. Many of the invitations are from Torah institutions and synagogues, and the audience is comprised of people who have some relationship to Torah, if only as financial supporters of institutions.

I can assure you, and this is not out of modesty or humility, but there are many Torah scholars who far, far surpass me in their knowledge of Torah. Many have an excellent knowledge of the writings of mussar and *chassidus*. If what was being sought was Torah insights, they would be called on as speakers more often than I. I strongly suspect that my attraction as a "draw" is related to the M.D. after my name rather than to the Rabbi before it. I believe that some people have greater respect for those who have achieved secular knowledge than those who have Torah knowledge, and this is a serious misconception. Too often we think that all a Torah scholar can give us is "old hat," but we should realize that the ancient teachings of Torah are eternal and have application today, and are far more reliable than new ideas. When a Torah scholar speaks and the auditorium is filled to capacity, that is when Torah is being honored.

We also honor those who study Torah when we are generous in our support of institutions of Torah learning. It is regrettable that teachers of Torah are at the bottom of the ladder in terms of salary. Underpaying teachers of Torah is not honoring Torah properly.

וּנְדַבֵּר עַתָּה מֵעִנְיַן הָאַהֲבָה, וַעֲנָפֶיהָ הֵם שְׁלשָׁה: הַשִּׂמְחָה, הַדְּבֵיקוּת, וְהַקִּנְאָה. וְהִנֵּה עִנְיַן הָאַהֲבָה הוּא שֶׁיִּהְיֶה הָאָדָם חוֹשֵׁק וּמִתְאַוֶּה מַמָּשׁ אֶל קִרְבָתוֹ יִתְבָּרֵךְ, וְרוֹדֵף אַחַר קְדֻשָּׁתוֹ כַּאֲשֶׁר יִרְדּוֹף אִישׁ אַחַר דָּבָר הַנֶּחְמָד מִמֶּנּוּ חֶמְדָּה עַזָּה, עַד שֶׁיִּהְיֶה לוֹ הַזְכָּרַת שְׁמוֹ יִתְבָּרֵךְ שַׁעֲשׁוּעַ וְעֹנֶג מַמָּשׁ, כְּמִי שֶׁאוֹהֵב אֶת אֵשֶׁת נְעוּרָיו אוֹ בְּנוֹ יְחִידוֹ אַהֲבָה חֲזָקָה אֲשֶׁר אֲפִלּוּ הַדִּבּוּר בָּם יִהְיֶה־לוֹ לְנַחַת וְתַעֲנוּג.

Let us now turn to ahavah, love of G-d, which is comprised of three branches: joy, communion, and zeal. Love of G-d means that a person has a passion and desire for closeness to Him, and pursues the Divine holiness just as one would pursue the object of his strongest desire, to the point that mere mention of the Divine Name and hearing His praises arouses an intense delight, much as one would feel about the wife of one's youth, or a beloved child, where even mention of them is pleasurable.

The Baal Shem Tov was asked, How is it possible to develop an intense love for G-d, inasmuch as He is not visible to the senses? Can one have love for an abstraction? The Baal Shem Tov replied, "One achieves love of G-d through *ahavas Yisrael*. If you love your neighbor, you will love G-d as well."

This truth was evident in the life of Rabbi Levi Yitzchak of Berditchev, whose love for his people is legendary. He often championed their cause, even challenging G-d that He has not dealt fairly with His children. Rabbi Levi Yitzchak also manifested his intense love for G-d in his prayers, during which he was unable to restrain himself, and often gesticulated wildly as he recited the prayers. Sometimes, in his fervor, he would embrace the stove that heated the synagogue. His opponents, suspecting him of dissimulating, once heated the stove to an intense degree. When Rabbi Levi Yitzchak embraced the fiery hot stove, his clothes were singed, and his skin began to sear, but he continued his prayer, totally oblivious that he was actually getting burned.

One of the sources of our love for G-d is G-d's love for us, based on the principle stated by Solomon "Just as water reflects an image, so does one heart reflect the feeling of another" (*Proverbs* 27:19). A *chassid* once asked a Rebbe, Why then do we not all feel this intense love for G-d, since His love for us is so great? The Rebbe replied, "You will note that Solomon does not say, 'Just as a *mirror* reflects,' but 'Just as *water* reflects.' The difference is that a mirror will reflect even a distant object, whereas water will reflect only that which is close to it. If we were closer to G-d, His love would arouse ours." All the steps in *Mesillas Yesharim* are concerned with teaching us how to come closer to G-d.

The chassidic master, Rabbi Baruch of Kosov, stated that if someone acts kindly towards someone whom you love, that makes you feel happy, whereas if someone inflicts pain on your loved one, it will cause you to feel sad. If someone truly loves G-d, then he will rejoice when he sees others do mitzvos, and he will be distressed when he sees someone sin. If we are indifferent to what others do, that indicates a lack of love for G-d.

Earlier we mentioned that the *neshamah*, the essence of man, is part of G-d Himself, and that just as a small flame held close to a larger one is attracted to the latter to the point that it can be totally absorbed by it, so it is with the *neshamah*, which is attracted to its source. If we do not feel this attraction, it is because of the many barriers, comprised of our physical desires, that obstruct this attraction, much as insulation will inhibit the attraction of a magnet for iron. As one observes Watchfulness and Abstinence, these barriers are eliminated, and one can then feel the inherent love for G-d.

There is one facet of love for G-d that needs a bit of elaboration. The books of mussar tell us that true love originates not from what someone does for you, but from what you do for the other person. Indeed, sometimes a recipient of kindness may react with resentment toward his benefactor rather than with love. If this is the case, then we can understand why G-d loves us, because He does everything for us and all we have is from Him. But how can we develop love for G-d, when there is nothing we can give Him? It is impossible for G-d to be lacking in anything.

The psalmist says, "Give strength unto G-d" (68:35), which some commentaries relate to the Talmudic statement that when Israel observes the Torah and mitzvos, they "add strength to G-d." There is thus a possibility of adding strength to G-d, but how are we to understand this?

G-d designed the universe with a system of justice, which binds everyone, including Himself. In a lengthy essay, Rabbi Yeruchem Levovitz explains that G-d does not deviate from justice, and even when He is merciful, it is within the confines of justice. G-d will not override His own laws.

Since G-d is infinitely benevolent, He wishes to bestow His blessings on all, yet human behavior is often such that the system of justice, which G-d observes, will not permit this. Divine mercy is thus contingent on finding some redeeming features which would merit mercy, so that G-d can be merciful without transgressing His rules of justice. When Israel disobeys the Torah, they do not have the meritorious deeds which would allow G-d to dispense His mercy. When we do His will, we are providing Him with that which He "needs" so that He may implement His infinite kindness, which is what G-d wishes to do. Thus, we *do* give strength to G-d. With our observance of Torah, we give Him that which is necessary for Him to be benevolent to us.

There are many references in the Talmud and Midrash to the Divine pleasure when people perform mitzvos and to the Divine distress when they do not. It is customary to precede performance of a mitzvah with the phrase, "I am hereby performing this mitzvah in order to provide a *nachas ruach* (pleasure) to my Creator." How an All-perfect G-d can have pleasure is a theological-philosophic mystery, but we are told it is so, and we may think of it as similar to the pleasure of parents when they see their children doing what is right. We thus *do* have a way of achieving love for G-d by what we do for Him.

וְהִנֵּה וַדַּאי שֶׁמִּי שֶׁאוֹהֵב אֶת בּוֹרְאוֹ אַהֲבָה אֲמִתִּית, לֹא יַנִּיחַ עֲבוֹדָתוֹ לְשׁוּם טַעַם שֶׁבָּעוֹלָם אִם לֹא יִהְיֶה אָנוּס מַמָּשׁ, וְלֹא יִצְטָרֵךְ רִצּוּי וּפִתּוּי לָעֲבוֹדָה, אֶלָּא אַדְּרַבָּה לִבּוֹ יִשָּׂאֵהוּ וִירִיצֵהוּ אֵלֶיהָ אִם לֹא יִהְיֶה עִכּוּב גָּדוֹל שֶׁיִּמְנָעֵהוּ . . .וְהִנֵּה זֹאת וַדַּאי, שֶׁאַהֲבָה זֹאת צָרִיךְ שֶׁלֹּא תִהְיֶה אַהֲבָה הַתְּלוּיָה בְדָבָר, דְּהַיְנוּ, שֶׁיֶּאֱהַב אֶת הַבּוֹרֵא יִתְבָּרֵךְ עַל שֶׁמֵּטִיב אֵלָיו וּמַעֲשִׁירוֹ וּמַצְלִיחַ אוֹתוֹ, אֶלָּא כְּאַהֲבַת הַבֵּן לְאָבִיו, שֶׁהִיא אַהֲבָה טִבְעִית מַמָּשׁ,

One who truly loves G-d will not allow anything to divert him from serving Him, unless there is some overwhelming distress that makes this impossible. To the contrary, his heart constantly elevates and motivates him to the service of G-d. (Ramchal cites several Scriptural references to this effect, e.g., "My soul thirsts for You; my flesh pines for You" (Psalms 63:2) . . .

Of course, this love must be pure, without ulterior motive for reward, but rather like that of a child for his father, which is an inherent, natural love.

The Rabbi of Kotzk was seen eating in the *succah* even though it was raining. He was asked why he did so, inasmuch as the *Shulchan*

Aruch says that one is exempt from eating in the *succah* when it rains. The Rabbi answered, "You don't understand the *halachah.* The exemption is granted because one must not be distressed in the *succah*, and since rain makes eating in the *succah* very unpleasant, one may eat in the house. For me, I am far more distressed eating in the house on Succos than sitting in the rain; hence I am not exempt." To the Rabbi of Kotzk, the joy of the mitzvah of *succah* surpassed any personal discomfort.

As we previously noted, following the Passover and Succos festivals, during which the *tefillin* are not worn, Rabbi Levi Yitzchak of Berditchev would sit up all night at the window watching for the first sign of dawn, at which time he would be able to perform the beloved mitzvah of *tefillin* again. These are examples of true love for Torah and mitzvos.

וּמִבְחַן הָאַהֲבָה הַזֹּאת הוּא בִּזְמַן הַדֹּחַק וְהַצָּרָה. וְכֵן אָמְרוּ ז״ל (ברכות נד, א): ,,וְאָהַבְתָּ אֵת ה׳ אֱלֹהֶיךָ בְּכָל־לְבָבְךָ, וּבְכָל־נַפְשְׁךָ (דברים ו, ה) אֲפִלּוּ נוֹטֵל אֶת נַפְשֶׁךָ, וּבְכָל מְאֹדֶךָ בְּכָל מָמוֹנֶךָ״ . . . ,,כָּל מַאי דְעָבְדִין מִן שְׁמַיָּא לְטָב״, (ברכות ו, ה) – אֲפִילוּ נוֹטֵל אֶת נַפְשֶׁךָ, וּבְכָל־מְאֹדֶךָ־בְּכָל מָמוֹנֶךָ״ . . . ,,כָּל מַאי דְעָבְדִין מִן שְׁמַיָּא לְטָב״, (ברכות ס, ב), וָזֶה, כִּי אֲפִלּוּ הַצַּעַר וְהַדֹּחַק הַנִּרְאֶה בְּעֵינָיו רָעָה, אֵינֶנּוּ בֶּאֱמֶת אֶלָּא טוֹבָה אֲמִתִּית . . . שֶׁאַף־עַל־פִּי שֶׁהַמַּעֲשֶׂה אַכְזָרִי לִכְאוֹרָה, אֵינוֹ אֶלָּא רַחֲמָנוּת בֶּאֱמֶת, לְהֵיטִיבוֹ בְּאַחֲרִיתוֹ.

The test of true love comes during times of trouble and distress. The Talmud makes this clear when it interprets the Scriptural verse "You shall love your G-d with all your heart and with all your soul" (Deuteronomy 6:5) to mean even if He takes your soul and "with all your might" to mean even if He takes all your possessions . . . A person should trust that everything G-d does is for an ultimate good (Berachos 60b), even when it involves suffering and distress. One who has true love for G-d knows that He would never harm him . . . and that any suffering he experiences is for some ultimate good that may be beyond his grasp at the time.

Ramchal states that the acid test of love for G-d is how one reacts to adversity. This is indeed a most exacting test, both of one's faith as well as his love for G-d.

We frequently see bad things happening to good people, and we cannot but wish to understand why. What sense does it make to say that "G-d reprimands those whom He loves" (*Proverbs* 3:12) or "Because G-d loves him, He causes him to suffer" (*Isaiah* 53:10)? We may spank a child when he is bad, and indeed we do so out of our love for him, to teach him to avoid wrong. But aside from this, is there any rationale in inflicting suffering on someone because you love him? Yet our sages state that a person may undergo suffering solely because G-d loves him (*Berachos* 5a). This is a most difficult concept to understand.

The explanation that is offered is that inasmuch as there is no human being that is perfect, and every person, regardless of how great a *tzaddik* he may be, has committed some transgressions, the Divine system of absolute justice, which does not allow for overlooking anything, demands that the person suffer the consequences of his misdeeds. Since G-d wishes that the *tzaddik* ultimately receive the greatest reward in *Gan Eden* (Paradise), He subjects him to suffering in this world so that he will enter the Eternal World without the slightest blemish.

This explanation does not suffice, else Moses would not have been denied an answer when he asked G-d why bad things happen to good people (*Berachos* 7a). We are told that Moses wrote the Book of Job, which analyzes the phenomenon of why the good suffer, and after all arguments have been exhausted and rebutted, the answer is that one must have faith. We must resign ourselves that we cannot fully understand this. I have mentioned elsewhere that I once observed a mother restraining her infant so that the doctor could inject him to immunize him against harmful diseases. The infant cried and struggled, and tried to bite and hit his mother. Yet, when the ordeal was over, the infant clutched his mother and held onto her for dear life. But why? Hadn't she just collaborated in causing him pain? The answer is that even though an infant cannot possibly understand that the pain which is being inflicted is for an ultimate good, to protect him from incurable diseases, he nevertheless knows that his mother cares for him and his trust in her love for him is not shaken by her assisting in causing him pain. That is how we must relate to G-d in times of adversity. Like the infant, there is no way we can understand the good in our misery, and we can only have faith in G-d that this suffering is a necessary step for some ultimate and far greater good. As Ramchal says, This is the acid test of faith and love.

אַךְ בַּעֲלֵי הַדֵּעָה הָאֲמִתִּית אֵינָם צְרִיכִים אֲפִלּוּ לַטַּעַם הַזֶּה, כִּי הֲרֵי אֵין לָהֶם כַּוָּנַת עַצְמָם כְּלָל, אֶלָּא כָּל תְּפִלָּתָם לְהַגְדִּיל כְּבוֹד שְׁמוֹ יִתְבָּרֵךְ וְלַעֲשׂוֹת נַחַת־רוּחַ לְפָנָיו. וְכָל מַה שֶׁיִּתְגַּבְּרוּ עִכּוּבִים נֶגְדָּם עַד שֶׁיִּצְטָרְכוּ הֵם יוֹתֵר כֹּחַ לְהַעֲבִירָם, הִנֵּה יֶאֱמַץ לִבָּם וְיִשְׂמְחוּ לְהַרְאוֹת תֹּקֶף אֱמוּנָתָם, כְּשַׂר צָבָא הָרָשׁוּם בִּגְבוּרָה אֲשֶׁר יִבְחַר לוֹ תָּמִיד בַּמִּלְחָמָה הַחֲזָקָה יוֹתֵר, לְהַרְאוֹת תָּקְפּוֹ בְּנִצְחוֹנָהּ.

People of more profound understanding do not require an explanation, because they have no self-interest at all, and their only aspiration is to bring glory to the Divine Name. The more obstacles placed in their path, the more courage and strength they muster to overcome them. It is much like a general who wishes to demonstrate his loyalty to the king, who seeks to be assigned the most challenging battles in order to be able to show his devotion to the king.

Here Ramchal is describing the response that may be expected from someone who has reached the spiritual level of *Chassidus*, who is so focused on doing the Divine will that his own status is irrelevant. To the contrary, the more challenges put in his way, the happier he is to master them to manifest his intense love for G-d.

The chassidic master, Rabbi Zusia, was once asked to explain the Talmudic passage that a person should be as grateful for the bad that happens to him as for the good (*Berachos* 54a). Rabbi Zusia shrugged, "I have no way of understanding that passage, because nothing bad has ever happened to me." Coming from a person who lived in abject poverty and whose body was racked with pain, Rabbi Zusia's answer represents the reaction to which Ramchal is referring as appropriate for a *Chassid*.

The person who has mastered this level of *Chassidus* has achieved equanimity. Other than the pursuit of doing the Divine will and coming closer to G-d, nothing is of significance, neither personal pleasure nor pain.

We may understand this a bit better by an analogy to physical pain. It has been proven many times, and I can attest to this from personal clinical experience, that a person can be rendered oblivious to intense pain by hypnosis. Major surgical procedures can be done without any anesthetic, with the patient not feeling even a twinge of pain. There are various explanations for the hypnotic phenomenon, one of them being that the mind is so focused on one thing that it does not register any other stimuli.

Even chemical relief of pain is somewhat similar to this phenomenon. Whereas the anesthesia of a local anesthetic is due to interfering with the ability of a nerve to conduct a sensation, the relief of pain by morphine is totally different. The pain stimuli are conducted to the brain, and if carefully questioned, the patient will state that he feels a sensation, but that it is not distressful. What morphine apparently does is it blocks the area of the brain that interprets these stimuli as painful.

In either case, hypnosis or morphine, there is no cognitive change; i.e., there is no interference with the body sensing the stimuli, and it is as if the patient were saying, "It hurts, but it doesn't bother me in the least." It is an affective change, or an alteration in the feeling response.

If this occurs with physical distress, it is easy to see why it can also occur with psychological distress, as when one suffers a personal loss of any kind. Cognition is intact, one knows reality, and has a clear perception of what is happening, but the effect is "That does not cause me distress." This can be achieved by focusing all one's strivings and feelings toward G-d.

The *Chassid* has yet another way of dealing with adversity. The Scripture states, "I am with him in distress" (*Psalms* 91:15), and the Talmud states that when a person suffers, G-d is distressed by this suffering, just as parents suffer when their beloved child is in pain. Of course, we might ask the obvious question: The parents may be powerless to relieve the child's pain, hence they suffer along with him; but G-d can relieve ours, and then there would be no need for us nor He to suffer. But we have already said that human suffering is an unsolvable mystery, and is an integral part of the unfathomable Divine system of justice. According to the latter, G-d must allow this suffering, but He suffers along with us.

A man who dealt in lumber once complained to his Rebbe that he had sustained a severe financial loss. He had purchased a forest at an inflated price, and the price of lumber then dropped precipitously. The Rebbe said, "You know that when you are in distress, G-d is in distress along with you, and when you grieve over your financial loss, you thereby cause G-d to grieve. Tell me now, are a few pieces of wood important enough to justify causing G-d to grieve?"

One who has reached the level of *Chassidus*, who has an intense love for G-d, would not want G-d to be in distress. If he accepts his suffering with equanimity, he thereby relieves G-d of this distress, hence the love for G-d can minimize or extinguish the pain reaction.

וּנְבָאֵר עַתָּה עַנְפֵי הָאַהֲבָה, הֵם הַשְּׁלֹשָׁה שֶׁזָּכַרְתִּי: הַדְּבֵקוּת, הַשִּׂמְחָה, וְהַקִּנְאָה. הַדְּבֵקוּת הוּא שֶׁיִּהְיֶה לִבּוֹ שֶׁל הָאָדָם מִתְדַּבֵּק כָּל־כָּךְ בִּשְׁמוֹ יִתְבָּרֵךְ, עַד שֶׁכְּבָר יָסוּר מִלְּפְנוֹת וּלְהַשְׁגִּיחַ אֶל שׁוּם דָּבָר זוּלָתוֹ . . . וְהִנֵּה תַּכְלִית הַמִּדָּה הַזֹּאת הוּא לִהְיוֹת הָאָדָם מִתְדַּבֵּק כָּךְ אֶל בּוֹרְאוֹ בְּכָל־עֵת וּבְכָל־שָׁעָה. אָמְנָם לְפָחוֹת בִּשְׁעַת עֲבוֹדָה, אִם אוֹהֵב הוּא אֶת בּוֹרְאוֹ, וַדַּאי שֶׁיִּהְיֶה לוֹ הַדְּבֵקוּת הַזֶּה . . . וְעַל הַדְּבֵקוּת הֻזְהַרְנוּ בַּתּוֹרָה פְּעָמִים רַבּוֹת.

Let us now return to the three branches of ahavah: communion, joy, and zeal. Communion means to cling so closely to G-d that one is not concerned with anything else . . . This should preferably be a constant attitude, but at the very least such communion should be achieved when one is engaged in the Divine service. The Scripture exhorts us many times in regard to communion (Ramchal cites several Scriptural references here).

One should not mistake Ramchal's advocacy of communion, defined as an all-absorbing striving for closeness to G-d which should eliminate all other concerns, to mean that one should isolate oneself from society and from all normal activities in a monastic manner. To the contrary, we have seen that Ramchal is critical of such withdrawal from life. Rather, we should engage in normal activities, but these should all be goal directed toward the Divine service.

A *tzaddik* once lodged at an inn, and in the morning, when the innkeeper was wearing his *tallis* and *tefillin*, a customer came in to purchase a quart of beer. The innkeeper proceeded to measure out the beer, and when the customer began to haggle about the price, he poured the beer back into the keg and continued his praying. The *tzaddik* later asked him to explain his behavior, and the innkeeper said, "When the man asked me for a quart of beer, I had the opportunity of fulfilling the mitzvah of giving an honest measure. But then he began haggling about the price, and that is business. Well, I don't do business when I'm wearing a *tallis* and *tefillin*."

One can transact with merchandise, and by dealing honestly, be performing a mitzvah which constitutes communion with G-d, and this is equally true of virtually all our actions. Nothing need be exempted from the Divine service, and one can be in communion while engaging in normal behavior.

The Talmud provides us with an important insight into communion.

On the verse "You shall cling unto G-d" (*Deuteronomy* 30:20), the Talmud asks, "How is it possible for a mortal to cling unto G-d?" and the Talmud answers, "If a person sees to it that his daughter marries a Torah scholar, and he helps support the study of Torah, he is thereby clinging unto G-d" (*Kesubos* 112b).

The kabbalists state that the Divine wisdom, unlike human wisdom, is not something which G-d acquired, because G-d is, was, and will be perfect eternally, and there can be no change in Him. He therefore could not have become wise or wiser. The Divine wisdom is not a trait such as human wisdom is, but is inseparable from G-d Himself, and since the Torah *is* the Divine wisdom, G-d and the Torah must be one and the same. Therefore, one who embraces Torah is embracing G-d. This is true not only of one who dedicates himself totally to study of Torah, but also of someone who is engaged in work or business for much of the day. This person, too, can embrace Torah by (a) supporting Torah study, and by raising his children in such a manner that their marriages foster a continuity of Torah, and by (b) conducting his daily affairs according to the strict requirements set down by the Torah. This, too, constitutes a communion with G-d.

הַשֵּׁנִי הוּא הַשִּׂמְחָה, וְהוּא עִקָּר גָּדוֹל בָּעֲבוֹדָה. וְהוּא מַה שֶּׁדָּוִד מַזְהִיר וְאוֹמֵר (תהילים ק, ב): ,,עִבְדוּ אֶת־ה׳ בְּשִׂמְחָה בֹּאוּ לְפָנָיו בִּרְנָנָה״ . . . וְאָמְרוּ רַבּוֹתֵינוּ ז״ל (שבת ל, ב): ,,אֵין הַשְּׁכִינָה שׁוֹרָה אֶלָּא מִתּוֹךְ שִׂמְחָה שֶׁל מִצְוָה״ . . . כִּי זֹאת הִיא הַשִּׂמְחָה הָאֲמִתִּית שֶׁיִּהְיֶה לִבּוֹ שֶׁל הָאָדָם עָלֵז עַל שֶׁהוּא זוֹכֶה לַעֲבוֹד לִפְנֵי אָדוֹן יִתְבָּרֵךְ שֶׁאֵין כָּמוֹהוּ, וְלַעֲסוֹק בְּתוֹרָתוֹ וּבְמִצְוֹתָיו שֶׁהֵם הַשְּׁלֵמוּת הָאֲמִתִּי וְהַיְקָר הַנִּצְחִי.

The second branch of avahah is simchah (joy), which is a fundamental principle in the Divine service, as David says in Psalms (100:2), "Serve G-d with joy, come before Him with song." . . . The Talmud says, "The Divine presence comes to rest only where there is joy in doing mitzvos" (Shabbos 30b). . . . True simchah results from the realization of how great a privilege one has to serve G-d and to participate in His Torah and mitzvos, which comprise the eternal and true perfection.

The joy which is so highly praised in Scripture and in the Talmud is not the levity which results from earthly pastimes, but the *simchah* of mitzvah, and it is this and only this that merits the imminent presence of G-d.

When Rabbi Mendel of Kotzk came as a fledgling student to Rabbi Bunim of Pshische, the latter asked him, "Young man, where is G-d?" Rabbi Mendel answered, "G-d is everywhere." Rabbi Bunim repeated the question, "Young man, I have asked you, where is G-d?" Rabbi Mendel said, "The Scripture says that His glory fills the universe." Rabbi Bunim persisted, "Young man, you are not answering my question. Where is G-d?" Rabbi Mendel responded, "If my answers are not adequate, then you tell me." Rabbi Bunim said, "G-d can be found wherever His presence is invited."

G-d is indeed everywhere as Rabbi Mendel said, but to have the Divine presence in a manner that one can sense it, this requires *simchah*. The Divine glory is not manifest where there is dejection.

Is it possible to generate joy? Is not joy contingent upon various happenings in a person's life? Obviously, if one were to win a large sum of money, one would be happy. If one were to suffer a severe financial loss, one would be sad. If there is a birth or a wedding in the family, one rejoices. If, G-d forbid, there is illness or a death in the family, one is sad. The emotions of happiness and sadness are thus dependent on what transpires in our lives, much of which is beyond our control. How, then, can there be a commandment, "You shall rejoice" (*Deuteronomy* 16:15), as if there were a button one could push to turn on *simchah*?

Perhaps there is no button to push, but we are capable of having far greater mastery of our emotions than we think.

We have mentioned two types of mental processes: (1) cognitive, or our knowledge of something, and (2) affective, or our feeling about something. Affect is largely dependent on cognition. We are happy when we win a huge prize because our cognition is that having money is good.

A bit of sound, sober thinking can enable a person to realize that not everything that he has thought of as being good is indeed so. If we rethink our values, then our cognition, our ideas of what is good, may change, and along with that our affects can change.

Ramchal began this work with the concept of what is man's purpose in the world, which, he states, is to do the Divine will, and thereby come close to G-d. A true and sincere conviction of this will thus result in *simchah*.

A man was once sentenced to twenty-five years of hard labor. His hands were shackled to a huge, heavy wheel in the wall which he had to turn all his waking hours. When his long sentence was completed, the weary, broken man went around the building to see what he had been accomplishing with his backbreaking work all these years, and when he saw that the wheel was not attached to anything, he collapsed.

"Twenty-five years of constant, backbreaking work," he cried, "all for nothing."

Just as futility is the nadir of dejection, so the awareness that one is accomplishing something truly substantial is the zenith of joy. While there are both pleasant and unpleasant happenings in life, these need not impinge heavily on a person's affect. An intelligent, thinking person will realize that physically enjoyable pastimes are but fleeting and ephemeral and achieve nothing. It is the fulfillment of the Divine will which is man's purpose on earth, and when he is engaged in achieving this purpose, there is reason for *simchah*.

People who feel deprived cannot have *simchah*, but the person who has reached the state of *Chassidus* has already mastered Abstinence, and since he has far fewer unmet needs, he can be happy. On the other hand, a person who feels he has many needs, some of which cannot be satisfied, will be deterred from *simchah* by his constant state of dissatisfaction. One whose needs are few can be grateful for whatever he has, and there is no envy of others to interfere with his *simchah*.

The chassidic master of Karlin said, "Whereas there is no explicit Torah commandment prohibiting dejection, it can cause a person to commit the most serious transgressions."

There is impressive clinical evidence that a happy attitude is conducive to recovery from severe illnesses, and that dejection can aggravate disease. There are more than just a few cases of patients who were able to lift their spirits and surprised their doctors by unexpected recovery.

Simchah is a potent and positive force, and is relatively easily achieved by one who has mastered the first few steps of spirituality. A firm faith in G-d and an austere lifestyle eliminate most of the common deterrents to *simchah*.

הֶעָנָף הַשְּׁלִישִׁי הוּא הַקִּנְאָה, שֶׁיִּהְיֶה הָאָדָם מְקַנֵּא לְשֵׁם קָדְשׁוֹ, שׂוֹנֵא אֶת מְשַׂנְאָיו . . . לְדַבֵּר בְּמִי שֶׁיֵּשׁ בְּיָדוֹ לִמְחוֹת וְאֵינוֹ מוֹחֶה, וְגָזְרוּ דִינוֹ לִתָּפֵס בַּעֲוֹן הַחוֹטְאִים עַצְמוֹ . . . וְזֶה פָּשׁוּט, כִּי מִי שֶׁאוֹהֵב אֶת חֲבֵרוֹ אִי־אֶפְשָׁר לוֹ לִסְבּוֹל שֶׁיִּרְאֶה מַכִּים אֶת חֲבֵרוֹ אוֹ מְחָרְפִים אוֹתוֹ, וּבְוַדַּאי שֶׁיֵּצֵא לְעֶזְרָתוֹ. גַּם מִי שֶׁאוֹהֵב שְׁמוֹ יִתְבָּרֵךְ, לֹא יוּכַל לִסְבּוֹל וְלִרְאוֹת שֶׁיְּחַלְּלוּ אוֹתוֹ חַס־וְחָלִילָה וְשֶׁיַּעַבְרוּ עַל מִצְוֹתָיו.

The third branch of avahah is zeal, that a person should be zealous for the glory of G-d, and despise those who are His enemies ... If a person has the opportunity to protest behavior that is adverse to the Divine will and does not do so, he is held culpable for those sins ... Just as one who sees a dear friend being harmed or insulted will certainly come to his aid, so will a person who loves G-d be zealous to oppose those who offend Him.

Zealousness is a double-edged sword, and must be wielded with utmost care and caution. Some people, believing that they are defending the honor of G-d, may actually defeat the purpose with reckless and thoughtless behavior.

There is no question that the Chafetz Chaim reached the highest levels of spirituality, which included being zealous for the honor of G-d. Yet, he never exhibited any form of objectionable behavior. This is equally true of all our great Torah personalities. Even zeal can be achieved with gentleness.

The Chafetz Chaim was told of a person who had deviated from Torah and no longer observed the mitzvos. He sent for the man, seated him near to him, put his hands into his, and softly said *"Shabbos, Shabbos,"* and as he did so, his tears began to flow profusely. He did not reprimand the man nor scold him, but the latter was profoundly touched to see how deeply the great sage was hurt by his deviation from Torah, and he soon returned to Torah observance.

Ramchal describes zealousness for G-d as similar to the feeling one would have upon seeing someone he loved being harmed or insulted, which would cause him great distress. Zealousness for G-d is based on a profound feeling of distress upon seeing the Divine will abused, and before one may undertake any act of zeal, he must feel this pain deeply and genuinely.

The ethical works repeatedly emphasize that our prayers should be motivated primarily by *tzaar haShechinah,* the distress and anguish of the Divine Presence, which went into exile along with Israel, and suffers along with Israel's suffering. G-d wishes to concentrate His presence in the Holy Land, in Jerusalem, and in His Sanctuary. Our lack of proper observance of Torah resulted in our being driven from our homeland, and like the devoted father, G-d went into exile along with His children. He suffered along with us the many persecutions we endured, and abiding by His absolute rules of justice, He did not intervene to prevent our anguish. It is much like the example cited earlier, of the mother who restrains her infant so that the doctor can administer the lifesaving although painful injection. She knows the child must receive this, and that it is to his ultimate advantage, but she feels the child's pain nevertheless.

The true *Chassid*, whose love for G-d surpasses his love for himself, and who would willingly sacrifice his life for G-d, does not pray for his own comfort and success, but rather that Israel should be relieved of its suffering, and that he as an individual should be relieved of his suffering, in order that G-d should be relieved of His distress of seeing His children suffer. Once a person has truly reached this point of devotion, then and only then is he ready for zeal. As long as his personal interests prevail and his primary motivation is not for the relief of the Divine distress, he had better avoid zealousness.

How cautious we must be in exercising zealousness can be seen by the episodes of Pinchas (*Numbers* 25:11) and Elijah (*II Kings* 19:10). In the first instance Pinchas slew an adulterer, and in the second one Elijah, whom the Midrash identifies with Pinchas, fled into the desert because he could not tolerate Israel's lapse into idolatry. Whereas in the first incident Pinchas received a Divine reward for his zeal, in the second episode Elijah was relieved of his leadership. The Midrash says that G-d said to Elijah, "You have always been a zealot!" One of the commentaries states that in episodes of zealous behavior, a person who is not by nature aggressive nor intolerant, and who must essentially overcome his natural inclination to be passive and tolerant, is indeed praiseworthy. Pinchas was rewarded because, like his grandfather Aaron, he was a lover of peace. When, as Elijah, he was again zealous, he was reprimanded. Why? Repetition of zealous behavior indicates that the person may have a characterological tendency to zeal, and that is not praiseworthy.

Those who would be zealous ought to examine themselves very thoroughly. The zealousness that is commendable is one that requires a struggle to overcome the resistance to take action. Characterological zealousness is not a desirable trait.

וְהִנֵּה בֵּאַרְנוּ עַד הֵנָּה הַחֲסִידוּת מַה שֶּׁתָּלוּי בְּמַעֲשֶׂה, וּבְאֹפֶן הָעֲשִׂיָּה. וּנְבָאֵר עַתָּה הַתָּלוּי בְּכַוָּנָה. וּכְבָר דִּבַּרְנוּ גַּם־כֵּן לְמַעְלָה מֵעִנְיַן לִשְׁמָהּ וְשֶׁלֹּא־לִשְׁמָהּ לְמַדְרֵגוֹתֵיהֶם. אָמְנָם וַדַּאי שֶׁמִּי שֶׁמִּתְכַּוֵּן בַּעֲבוֹדָתוֹ לְטַהֵר נַפְשׁוֹ לִפְנֵי בּוֹרְאוֹ לְמַעַן תִּזְכֶּה לָשֶׁבֶת אֶת פָּנָיו בִּכְלָל הַיְשָׁרִים וְהַחֲסִידִים, ,,לַחֲזוֹת בְּנוֹעַם ה׳ וּלְבַקֵּר

בְּהֵיכָלוֹ״ (תהילים כז, ד) וּלְקַבֵּל הַגְּמוּל אֲשֶׁר בָּעוֹלָם־הַבָּא, לֹא נוּכַל לוֹמַר שֶׁתִּהְיֶה הַיּוֹתֵר טוֹבָה, כִּי עַד שֶׁהָאָדָם מִתְכַּוֵּן לְטוֹבַת עַצְמוֹ, סוֹף־סוֹף עֲבוֹדָתוֹ לְצֹרֶךְ עַצְמוֹ. אַךְ הַכַּוָּנָה הָאֲמִתִּית הַמְּצוּיָה בַּחֲסִידִים אֲשֶׁר טָרְחוּ וְהִשְׁתַּדְּלוּ לְהַשִּׂיגָהּ, הוּא שֶׁיִּהְיֶה הָאָדָם עוֹבֵד רַק לְמַעַן אֲשֶׁר כְּבוֹדוֹ שֶׁל הָאָדוֹן בָּרוּךְ־הוּא יִגְדַּל וְיִרְבֶּה . . . שֶׁזֹּאת הִיא הַכַּוָּנָה הַמְּעֻלָּה שֶׁהִיא רְחוֹקָה לְגַמְרֵי מִכָּל הֲנָאַת עַצְמוֹ, וְאֵינָהּ אֶלָּא לִכְבוֹדוֹ שֶׁל מָקוֹם וּלְקִדּוּשׁ שְׁמוֹ יִתְבָּרֵךְ הַמִּתְקַדֵּשׁ בִּבְרִיּוֹתָיו בְּשָׁעָה שֶׁעוֹשִׂים רְצוֹנוֹ . . . וְהִנֵּה הֶחָסִיד כָּזֶה מִלְּבַד הָעֲבוֹדָה שֶׁהוּא עוֹבֵד בְּמַעֲשֵׂה מִצְוֹתָיו עַל הַכַּוָּנָה הַזֹּאת, הִנֵּה וַדַּאי צָרִיךְ שֶׁיִּצְטַעֵר תָּמִיד צַעַר מַמָּשׁ עַל הַגָּלוּת וְעַל הַחָרְבָּן, מִצַּד מַה שֶּׁזֶּה גּוֹרֵם מִעוּט כִּבְיָכוֹל לִכְבוֹדוֹ יִתְבָּרֵךְ.

Thus far we have dealt with the acts of Chassidus, and we will now discuss what Chassidus requires in the area of kavannah (intention and motivation).

There are various degrees of kavannah, with and without ulterior motives. For example, if a person serves G-d so that he can merit being with the righteous in the World to Come and bask in the glory of G-d, we can hardly consider that an improper kavannah. Yet, there is no denying that it is self-serving, because the ultimate intent is for his own needs. The true kavannah of the Chassid is to serve G-d without any intent of personal gain, but solely and only because He is Master of the Universe.

The Chassid will rejoice whenever he sees the Divine Name honored, and he will be distressed when it is otherwise ... His prayers are for the return of the Divine presence to Jerusalem, and he bemoans the exile of Israel because it is a dishonor to G-d that His people are in exile.

Chassidus is essentially the full implementation of what Ramchal posited in Chapter One, the fulfillment of man's obligation on earth. As one progresses in spirituality, one becomes more single minded in directing everything toward this goal. His own interests are set aside, first in Watchfulness, and then in Abstinence, and now it is required that even his performance of mitzvos must be elevated to the point of total lack of self-interest. Even though the self-interest may be of a spiritual nature, e.g., to merit the reward of enjoying the Divine presence in *Gan Eden*, it is nevertheless a self-interest, which detracts from the highest state of purity. There is a fine distinction between wishing to merit reward for one's self-interest, or doing so because one knows that in His infinite benevolence, G-d wishes to bestow rewards, but that if we do not do the Divine will, the absolute system of justice does not provide the opportunity for G-d to exercise His benevolence. By doing the mitzvos wholeheartedly, one is giving G-d the opportunity to be benevolent, and a *Chassid* may work for reward not for his own sake, but in order to give pleasure to G-d Who wishes to reward His children. It is important that we do not deceive ourselves to think we are doing the latter, when we are still at the self-interest level.

The *Chassid* is sensitive to the Divine distress because of the exile of Israel, and pious Jews have traditionally arisen at midnight to recite the prayers which express our anguish at the desecration of the Divine Name resulting from Israel's exile. A specific time was set aside for mourning the loss of the Sanctuary, but for the remainder of the day, a person should feel *simchah*. One of the chassidic masters gave a parable of a king who was exiled, and who took lodging with one of his devoted subjects. The latter was deeply saddened by the fact that his king was in exile, but thrilled and highly honored that the king was in his home. That is how we are to feel about the exile of the Divine Presence: It pains us deeply, but we rejoice in knowing that G-d dwells among us.

וְאִם יֹאמַר אָדָם: מִי אֲנִי וּמָה אֲנִי סָפוּן, שֶׁאֶתְפַּלֵּל עַל הַגָּלוּת וְעַל יְרוּשָׁלַיִם? הֲמִפְּנֵי תְפִלָּתִי יְכֻנְּסוּ הַגָּלֻיּוֹת וְתִצְמַח הַיְשׁוּעָה? תְּשׁוּבָתוֹ בְּצִדּוֹ, כְּאוֹתָהּ שֶׁשָּׁנִינוּ (סנהדרין לז, א): „לְפִיכָךְ נִבְרָא אָדָם יְחִידִי, כְּדֵי שֶׁכָּל אֶחָד יֹאמַר: בִּשְׁבִילִי נִבְרָא הָעוֹלָם". וּכְבָר נַחַת־רוּחַ הוּא לְפָנָיו יִתְבָּרֵךְ, שֶׁיִּהְיוּ בָּנָיו מְבַקְשִׁים וּמִתְפַּלְלִים עַל זֹאת. וְאַף שֶׁלֹּא תֵעָשֶׂה בַקָּשָׁתָם מִפְּנֵי שֶׁלֹּא הִגִּיעַ הַזְּמָן אוֹ מֵאֵיזֶה טַעַם שֶׁיִּהְיֶה, הִנֵּה הֵם עָשׂוּ אֶת שֶׁלָּהֶם וְהַקָּדוֹשׁ־בָּרוּךְ־הוּא שָׂמֵחַ בָּזֶה.

If a person says, "But who am I, and what am I worth that my prayers for redemption should be effective? Will salvation come because I pray for it?" The answer was given by the Talmud: Man was created as a single individual to teach us that one person can be an entire world (Sanhedrin 37a). If our prayers have not yet been effective because the time for redemption, according to the Divine wisdom, has not arrived, we have nevertheless been faithful in praying for it."

The efficacy of prayers has been questioned on the grounds, "Can human prayer cause G-d to change His mind, to do something that

He would not otherwise have done?" Various answers to this question have been given. The Divine will does not change, but G-d may have decreed that certain things will be given to an individual when he has reached a particular state of spirituality, or when he has achieved sufficient merits. The Talmud states that the matriarchs were barren for many years because G-d desired their prayer. Why? Because their prayer elevated them to a higher level of spirituality, and the mothers of Isaac and Jacob had to be at this level to beget and raise the patriarchs of our people.

Rabbi Elimelech of Lizensk said that the reason prayer is effective is because G-d always implements the Divine system of justice. Suppose that for whatever reason, Person "A" meets with adversity, which occurred according to the Divine system of justice. Person "B" learns of "A's" distress, and he so identifies with "A" and so feels his suffering, that he is now in distress. But since it had not been decreed that "B" should suffer, the Divine system of justice requires that G-d should intervene to relieve "A," so that "B" should not suffer. This is how feeling another's pain and praying for him can be effective.

No one should think that his prayer is insignificant. Countless stories have been handed down about the efficacy of a single individual's prayer, and not necessarily only that of a great *tzaddik*. Every person's prayer counts.

There is a story of one congregation that ran short of funds to buy sacramental wine, and they decided that each worshiper would donate one glass of wine and pour it into a large container. Yankel thought, "No one will know the difference if I pour in a glass of water. It will hardly dilute the wine at all." But Shmulik had the same idea, as did Berel, and David, and Boruch, etc. When they went to fetch wine for *kiddush*, all they found was pure water.

If I neglect to pray because my prayer does not count, why should anyone else feel differently? The result will be that no one will pray!

הֲרֵי כָּאן שֶׁחַיָּבִים אֲנַחְנוּ בָּזֶה וְאֵין לָנוּ לִפָּטֵר מִפְּנֵי מִעוּט כֹּחֵנוּ, כִּי עַל כַּיּוֹצֵא בָּזֶה שָׁנִינוּ (אבות ב, טז): ,,לֹא עָלֶיךָ הַמְּלָאכָה לִגְמוֹר וְאִי־אַתָּה בֶן־חוֹרִין לִבָּטֵל הֵימֶנָּה".

We have an obligation to pray, and we cannot excuse ourselves because we think our strength is inadequate. The Talmud says, "The work is not yours to complete, but you do not have the freedom to abstain from it" (Ethics of the Fathers 2:21).

In mundane activities, we expect a product from our efforts, and we do not go through motions for no tangible purpose whatever. However, this is only if we are free and work at our own behest. If one is a servant, he must follow the master's instructions, and he need not necessarily know why the master wants something done and what will result from the work. Even a hired person may be paid to do a task, the ultimate result of which is unknown to him.

We are servants of G-d, and we are to follow His commandments. The Torah is very explicit, "The Israelites are My servants, whom I have delivered from the land of Egypt" (*Leviticus* 25:55).

It is related that on Passover at the *seder*, a child asked the traditional four questions: "Why is this night different than all other nights?" The father responded by reciting the *Haggadah*, "We were slaves to Pharaoh in Egypt." The child interrupted, "How is that an answer to my question?" The father responded, "Look, when we were slaves to Pharaoh, we did as we were told, and did not ask why. G-d delivered us from Egypt and we now serve Him as our Master. We should not ask 'why' about the Divine commandments anymore than we did about Pharaoh's orders."

There are some who are zealous in championing liberty, who contend that if a person is bound by Torah, he is not free, since there are so many restrictions on his behavior. This shows a very shallow understanding of human psychology and behavior. Our sages knew far better when they said, "One is not free unless he observes Torah" (*Ethics of the Fathers* 6:2).

Animals are not free creatures, because they are totally dominated by their physical drives. An animal cannot make a choice, certainly not a moral choice. The hungry animal must go in search of food, and cannot decide whether or not it should eat. A human being, on the other hand, may choose to resist the craving for food, and fast even when he is hungry. An animal will take whatever food it can get, unless it is frightened away by a more powerful animal who has the food in its possession, because there is no moral constraint against taking the belongings of another. A human being, on the other hand, even in absence of threat of punishment, may decide not to take the belongings of someone else, even if he should desire them, because it is wrong to do so. The only creature that can choose how it wishes to behave is man.

Man, too, has an animal body, with all the desires and predilections inherent in it. What distinguishes man from animal is that man has a spirit, which gives him the capacity to resist the force of physical drives. This spirit was implanted in man by G-d, and man was given a set of laws by which he should abide. For the Noahites there is a more limited set of laws, and for the Jews it is the Torah. The Torah indeed prescribes laws which apply to virtually every facet of life, but it thereby elevates man into a truly spiritual being.

A person, of course, is free to reject Torah, but he then subjects himself to domination by his animal body. Similarly, a person is free to take all his valuable belongings and throw them in the river, and although this is clearly irrational, he does have the freedom to do so, although no one would call such behavior commendable. A person may discard valuable things because he is totally unaware of their true worth.

The Jew chooses to accept Torah and servitude to G-d. This is a free choice, which a person must make each and every day. When we read the *Shema* every day, we thereby accept the "yoke of obedience to G-d." Since this is a daily requirement, it means that we cannot observe the Torah today merely as a continuation of what we did yesterday or as a habit. Each day there must be a new acceptance, and since a person should constantly be advancing himself spiritually, each day the acceptance should be at a higher level than that of the previous day. Each day a person has the freedom to make a decision, and each day the choice of subjugating oneself to the "yoke of obedience to G-d" is a free choice. This is the significance of the Talmudic statement that the only truly free person is one who observes Torah. Failure to do so renders one a slave to one's physical and essentially animal self.

וְאָמְנָם עוֹד עִקָּר שֵׁנִי יֵשׁ בְּכַוָּנַת הַחֲסִידוּת וְהוּא טוֹבַת הַדּוֹר, שֶׁהִנֵּה רָאוּי לְכָל חָסִיד שֶׁיִּתְכַּוֵּן בְּמַעֲשָׂיו לְטוֹבַת דּוֹרוֹ כֻּלּוֹ לְזַכּוֹת אוֹתָם וּלְהָגֵן עֲלֵיהֶם . . . שֶׁאֵין הַקָּדוֹשׁ־בָּרוּךְ־הוּא חָפֵץ בְּאָבְדַן הָרְשָׁעִים, אֶלָּא מִצְוָה מֻטֶּלֶת עַל הַחֲסִידִים לְהִשְׁתַּדֵּל לְזַכּוֹתָם וּלְכַפֵּר עֲלֵיהֶם . . . וּלְלַמֵּד סַנֵּגוֹרְיָא עַל הַדּוֹר כֻּלּוֹ . . . כִּי אֵין הַקָּדוֹשׁ־בָּרוּךְ־הוּא אוֹהֵב אֶלָּא לְמִי שֶׁאוֹהֵב אֶת יִשְׂרָאֵל . . . וְאֵלֶּה הֵם הָרוֹעִים הָאֲמִתִּיִּים שֶׁל יִשְׂרָאֵל שֶׁהַקָּדוֹשׁ־בָּרוּךְ־הוּא חָפֵץ בָּהֶם הַרְבֵּה, שֶׁמּוֹסְרִים עַצְמָם עַל צֹאנוֹ, וְעוֹמְדִים תָּמִיד בַּפֶּרֶץ לְהִתְפַּלֵּל עֲלֵיהֶם לְבַטֵּל הַגְּזֵרוֹת הַקָּשׁוֹת, וְלִפְתּוֹחַ עֲלֵיהֶם שַׁעֲרֵי הַבְּרָכָה.

Another important principle of Chassidus is caring for the welfare of one's generation, to direct one's actions for the good of the generation, to benefit and protect them ... G-d does not want the wicked to perish, and it is incumbent upon a Chassid to pray for and seek forgiveness for those who violate the Torah ... A Chassid should also seek to defend his generation ... because G-d loves Israel, and whoever loves Israel finds favor before G-d ... These were the true leaders and shepherds of Israel, who constantly sought Israel's betterment and prayed for them to revoke any harsh decrees.

The prototype for this aspect of *Chassidus* is none other than Moses, who repeatedly interceded before G-d on behalf of the sinful Israelites, to the point of willingness to sacrifice his life for them. Noah, on the other hand, who saved himself and did not pray adequately to save his generation, is taken to task for this, and the deluge is referred to in the Prophets as "The Waters of Noah" (*Isaiah* 54:9) holding him responsible for the flood because he did not pray to avert it as Moses would have done. The patriarch Abraham, too, sought to gain a reprieve for the corrupt cities of Sodom and Ammorah (*Genesis* 18:23).

This theme is repeated throughout the Talmud, and was greatly emphasized by the Baal Shem Tov. In his time there were itinerant rabbis who would circulate among small communities and preach to the people, often sharply reprimanding them for lack of diligence in the study of Torah and performance of mitzvos. The Baal Shem Tov was intolerant of them and rebuked them, telling them that they should deliver messages of hope and courage to uplift the spirits of the Jews who lived under feudal oppression. To one preacher who was critical of people's lack of *kavannah* in praying hastily, the Baal Shem Tov said, "Do you realize that when a Jew hurries home breathless after a hard day's work and says, 'I have only a few minutes left to recite *Minchah* (the afternoon service), do you realize that the heavenly angels tremble before the holiness of his prayer?" One time, upon hearing one of the preachers deliver a scathing sermon, the Baal Shem Tov rushed up to the Ark and said, "Master of the Universe, do not listen to this man. Your children are good and loyal. This man sermonizes because he needs to raise money to marry off his daughter. Please bless him with money, and he will stop preaching harshly about Your children."

While all the chassidic masters followed this pattern of looking for the good in people, the outstanding master was Rabbi Levi Yitzchak of Berditchev, who excelled in this. Stories abound of how Rabbi Levi Yitzchak would intercede for people, showing G-d their merits and pleading for them. One of the chassidic masters said that as far as Rabbi Levi Yitzchak was concerned, G-d had not dealt fairly with even a single Jew!

On *Tishah B'Av* (a fast day commemorating the destruction of the Sanctuary), Rabbi Levi Yitzchak saw someone eating. "My child," he said, "you must certainly have forgotten that today is *Tishah B'Av*. The man replied, "No, I know it is *Tishah B'Av*."

"Ah," Rabbi Levi Yitzchak said, "then you undoubtedly were instructed by your doctor not to fast."

"No," the man said, "I have no use for a doctor. I am in perfect health."

Rabbi Levi Yitzchak turned his eyes to Heaven. "Master of the Universe," he said, "I have just given this man two valid reasons to excuse his behavior, yet because he so loves the truth, he did not take advantage of them. Since You are a G-d of truth, You must recognize this man's virtues and reward him accordingly."

Rabbi Levi Yitzchak used to say, "Since G-d has chosen Israel as His people, no one has the right to say anything negative about them."

One *Shavuos* Rabbi Levi Yitzchak said, "Master of the Universe, perhaps on Rosh Hashanah and Yom Kippur You may not have granted forgiveness to those who offended You because on these days You function as a king, and the *halachah* is that a king may not forgive an offense against the crown. But today is the day on which You give us the Torah, and today You function as a teacher rather than as a king, and a teacher certainly does have the right to forgive an offense. Therefore, today You should grant forgiveness to everyone."

וְהִנֵּה כְּבָר בֵּאַרְנוּ חֶלְקֵי הַחֲסִידוּת הָרָאשִׁיִּים, וּפְרָטֵיהֶם מְסוּרִים לְכָל בַּר־שֵׂכֶל וּלְכָל לֵב טָהוֹר לְהִתְנַהֵג בָּם בַּדֶּרֶךְ הַיָּשָׁר.

We have now explained the major components of Chassidus. The details are left for each intelligent person of pure heart to work out and conduct himself accordingly.

How much is included in these two attributes: intelligence and of pure heart! There is no dearth of people who have demonstrated vast intellectual capacity, yet this by no means assures proper behavior. The atrocities of the Holocaust were committed by Germany, which boasted of its leading universities, scientists, philosophers, and authors. On the other hand, people of pure heart who may be well motivated may lack the intelligence necessary for proper behavior, and their good intentions may go astray.

The combination of both intelligence and purity of heart is not too common. To help us implement *Chassidus*, Ramchal therefore provides further analysis in the following chapter.

20

בְּמִשְׁקַל הַחֲסִידוּת

The Balance of Chassidus

מַה שֶּׁצָּרִיךְ לְבָאֵר עַתָּה הוּא מִשְׁקַל־הַחֲסִידוּת הַזֶּה, וְהוּא עִנְיָן עִקָּרִי מְאֹד מְאֹד. וְתֵדַע בֶּאֱמֶת שֶׁזּוֹהִי הַמְּלָאכָה הַקָּשָׁה שֶׁבַּחֲסִידוּת, כִּי דַקּוּתוֹ רַב, וְיֵשׁ לַיֵּצֶר בַּדָּבָר הַזֶּה כְּנִיסָה גְדוֹלָה, עַל כֵּן נִמְצֵאת סַכָּנָתוֹ עֲצוּמָה, כִּי הַרְבֵּה דְּבָרִים טוֹבִים יוּכַל הַיֵּצֶר לְרַחֵק כְּאִלּוּ הֵם רָעִים, וְהַרְבֵּה חֲטָאִים לְקָרֵב כְּאִלּוּ הֵם מִצְוֹת גְּדוֹלוֹת.

We must now clarify the balance of Chassidus, which is a most fundamental subject and represents the most difficult process in Chassidus. This is a very delicate balance, and allows for many areas of infiltration by the yetzer hara. This is a precarious area, fraught with great danger because the yetzer hara can reject many good things as being bad, and seduce one to do something evil by making it appear to be a great mitzvah.

Ramchal has struck a chord of the greatest importance, and is very emphatic about it. Someone who lives essentially according to the *Shulchan Aruch*, by the letter of the law, has fairly firm guidelines for his behavior, because so much of it is described in the *Shulchan Aruch* as being either obligatory as a mitzvah, forbidden as a sin, or something neutral and permissible. Thus, one can know that it is a mitzvah to hear the *shofar* on Rosh Hashanah, it is a sin to eat *treifah*, and those things which are not listed as either mitzvos nor sins are permissible.

When one practices *Chassidus*, however, one wishes to do more than that which the *Shulchan Aruch* prescribes. For these things there are no hard and fast guidelines, and in absence of these, the *yetzer hara* has considerable leeway in influencing one's behavior, since one cannot appeal to an authority as to whether the behavior is desirable or undesirable. Ramchal has already noted that some people have distorted notions about *Chassidus*, and engage in fasting and excessive confessions. The *Shulchan Aruch* neither forbids nor advocates such practices, and one may therefore think that one is doing something very praiseworthy, doing much more than is required by the letter of the law. Ramchal has pointed out that such behavior is most unwise, and is a corruption of *Chassidus*.

The concept of misguided *Chassidus* is found in the Talmud, which gives two examples of ill-advised and foolish piety, such as someone who is reluctant to save a drowning woman because he is afraid that physical contact with a woman will arouse his lust (*Sotah* 21b), or someone who delays coming to another's rescue until he first takes off his *tefillin* (*Talmud Yerushalmi*, Sotah 3:4).

While giving *tzedakah* is a mitzvah of the highest caliber, *halachah* designates a limit of one-fifth of a person's earnings that may be given to *tzedakah*. I recall, as a youngster, a man of meager earnings who went into debt to give far greater amounts of *tzedakah* than was within his means. People respected him highly for his self-sacrifice, but one time there was an appeal for a worthy cause in our shul, and this man brought in a donation of one hundred dollars, which my father refused to accept. My father said to me, "Solomon says, 'Do not be a *tzaddik* to excess' (*Ecclesiastes* 7:16), which is what this man is doing. This is not normal and it is not right." I did not realize how right my father was until many years later, when this man had a favorable turn of fortune, acquired much property, and became very wealthy. How disappointed everyone was when he turned out to be a miser, and one could not extract from him a single cent for *tzedakah*! Rambam was right: Virtue is a mean, and neither extreme is virtuous.

As was already mentioned, the Chafetz Chaim would come into the study hall at night, and send the students off to sleep. He stated that the urge to continue learning into the wee hours of the morning is quite likely the cunning of the *yetzer hara*, to cause one to be so exhausted from lack of sleep that the following day would be wasted. There may be isolated individuals who are able to tolerate a more stringent schedule without negative effects, but the Chafetz Chaim felt that this was not proper conduct for the average student. No doubt others would have considered late-night study to be praiseworthy, but the Chafetz Chaim did not hold this to be *Chassidus*.

In regard to zealousness, we have already noted that zeal can be counterproductive. There are some people who have brought dishonor to Judaism by their thoughtless behavior, which they assumed to be a mitzvah because they were "defending" the Torah. Numerous examples can be cited of misguided piety resulting from the lack of explicit guidelines for *Chassidus*.

וּבֶאֱמֶת שֶׁלֹּא יוּכַל אִישׁ לְהַצְלִיחַ בְּמִשְׁקָל הַזֶּה, אֶלָּא בִּשְׁלֹשָׁה דְּבָרִים: שֶׁיִּהְיֶה לִבּוֹ יָשָׁר שֶׁבַּלְּבָבוֹת, שֶׁלֹּא תִהְיֶה פְּנִיָּתוֹ אֶלָּא לַעֲשׂוֹת נַחַת־רוּחַ לְפָנָיו יִתְבָּרֵךְ, וְלֹא זוּלַת זֶה כְּלָל. וְשֶׁיִּהְיֶה מְעַיֵּן עַל מַעֲשָׂיו עִיּוּן גָּדוֹל, וְיִשְׁתַּדֵּל לְתַקְּנָם עַל־פִּי הַתַּכְלִית הַזֶּה, וְאַחַר כָּל זֹאת יִהְיֶה מַשְׁלִיךְ יְהָבוֹ עַל ה׳.

[In the absence of written guidelinges. . .] In order for a person to succeed in Chassidus, he must meet three requirements: (1) He must be of utmost sincerity, and have no ulterior motive other than to do that which is pleasing to G-d; (2) he must carefully scrutinize his actions and try his utmost to direct them toward this goal; (3) after all this has been done, he must throw his burden on G-d (i.e., he has done all he can do and done it properly and the rest is in G-d's hands).

The steps of spirituality proceed in an unalterable sequence. One must master *Nekiyus* before one can approach *Chassidus*. As we will recall, *Nekiyus* requires a single-mindedness of intention in all one's acts, with elimination of all traces of personal interest. Secondly, a *Chassid* cannot act out of habit, because habitual behavior is performed without proper thought and deliberation. Ramchal had cited the Talmudic description of the prayer of a *Chassid*, which is preceded by an hour of meditation. Prayers which are recited out of rote are not the prayers of a *Chassid*, and this holds true not only for performance of other mitzvos, but for all of one's actions. A *Chassid* thinks about what he does before he does it, and constantly scrutinizes his behavior as to whether it indeed contributes anything to the ultimate goal.

Finally, a *Chassid's* trust in G-d must be absolute. The Talmud does indeed state that it is not considered blasphemy if a person feels angry at G-d when in severe distress (*Bava Basra* 16b), but while the suffering person is exonerated from sin, he is not considered a *Chassid*. A perfect trust in G-d means that one totally defers to the Divine wisdom and judgment as being not only just but also benevolent. The *Chassid* is one who can praise G-d for the bad that he experiences as well as for the good. This can occur only in someone who has divested himself of all personal interests, because as long as the latter is present, one cannot achieve acceptance of adversity with equanimity.

A *Chassid* does not experience Abstinence as a self-denial, because there is no "self" which is being denied anything. The "self" is nothing but an extension of G-d that was created in this particular form in order to carry out G-d's will. This is a total self-effacement which logically leads to the next step on the ladder of spirituality: Humility.

וְהִנֵּה מַה שֶּׁצָּרִיךְ לְהָבִין הוּא, כִּי אֵין לָדוּן דִּבְרֵי הַחֲסִידוּת עַל מַרְאֵיהֶן הָרִאשׁוֹן, אֶלָּא צָרִיךְ לְעַיֵּן וּלְהִתְבּוֹנֵן עַד הֵיכָן תּוֹלְדוֹת הַמַּעֲשֶׂה מַגִּיעוֹת, כִּי לִפְעָמִים הַמַּעֲשֶׂה בְּעַצְמוֹ יֵרָאֶה טוֹב, וּלְפִי שֶׁהַתּוֹלָדוֹת רָעוֹת, יִתְחַיֵּב לְהַנִּיחוֹ. וְאִם יַעֲשֶׂה אוֹתוֹ, יִהְיֶה חוֹטֵא וְלֹא חָסִיד. הִנֵּה מַעֲשֵׂה גְּדַלְיָה בֶּן אֲחִיקָם (ירמיה מא, טז) גָּלוּי לְעֵינֵינוּ, שֶׁמִּפְּנֵי רוֹב חֲסִידוּתוֹ שֶׁלֹּא לָדוּן אֶת יִשְׁמָעֵאל לְכַף חוֹבָה אוֹ שֶׁלֹּא לְקַבֵּל לְשׁוֹן הָרָע, אָמַר לְיוֹחָנָן בֶּן קָרֵחַ: ,,שֶׁקֶר אַתָּה דוֹבֵר אֶל יִשְׁמָעֵאל.'' וּמַה גָּרַם? גָּרַם שֶׁמֵּת הוּא וְנִפְזְרוּ יִשְׂרָאֵל, וְכָבָה גַּחַלְתָּם הַנִּשְׁאָרָה. וּכְבָר יִחֵס הַכָּתוּב אֵלָיו הֲרִיגַת הָאֲנָשִׁים אֲשֶׁר נֶהֶרְגוּ, כְּאִלּוּ הֲרָגָם הוּא.

What must be understood is that acts of Chassidus should not be judged superficially, but rather with careful reflection on what their long-term effects may be. At times an action in itself may appear to be good, but the eventual consequences are bad, and if one follows the course of action he will be a sinner rather than a Chassid.

(When Jerusalem fell to the Babylonians, they appointed Gedaliah ben Ahikam as governor of Judea. Gedaliah was warned that Yishmael ben Netaniah had been hired by the king of Ammon to assassinate him.) Because of his great piety, Gedaliah refused to accept lashon hara about Yishmael (Jeremiah 40:16). This resulted in Gedaliah's death and the dispersion of the remnants of Israel. The Talmud holds Gedaliah responsible for this calamity, as though he was the guilty one (for his refusal to heed the warning).

While Ramchal's admonition requiring the necessity for considering the long-range consequences of one's action is certainly appropriate for *Chassidus*, it also has much wider application, and is an important guideline even for people who have not advanced to this stage of spirituality. The Talmud says, "Who is a wise person? One who can foresee the consequences of one's behavior" (*Tamid* 32a).

Many people act according to what they see as immediately advantageous, and fail to give adequate consideration to what may be the ultimate results of their actions. Ramchal had referred to the distorting influences of desire and temptation and that these may blind a person even to the immediate harmful effects of his behavior, let alone the possible deleterious results in the remote future.

A wise person does not act on whim, but gives much thought to his actions, whereas the foolish person is likely to act impulsively. The wise Solomon repeatedly emphasizes this point. "All the ways of a person are just in his own eyes" (*Proverbs* 21:2). "The way of a fool is straight in his own eyes" (ibid. 12:15). "Listen to advice and accept instruction, that you may be wise in the end" (ibid. 19:20). "A way may seem straight to a man, yet its end is the way of death" (ibid. 14:12).

Clinically, I regularly see individuals who act destructively because of an immediate gain or pleasure, as is characteristic of the alcoholic, the drug addict, the cigarette smoker, or the compulsive overeater. One recovered alcoholic said, "I never in my life took a drink unless I thought it was right thing to do at the time." Short-sighted behavior is by no means restricted to people with chemical or food addictions. Many people fall prey to harmful behavior by focusing only on the immediate gratification. The sages of the Talmud were well aware of this, and Rabbi Yehudah HaNasi advises: "Consider the loss sustained in performance of a mitzvah as opposed to the ultimate gain, and the gain in committing a sin as opposed to the ultimate loss" (*Ethics of the Fathers* 2:1). The counsel of Ramchal to avoid myopic judgment is thus appropriate for every person.

Ramchal's singling out the *Chassid* for this precaution is because the *Chassid*, lacking firm guidelines (as noted above), is particularly vulnerable to being misled because of his belief that what he is doing is indeed the will of G-d. While accepting *lashon hara* is indeed a grievous sin, it is foolish to fail to heed warnings that one is in danger of harm, and Gedaliah's piety was ill advised. The Chafetz Chaim in his magnum opus on *lashon hara* provides guidelines as to when one must pay attention to what might appear to be *lashon hara*, and when one must warn others of possible danger to them, even though this may appear to be *lashon hara*.

I frequently receive calls where the question is posed, "I received an inquiry regarding a *shidduch* (matrimonial match), because I am friendly with the family. I happen to know that the young man (or young woman, or a close family member) had an episode of mental illness for which they were hospitalized. Am I permitted to reveal this?"

This issue has been dealt with by *halachic* authorities, and it is their opinion that one is *obligated* to provide this information, and that failure to do so violates the Scriptural commandment "Do not stand idly by and see your brother's blood being spilled" (*Leviticus* 19:16), which the Talmud interprets to mean that one has an obligation to avert harm that may occur to someone else. Those who are squeamish about this should think of it this way. Suppose you had made an inquiry about a proposed match for your daughter, and someone withheld important information about the young man or his family. After there are several children to this marriage the young man suffers a relapse of a preexisting condition, and your daughter is now in a dilemma which could have been avoided, or for which she could have been better prepared to cope. How would you feel about those people who withheld this information from you?

I cannot help but wonder why this is the only time people are concerned about *lashon hara*. If people would consult a rabbi every time they were about to say something negative about someone else as to its permissibility, the telephone company would have to erect a huge, fully computerized building to handle the volume of calls. Is it not strange that the only time people raise the question about revealing a possible defect in someone else is when it is in fact permissible to do so?

וְהַבַּיִת הַשֵּׁנִי גַּם־הוּא חָרַב עַל־יְדֵי חֲסִידוּת כָּזֶה אֲשֶׁר לֹא נִשְׁקַל בְּמִשְׁקַל צֶדֶק. בְּמַעֲשֶׂה דְּבַר־קַמְצָא (גיטין נו, א) אָמְרוּ, „סְבוּר רַבָּנָן לְקָרוּבֵהּ. אָמַר לָהֶם רַבִּי זְכַרְיָה בֶּן אֶבְקוּלַס, יֹאמְרוּ: בַּעֲלֵי מוּמִין קְרֵבִין לְגַבֵּי מִזְבֵּחַ. סְבוּר לְמִקְטְלֵהּ, אָמַר לָהֶם רַבִּי זְכַרְיָה בֶּן אֶבְקוּלַס, יֹאמְרוּ: מַטִּיל מוּם בְּקָדָשִׁים יֵהָרֵג". בֵּין כָּךְ וּבֵין־כָּךְ הָלַךְ אוֹתוֹ־רָשָׁע וְהִלְשִׁין אֶת יִשְׂרָאֵל. בָּא הַקֵּיסָר וְהֶחֱרִיב יְרוּשָׁלַיִם. וְהוּא מַה שֶּׁאָמַר רַבִּי יוֹחָנָן עַל זֶה, „עַנְוְתָנוּתוֹ שֶׁל רַבִּי זְכַרְיָה הֶחֱרִיבָה אֶת בֵּיתֵנוּ וְשָׂרְפָה אֶת הֵיכָלֵנוּ וְהִגְלַתְנוּ לְבֵין הָאֻמּוֹת".

The second Temple was destroyed because of ill-advised Chassidus. (A vengeful person who bore a grudge against the rabbis told the emperor that the Jews were rebelling against him, and as proof of his charge, he stated that the Jews would refuse to accept a sacrificial offering from him. When the emperor sent a sheep for sacrifice, this person inflicted a slight defect in the animal's eye, which although hardly visible, disqualified the animal for the Altar according to halachah. Fearing that refusal to sacrifice the emperor's offering would incite his wrath, the rabbis suggested processing the offering in spite of its defect.) Rabbi Zechariah said, "This will set a precedent that defective offerings are permissible." It was then suggested that they do away with this vengeful person (so that he does not inform the emperor that his offering was rejected), whereupon Rabbi Zechariah said, "This will set a precedent that one who inflicts a defect on an offering is put to death." This evil person did indeed inform the emperor, who vented his wrath by destroying Jerusalem. Rabbi Yochanan said, "Rabbi Zechariah's excessive piety caused the destruction of the House of G-d and drove us into exile."

Whereas no one has the authority to set aside any Torah restriction, the Sanhedrin (Supreme Court) was empowered under exceptional circumstances and as an isolated incident only, to do what was expedient. A classic example of this is Elijah's bringing a sacrificial offering outside of the Sanctuary (*I Kings* 18:23-39). Elijah did not say that it was permissible to do so, but that circumstances required this unusual action. Had Elijah said that the Torah restriction was no longer operative, his words would have been ignored and he would have been punished. Similarly, the danger of inciting the wrath of the emperor and bringing about a calamity warranted overriding one of the prohibitions for this single event. Rabbi Zechariah insisted on being more pious than the Sanhedrin, and his ill-fated counsel was disastrous to our nation.

Decisions of Torah authorities are bound by the regulations of *halachah*, and there is no mechanism in Judaism for granting a dispensation or altering the *halachah*. However, when there are circumstances which the Torah authorities consider to constitute a matter of life and death, they may apply the *halachah* that with the exception of the three cardinal sins (adultery, idolatry, and murder) the danger to life overrides all other prohibitions. For someone to insist on being superpious and to reject the opinion of the Torah authorities is a sin and not *Chassidus*.

הִנֵּה הַתּוֹרָה צִוְּתָה (ויקרא יט, יז): ,,הוֹכֵחַ תּוֹכִיחַ אֶת עֲמִיתֶךָ'', וְכַמָּה פְּעָמִים יִכָּנֵס אָדָם לְהוֹכִיחַ חוֹטְאִים בְּמָקוֹם אוֹ בִזְמַן שֶׁאֵין דְּבָרָיו נִשְׁמָעִים, וְגוֹרֵם לָהֶם לְהִתְפָּרֵץ יוֹתֵר בְּרִשְׁעָם וּלְחַלֵּל ה' לְהוֹסִיף עַל חַטָּאתָם פֶּשַׁע. הִנֵּה בְּכַיּוֹצֵא בָזֶה אֵינוֹ מִן הַחֲסִידוּת אֶלָּא לִשְׁתּוֹק. וְכָךְ אָמְרוּ ז"ל (יבמות סה, ב): ,,כְּשֵׁם שֶׁמִּצְוָה לוֹמַר דָּבָר הַנִּשְׁמָע, כָּךְ מִצְוָה שֶׁלֹּא לוֹמַר אֶת שֶׁאֵינוֹ נִשְׁמָע''.

The Torah commands us to reprimand a person who is behaving improperly (Leviticus 19:17). Yet, how often will a person rebuke others at a time or place where it is evident that they will not listen, and he thereby provokes them to further sinfulness and to desecrate the Divine Name. Here Chassidus advocates being silent, as the Talmud says, "Just as it is a mitzvah to say what will be listened to, so it is a mitzvah to refrain from saying what will not be listened to" (Yevamos 65b).

We dealt with this subject in our discussion of Zealousness. There is a proper time and place for rebuke, as well as a proper technique. One must be able to empathize before rebuking another person, and the simplest way to determine if rebuke is appropriate is to identify with that person. Think of yourself as being in his position. How would you react to rebuke if you were in his place?

With rare exceptions, rebuke should always be administered in private, to avoid humiliating anyone before others. Firstly, publicly humiliating a person is a grievous sin (*Ethics of the Fathers* 3:11), and secondly the person who is embarrassed will be so hurt and angry that he cannot possibly accept a reprimand. Wait until you have the opportunity to be alone with the person, and then deliver your message softly and gently, in the same manner you would wish someone to speak to you. The person is then much more likely to appreciate your consideration in delaying your rebuke so as not to humiliate him, and this in itself may encourage him to listen to you. Furthermore, if you dislike the person, leave the rebuke to others. Constructive rebuke will occur only if one corrects others just as one would correct his own child, with an intense love, and with the rebuke stemming from a sincere desire to help the other person rather than from anger that he is behaving in a manner inimical to you.

Solomon says, "Do not rebuke a scoffer lest he hate you. Rebuke a wise person, and he will love you" (*Proverbs* 9:8). One of the commentaries explains that if you rebuke someone by degrading and insulting him, he will hate you and reject your words. If, however, you rebuke him by appealing to his pride and by trying to elevate his self-esteem, he will appreciate your words. Solomon is thus saying, "Do not rebuke someone by calling him a scoffer or a sinner. Instead, praise him for his wisdom, and help him see that his behavior is not in accordance with his wisdom."

I can personally attest to the efficacy of this method. I recall that as a child, when I did something of which my father disapproved, he would gently say, *"Es past nisht,"* meaning "That behavior does not become you. It is beneath your dignity. You are too good for that." I was never put in a position to resent a reprimand, and I remember my father's rebukes with great fondness.

It is futile to dissimulate. If you do not sincerely love a person and are not correcting him for his own good, do not act as if you did. If you do not believe that the behavior is beneath the other person's dignity because you do not hold him in high esteem, do not say it. In such cases, keep your silence and leave the rebuke to others.

רְאֵה, פָּשׁוּט הוּא שֶׁרָאוּי לְכָל אָדָם לִהְיוֹת מַקְדִּים וְרָץ לִדְבַר־מִצְוָה וּלְהִשְׁתַּדֵּל לִהְיוֹת מִן הָעוֹסְקִים בָּהּ. אַךְ הִנֵּה לִפְעָמִים יָכוֹל לְהִוָּלֵד מִזֶּה מְרִיבָה, שֶׁיּוֹתֵר תִּתְבַּזֶּה הַמִּצְוָה וְיִתְחַלֵּל בָּהּ שֵׁם־שָׁמַיִם מִמַּה שֶּׁיִּתְכַּבֵּד. בְּכַיּוֹצֵא בָּזֶה, וַדַּאי שֶׁחַיָּב הֶחָסִיד לְהַנִּיחַ אֶת הַמִּצְוָה וְלֹא לִרְדּוֹף אַחֲרֶיהָ.

It is of course desirable that a person should be diligent in pursuit of doing a mitzvah, but at times this may result in quarrels and strife, and can bring dishonor rather than honor to the Divine Name. In such instances, a Chassid is better advised to leave the mitzvah rather than pursue it.

If one truly loves G-d, one would avoid doing anything which might displease Him. Ramchal had indicated that *Chassidus* requires a delicate balance, and that one might be so misled by his intense desire to do a mitzvah that he ends up committing a grievous sin. The Talmud tells of an incident where two *kohanim* (priests) were racing to do the Divine service in the Temple, and when one saw that the other would beat him to it, he stabbed him to death (*Yoma* 23a). This represents a very sick mentality, and a grossly corrupted concept of what it is that G-d wishes us to do.

Rabbi Yisrael of Salant was seen washing his hands before a meal, using the very minimum of water required by *halachah*. When asked why he does not abide by the *Shulchan Aruch's* commendation for those who use more than just the bare minimum amount, Rabbi Yisrael replied, "I cannot be a *Chassid* at the expense of the water carrier, whose back aches under the burden of buckets of water." One must be a *Chassid* at one's own expense, not that of others.

It is customary on Friday evening, before the meal, to review the Torah portion and study the Zohar in preparation for sanctifying Shabbos by the *kiddush*. My father would tell of a chassidic master who had taken upon himself voluntary exile, wandering from town to town, and who was once very hungry on Friday night, and had to wait to eat until the host had finished meditating. When this master returned to his home and had guests for Shabbos, he would begin *"Shalom Aleichem"* (the introductory hymn for *kiddush*) while the reader was closing the evening service, so that he could make *kiddush* and serve his guests without delay.

We invariably had guests at our Shabbos table, and my father rarely took the time to prepare for *kiddush*, because some of the guests were itinerant rabbis who had not eaten much that day. He would say, "I cannot study the Zohar at the expense of those who are hungry." I recall that at times, when he felt it absolutely necessary to meditate and prepare for *kiddush*, he would have the guests make *kiddush* first and have the first course served. After they had eaten something he would excuse himself and return to his study to prepare for *kiddush*.

The first order of priority for *Chassidus* is consideration for others.

הִנֵּה חַיָּב הָאָדָם לִשְׁמוֹר כָּל הַמִּצְוֹת בְּכָל דִּקְדּוּקֵיהֶם לִפְנֵי מִי שֶׁיִּהְיֶה וְלֹא יִירָא וְלֹא יֵבוֹשׁ . . . אָמְנָם גַּם בָּזֶה צָרִיךְ חִלּוּק וְהַבְחָנָה, כִּי כָּל זֶה נֶאֱמַר עַל גּוּפֵי הַמִּצְוֹת שֶׁחַיָּבִים אֲנַחְנוּ בָּהֶם חוֹבָה גְמוּרָה, שֶׁבָּהֶם יָשִׂים פָּנָיו כַּחַלָּמִישׁ. אַךְ יֵשׁ אֵיזֶה תּוֹסְפוֹת חֲסִידוּת, שֶׁאִם יַעֲשֶׂה אוֹתָם הָאָדָם לִפְנֵי הֲמוֹן הָעָם, יִשְׂחֲקוּ עָלָיו וְיִתְלוֹצְצוּ, וְנִמְצְאוּ חוֹטְאִים וְנֶעֱנָשִׁים עַל יָדוֹ, וְהוּא הָיָה יָכוֹל לְהַנִּיחַ מִלַּעֲשׂוֹת הַדְּבָרִים הָהֵם, כִּי אֵינָם חוֹבָה מֻחְלֶטֶת. הִנֵּה דָּבָר כָּזֶה, וַדַּאי שֶׁיּוֹתֵר הָגוּן הוּא לֶחָסִיד שֶׁיַּנִּיחֵהוּ מִשֶּׁיַּעֲשֵׂהוּ.

A person is obligated to observe all the mitzvos with all of their specifications, regardless in whose presence he finds himself, and one should feel no shame (if others ridicule him) . . . But this applies only to whatever is obligatory, in which case a person should have a rock-like obstinacy. However, for things which are not obligatory and which a person does for reasons of Chassidus, if he feels that others will mock him, he should refrain from this practice and not cause others to sin (by mocking him).

This statement requires some clarification. It might appear at first glance that Ramchal is advocating yielding to public pressure or prevailing lifestyles so as not to be ridiculed, as long as one does not frankly violate Torah law. This is not the case. The Midrash states that the reason our ancestors merited deliverance from the bondage of Egypt is because they maintained their Jewish identity, retaining their Jewish garb, their language, and their Jewish names. While there may not be an explicit law that requires a Jew to dress in a certain way, it is important to maintain a Jewish identity to avoid assimilation. Ramchal does not mean, for example, that a person who wishes to have a beard should shave it (even in an *halachically* permissible way) in order to avoid people poking fun at him.

What Ramchal is referring to is the manner in which mitzvos are performed. There are a variety of customs in different communities regarding the ways in which mitzvos are performed, all of which are legitimate. If a person finds himself in an environment where people will not understand why he is doing the mitzvah so differently than they, and if this would provoke ridicule, it is better to follow the local custom. For example, many people put on a second pair of *tefillin* after morning services to comply with an opinion which is not binding in *halachah*. Some people wear two pair of *tefillin* simultaneously. If someone who has this practice finds himself in a community where this would appear to others to be weird, it is better that he not make himself conspicuous, and let him rather put the two pair of *tefillin* on in sequence rather than together. It is these different ways of doing mitzvos that Ramchal is referring to when he advocates adjusting to local custom rather than arousing amazement by doing things one's own way, if this is not required by *halachah*.

וּמַעֲשֶׂה דְרַבִּי טַרְפוֹן (ברכות י, ב) יוֹכִיחַ, שֶׁהֶחְמִיר לְהַטּוֹת כְּבֵית־שַׁמַּאי, וְאָמְרוּ לוֹ: ,,כְּדַאי הָיִיתָ לָחוּב בְּעַצְמְךָ שֶׁעָבַרְתָּ עַל דִּבְרֵי בֵית־הִלֵּל״, אַף־עַל־פִּי שֶׁמַּחְמִיר הָיָה. וָזֶה, שֶׁעִנְיַן מַחֲלֹקֶת בֵּית־שַׁמַּאי וּבֵית־הִלֵּל הָיָה עִנְיָן כָּבֵד לְיִשְׂרָאֵל, מִפְּנֵי הַמַּחֲלֹקֶת הַגְּדוֹלָה שֶׁרָבְתָה בֵּינֵיהֶם, וְסוֹף־סוֹף נִגְמַר שֶׁהֲלָכָה כְּבֵית־הִלֵּל

לְעוֹלָם. הִנֵּה קִיּוּמָהּ שֶׁל תּוֹרָה, שֶׁגְּמַר־דִּין זֶה יִשָּׁאֵר בְּכָל תֹּקֶף לָעַד וּלְעוֹלְמֵי עוֹלָמִים, וְלֹא יֶחֱלַשׁ בְּשׁוּם פָּנִים, שֶׁלֹּא תֵּעָשֶׂה תּוֹרָה חָס־וְחָלִילָה כִּשְׁתֵּי תוֹרוֹת. וְעַל־כֵּן לְדַעַת הַמִּשְׁנָה הַזֹּאת, יוֹתֵר חֲסִידוּת הוּא לְהַחֲזִיק כְּבֵית הִלֵּל אֲפִלּוּ לְקֻלָּא, מִלְּהַחֲמִיר כְּבֵית־שַׁמַּאי. וְזֶה לָנוּ לְעֵינַיִם לִרְאוֹת אֵיזֶה דֶּרֶךְ יִשְׁכּוֹן אוֹר בֶּאֱמֶת וּבֶאֱמוּנָה, לַעֲשׂוֹת הַיָּשָׁר בְּעֵינֵי ה׳.

(The Talmud cites a dispute between the House of Hillel and the House of Shammai as to the proper position for reciting the evening Shema, with the former saying that there is no requirement for a specific position, while the latter contending that the evening Shema must be recited while reclining. The Talmud accepts the opinion of the House of Hillel as the final halachah).

Rabbi Tarfon wished to satisfy both opinions, and was sharply rebuked for this by his peers (Berachos 10b). They felt that trying to satisfy the opinion of the House of Shammai might cause doubt in people's minds on the acceptance of the opinion of the House of Hillel as being the halachah. This is an example where excessive piety was disapproved because it threatened to undermine the established authority.

One must be extremely careful in trying to satisfy all opinions, even those that were rejected by the final *halachic* authorities. Sometimes this is permissible, but if doing so may lead to causing doubt as to what is *halachically* binding, it is better to not be in compliance with all opinions rather than to undermine authority.

21

בְּדַרְכֵי קְנִיַּת הַחֲסִידוּת

Acquisition of Chassidus

הִנֵּה מִמַּה שֶׁיּוֹעִיל הַרְבֵּה לִקְנוֹת הַחֲסִידוּת, הוּא גֹּדֶל הַהִסְתַּכְּלוּת וְרוֹב הַהִתְבּוֹנְנוּת. כִּי כַּאֲשֶׁר יַרְבֶּה הָאָדָם לְהִתְבּוֹנֵן עַל גֹּדֶל רוֹמְמוּתוֹ יִתְבָּרֵךְ וְתַכְלִית שְׁלֵמוּתוֹ, וְרוֹב הַהֶרְחֵק הַבִּלְתִּי מְשֹׁעָר שֶׁבֵּין גְּדֻלָּתוֹ וּבֵין שִׁפְלוּתֵנוּ, יִגְרוֹם לוֹ שֶׁיִּמָּלֵא יִרְאָה וּרְעָדָה מִלְּפָנָיו. וּבְהִתְבּוֹנְנוֹ עַל רוֹב חֲסָדָיו עִמָּנוּ וְעַל גֹּדֶל אַהֲבָתוֹ יִתְבָּרֵךְ לְיִשְׂרָאֵל וְעַל קִרְבַת הַיְשָׁרִים אֵלָיו וּמַעֲלַת הַתּוֹרָה וְהַמִּצְוֹת וְכַיּוֹצֵא מִן הָעִיּוּנִים וְהַלִּמּוּדִים, וַדַּאי שֶׁתִּתְלַהֵט בּוֹ אַהֲבָה עַזָּה וְיִבְחַר וְיִתְאַוֶּה לִדָּבֵק בּוֹ. כִּי בִרְאוֹתוֹ שֶׁהַשֵּׁם יִתְבָּרֵךְ הוּא לָנוּ לְאָב מַמָּשׁ וּמְרַחֵם עָלֵינוּ כְּאָב עַל בָּנִים, יִתְעוֹרֵר בּוֹ בְּהֶמְשֵׁךְ, הַחֵפֶץ וְהַתְּשׁוּקָה לִגְמוֹל לוֹ כְּבֵן אֶל אָבִיו . . . וְהִנֵּה וַדַּאי שֶׁיַּעַזְרֵהוּ לָזֶה רוֹב הַהַתְמָדָה וְהָעִיּוּן בְּמִזְמוֹרֵי דָוִד עָלָיו־הַשָּׁלוֹם וְהַהִתְבּוֹנְנוּת בָּם בְּמַאַמְרֵיהֶם וְעִנְיָנָם. כִּי בִּהְיוֹתָם כֻּלָּם מְלֵאִים אַהֲבָה וְיִרְאָה וְכָל מִינֵי חֲסִידוּת, הִנֵּה בְּהִתְבּוֹנְנוֹ בָּם, לֹא יִמָּנַע מֵהִתְעוֹרֵר בּוֹ הִתְעוֹרְרוּת גָּדוֹל לָצֵאת בְּעִקְּבוֹתָיו וְלָלֶכֶת בִּדְרָכָיו. וְכֵן תּוֹעִיל הַקְּרִיאָה בְּסִפּוּר מַעֲשֵׂה הַחֲסִידִים בָּאַגָּדוֹת אֲשֶׁר בָּאוּ שָׁם, כִּי כָּל אֵלֶּה מְעוֹרְרִים אֶת הַשֵּׂכֶל לְהִתְיַעֵץ וְלַעֲשׂוֹת כְּמַעֲשֵׂיהֶם הַנֶּחְמָדִים.

What is most helpful in acquiring Chassidus is profound thought and much reflection on the infinite majesty of G-d, the enormous, incalculable gap between His majesty and mortal man's lowliness, which will inspire a person to great awe. As one reflects on G-d's infinite benevolence and His tremendous love for us, and on the nobility of Torah and mitzvos, one is aroused to an intense love for G-d and a desire to be united with Him. As one recognizes His caring for us like a father for a child, one will respond with the love of a child for his father . . . It is also of great help to study the Psalms of David, which inspire us to reverence and love for G-d, and to read about the lives of our tzaddikim, because these stimulate a person to emulate them.

Rambam states that the way to acquire love for G-d is to reflect on the wonders of creation, which will reveal the infinite Divine wisdom and inspire a person to wish to come to a greater knowledge of G-d (*Yesodei Hatorah* 2:2). Rambam is referring not only to the great wisdom of G-d one can discover through a careful study of the universe, which science has now made more evident to us as we discover the unbelievable, genius complexity in the structure of submicroscopic molecules as well as the awesome composition of galaxies, some of which are a trillion times greater than the solar system, and the precise, immutable laws which the universe obeys, as we say in our morning prayers on Shabbos, "He created them with knowledge, understanding, and wisdom. . .they fulfill with reverence the will of their Master." Rambam goes on with a rather brief description of the various levels of creation, including the spiritual, celestial spheres.

It is generally assumed that Rambam did not have access to *kabballah*. Ramchal, on the other hand, was extremely proficient in *kabballah* and wrote profusely on the subject. Ramchal is highly critical of those who neglect the study of *kabballah*, and feels that its study is essential to come to the greatest knowledge about G-d that is accessible to the human mind. His other great works, *The Way of G-d*, *The Wisdom of Understanding*, and *The One-Hundred-Thirty-Eight Portals to Wisdom*, draw heavily upon *kabballah*. It is through the revelations of *kabballah* that man was given an insight, not into the essence of G-d which is unknowable, but into the Divine wisdom in the creation and operation of the universe.

The study of *kabballah* has been a matter of controversy since the earliest times. The revealed aspects of Torah are generally amenable to logical understanding, and it is even possible for a person to study the Talmud on his own. *Kabballah*, on the other hand, is esoteric and involves concepts which may require more imagination than logic. It is only a stone's throw from imagination to imagery, and the Torah repeatedly warns against applying imagery to G-d. "For you have not seen any image" (at Sinai, *Deuteronomy* 4:16). *Kabballah* cannot be learned on one's own, and one must be guided by a competent instructor.

The delicate nature of the hidden secrets of creation and the makeup of the celestial spheres makes it highly vulnerable to dangerous distortion. The Talmud states that four of the greatest sages became involved in these esoteric pursuits. Ben Azai died, Ben Zoma became irrational, Elisha ben Avuyah became a heretic, and only Rabbi Akiva emerged unscathed.

The dangers of delving into the *kabballah* became evident with the debacle of Shabbtai Zevi (1620-1676), a brilliant scholar and student of *kabballah*, who developed the delusion that he was the Messiah. With his erudition and charisma, and particularly in view of the aftermath of the terrible pogroms of 1648, he attracted a large following, including some of the prominent Jewish authorities. The tragic denouement came when he converted to Islam, taking many of his followers along with him and leaving many others in disillusion and despair. Ramchal and Baal Shem Tov, who lived only several decades after Shabbtai Zevi and both of whom advocated the study of *kabballah*, suffered much persecution because of the fears that this might result in similar false messianic cults.

It is generally accepted that while the study of *kabballah* is indeed important, several safeguards must be taken to avoid misunderstanding of these delicate concepts. They are: (1) a thorough knowledge of Talmud and *halachah*; (2) learning only from a recognized authoritative instructor; and (3) preferably delaying its study until after age forty, when one has gained greater maturity and is less likely to be carried away by impetuous imagination.

Ramchal also recommends learning about the lifestyles of our great *tzaddikim*. The potency of this cannot be overestimated, and we have already referred to the Talmudic statement that the narratives of the servants of the patriarchs supersede in importance the learned discussions of their scholarly descendants, because describing the way the patriarchs lived their daily lives provides the essence of the spiritual life which G-d desires of man. I recall as a child being deeply impressed by stories about our great *tzaddikim*, and the heights of spirituality attained by people who lived, not in the times of the prophets or of the Talmud, but in our very own era, which taught me that these spiritual levels are not beyond reach even in our own day and age.

אַךְ מַפְסִידֵי הַחֲסִידוּת, הֵם הַטְּרָדוֹת וְהַדְּאָגוֹת. כִּי בִּהְיוֹת הַשֵּׂכֶל טָרוּד וְנֶחְפָּז בְּדַאֲגוֹתָיו וּבַעֲסָקָיו, אִי־אֶפְשָׁר לוֹ לִפְנוֹת אֶל הַהִתְבּוֹנְנוּת הַזֶּה. וּמִבְּלִי הִתְבּוֹנְנוּת לֹא יַשִּׂיג הַחֲסִידוּת. וַאֲפִילוּ אִם הִשִּׂיגוֹ כְּבָר, הִנֵּה הַטְּרָדוֹת מַבְרִיחוֹת אֶת הַשֵּׂכֶל וּמְעַרְבְּבוֹת אוֹתוֹ וְאֵינָם מַנִּיחוֹת אוֹתוֹ לְהִתְחַזֵּק בְּיִרְאָה וּבְאַהֲבָה וּבִשְׁאָר הָעִנְיָנִים הַשַּׁיָּכִים אֶל הַחֲסִידוּת כַּאֲשֶׁר זָכַרְתִּי. עַל־כֵּן אָמְרוּ ז״ל (שבת ל, ב): „אֵין הַשְּׁכִינָה שׁוֹרָה לֹא מִתּוֹךְ עַצְבוּת וכו׳ ״.

Deterrents to Chassidus are worries and preoccupation, because when the mind is preoccupied with worries, one cannot devote one's thoughts to the reflection which is vital to Chassidus. Even if one has already attained Chassidus, worries and preoccupation confuse one's thoughts and do not allow one to grow in reverence and love for G-d. This is why the Talmud says, "The Divine Presence does not reside in the midst of dejection" (Shabbos 30b).

We have already discussed the paralyzing effects of depression on both thought and action. The Baal Shem Tov and subsequent chassidic masters all emphasized the need to overcome dejection and reinforce oneself in *simchah* by strengthening one's faith and trust in G-d.

It is important to present some clinical information at this point. A person may feel dejected because of adverse circumstances in life. This dejection is in the nature of a grief reaction, and is usually a response to some adverse circumstances: loss of job, illness, financial reversal, or loss of a family member. While these feelings of sadness are indeed distressing, they are normal, not an illness, and do not require "treatment." These require support from family, compassionate friends, helpful counseling, and an increased faith and trust in the Divine benevolence and wisdom.

There is another type of depression, however, which, while resembling the grief reaction in many ways, is quite different in origin and management. There are certain chemical changes in the body that can produce depression, at all ends of the spectrum from mild dejection to severe despair. Along with the sad mood there may be sleep disturbance, loss of interest, inability to concentrate, dry mouth, constipation, loss of appetite, fatigue, and death wishes. This depressive disease may not have anything to do with adverse occurrences in the person's life, and may come out of the blue without any discernible cause. It may also follow any physical exhaustion, such as a severe virus, hepatitis, infectious mononucleosis, childbirth, miscarriage, menopause, or a surgical procedure. These conditions may have a genetic factor. If untreated, the depression may clear on its own, but since the symptoms are so severe and disabling, it is simply inhuman to allow anyone to suffer for months. The "talking cure" or traditional psychotherapy is usually of little help, and what is necessary is appropriate medication to correct the body chemistry. Fortunately, many effective medications are now available.

Whether one experiences sadness due to circumstances or whether it is the result of a chemical upset in the body, appropriate measures should be taken to relieve the depression. As Ramchal points out, depression and worry can seriously interfere with a person's spiritual progress, as well as with every other facet of his life.

כָּל־שֶׁכֵּן הַהֲנָאוֹת וְהַתַּעֲנוּגִים שֶׁהֵם הַפְּכִּיִּים מַמָּשׁ אֶל הַחֲסִידוּת, כִּי הִנֵּה הֵם מְפַתִּים הַלֵּב לִמְשֹׁךְ אַחֲרֵיהֶם וְסָר מִכָּל עִנְיְנֵי הַפְּרִישׁוּת וְהַיְדִיעָה הָאֲמִתִּית.

It goes without saying that indulgence in physical pleasures is the polar opposite of Chassidus, since these seduce a person to pursue them, and distract him from abstinence and pursuit of truth.

The Vilna Gaon said that there is not a single superfluous word in *Path of the Just*. Ramchal counted his words, and although he assumes that one should have no doubt that Abstinence and *Nekiyus* are necessary prerequisites for *Chassidus*, he nevertheless mentions it again. Why?

We have previously alluded to the capacity for a person to delude himself. A person can behave in such a manner as to convince himself that he is at a high level of spirituality. There is a simple litmus test to determine whether one is indeed there or not. Does one look forward to enjoying various physical experiences? Does it make a difference whether the food one will be served is delightful or simply edible although quite tasteless? If one is aware of a desire for and/or a response to physical pleasures, one should know that he has not yet achieved the spiritual level of *Chassidus*.

Let us remember that pursuit of *Chassidus* is not obligatory and that the highest levels of *Chassidus* are not attainable by everyone.

Therefore if a person wishes to abide by the letter of the law regulating his performance of mitzvos that is his prerogative. Nonetheless, he is to be commended for each level in which he does master, but he should not deceive himself and assume that he is at a higher level than is the case.

אָמְנָם מַה שֶׁיּוּכַל לִשְׁמוֹר אֶת הָאָדָם וּלְהַצִּילוֹ מִן הַמַּפְסִידִים הָאֵלֶּה, הוּא הַבִּטָּחוֹן, וְהוּא שֶׁיַּשְׁלִיךְ יְהָבוֹ עַל ה׳ לְגַמְרֵי, בַּאֲשֶׁר יֵדַע כִּי וַדַּאי אִי־אֶפְשָׁר שֶׁיֶּחְסַר לָאָדָם מַה שֶּׁנִּקְצַב לוֹ . . . וּכְבָר הָיָה הָאָדָם יָכוֹל לִהְיוֹת יוֹשֵׁב וּבָטֵל וְהַגְּזֵרָה הָיְתָה מִתְקַיֶּמֶת, אִם לֹא שֶׁקָּדַם הַקְּנָס לְכָל־בְּנֵי־אָדָם: ,,בְּזֵעַת אַפֶּיךָ תֹּאכַל לֶחֶם׳׳ (בראשית ג, יט) . . . אַךְ לֹא שֶׁהַהִשְׁתַּדְּלוּת הוּא הַמּוֹעִיל, אֶלָּא שֶׁהַהִשְׁתַּדְּלוּת מֻכְרָח. וְכֵיוָן שֶׁהִשְׁתַּדֵּל, הֲרֵי יָצָא יְדֵי־חוֹבָתוֹ, וּכְבָר יֵשׁ מָקוֹם לְבִרְכַּת־שָׁמַיִם שֶׁתִּשְׁרֶה עָלָיו וְאֵינוֹ צָרִיךְ לְבַלּוֹת יָמָיו בַּחֲרִיצוּת וְהִשְׁתַּדְּלוּת . . . אֶלָּא הַדֶּרֶךְ הָאֲמִתִּי הוּא דַּרְכָּם שֶׁל הַחֲסִידִים הָרִאשׁוֹנִים, עוֹשִׂים תּוֹרָתָן עִקָּר וּמְלַאכְתָּן טְפֵלָה, וְזֶה וָזֶה נִתְקַיֵּם בְּיָדָם. כִּי כֵיוָן שֶׁעָשָׂה אָדָם קְצָת מְלָאכָה, מִשָּׁם וָהָלְאָה אֵין לוֹ אֶלָּא לִבְטֹחַ בְּקוֹנוֹ וְלֹא לְהִצְטַעֵר עַל שׁוּם דָּבָר עוֹלָמִי.

The most effective protection against these deterrents is a firm, unwavering trust in G-d. A person must know that he will receive whatever was preordained for him, and that no one can take away an iota of what was destined to be his . . . Man could have lived without work if not for the penalty to Adam, "By the sweat of your brow shall you eat your bread" (Genesis 3:19) . . . Man must therefore abide by the Divine decree to earn his living, but should know that how much he earns is a Divine blessing, and is not dependent on the extent of his efforts . . . A person should therefore limit his exertion to gain profit, and devote the majority of his time to Torah and spirituality, and not be troubled by worldly matters (which are not within his control).

Ramchal is providing us with the antidote against worry. There are actually two kinds of worry, constructive and destructive. An example of constructive worry is a student who is concerned about receiving a good grade on his exam. This concern leads him to devote his time to studying for the exam and preparing himself adequately, instead of wasting it in pastimes. However, once the exam is over and he must wait for the grade, worrying about what the grade will be is futile.

All the worry in the world will not affect the grade in the least. What point is there in wasting energy on something so futile? Worrying that is futile is destructive, and it is this kind of worry that not only detracts from pursuit of *Chassidus*, but can also contribute to various diseases, such as migraine headache, peptic ulcer, high blood pressure, and coronary artery disease.

One gentleman told me that he used to suffer with insomnia, worrying all night about his business transactions. "Then I discovered that G-d never sleeps, and since He is going to be up anyway, there was no need for both of us to be up, so I went to sleep."

Ramchal's advice is simply good logic. Do not worry about things that are beyond your control. Trust G-d to take care of them.

22

בְּבֵאוּר מִדַּת הָעֲנָוָה

The Trait of Humility

הִנֵּה כְּבָר דִּבַּרְנוּ לְמַעְלָה מִגְּנוּת הַגַּאֲוָה, וּמִכְּלָלָהּ נִשְׁמַע שֶׁבַח הָעֲנָוָה. אַךְ עַתָּה נְבָאֵר יוֹתֵר עִקַּר הָעֲנָוָה וְתִתְבָּאֵר הַגַּאֲוָה מֵאֵלֶיהָ.

הִנֵּה כְּלָל הָעֲנָוָה הוּא הֱיוֹת הָאָדָם בִּלְתִּי מַחֲשִׁיב עַצְמוֹ מִשּׁוּם טַעַם שֶׁיִּהְיֶה, וְזֶה הֵפֶךְ הַגַּאֲוָה מַמָּשׁ. וְהַתּוֹלָדוֹת הַנִּמְשָׁכוֹת מִזֶּה, תִּהְיֶינָה הַהֲפָכִיּוֹת שֶׁל תּוֹלְדוֹת הַגַּאֲוָה. וּכְשֶׁנְּדַקְדֵּק, נִמְצָא שֶׁתְּלוּיָה בְּמַחֲשָׁבָה וּבְמַעֲשֶׂה. כִּי בַּתְּחִלָּה צָרִיךְ שֶׁיִּהְיֶה הָאָדָם עָנָיו בְּמַחֲשַׁבְתּוֹ, וְאַחַר־כָּךְ יִתְנַהֵג בְּדַרְכֵי הָעֲנָוִים. כִּי אִם לֹא יִהְיֶה עָנָיו בְּדַעְתּוֹ וְיִרְצֶה לִהְיוֹת עָנָיו בְּמַעֲשֶׂה, לֹא יִהְיֶה אֶלָּא מִן הָעֲנָוִים הַמְדַמִּים וְהָרָעִים שֶׁזָּכַרְנוּ לְמַעְלָה, שֶׁהֵם מִכְּלַל הַצְּבוּעִים אֲשֶׁר אֵין בָּעוֹלָם רַע מֵהֶם.

We have already discussed the repulsiveness of vanity, and from that we can infer the praiseworthiness of Humility. Let us now discuss Humility directly.

The essence of Humility is that a person should not attach importance to himself, which is the very opposite of vanity. The consequences of Humility are the opposites to those of vanity. Humility must be exercised both in thought and in deed, because acting humble without feeling humble is deceitful and hypocritical.

The trait of Humility is given the utmost importance by all our ethicists. The Talmud says "Be very, very humble" (*Ethics of the*

Fathers 4:4), and many ethicists comment that whereas Rambam states that for every trait, virtue is the mean between two extremes, Humility is an exception to the rule, and the virtue of Humility is found at one of the extreme poles; hence the Talmudic expression "Be very, very humble." It is therefore important that we understand what is meant by Humility, because it can be easily confused with feelings of inadequacy and worthlessness, which are by no means virtuous. We alluded to this in the discussion of vanity, but just as Ramchal finds it necessary to review Humility again, we will follow his direction and elaborate upon it a bit.

Bear in mind that the essence of spirituality is truth, and that deviation from truth cannot be virtuous. Hence it is essential for spirituality that a person not delude himself, because delusion is the opposite of truth. A person must therefore be aware of his talents, skills, capacities, and strengths, and knowing all his positive endowments, nevertheless be utterly humble.

A person must also have a feeling of worth. We are children of G-d, and every person bears within himself a Divine soul, which, being the breath of G-d (*Genesis* 2:7), is of G-d's essence. Hence, every person is G-dly. Furthermore, even if one has strayed from the Divine will, he does not forfeit this Divine essence within him, and the awareness of this should avoid the paralytic effect of despair, of feeling useless and worthless. I elaborated on this theme in *Let Us Make Man*, distinguishing self-esteem from vanity and Humility from unwarranted feelings of inadequacy and worthlessness. This is a crucial distinction, and here as nowhere else, the lives of our great *tzaddikim* can be a beacon of light to guide us to true Humility and avoid the pitfalls of low self-esteem.

Lives of *tzaddikim* can help us with Humility in two ways. Firstly, the more we realize the great spiritual levels they reached and their total devotion to Torah and mitzvos, the more we realize how pathetically little we have achieved. Secondly, there are many accounts of the profound humility of these great people, and if with all the enormity of their achievements they were truly humble and did not consider themselves deserving of honor and praise, we should certainly not have any claim to the latter.

The great Talmudist, Rabbi Shlomo Luria, lived above a vegetable store, whose proprietor was a G-d-fearing man, assumed to be sincere but unlearned. Rabbi Luria once awoke in the middle of the night and heard someone studying Talmud with the traditional melody. Curious, he followed the sound of the voice, and found that it was the proprietor studying Talmud in the wee hours of the morning, and as he listened, he found him to be an accomplished scholar. Rabbi Luria confronted him about this, and the man pleaded with him and extracted a promise not to expose him. Shortly before Rabbi Luria's death, he called the community leaders together and revealed the secret of the vegetable store proprietor's true abilities, instructing them to appoint him as his successor as Rabbi of Lublin. This outstanding Torah scholar had shunned the honor he richly deserved.

The renowned scholar and *kabbalist*, Rabbi Sholom Sharabi, came to Jerusalem from Yemen, and took a job as a caretaker of a *shul*, concealing his enormous erudition. When Torah classes were held, he sat quietly in a corner reciting *Psalms*, but could not help overhearing the Talmudic discussions. Once all the scholars, including their instructor, were stumped by a difficult problem in the Talmud that they were unable to resolve. Later than night, when everyone had left, and Rabbi Sholom was putting the books away, he wrote a brief note explaining the solution to the thorny problem, and inserted it in the instructor's book. This occurred several times, and no one knew who the mysterious scholar was. The instructor's daughter, curious and anxious to get to the root of the mystery, kept a close watch on the *shul*, and noted that the caretaker occasionally slipped a note into her father's volume. Only this way was Rabbi Sholom's outstanding Torah knowledge revealed.

Many of our Torah luminaries had great difficulty accepting the honors accorded to them in their position, yet could not avoid them because the authority of the position and the respect which it commanded necessitated this. They were truly distressed by the honor accorded them, as countless anecdotes testify.

The Chafetz Chaim often had students new to Radin's yeshivah sleep in his house until they were able to arrange for regular lodging. Once a student reported that one night he awoke and heard the great sage tearfully soliloquizing: "Yisroel Meir, do you deserve the honors being given to you? Have you fulfilled even one-hundredth of what a Jew is suppose to do? Why then do you deserve honor? You are but a simple person and a frightful sinner."

I was fortunate to make the acquaintance of the great Steipler Gaon, with whom I kept up a correspondence. He pleaded with me not to address him with lavish, honorary titles. "The Talmud says, 'Woe to a person who people mistakenly assume to be learned.'" This great *tzaddik*, as many other *tzaddikim*, was aware of his erudition in Torah, yet did not feel that this was grounds for being praised. In fact, he considered the praise accorded him as groundless and this caused him great distress.

הָעֲנָוָה בְּמַחֲשָׁבָה הִיא שֶׁיִּתְבּוֹנֵן הָאָדָם וְיִתְאַמֵּת אֶצְלוֹ אֲשֶׁר אֵין הַתְּהִלָּה וְהַכָּבוֹד רְאוּיִים לוֹ . . . כִּי אִי־אֶפְשָׁר לָאָדָם, בְּאֵיזֶה מַדְרֵגָה שֶׁיִּהְיֶה מִן הַשְּׁלֵמוּת, שֶׁלֹּא יִהְיוּ בוֹ חֶסְרוֹנוֹת רַבִּים . . . שֶׁ,,אָדָם אֵין צַדִּיק בָּאָרֶץ אֲשֶׁר יַעֲשֶׂה טּוֹב וְלֹא יֶחֱטָא'' (קהלת ז, כ) . . . אֲפִלּוּ יִהְיֶה בַּעַל־מַעֲלוֹת רַבּוֹת, כִּי כְּבָר עִנְיְנֵי הַחֶסְרוֹנוֹת הָאֵלֶּה יַסְפִּיקוּ לְהַחֲשִׁיכָם.

Humility in thought consists of a person reflecting upon and recognizing that he does not merit being praised and honored by others . . . There is no person without defects . . . as Solomon says, "There is no righteous person in the land that does all good and does not sin" (Ecclesiastes 7:20) . . . Regardless how many virtues a person possesses, these faults should suffice to prevent vanity.

There is a beautiful Midrash which states that when King David completed composition of his psalms, he said, "Master of the Universe! Has there ever been a creature that sang Your praises as I have done?" Just then a frog appeared and said, "David, do not be vain! The beauty of my praises to G-d far surpasses yours" (*Perek Shirah*).

This Midrash says it all. A frog is a perfect creature. It does not sin, and it fulfills whatever purpose it was created for. What human being can make this claim? The prophet says, "G-d does not trust that even the holiest will not sin" (*Job* 4:18). Man has the capacity for near-perfection, but the Talmud lists only four people in all of history who were completely without sin: Benjamin, the son of Jacob; Amram, father of Moses; Yishei, father of David; and Chilav, son of David (*Shabbos* 55b). It is noteworthy that neither the patriarchs nor Moses nor many of the other great *tzaddikim* are included in this list. If they are considered to have sinned, what shall we say?

Let us suppose that an individual thinks of himself as having rather few sins, although this is probably due to an inaccurate accounting. Would someone appear at a social event with a fine suit or dress that has several stains on it? Would we accord honor to someone who appears in public in such a garment? Our sins are stains on our persons, and since we undoubtedly have an abundance of these rather than just a few, how can we consider ourselves deserving of praise and honor?

I have often thought that the worst punishment that can be inflicted on a person on Judgment Day is to show him a video, a playback of his entire life. If he is deserving of an even greater punishment, an audience will be invited to watch it along with him. Would we not bury our heads in shame if someone were to witness a play-by-play video of our entire life? If we expect others to praise and honor us, would we expect this from them if they watched our video and knew everything about us? If we will be honest with ourselves, we will admit that the only way we can make a claim to honor and praise is that people do not know the entire truth about us. How can a person be vain if he knows that it is all based on a lie?

הִנֵּה הַחָכְמָה הִיא הַמְּבִיאָה יוֹתֵר אֶת הָאָדָם לִידֵי הִתְנַשְּׂאוּת וְגַאֲוָה, לְפִי שֶׁכְּבָר הִיא מַעֲלָה שֶׁבָּאָדָם עַצְמוֹ, בַּחֵלֶק הַנִּכְבָּד שֶׁלּוֹ דְּהַיְנוּ הַשֵּׂכֶל. וְהִנֵּה אֵין לְךָ חָכָם שֶׁלֹּא יִטְעֶה וְשֶׁלֹּא יִצְטָרֵךְ לִלְמוֹד מִדִּבְרֵי חֲבֵרָיו, וּפְעָמִים רַבּוֹת אֲפִילוּ מִדִּבְרֵי תַלְמִידָיו. אִם כֵּן, אֵפוֹא, אֵיךְ יִתְנַשֵּׂא בְּחָכְמָתוֹ? וְאָמְנָם מִי שֶׁהוּא בַּעַל שֵׂכֶל יָשָׁר, אֲפִלּוּ אִם זָכָה לִהְיוֹת חָכָם גָּדוֹל וּמֻפְלָג, בֶּאֱמֶת כְּשֶׁיִּסְתַּכֵּל וְיִתְבּוֹנֵן, יִרְאֶה שֶׁאֵין מָקוֹם לְגַאֲוָה וְהִתְנַשְּׂאוּת. כִּי הִנֵּה מִי שֶׁהוּא בַּעַל־שֵׂכֶל שֶׁיּוֹדֵעַ יוֹתֵר מֵהָאֲחֵרִים, אֵינוֹ עוֹשֶׂה אֶלָּא מַה שֶּׁבְּחֹק טִבְעוֹ לַעֲשׂוֹת, כָּעוֹף שֶׁמַּגְבִּיהַּ לָעוּף, לְפִי שֶׁטִּבְעוֹ בְּכָךְ, וְהַשּׁוֹר מוֹשֵׁךְ בְּכֹחוֹ, לְפִי שֶׁחֻקּוֹ הוּא. כֵּן מִי שֶׁהוּא חָכָם, הוּא לְפִי שֶׁטִּבְעוֹ מְבִיאוֹ לָזֶה. וְאִלּוּ אוֹתוֹ שֶׁעַכְשָׁיו אֵינוֹ חָכָם כָּמוֹהוּ הָיָה לוֹ שֵׂכֶל טִבְעִי כָּמוֹהוּ, הָיָה מִתְחַכֵּם גַּם־הוּא כָּמוֹהוּ. אִם־כֵּן, אֵין כָּאן לְהִתְנַשֵּׂא וּלְהִתְגָּאוֹת. אֶלָּא אִם יֶשׁ־בּוֹ חָכְמָה רַבָּה, הִנֵּה הוּא מְחֻיָּב לְלַמְּדָהּ לְמִי שֶׁצָּרִיךְ אֵלֶיהָ.

The factor most responsible for vanity is pride in one's intelligence, since the rational mind is the distinctive human feature. Yet, which wise man has never erred, and misused his rational mind? What grounds are there then for vanity? But even if one were extremely wise and did not err, is this any reason for vanity? Should a bird be vain because of its capacity to fly, or the ox because of his strength to pull a plow? Wisdom, like these traits, is a natural, G-d-given capacity. How can one take pride in what was given to him? Rather, one should make certain that he shares his wisdom and other talents with those in need of them. There is no place for vanity here.

In his famous letter to his son, Ramban states that one should never feel superior to others. "Those who are wiser than you, you must respect and feel humble in their presence. And if you are wiser than others, then you must realize that their mistakes can be more easily forgiven than yours, because they lack your intelligence; hence they are more virtuous than you."

The chassidic master, Rabbi Chaim of Chernovitz, asks, "The Torah states that Moses was the most humble of all men on earth (*Numbers* 12:3). How could this be? Was Moses not aware of his incomparable knowledge and prophetic powers, and that he alone of all mankind was privileged to speak directly with G-d?" Rabbi Chaim answers that Moses reasoned that his great capacities came about because he was taken up to Heaven, in the company of the heavenly angels and afforded intimate contact with the Divine presence. If other people were less spiritual than he, it was because they had not been exposed to these celestial phenomena. Had others been given his privileges, he thought, they would certainly have made better use of them and would have reached a higher level of spirituality than he.

The Talmud says, "Wherever one finds the greatness of G-d, there one also finds His humility" (*Megillah* 31a). True greatness and Humility are inseparable. Those who allow their wisdom and achievements to result in vanity are actually deficient in wisdom. Furthermore, the Talmud says that whoever is humble, G-d elevates him, but whoever is arrogant, G-d lowers him (*Eruvin* 13b).

Humility is not only a virtue, but also the key to clarity of thought. As long as there is an ego factor, one is preoccupied with oneself, and wherever there is an element of self-interest, one's thought processes are invariably influenced in that direction. It is for this reason that Rabbi Pinchas ben Yair placed Humility on the ladder of spirituality after Abstinence and *Nekiyus*, the achievement of which should eliminate self-interest, at least in the physical sphere, and allow for development of Humility, which lies primarily in the intellectual sphere. It is for this reason, the Talmud says, that in the many *halachic* disputes between the House of Hillel and the House of Shammai the decisive decision is that of Hillel, because they were more humble (*Eruvin* 13b). How does Humility affect the correctness of a *halachah*? Because a humble person, who is devoid of any ego influences, can be far more objective and have more cognizance of the truth. Indeed, the father of this school, Hillel himself, is described in the Talmud as a paragon of Humility, and likened onto Moses. It is therefore characteristic of Hillel to say, "Humility can elevate me, and vanity can depress me" (*Shemos Rabbah* 45:5).

In *Let Us Make Man* I elaborated on the distinction between vanity and self-esteem, and I alluded to this earlier in this book. I mention it here only because it was Hillel, the most humble human second only to Moses, who nevertheless said, "If I am here, all is here" (*Succah* 53a). Self-effacement and Humility are not at all incompatible with an honest self-appraisal.

As a practical example of how one's ego can be obstructive, let me quote an observation of a highly accomplished professional person who recovered from severe alcoholism. "There is no way I could have recovered by my own efforts. I know that G-d did it for me. He was always trying to do it for me, but I kept getting in His way. What the recovery program accomplished is to enable me to get out of the way so that G-d could do His thing without my obstructing Him." A humble person can recognize his achievements, but he also knows where they came from.

וְהִנֵּה דִּבַּרְנוּ עַד־הֵנָּה מֵעֲנְוַת־הַמַּחֲשָׁבָה. נְדַבֵּר עַתָּה מֵעַנְוַת־הַמַּעֲשֶׂה . . . הָאֶחָד הוּא, בְּהִתְנַהֵג בִּשְׁפְלוּת. וְזֶה רָאוּי שֶׁיִּהְיֶה: בְּדִבּוּרוֹ, בַּהֲלִיכָתוֹ, בְּשִׁבְתּוֹ, וּבְכָל תְּנוּעוֹתָיו. בְּדִבּוּרוֹ, אָמְרוּ ז״ל: (יומא פו, א) ,,לְעוֹלָם יִהְיֶה דִּבּוּרוֹ שֶׁל אָדָם בְּנַחַת עִם הַבְּרִיּוֹת.״ וּמִקְרָא מָלֵא הוּא (קהלת ט, יז): ,,דִּבְרֵי חֲכָמִים בְּנַחַת נִשְׁמָעִים.״ צָרִיךְ שֶׁיִּהְיוּ דְבָרָיו דִּבְרֵי־כָבוֹד וְלֹא דִבְרֵי־בִזָּיוֹן. וְכֵן הוּא אוֹמֵר (משלי יא, יב): ,,בָּז לְרֵעֵהוּ חֲסַר־לֵב.״

Let us now turn to Humility in conduct . . . One's speech, gait, and all one's movements should reflect Humility. The Talmud says, "A person should always speak gently" (Yoma 86a), and Solomon says, "The words of the wise, spoken gently, are accepted" (Ecclesiastes 9:17). Furthermore, one should speak respectfully, avoiding insulting language. "One who shames his friend is a heartless person" (Proverbs 11:12).

Ramchal is providing not only teachings in *Chassidus*, but also a lesson in effective communication.

One of my patients was a high-powered executive whom I treated for psychosomatic chest pain. In the course of treatment I discovered that at the office he was a tyrant, and that he would scream at his subordinates during executive meetings. I used the relaxation technique to help him subdue his outbursts, and to learn how to deliver a message in a gentle manner. I pointed out to him that the content of his message was invariably good, but that when he began shouting and berating others, they became defensive and simply tuned him out, so that his message never got across. He gradually changed his technique, and the entire atmosphere at the office underwent a marked change. One day when I called to change an appointment, his secretary said, "Whatever you are doing with him, keep on doing it. He is a different man, and a delight to work for." It is thus not only in the interest of spirituality that one should be humble in speech, but also for very self-serving reasons.

בַּהֲלִיכָתוֹ . . . וְלֹא יֵלֵךְ בְּקוֹמָה זְקוּפָה, וְלֹא בִכְבֵדוּת גָּדוֹל עָקֵב בְּצַד גֹּדֶל, אֶלָּא כְּדֶרֶךְ כָּל הוֹלֵךְ לַעֲסָקָיו. וְכֵן אָמְרוּ ז״ל (קידושין לא, א): ,,כָּל הַהוֹלֵךְ בְּקוֹמָה זְקוּפָה, כְּאִלּוּ דוֹחֵק רַגְלֵי הַשְּׁכִינָה״ . . . בְּשִׁבְתּוֹ, שֶׁיְּהֵא, מְקוֹמוֹ בֵּין הַשְּׁפָלִים, וְלֹא בֵין הָרָמִים . . . זֶה אָמְרוּ (ילקוט יחזקאל שס״א): ,,כָּל מִי שֶׁהוּא גָדוֹל בָּעוֹלָם־הַזֶּה, קָטָן בָּעוֹלָם־הַבָּא״ . . . וְאָמְרוּ (סוטה ה, א): ,,לְעוֹלָם יִלְמַד אָדָם מִדַּעַת קוֹנוֹ, שֶׁהֲרֵי הִנִּיחַ הַקָּדוֹשׁ־בָּרוּךְ־הוּא כָּל הָרִים וּגְבָעוֹת וְהִשְׁרָה שְׁכִינָתוֹ עַל הַר־סִינָי.״

One's gait should be humble, not strutting with an air of pride. Our sages have said, "One who struts with pride is as if he is pushing away the Divine Presence" (Kiddushin 31a) ... One should not seek to be seated among the notables ... The Talmud tells us that G-d taught us Humility by bringing the Divine Presence down on the lowest mountain in the Sinai range when he gave the Torah (Sotah 5a) ... One should remember, "Those who are high in this world are lowly in the World to Come" (Yalkut Ezekiel 361).

If people who strut like peacocks and try to impress others with their importance would only realize how absurd they look, and that instead of impressing others with their importance, they convey an attitude of foolishness, perhaps they would avoid such postures. The same is true of people who insist that they be given a seat with or near the dignitaries at an event. Those who arrange the seating generally say, "Don't forget that we've got to put Mr. X up front. You know how he gets if he doesn't get what he thinks he deserves. What a pompous idiot!" Since many people have at one time or another served on an arrangement committee, they may paradoxically not think too highly of those people who are always seated up front. Again, over and above *Chassidus*, Ramchal is teaching us behavior that will work to our own advantage.

הַחֵלֶק הַשֵּׁנִי הוּא סְבִילַת הָעֶלְבּוֹנוֹת. וְהִנֵּה בְּפֵרוּשׁ אָמְרוּ ז״ל (שם): ,,לְמִי נוֹשֵׂא עָוֹן, לְמִי שֶׁעוֹבֵר עַל פֶּשַׁע.״ וְאָמְרוּ עוֹד (שבת פח, ב): ,,הַנֶּעֱלָבִים וְאֵינָם עוֹלְבִים, שׁוֹמְעִים חֶרְפָּתָם וְאֵינָם מְשִׁיבִים, עֲלֵיהֶם הַכָּתוּב אוֹמֵר (שופטים ה, לא) ,,וְאוֹהֲבָיו כְּצֵאת הַשֶּׁמֶשׁ בִּגְבֻרָתוֹ.״

Humble conduct includes being able to bear an insult without responding in anger. Our sages said, "Whom does G-d forgive? Those who overlook offenses against them" (Megillah 28a). And again, "Those who are insulted and do not return the insult, of them it is said 'those who love G-d are like the sun at its greatest strength' " (Shabbos 88b).

The Talmud and the ethical writings abound with anecdotes of *tzaddikim* who bore insults in silence. This requires a great deal of restraint, and one must learn to control the impulse to strike back. But let us think a moment. If we react impulsively when provoked, how is our behavior different than that of a brute beast? Of what use is our knowledge and intelligence if it does not elevate us above the level of animal behavior?

Here again the practice of *Chassidus* is a lesson in optimal behavior. If we return an insult, we will provoke the antagonist, who in return will respond in kind, resulting in a vicious cycle. In addition, bystanders are apt to be drawn in, taking sides and resulting in a verbal if not physical melee. The antagonist will walk away feeling victimized and self-righteous.

Think of what will happen if you keep your silence. The antagonist remains with his offensive remarks, does not feel victimized, and if there are any observers, they will think poorly of him and highly of you. Not only will there not be a melee, but it is likely that after a while, the one who offended you will realize his foolishness and call to apologize.

Let us also remember that none of us are free of offenses against G-d. The Divine system of justice operates on a principle of dealing with a person according to one's own behavior. If we are quick to forgive others, we will merit that G-d will be quick to forgive us.

שִׂנְאַת הָרַבָּנוּת וּבְרִיחַת הַכָּבוֹד . . . וְאָמְרוּ (עירובין יג, ב): ,,כָּל הָרוֹדֵף אַחַר הַכָּבוֹד, הַכָּבוֹד בּוֹרֵחַ מִמֶּנּוּ״ . . . הוּא מַה שֶּׁאָמְרוּ בְּפָרָשַׁת כֹּהֵן־מָשׁוּחַ, זֶה לְשׁוֹנָם (הוריות י, א): ,,כְּמְדַמִּין

שֶׂשְּׂרָרוּת אֲנִי נוֹתֵן לָכֶם?! עַבְדוּת אֲנִי נוֹתֵן לָכֶם.״ וְאָמְרוּ עוֹד (פסחים פז, ב): ,,אוֹי לָהּ לָרַבָּנוּת שֶׁמְּקַבֶּרֶת אֶת בְּעָלֶיהָ.״

Humility includes despising positions of dominance and fleeing from honor . . . The Talmud says "Whoever pursues honor, the honor will flee from him." (Eruvin 13b) . . . and "The position of lordship is actually a position of servitude" (Horayos 10a), and "Woe unto lordship, which buries its possessors" (Pesachim 87b).

We may envy people who have achieved positions of power, but it is a foolish jealousy. Even if the glory of the position does provide one with a sense of well-being, it is really not much different than the euphoria the drug addict obtains from narcotics. The good feeling is evanescent, one constantly wants more, one is never satisfied, and the consequences are generally most unpleasant. People who pursue positions of authority must have a very low self-esteem, that they are in such desperate need to have others acknowledge them as being worthwhile. Our greatest leader, Moses, was the most humble man on earth, and it is characteristic that he struggled to avoid the mantle of leadership (*Exodus* 3:10-4:17).

The great Talmudist, Rabbi Akiva Eiger, was able to study Torah and avoid taking on a rabbinical position because he had a source of income from a dowry. All his belongings were lost in a fire, and he was compelled to accept a rabbinical appointment. He writes, "I would like to find peace, to cast off the yoke of the rabbinate and to be just an average citizen. Only G-d knows how I despise the position of authority. As soon as our children will be independent, my wife has agreed with me that I can take on a position of caretaker of a *shul* and earn my sustenance rather than being a rabbi."

If what you are looking for is peace and tranquility, do not seek to be master over others. The more people who are subordinate to you, the greater is your burden, since you carry ultimate responsibility for their actions, most of which you cannot control. I can speak of this from personal experience. My responsibilities as director of a large psychiatric service were more than enough, but when we received a federal grant to expand services and open a large community mental health center, we added a huge staff. At the close of one busy day, the hospital administrator met me and said, "You look exhausted. You should hire an assistant." My response was, "One more assistant and I quit." The less responsibility you carry for the actions of others, the happier you will be. Glory and power are indeed a lure, but they are very much like quicksand, and the Talmudic statement is absolutely true: "Woe unto lordship, for it buries those who possess it."

הַחֵלֶק הָרְבִיעִי הִיא חִלּוּק הַכָּבוֹד לְכָל אָדָם. וְכֵן שָׁנִינוּ (אבות ד, א): ,,אֵיזֶהוּ מְכֻבָּד? הַמְכַבֵּד אֶת הַבְּרִיּוֹת" . . . וְעוֹד שָׁנִינוּ (אבות ד, טו): ,,הֱוֵי מַקְדִּים בִּשְׁלוֹם כָּל אָדָם" . . . וּכְבָר סִפְּרוּ ז"ל (יבמות סב, ב) מֵעֶשְׂרִים וְאַרְבָּעָה אֶלֶף תַּלְמִידֵי רַבִּי עֲקִיבָא שֶׁמֵּתוּ, עַל שֶׁלֹּא הָיוּ נוֹהֲגִין כָּבוֹד זֶה לָזֶה . . . וְהִנֵּה וַדַּאי, שֶׁהָעֲנָוָה מְסִירָה מִדֶּרֶךְ הָאָדָם מִכְשׁוֹלוֹת רַבִּים וּמְקָרֶבֶת אוֹתוֹ אֶל טוֹבוֹת רַבּוֹת, כִּי הֶעָנָיו יָחוּשׁ מְעַט עַל דִּבְרֵי הָעוֹלָם וְלֹא יְקַנֵּא בַּהֲבָלָיו. וְעוֹד שֶׁחֶבְרַת־הֶעָנָיו נָאָה עַד־מְאֹד וְרוּחַ הַבְּרִיּוֹת נוֹחָה הֵימֶנּוּ, בְּהֶכְרֵחַ לֹא יָבוֹא לִידֵי כַּעַס וְלֹא לִידֵי מְרִיבָה אֶלָּא הַכֹּל בְּהַשְׁקֵט, הַכֹּל בִּמְנוּחָה. אַשְׁרֵי שֶׁזּוֹכֶה לְמִדָּה זוֹ.

Another aspect of Humility is being respectful to others. The Talmud says, "Who is an honorable person? One who gives honor to others" (Ethics of the Fathers 4:1) . . . "Always be the first to greet others" (ibid. 4:15) . . . We are also told that Rabbi Akiva had twenty-four thousand students who perished because they did not act respectfully to one another (Yevamos 62b) . . .

It is unquestionable that Humility removes many obstacles from a person's path in life, and brings him closer to much that is good. He is little affected by worldly affairs, and his company is enjoyable. He does not become angry nor is he drawn into arguments. Fortunate is one who has achieved this trait.

How different Torah values are from secular values! The average person undoubtedly thinks that an honorable person is one who *receives* much honor from others, whereas the Torah attitude is the reverse: It is one who *gives* honor. Similarly, the world considers a wealthy person to be one who has accumulated a great fortune, whereas the Torah attitude is that true wealth consists of being satisfied with what you have.

Ramchal cites the tragic episode of Rabbi Akiva's disciples. We commemorate this unfortunate event every year by observing various mourning practices in the weeks between Passover and Shavuos, the time period during which they died. Why this practice? To teach us that even people of great scholarship may be vulnerable to acting with lack of respect to others.

It is unfortunate that so relatively little of the lives of our sages has been preserved for posterity, but whatever we do have is precious. Rabbi Akiva Eiger, in a letter to his son who edited his manuscripts of responsa for publication, writes, "You will see among the correspondence letters from people who identify themselves as having learned in my yeshivah. *Do not refer to any of them as my students*. I have never called anyone my student, because how do I know that I have not learned more from him than he from me?"

Rabbi Yisrael of Salant, one of the greatest Torah luminaries of his generation, was always the first to greet any scholar who came to town, in spite of the accepted protocol that the guest visits the Rabbi of the city first. Rabbi Yisrael said, "In no way can I make sense of this business of who visits whom first. What is this? Some kind of childish game with rules of play?"

In his last will, Rabbi Elijah Tumim-Rabinowitz tells his children, "I always kept before my eyes the Talmudic statement 'Let your neighbor's honor be as dear to you as your own.' Also, 'Whoever knows that another person surpasses him in any one way is obligated to give that person respect.' I was therefore extremely cautious to give respect to every person, regardless of who it might be."

My grandfather, the Rabbi of Bobov, resided for a period in Tshebin, and was at a gathering with the renowned scholar Rabbi Weidenfeld, who was the local rabbi and dean of the yeshivah. My grandfather made a comment and quoted Tosafos (a commentary on the Talmud) as his source, whereupon Rabbi Weidenfeld, whose knowledge of Talmud was vast, said, "There is no such statement in *Tosafos.*" Months later, while lecturing on Talmud to his students, he came across the *Tosafos* from which my grandfather's statement could be inferred. He then exclaimed to his students, "Look at the restraint the Rabbi of Bobov exercised! He had the correct source which I had overlooked, yet did not wish to embarrass me by proving himself to be right."

Ramchal closes this chapter with a brief summary, citing the great good that can flow from the trait of Humility. Little wonder that of all the enormous virtues of Moses, the Torah cites only one: Humility. This trait assures a person the best of both worlds: peace in this world and closeness to G-d in the World to Come.

23

בְּדַרְכֵי קְנִיַּת הָעֲנָוָה
How Humility Can Be Acquired

שְׁנַיִם הֵם הַמַּרְגִּילִים אֶת הָאָדָם אֶל הָעֲנָוָה: הָרְגִילוּת וְהַהִתְבּוֹנֵן. הָרְגִילוּת הוּא, שֶׁיִּהְיֶה הָאָדָם מַרְגִּיל עַצְמוֹ מְעַט־מְעַט בְּהִתְנַהֵג בְּשִׁפְלוּת עַל הַדֶּרֶךְ שֶׁזָּכַרְנוּ: בִּישִׁיבַת הַמְּקוֹמוֹת הַפְּחוּתִים וְלָלֶכֶת בְּסוֹף הַחֶבְרָה, לִלְבּוֹשׁ בְּגָדִים צְנוּעִים, דְּהַיְנוּ מְכֻבָּדִים אַךְ לֹא מְפֹאָרִים. כִּי בְּהִתְרַגְּלוֹ בַּדֶּרֶךְ הַזֶּה, תִּכָּנֵס וְתָבוֹא הָעֲנָוָה בְּלִבּוֹ מְעַט־מְעַט עַד שֶׁתִּקָּבַע בּוֹ כָּרָאוּי. כִּי הִנֵּה בִּהְיוֹת טֶבַע לֵב הָאָדָם לָזוּחַ וּלְהִתְנַשֵּׂא, קָשֶׁה עָלָיו לַעֲקוֹר הַנְּטִיָּה הַטִּבְעִית הַזֹּאת מֵעִקָּרָהּ, אֶלָּא־אִם־כֵּן בִּפְעֻלּוֹת הַחִיצוֹנוֹת הַמְּסוּרוֹת בְּיָדוֹ, יִמְשׁוֹךְ מְעַט־מְעַט הַדָּבָר בִּפְנִימִיּוּתוֹ הַבִּלְתִּי מָסוּר לוֹ כָּל־כָּךְ.

There are two factors which lead to Humility: (1) practice and (2) reflection. Practice means that a person should gradually adopt humble conduct as was described earlier; i.e., sitting in a less prominent place, remaining toward the back of a group rather than pushing himself to the forefront, and dressing modestly. As he does this, Humility will develop within. Inasmuch as it is natural for a person to seek recognition and honor, one cannot annihilate this tendency unless one practices behavior which will impact upon his inner feelings.

Ramchal's understanding of human psychology is profound, and in this single paragraph he demonstrates that he knew more than many learned psychologists who for so long have advocated changing behavior by understanding its source. Ramchal says that such efforts are futile, because, contrary to traditional psychological teaching, we have no way of reaching into ourselves and extirpating the source. One can only begin by changing behavior, which will then bring about the desired internal change.

We have dealt with this issue earlier in this book, and pointed out that some of the more recent schools of psychology, no doubt because they observed the inefficacy of traditional psychotherapy, have taken a more behavioristic approach working from the outside-in rather than from the inside-out. In fact, it is in regard to development of the trait of Humility that Ramban begins his letter to his son with the instruction to control his rage reaction, which will then lead to Humility. Ramchal echoes this concept and states it explicitly: *Feelings are not under our control, whereas actions are.* Trying to control the uncontrollable is futile, and the only sensible approach is to change that which is amenable to change and control; i.e., action, and then allowing the action to impact on one's feelings.

אַךְ הַהִתְבּוֹנֵן הוּא עַל עִנְיָנִים שׁוֹנִים: הָאֶחָד הוּא הַמֻּזְכָּר בְּדִבְרֵי עֲקַבְיָא בֶּן־מַהֲלַלְאֵל (אבות ג, א): ,,דַּע מֵאַיִן בָּאתָ, מִטִּפָּה סְרוּחָה. וּלְאָן אַתָּה הוֹלֵךְ, לִמְקוֹם עָפָר רִמָּה וְתוֹלֵעָה. וְלִפְנֵי מִי אַתָּה עָתִיד לִתֵּן דִּין וְחֶשְׁבּוֹן, לִפְנֵי מֶלֶךְ־מַלְכֵי־הַמְּלָכִים הַקָּדוֹשׁ־בָּרוּךְ־הוּא.״

Reflection involves several considerations. (1) The statement of Akavia ben Malhallel, "Know whence you derive, from a putrid drop, where you are destined, to a wormy grave, and before whom you will have to give an account of your life, before the King of kings" (Ethics of the Fathers 3:1).

There is reason to believe that vanity is but a reaction to an intolerable feeling of worthlessness. It is only people who feel small that endeavor to be seen as big. Anyone familiar with juvenile behavior knows that a small child will climb on a chair and declare loudly, "Look, Mommy and Daddy! Look how big I am!" A child is thrilled when an adult seats him on his shoulders so that he is taller than anyone else. While adults do not engage in such behavior physically, they often do so psychologically, but the reason is the same.

As we have pointed out, one can feel "big" with a healthy self-esteem and not be vain. To the contrary, a healthy self-esteem will avoid the need for vanity. Someone who feels "big" does not have to climb on a chair or do its psychological equivalent. Healthy self-esteem consists of knowing one's value and strengths, one's inherent greatness as being the possessor of a Divine soul, as one commissioned by G-d to carry out a specific mission in the universe.

Our ethical writers point out that man is actually superior to the Heavenly angels. While angels are indeed holy, they have no option to be otherwise, because they were created as holy, pure spiritual beings. Their holiness is not something they worked for and achieved, and an angel can neither improve on his state of holiness nor advance himself in spirituality.

Man, on the other hand, is created with a great potential for holiness, having within him a Divine soul. But as we know only too well, the demands of the physical body can easily dominate the soul and degrade man to the level of being what science classifies him, *homo sapiens*, a gorilla with intellect. For man to be more than an animal with intellect, he must struggle against the powerful physical forces that pull him down, and this is a relentless battle that continues to the very day of his death. In contrast to angels, man develops his spirituality and earns his holiness by sheer effort. Again in contrast to angels, man does not have to remain in a fixed state of spirituality, but can advance infinitely.

The chassidic writers point out that whereas angels are indeed created by G-d, they are essentially objects like all other objects of creation, and it is only of man that the Torah says, "G-d blew a breath of life into him," upon which the Zohar comments that man exhales from deep within himself. Thus, the breath of life that animates man is part of G-d Himself, a matter of fact which does not apply to angels.

In the beginning of *Mesillas Yesharim*, Ramchal posited the ultimate goal of man as becoming united with G-d, which is actually a re-union, with the Divine soul returning to its source in G-d. Such a re-union is possible only for man, who has this Divine soul, and not for angels. Man is thus capable of achieving a goal that is inaccessible even to the Heavenly angels.

This is what Akavia is saying. In contrast to spiritual angels, who were created in the state of perfection, man's origin is the most humble possible, and his physical self is a nothingness which will disintegrate into its elements. Yet it is he who will be privileged to stand before the King of kings. It is man who will be called upon to give an accounting of his life, a report on the success of his mission, because it is only man who has the capacity to fulfill such a mission and to be in the immediate presence of G-d, closer to G-d than even the angels.

Man should reflect upon himself and at once become aware of both his smallness and his greatness. This self-esteem should obviate any need for defensive vanity, for figuratively climbing on a chair to show everyone how tall he is. At the same time, the awesomeness of his responsibility, that he will be standing before G-d to present an accounting of himself, should subdue any juvenile feelings of "Just look what I have done" with a request for applause. This is an excellent formula for Humility.

הַשֵּׁנִי הוּא עִנְיַן חִלּוּף תּוֹלְדוֹת הַזְּמָן וְרוֹב תְּמוּרוֹתֵיהֶם, כִּי הֶעָשִׁיר קַל לִהְיוֹת עָנִי, וְהַמּוֹשֵׁל לְעֶבֶד, וְהַמְּכֻבָּד לְנִקְלֶה, וְאִם הוּא יָכוֹל כָּל־כָּךְ עַל נְקַלָּה לָשׁוּב אֶל הַמַּצָּב הַנִּבְזֶה בְּעֵינָיו הַיּוֹם, אֵיךְ יִגְבַּהּ לִבּוֹ עַל מַצָּבוֹ אֲשֶׁר אֵינוֹ בָּטוּחַ עָלָיו? כַּמָּה מִינֵי חֳלָאִים יְכוֹלִים, חָס־וְחָלִילָה, לָבוֹא עַל הָאָדָם שֶׁיִּצְטָרֵךְ בְּמוֹ פִּיו לְהִתְחַנֵּן לְמִי שֶׁיַּעֲזוֹר אוֹתוֹ וִיסַיְּעֵהוּ וְיָקֵל לוֹ בְּמִקְצָת?! כַּמָּה צָרוֹת, חָס וְחָלִילָה, יְכוֹלִים לָבוֹא עָלָיו שֶׁיִּצְטָרֵךְ לָלֶכֶת לְשַׁחֵר פְּנֵי רַבִּים אֲשֶׁר מָאַס לִפְעָמִים לָתֵת לָהֶם שָׁלוֹם, לְמַעַן יִהְיוּ לוֹ לְמוֹשִׁיעִים?! וּדְבָרִים אֵלֶּה אֲנַחְנוּ רוֹאִים בְּעֵינֵינוּ דְּבַר־יוֹם בְּיוֹמוֹ, כְּדַאי הֵם לְהָסִיר מִלֵּב הָאָדָם גַּאֲוָתוֹ וּלְהַלְבִּישׁוֹ עֲנָוָה וְשִׁפְלוּת.

A second consideration is the changeability and unpredictability of time and circumstances. How simple it is for the wealthy to become destitute, for the ruler to become a slave, for the honored to be disgraced! How then can one be vain if his state of greatness is so precarious? How many diseases (G-d forbid) may suddenly cause one to be helpless and dependent on others! How many troubles (G-d forbid) can afflict a person so that he may have to appeal for help to people he had formerly belittled! Witnessing such happenings daily, is this not enough to rid a person of vanity and make him feel humble?

This graphic paragraph hardly needs any comment. We have all seen how the mighty have fallen, and only a fool will say, "It will never happen to me." Medically speaking, all it takes is a minute clot of blood, perhaps only one millimeter in size, to clog a crucial blood vessel to the brain, and instantaneously transform an intellectual genius into a mentally defective person and a high-powered executive into a virtual vegetable state. With such fragility, how can one possibly be vain?

וּכְשֶׁיִּתְבּוֹנֵן עוֹד הָאָדָם עַל חוֹבָתוֹ לְפָנָיו יִתְבָּרֵךְ, וְכַמָּה הִיא נֶעֱזֶבֶת מִמֶּנּוּ וְכַמָּה הוּא מִתְרַשֵׁל בָּהּ, וַדַּאי שֶׁיֵּבוֹשׁ וְלֹא יִתְגָּאֶה, יִכָּלֵם וְלֹא יָרוּם לְבָבוֹ . . . וְעַל הַכֹּל יִתְבּוֹנֵן תָּמִיד לְהַכִּיר חֻלְשַׁת־הַשֵּׂכֶל־הָאֱנוֹשִׁי וְרוֹב טָעֻיּוֹתָיו וּכְזָבָיו, שֶׁיּוֹתֵר קָרוֹב לוֹ תָּמִיד הַטָּעוּת מֵהַיְדִיעָה הָאֲמִיתִית. עַל־כֵּן יִירָא תָּמִיד מֵהַסַּכָּנָה הַזֹּאת וִיבַקֵּשׁ לִלְמוֹד תָּמִיד מִכָּל־אָדָם וְלִשְׁמוֹעַ תָּמִיד לְעֵצָה פֶּן יִכָּשֵׁל. וְהוּא מַה שֶּׁאָמְרוּ ז״ל (אבות ד, א): „אֵיזֶהוּ חָכָם, הַלּוֹמֵד מִכָּל אָדָם.״

If a person reflects on his duties in relation to G-d, how neglectful he has been and how weak he has been in his performance, he is certain to feel ashamed and not vain.... Above all, he should realize the limitations of the human mind, how vulnerable one is to errors and to falsehood, and that one is always closer to error than to truth. This should result in a constant state of concern, to be on the alert to learn from everyone and to accept advice so that one does not go astray, as the sages say, "Who is a wise person? One who learns from everyone" (Ethics of the Fathers 4:1).

In the account of creation, G-d said, "Let us make man" (*Genesis* 1:26). Rashi comments that G-d was not in need of any assistance, and that the expression "Let us" is used because He took counsel with the angels about the creation of man. Obviously, G-d is not in need of advice from anyone, and did so only to teach us that even the greatest and wisest person should not hesitate to seek advice from those of lesser status.

In medicine, patients may ask their attending physician to request the opinion of a consultant. Pompous doctors who think they are the greatest may take offense at such a request, and if they agree to a consultation, they will only call upon the chief of the department in the university or some other outstanding physician. To seek the counsel of anyone of lesser prestige is demeaning and an affront to their dignity. It does not take profound psychological insight to recognize that this is a defensive attitude, the reaction of a person who basically thinks of himself as inadequate, who feels threatened by having to ask for counsel. A physician with a healthy self-esteem will gladly confer with anyone who may have something to offer. This is what "Let us make man" teaches us. If one is truly competent, asking for counsel from others who have not equaled his level should not pose a threat.

During my first year of training as a psychiatric resident, I had the opportunity to refer a friend to an internationally famous psychiatrist.

Imagine my surprise when, several days later, I received a long distance call from this noted world authority, to discuss the case with me. I stammered, "Doctor, perhaps you are not aware that I am not a psychiatrist. I am just a beginning resident, and I have not yet learned anything about psychiatry." The noted psychiatrist responded, "Oh, yes, I know psychiatry well enough, but you have a better acquaintance of this patient than I do." We then proceeded to discuss the case, and based on the information I was able to provide him, he decided on a particular course of treatment.

Overwhelmed by this experience, I went to our director of education and said, "Guess from whom I received a request for consultation!" and went on to describe the call. The director smiled and said, "Doctor Twerski, the only person who would call a first-year resident to ask for advice on a case is the widely acclaimed world authority who wrote the book on the subject. He did not feel in the least threatened by asking your opinion."

This is just another indication that true Humility is a sign of greatness.

Ramchal's excellent advice on acquisition of Humility notwithstanding, it is germane to cite a conversation between the Baal Shem Tov and his disciples. Shortly before his death, when he bade farewell to his beloved students, they tearfully asked "How can you abandon us? Who is to be our guide and teacher?" The Baal Shem Tov answered, "In your search for a teacher, ask him what you can do to escape from the clutches of vanity. If anyone provides you with techniques and methods to do so, he is not your leader. The one who will tell you, 'Pray intensely and with desperation, just as a drowning person pleads to be saved,' he is your true leader. Man's penchant for vanity is so powerful that only G-d can help him overcome it." Let us be aware then, that just as one's efforts in any area of endeavor are necessary, but that success in any venture is the result of Divine aid, so it is with Humility. The techniques Ramchal suggests constitute the efforts we must make, but we must remember to pray fervently for Divine assistance in achieving Humility.

אַךְ מַפְסִידֵי הַמִּדָּה הַזֹּאת, הוּא הָרִבּוּי וְהַשְּׂבִיעָה בְּטוֹבוֹת הָעוֹלָם הַזֶּה. וּכְעִנְיַן הַכָּתוּב שֶׁבְּפֵרוּשׁ אוֹמֵר (דברים ח, יב): ,,פֶּן-תֹּאכַל וְשָׂבָעְתָּ וגו׳ ״. עַל-כֵּן מָצְאוּ לָהֶם הַחֲסִידִים טוֹב לִהְיוֹת הָאָדָם מְעַנֶּה נַפְשׁוֹ לִפְעָמִים, לְמַעַן הַשְׁפִּיל יֵצֶר הַגַּאֲוָה, אֲשֶׁר אֵינֶנּוּ מִתְגַּבֵּר אֶלָּא מִתּוֹךְ הָרִבּוּי. וְכָעִנְיָן שֶׁאָמְרוּ ז״ל (ברכות לב,

א): ,,אֵין אֲרִי נוֹהֵם מִתּוֹךְ קֻפָּה שֶׁל תֶּבֶן אֶלָּא מִתּוֹךְ קֻפָּה שֶׁל בָּשָׂר״.

Among deterrents to Humility is indulgence in worldly pleasures, as the Scripture admonishes us (Deuteronomy 8:12), "Beware lest you eat and be satisfied. . . (ibid. v. 14) *and you will feel yourself superior." This is the reason why some Chassidim felt that occasional fasting was beneficial, because they felt that vanity occurs only amidst abundance, as the Talmud says, "A lion does not roar over a heap of straw, but only over a heap of meat" (Berachos 32a).*

In several places, Ramchal has discouraged fasting and other practices of mortification of the flesh as being a foolish distortion of *Chassidus*. Yet, everything has its place. The criticism of fasting lay in the fact that people might assume that this ***is*** the essence of *Chassidus*, and Ramchal has gone to great pains to point out what *Chassidus* is really all about, and that it can be achieved without excessive fasting. Ironically, one who feels hungry and exhausted due to fasting might think, "Just see how much I sacrificed for G-d. I am a real *tzaddik*," and instead of resulting in *Chassidus*, this may lead to vanity, the very antithesis of *Chassidus*.

In selected cases, where one has advanced through all the steps up to and including *Chassidus*, and feels that his physical being is still demanding too much and that he must "teach it a lesson," occasional fasting may be helpful. As Ramchal has pointed out, *Chassidus* is without firm written guidelines, and it is easy to go astray and think one is doing good when the opposite is the case. Anyone contemplating fasting would do well to seek the counsel of a competent spiritual mentor, in order to avoid the pitfalls incident to self-flagellation.

עוֹד מִמַּפְסִידֵי הָעֲנָוָה הוּא הַהִתְחַבְּרוּת אוֹ הַהִשְׁתַּמֵּשׁ בִּבְנֵי־אָדָם חֲנֵפִים אֲשֶׁר לִגְנוֹב לִבּוֹ בַּחֲנֻפָּתָם, לְמַעַן יֵיטַב לָהֶם, יְשַׁבְּחוּהוּ וִירוֹמְמוּהוּ, בְּהַגְדִּיל מַה שֶׁיֶּשׁ־בּוֹ מִן הַמַּעֲלוֹת עַד הַתַּכְלִית, וּבְהוֹסִיף עָלָיו מַה שֶׁאֵין בּוֹ כְּלָל. וְלִפְעָמִים שֶׁמַּה־שֶּׁיֶּשׁ־בּוֹ, הוּא הַהֵפֶךְ מִמַּה שֶּׁמְּשַׁבְּחִין אוֹתוֹ, וְהִנֵּה סוֹף־סוֹף דַּעַת הָאָדָם קַלָּה וְטִבְעוֹ חַלָּשׁ וּמִתְפַּתֶּה בְּנָקֵל, כָּל־שֶׁכֵּן בְּדָבָר שֶׁאֵלָיו הוּא נוֹטֶה בְּטֶבַע עַל כֵּן בְּשָׁמְעוֹ אֶת הַדְּבָרִים הָאֵלֶּה יוֹצְאִים מִפִּי שֶׁהוּא מַאֲמִין לוֹ, יִכָּנְסוּ בוֹ כְּאֶרֶס וָעֶכֶס, וְנִמְצָא נוֹפֵל בְּרֶשֶׁת־הַגַּאֲוָה וְנִשְׁבָּר . . . עַל כֵּן מִי שֶׁעֵינָיו בְּרֹאשׁוֹ, יוֹתֵר יִזָּהֵר וִיעַיֵּן בְּמַעֲשֵׂי מִי שֶׁרוֹצֶה לִקְנוֹתוֹ לוֹ לְחָבֵר אוֹ לְיוֹעֵץ אוֹ לְפָקִיד עַל בֵּיתוֹ, יוֹתֵר מִמַּה

שֶׁיִּזָּהֵר וִיעַיֵּן בְּמַאֲכָלוֹ וּבְמִשְׁתָּיו, כִּי הַמַּאֲכָל וְהַמִּשְׁתֶּה יוּכַל לְהַזִּיק לְגוּפוֹ בִלְבָד, וְהַחֲבֵרִים אוֹ הַפְּקִידִים יוּכְלוּ לְהַשְׁחִית נַפְשׁוֹ וּמְאוֹדוֹ וְכָל כְּבוֹדוֹ. וְדָוִד הַמֶּלֶךְ עָלָיו הַשָּׁלוֹם אוֹמֵר (תהלים קא, ו): ,,הֹלֵךְ בְּדֶרֶךְ תָּמִים הוּא יְשָׁרְתֵנִי. לֹא יֵשֵׁב בְּקֶרֶב בֵּיתִי עֹשֵׂה רְמִיָּה״. וְאֵין טוֹב לָאָדָם אֶלָּא שֶׁיְּבַקֶּשׁ־לוֹ חֲבֵרִים תְּמִימִים שֶׁיָּאִירוּ עֵינָיו בְּמֶה שֶׁהוּא עִוֵּר בּוֹ וְיוֹכִיחוּהוּ בְּאַהֲבָתָם, וְנִמְצְאוּ מַצִּילִים אוֹתוֹ מִכָּל רָע. כִּי מַה־שֶּׁאֵין הָאָדָם יָכוֹל לִרְאוֹת לְפִי שֶׁאֵינוֹ רוֹאֶה חוֹבָה לְעַצְמוֹ, הֵם יִרְאוּ וְיָבִינוּ וְיַזְהִירוּהוּ וְנִשְׁמָר.

Another deterrent to Humility is keeping company with flatterers, who for their own self-interest may praise a person, both exaggerating his virtues and even adding some non-existing ones. The human psyche is very vulnerable and is readily seduced, and one can easily begin to believe these praises, which enter into one's system like a venom and trap one into vanity.

The wise person will therefore be cautious about whom he chooses as a friend, an advisor, or as an overseer of his affairs, using even greater vigilance than he would for someone to advise him on his food and drink, because the latter can affect only his body, whereas companions can negatively affect one's soul, might, and very honor. David said, "Only one who walks uprightly shall serve me. A deceiver will not dwell in my house" (Psalms 101:6-7). There is nothing better than sincere friends who will alert one to things which he does not see, and in their love for him rebuke him to save him from harm. A person may be blind to his own defects, which others can see and warn him so that he can be saved.

The more we read Ramchal, the more admiration we have for his psychological insights. Even people who are humble are not in a safe harbor, because the vulnerability that pride and honor may turn one's head is very great. Almost in spite of ourselves, we may wish to hear others sing our praises. The aphorism "Flattery will get you nowhere" is by no means always true. Flattery can often achieve much, and people will use it to their own advantage.

We have already noted the efforts expended by our great Torah personalities to avoid falling into the trap of vanity. Some would fold the top of the letters they received in order to avoid reading the lavish titles by which they were being addressed. Many took great pains to avoid public acclaim.

On the return from a rabbinic convention, a number of the Torah leaders were on the same train, and at each stop they were greeted by an enthusiastic throng who wished to cast their eyes on these *tzaddikim*. The Chafetz Chaim was one of the sages, and refused to go out to the platform.

Rabbi Meir Shapiro of Lublin approached the Chafetz Chaim. "Why do you not go out? The people wish to see you."

The Chafetz Chaim responded, "Why should they wish to see me? I don't have horns on my head. It is only because they are under the false impression that I am someone special, and if I go out I am confirming this delusion. This is nothing but sheer vanity."

"And what is so wrong about vanity?" Rabbi Meir asked.

The Chafetz Chaim was shocked. "Why, vanity is the worst of all sins," he said. "We will be punished eternally in hell for being vain."

Rabbi Meir then said, "But the people wish to see you. Can you not accept some punishment in hell in order to grant people the enjoyment of seeing you?"

The Chafetz Chaim was electrified, and promptly went out to the platform. The acclaim he received hurt him deeply, but he was willing to bear this distress if it gave others pleasure.

Ramchal observes that a true friend is one who will call your faults to your attention so that you can improve upon them, rather than one who flatters you. Failure to alert a person to his character defects is a gross mistake, because he may continue to unwittingly harm himself.

In my book discussing the problems of alcoholism among physicians, *It Happens to Doctors, Too* (Hazelden 1982), I included a chapter where one doctor narrates how he was hospitalized for alcoholism five times over a period of years, the last time following a serious suicide attempt. On each of his hospitalizations his colleagues tried to "help" him by covering up his alcoholism and giving him other diagnoses to "protect" his career. He says, "My friends almost killed me with their kindness." This can be true within the family as well as among friends. We may possibly risk alienating someone if we point out his defects to him, but a wise person will essentially be grateful for constructive criticism, delivered with sincere care for one's welfare.

Rabbi Zusia of Hanipoli was only one of many *tzaddikim* who hired someone to reprimand him, knowing that others might be hesitant to do so. Solomon says, "Reverence for G-d is the beginning of wisdom, but fools despise wisdom and admonition" (*Proverbs* 1:7). "One who loves rebuke is a lover of wisdom. One who hates admonition is a fool" (ibid. 12:1).

24

בְּבֵאוּר יִרְאַת חֵטְא

Fear of Sin

הִנֵּה רְאוּתֵנוּ הַמִּדָּה הַזֹּאת נִמְנֵית אַחַר כָּל הַמִּדּוֹת הַטּוֹבוֹת אֲשֶׁר זָכַרְנוּ עַד־הֵנָּה, דַּי לָנוּ לְהָעִירֵנוּ עַל עִנְיָנָהּ שֶׁרָאוּי שֶׁיִּהְיֶה וַדַּאי עִנְיָן נִכְבָּד וְעִקָּרִי מְאֹד וְקָשֶׁה לְהַשִּׂיג אוֹתוֹ, שֶׁכְּבָר לֹא יוּכַל לְהַגִּיעַ אֵלָיו אֶלָּא מִי שֶׁכְּבָר הִשִּׂיג כָּל הַמִּדּוֹת שֶׁקָּדַם זִכְרָם.

The fact that this trait (Fear of Sin) is placed in the order after all the preceding traits should alert us that it must indeed be a difficult one to attain, and one cannot reach it until one has mastered all the previous traits.

Ramchal's conclusion cannot be avoided. We might think that Fear of Sin is elementary, and indeed, was this not the topic of Watchfulness, the very first step in the ladder of spirituality? In the discussion of Watchfulness the emphasis was on the need to take all possible precautions not to inadvertently transgress Torah law. Why then does Fear of Sin appear so late in the scheme, which indicates that we must have already mastered the seven preceding traits? The answer can only be that there are degrees or variations in Fear of Sin, one which is rather primitive, and others which require much greater spiritual preparation.

אָמְנָם צָרִיךְ שֶׁנַּקְדִּים כִּי מִינֵי הַיִּרְאָה הֵם שְׁנַיִם שֶׁהֵם שְׁלֹשָׁה. הָרִאשׁוֹנָה קַלָּה מְאֹד לְהַשִּׂיגָהּ, אֵין דָּבָר קַל כָּמוֹהוּ. וְהַשְּׁנִיָּה קָשָׁה מִן הַכֹּל וּשְׁלֵמוּתָהּ כְּמוֹ־כֵן שְׁלֵמוּת גָּדוֹל מְאֹד. יֵשׁ יִרְאַת־הָעֹנֶשׁ וְזֶהוּ הַמִּין הָרִאשׁוֹן. וְיֵשׁ יִרְאַת־הָרוֹמְמוּת . . . יִרְאַת־הָעֹנֶשׁ כִּפְשׁוּטָהּ, שֶׁאָדָם יִירָא מֵעֲבוֹר אֶת פִּי ה׳ אֱלֹהָיו, מִפְּנֵי הָעֳנָשִׁים אֲשֶׁר לָעֲבֵרוֹת, אִם לַגּוּף וְאִם לַנֶּפֶשׁ. וְהִנֵּה זֹאת קַלָּה וַדַּאי, כִּי כָּל אָדָם אוֹהֵב אֶת עַצְמוֹ וְיָרֵא לְנַפְשׁוֹ, וְאֵין דָּבָר שֶׁיַּרְחִיק אוֹתוֹ מֵעֲשׂוֹת דָּבָר אֶחָד יוֹתֵר מִן הַיִּרְאָה, שֶׁלֹּא תְבוֹאֵהוּ בוֹ אֵיזֶה רָעָה. וְאֵין יִרְאָה זוֹ רְאוּיָה אֶלָּא לְעַמֵּי־הָאָרֶץ וְלַנָּשִׁים אֲשֶׁר דַּעְתָּן קַלָּה.

There are essentially two types of fear, and the second is again subdivided into two. The first type is relatively easy to attain, while the second type is quite difficult, and its perfection is of a very high order. The first type is the fear of punitive consequences resulting from sin. There is also a second type of fear, which is reverence for the Divine majesty . . .

Fear of the punitive consequences of sin means that a person is fearful of suffering harmful consequences of sin, whether they affect the body or the soul. Since every person loves himself and wishes to avoid distress, he will avoid sin because of the fear of being harmed. This is a primitive type of fear.

Seeing the world as it is today, we would be fortunate if more people would reach at least this level of primitive Fear of Sin. What we have today, and perhaps this is not a new phenomenon in history, is a population largely occupied with the pleasure of the moment, with disregard for the future. We see this in the large number of people who turn to alcohol and drugs (even legitimate drugs when they are abused) for relief of discomfort of any type. We see this in people who smoke even with the undeniable evidence of the disastrous long-term effects of smoking. We see this in people who risk their health and lives by promiscuity, and we see this in people who overeat. We see this in people who allow the violence and immorality of television into their homes, ignoring the dangerous impact this may have on their children, and we see this in the gross abuse of the environment, even in the face of the ominous warnings that our current lifestyle is threatening the future of life on earth.

The frightening thing is that there appears to be no way to turn society around. Anything that threatens to deprive people of pleasure is rejected, albeit that such action may receive lip service. Our culture appears wedded to live for the moment. I believe we would settle for the Fear of Sin which Ramchal considers primitive.

But Ramchal is writing for those who wish to live a spiritual life, rather than those who are content with being *homo sapiens*. For them, motivation that is only for avoidance of harm is just another manifestation of self-love, and for those who have as their ultimate goal in life reuniting with G-d, and who value the self only for what it can do to bring them closer to G-d, there is a totally different concept of Fear of Sin.

הַמִּין הַשֵּׁנִי הוּא יִרְאַת־הָרוֹמְמוּת, וְהוּא שֶׁהָאָדָם יִרְחַק מִן הַחֲטָאִים וְלֹא יַעֲשֵׂם מִפְּנֵי כְּבוֹדוֹ הַגָּדוֹל יִתְבָּרֵךְ שְׁמוֹ . . . וְהִנֵּה זֹאת הַיִּרְאָה אֵינָהּ כָּל־כָּךְ קַלָּה לְהַשִּׂיג אוֹתָהּ כִּי לֹא תִוָּלֵד אֶלָּא מִתּוֹךְ יְדִיעָה וְהַשְׂכָּלָה לְהִתְבּוֹנֵן עַל רוֹמְמוּתוֹ יִתְבָּרֵךְ וְעַל פְּחִיתוּתוֹ שֶׁל הָאָדָם . . . וְהִיא . . . מֵחֶלְקֵי הַחֲסִידוּת . . . יִרְאַת הַחֵטְא הִיא כְּמוֹ חֵלֶק מִיִּרְאַת־הָרוֹמְמוּת שֶׁזָּכַרְנוּ וּכְמוֹ מִין בִּפְנֵי עַצְמוֹ. וְהַיְנוּ, כִּי עִנְיָנָהּ הוּא שֶׁיִּהְיֶה הָאָדָם יָרֵא וְדוֹאֵג תָּמִיד עַל מַעֲשָׂיו . . . כִּי יִרְאַת־הָרוֹמְמוּת הוּא בִּשְׁעַת־הַמַּעֲשֶׂה, אוֹ בִּשְׁעַת־הָעֲבוֹדָה אוֹ הָעֲבֵרָה . . . אַךְ יִרְאַת־הַחֵטְא הִיא בְּכָל עֵת וּבְכָל שָׁעָה, שֶׁהִנֵּה בְּכָל רֶגַע הוּא יָרֵא פֶּן יִכָּשֵׁל וְיַעֲשֶׂה דָבָר אוֹ חֲצִי־דָבָר שֶׁיִּהְיֶה נֶגֶד כְּבוֹד שְׁמוֹ יִתְבָּרֵךְ. וְעַל־כֵּן נִקְרֵאת יִרְאַת־חֵטְא, כִּי עִקָּרָהּ – יִרְאָה מִן הַחֵטְא שֶׁלֹּא יִכָּנֵס וְיִתְעָרֵב בְּמַעֲשָׂיו מֵחֲמַת פְּשִׁיעָה וְהִתְרַשְּׁלוּת אוֹ מֵחֲמַת הֶעְלֵם, יִהְיֶה בְּאֵיזֶה־דֶרֶךְ שֶׁיִּהְיֶה . . . אַךְ חֶלְקֵי הַיִּרְאָה הַזֹּאת, שְׁנַיִם: הָאֶחָד הוּא בַּהֹוֶה אוֹ עָתִיד, וְהַשֵּׁנִי בֶּעָבָר. בַּהֹוֶה הוּא . . . וּכְמוֹ שֶׁהִזְכַּרְתִּי לְמַעְלָה. בֶּעָבָר הוּא שֶׁיִּהְיֶה הָאָדָם חוֹשֵׁב תָּמִיד עַל מַה שֶּׁכְּבָר עָשָׂה, וְיִירָא וְיִדְאַג פֶּן יָצָא מִתַּחַת יָדָיו אֵיזֶה חֵטְא בְּלֹא שֶׁיֵּדַע.

The Fear of Sin we are now addressing is the overwhelming sensation of standing before the majesty of G-d, which we had discussed as a component of Chassidus ... This is not easily attainable, because it is dependent on a profound understanding of the infinite majesty of G-d and the lowliness of man ...

The specific type of Fear of Sin (which goes beyond that discussed under Chassidus) refers to a constant concern that even a hint of impropriety may have entered one's actions

. . . Whereas the sensation of the majesty of G-d occurs either at the time one is doing a mitzvah or praying, or occurs as a deterrent when one is confronted by the possibility of sin, the Fear of Sin we are now discussing is constant. I.e., a person is always on the alert that nothing remotely related to sin should enter his behavior, and this requires a constant, unrelenting vigilance before one acts, and a reflection on one's previous actions. This is why the term "Fear of Sin" is appropriate, because one who truly fears something is constantly alert to avoid danger.

There are ways to gauge how much one understands the gravity of sin. Let us take an analogy. If a person has a minor ailment, say a cold, a muscle ache, or a slight infection, he is likely to go to his family physician, who is fully competent to treat these conditions. If he has a severe heart problem, and especially if he may require a surgical procedure on his heart, he is not likely to rely on his family physician alone, and will consult the finest cardiologist available. Why? Because when the heart is involved, even a minute error can be fatal. With many other illnesses there is much greater margin of error that is tolerable, hence one need not be so concerned, because a small mistake is not life threatening. The greater the risk, the greater are the precautions one takes.

I have used this analogy for people who bring questions about Judaism to rabbis whose familiarity with *halachah* is not of the highest order. Would they accept a similar level of competence if they were consulting a medical authority for a heart problem? Their answer is that my analogy is not valid, because the questions they bring to the rabbi are not of the same life and death magnitude. This is precisely the point I wish to make. To someone who sees Torah and mitzvos as being the very essence of life, the alpha and omega of life itself, to someone who has as his goal in life that posited by Ramchal in the opening chapter, issues in Torah observance are very much a matter of life and death, and one seeks an authoritative opinion from someone comparable in medicine to the finest heart specialist.

This can help us understand Ramchal's category of Fear of Sin. Many people maintain limited vigilance over their homes, being satisfied with locked doors and windows. Others may install a security system, with an alarm and automatic notification of police. Banks, who are at greater risk of being robbed, have security guards and surveillance cameras. Government buildings and other establishments that are possible targets for terrorist attacks have more elaborate security systems, with cameras installed on all sides of the building, and a security person constantly viewing six monitoring screens, constantly on the alert for anyone or anything that appears even remotely suspicious.

A person who has a concept of sin as being harmful, and even one who has some concept of the Divine majesty which deters him from sin, will implement various degrees of Watchfulness. The person who has developed a level of spirituality beyond *Chassidus* and Humility, has an understanding that even the minutest hint of sin can be devastating, and that it is akin to a terrorist attack. He will therefore exercise a level of constant vigilance similar to that of those who are at risk of a terrorist attack, with "surveillance cameras" and the most elaborate early warning security system. This level of Fear of Sin sees even the faintest hint of sin as being a break in one's defenses.

One of the chassidic masters, arising from the *Shabbos* table on Friday night, accidentally jarred the table causing one of the candles to fall and extinguish, whereupon he began to weep bitterly that he had caused a violation of *Shabbos*. His followers tried to console him, that this was hardly a grievous sin deserving so severe a reaction, inasmuch as he had no intention of bumping the table, let alone causing the candle to fall. The rabbi responded, "It is not this sin that bothers me. However, the Talmud says, 'Sin begets sin,' and I am worried about what great transgression this may bring in its wake."

The rabbi understood the Talmudic statement correctly. "Sin begets sin" is a fact of nature, as immutable as the law of gravity, and unless even the minutest sin is eradicated by proper *teshuvah*, there is no telling what it may lead to. It is much like preparing a patient for surgery, where precautions are taken to make the entire operative area absolutely sterile. It is not enough that millions of bacteria are removed, because a single remaining germ can reproduce and cause a life-threatening infection. Similarly, absence of sin must be absolute because, like bacteria, even a single, "weak" sin can have grave consequences.

As I have previously noted, one of my patients was an alcoholic who had experienced several relapses, and was given "one last chance" by his employer to straighten out. This finally brought home the gravity of his drinking problem, because he knew that at his age and with his poor performance record, he would hardly be hired elsewhere. He knew that the loss of the job might also terminate a fragile marriage which had been severely affected by his drinking. He appeared most sincere about doing everything to avoid another relapse. He was given a rigid recovery program to follow, and was told that even one drink could initiate a severe relapse, because that is the nature of the addictive disease. A single drink can act like a spark in a volatile explosives factory.

This patient maintained his sobriety and followed the recommended recovery regimen faithfully. About eight months later he called in a state of panic. He had been invited to a friend's wedding reception, and was offered an alcoholic drink which he refused, but he did accept a glass of punch. One sip of the punch told him that it had been "spiked" with alcohol. He promptly put the glass down and ran to call me. "What should I do? I accidentally swallowed some alcohol. I don't want to lose my job and my family! What can I do to prevent this from becoming a full-blown relapse? Should I sign myself into the hospital for a few days?"

What this man realized about alcohol is what most people do not understand about "sin begets sin," something which the chassidic master did understand. A minor infraction may be minor only on its own, but there is no telling what series of events it may set in motion that could have grave consequences.

This is the Fear of Sin which Ramchal is now discussing. A person who has reached a high level of spirituality and realizes that everything might be lost by even a single "bacterium" of sin will be on constant vigilance to prevent such an occurrence, and will constantly review past actions to determine whether such an act might not have surreptitiously occurred, which he would then try to extirpate by proper *teshuvah.*

> (Ramchal cites a number of references to great *tzaddikim* who were concerned that there might have been slight defects in their performance of mitzvos, because an inadequately performed mitzvah is also a kind of "sin.")

וְהִיא זֹאת הַיִּרְאָה הָאֲמִתִּית שֶׁאָמְרוּ עָלֶיהָ (ברכות לג, ב): ,,אֵין לוֹ לְהַקָּדוֹשׁ־בָּרוּךְ־הוּא בְּעוֹלָמוֹ אֶלָּא אוֹצָר שֶׁל יִרְאַת שָׁמַיִם בִּלְבַד'', שֶׁרַק לְמֹשֶׁה הָיָה קַל לְהַשִּׂיגָהּ מִפְּנֵי רוֹב דְּבֵקוּתוֹ בּוֹ יִתְבָּרֵךְ שְׁמוֹ, כִּי הָאֲחֵרִים וַדַּאי שֶׁהַחֹמֶר מוֹנֵעַ גָּדוֹל הוּא לָהֶם. אָמְנָם כָּל חָסִיד וְחָסִיד רָאוּי לוֹ לְהִשְׁתַּדֵּל לְהַשִּׂיג מִמֶּנָּה כָּל־מַה־שֶּׁיּוּכַל.

The Talmud says, "All that G-d has in His storage house is a treasure of fear of heaven" (Berachos 33b). This is the kind of fear to which the Talmud was referring, which was attainable easily only by Moses. Others who are deterred by their earthly needs will find this more difficult. Nevertheless, anyone who pursues Chassidus should attempt to reach whatever level possible in the area of this type of Fear of Sin.

Moses said, "What does G-d ask of you but to fear Him?" (*Deuteronomy* 10:12), on which the Talmud comments that Moses appears to be minimizing the Fear of Sin as if this were easily attainable. The Talmud answers that "by Moses it was simple" (*Berachos* 33b), which leads the commentaries to remark, "Even if it were simple for Moses, that does not mean that it would be simple for the Israelites."

One of the explanations given is that the Talmud is saying that for those who were by (near) Moses, achieving this level of Fear of Sin was simple. In other words, being in the presence of Moses, and seeing how a person who had reached the highest level of spirituality possible for a human being was nevertheless concerned about possible infractions, one would be impressed that being so far removed from this level of spirituality, one should certainly be concerned about possible transgressions.

The message here is that if we make it our business to be in the presence of *tzaddikim*, and we see how vigilant they are even though they have achieved a level of spirituality which makes the likelihood of even the minutest sin most improbable, then we will understand how much vigilance we must exercise on our lives, since we are so much more prone to sin than they are.

The Scripture says, "Let your eyes see your teacher" (*Isaiah* 30:20). While studying works of mussar and *chassidus* is certainly important, it is not a substitute for personal contact with a Torah personality, with a *tzaddik*.

A friend of mine once came to see the Steipler Gaon, and when there was no answer to his knock on the door, he gently pushed the door open. The Steipler Gaon, who was very hard of hearing, had not heard the knock. He was sitting alone in the room, without any books in his hand, swaying to and fro and mumbling to himself. Since he was clearly not praying, my friend was curious as to what he was doing, and tiptoed softly until he was close enough to hear the Gaon say to himself, "*Ani maamin*, I believe, *SheHaborei Yisborach Shemo*, that the Creator, Blessed is His Name, *Hu Yachid*, is One, etc." The Steipler Gaon was reciting the thirteen principles of faith in Hebrew, and translating them for himself into Yiddish!

This great Torah scholar, who never let a moment pass without Torah study, found it necessary to take time away from his study to reinforce his belief in G-d and in the thirteen principles of faith! Although he knew the Hebrew well, he nevertheless translated each word into Yiddish for even greater impact.

How many of us recite the thirteen principles of faith daily? How many of us feel that we need our faith reinforced daily? If one sees a *tzaddik* doing so, one can begin to realize how important it is for people of lesser spirituality to take such measures.

Lo alman Yisrael. Israel is never bereft of *tzaddikim*, and in every generation there are Torah luminaries whose lives can be an inspiration to us. We need only to look for them.

25

בְּדֶרֶךְ קְנִיַּת הַיִּרְאָה

The Acquisition of Fear of Sin

אַךְ דֶּרֶךְ קְנִיַּת הַיִּרְאָה הַזֹּאת, הוּא הַהִתְבּוֹנֵן עַל שְׁנֵי עִנְיָנִים אֲמִתִּיִּים: הָאֶחָד הוּא הֱיוֹת שְׁכִינָתוֹ יִתְבָּרֵךְ נִמְצֵאת בְּכָל מָקוֹם שֶׁבָּעוֹלָם, וְשֶׁהוּא יִתְבָּרֵךְ מַשְׁגִּיחַ עַל כָּל דָּבָר קָטֹן וְגָדוֹל . . . וְכֵיוָן שֶׁיִּתְבָּרֵר לוֹ שֶׁבְּכָל מָקוֹם שֶׁהוּא, הוּא עוֹמֵד לִפְנֵי שְׁכִינָתוֹ יִתְבָּרֵךְ, אָז מֵאֵלֶיהָ תָּבוֹא בוֹ הַיִּרְאָה וְהַפַּחַד פֶּן יִכָּשֵׁל בְּמַעֲשָׂיו שֶׁלֹּא יִהְיוּ כָּרָאוּי לְפִי רוֹמְמוּת כְּבוֹדוֹ . . . וְאָמְנָם הַדָּבָר הַזֶּה אֵינוֹ מִצְטַיֵּר הֵיטֵב בְּשֵׂכֶל הָאָדָם אֶלָּא עַל־יְדֵי הַתְמָדַת הַהִתְבּוֹנְנוּת וְהַהִסְתַּכְּלוּת הַגָּדוֹל. כִּי כֵיוָן שֶׁהַדָּבָר רָחוֹק מֵחוּשֵׁינוּ, לֹא יְצַיְּרֵהוּ הַשֵּׂכֶל אֶלָּא אַחַר רוֹב הָעִיּוּן וְהַהַשְׁקָפָה. וְגַם אַחַר שֶׁיְּצַיְּרֵהוּ יָסוּר הַצִּיּוּר מִמֶּנּוּ בְּנָקֵל אִם לֹא יַתְמִיד עָלָיו הַרְבֵּה. וְנִמְצָא, שֶׁכְּמוֹ שֶׁרוֹב הַהִתְבּוֹנֵן הוּא הַדֶּרֶךְ לִקְנוֹת הַיִּרְאָה הַתְּמִידִית, כֵּן הֶסֵּחַ־הַדַּעַת וּבִטּוּל הָעִיּוּן הוּא הַמַּפְסִיד הַגָּדוֹל שֶׁלָּהּ, יִהְיֶה מֵחֲמַת טְרָדוֹת אוֹ בְרָצוֹן. כָּל הֶסֵּחַ־הַדַּעַת בִּטּוּל הוּא לַיִּרְאָה הַתְּמִידִית. הוּא מַה־שֶּׁצִּוָּה הַקָּדוֹשׁ־בָּרוּךְ־הוּא אֶל הַמֶּלֶךְ (דברים יז, יט): „וְהָיְתָה עִמּוֹ וְקָרָא בוֹ כָּל־יְמֵי חַיָּיו לְמַעַן יִלְמַד לְיִרְאָה אֶת־ה' אֱלֹהָיו". הָא לָמַדְתָּ, שֶׁאֵין הַיִּרְאָה נִלְמֶדֶת אֶלָּא מִן הַקְּרִיאָה הַבִּלְתִּי נִפְסֶקֶת. וּתְדַקְדֵּק שֶׁאָמַר: „לְמַעַן יִלְמַד לְיִרְאָה", וְלֹא אָמַר: „לְמַעַן יִירָא", אֶלָּא לְפִי שֶׁאֵין הַיִּרְאָה הַזֹּאת מֻשֶּׂגֶת בְּטֶבַע, כִּי אַדְּרַבָּה רְחוֹקָה הִיא מִמֶּנּוּ מִפְּנֵי גַּשְׁמִיּוּת הַחוּשִׁים, וְאֵינָהּ נִקְנֵית אֶלָּא עַל־יְדֵי לִמּוּד.

This level of Fear of Sin can be acquired by keeping two truths in mind: (1) The Divine presence is everywhere and (2) G-d looks upon all things, great and small, and nothing is hidden from Him (Ramchal cites Scriptural verses attesting to this) . . .

Once a person truly realizes that he is always in the presence of G-d Who scrutinizes his every thought and action, he will be fearful lest he do something that is improper before the Divine majesty . . . However, since these truths are not evident to the senses, they require much meditation and concentration to acquire them, and continued reflection to maintain them. Distraction from reflection on these truths, whether intentional or unintentional, results in attenuation of Fear of Sin. The Scripture states, "(The king of Israel) shall read it (his personal Torah scroll) all the days of his life, so that he may learn to fear G-d" (Deuteronomy 17:19). One must learn to fear G-d, and one must pursue this learning regularly.

Earlier we cited the dialogue wherein Rabbi Bunim of Pshische said to Rabbi Mendel of Kotzk that although G-d is Omnipresent, His presence is only felt where it is invited. Deviating in any way from absolute adherence to Torah and mitzvos erects a barrier between man and G-d, and essentially "disinvites" the Divine presence.

The Talmud states, "A person does not commit a sin unless he is overtaken by a spirit of folly" (*Sotah* 3a). Rabbi Shneur Zalman explains that the *neshamah* of every Jew craves closeness to G-d, and that the only reason a person sins is because he does not realize that sin causes a distancing from and a detachment from G-d. The "spirit of folly" that allows sin to occur is the mistaken belief that one can do as one pleases yet maintain a close contact with G-d.

A person who is dependent on a supply of oxygen in order to live will take great caution that nothing impinges on the tubing which conveys the life-sustaining substance to his lungs. Only a fool would allow the tube to be obstructed on the assumption that this would not interrupt the flow of oxygen. Similarly, a person who knows that imminent contact with G-d will be lost if he sins would never allow that to occur.

A spiritual person who is wise and does not harbor foolish ideas is aware that although he is always in the Divine presence, he may lose contact with G-d if any deviation from devotion to His will occurs. Yet, there are so many distractions in daily life that one is at risk of losing this perspective. The oxygen tubing is visible and tangible; hence one can easily note if an impediment to the flow occurs. As Ramchal points out, the Divine presence is not amenable to sense perception; hence constant reflection and meditation are necessary to avoid actions that might erect a barrier between man and G-d.

The opening paragraph of *Shulchan Aruch* quotes the verse of *Psalms*, "I constantly see G-d before me" (16:8). A person is required never to lose conscious contact with G-d.

The chassidic master of Pshische was a disciple of the Seer of Lublin, and one time found the Seer to be weeping inconsolably. The Seer explained to his student, "What has become of me? How could I have fallen into such depths? There have been moments when I have lost conscious contact with G-d, something which is an elementary requirement of a Jew. What kind of creature am I that I could have forgotten G-d even for a moment?" Help me, Yaakov Yitzchak, help me."

The young master of Pshische replied, "Will my master allow me to quote a *halachah*?"

"Of course," the Seer said.

"In the Torah there is a mitzvah of abandoning a forgotten sheaf of grain to the poor. If one discovers that in taking in the harvest, he forgot a sheaf, he may not return to retrieve it and must leave it to the poor. However, the *halachah* says, if there is something so unique about a particular sheaf that the farmer would be certain to quickly remember it, the momentary lapse of memory is not considered 'forgetting,' and he is permitted to retrieve it," the young master of Pshische said. "This teaches us that a momentary loss of conscious contact where an individual is certain to return quickly to conscious contact is not considered forgetting.

"If the master's mind was momentarily occupied by something else, this does not constitute a loss of conscious contact with G-d, as the *halachah* specifies," said the young Yaakov Yitzchak.

The Seer wiped away his tears and embraced his disciple. "You have consoled me, Yaakov Yitzchak."

We can now understand why David said, "The beginning of wisdom is the fear of G-d" (*Psalms* 111:10). One might ask, Fear of G-d is obviously related to piety and religious devotion, but what is its relationship to wisdom? In the light of Rabbi Shneur Zalman's remark, we can understand that wisdom is indeed related to fear of G-d, because only one totally bereft of wisdom would assume that disobeying the Divine will will not interfere with his contact with G-d, the source of all life.

26

בְּבֵאוּר מִדַּת הַקְּדֻשָּׁה
The Trait of Holiness

עִנְיַן הַקְּדֻשָּׁה כָּפוּל הוּא, דְּהַיְנוּ, תְּחִלָּתוֹ עֲבוֹדָה וְסוֹפוֹ גְמוּל, תְּחִלָּתוֹ הִשְׁתַּדְּלוּת וְסוֹפוֹ מַתָּנָה. וְהַיְנוּ: שֶׁתְּחִלָּתוֹ הוּא מַה־שֶּׁאָדָם מְקַדֵּשׁ עַצְמוֹ, וְסוֹפוֹ מַה־שֶּׁמְּקַדְּשִׁים אוֹתוֹ. וְהוּא מַה־שֶּׁאָמְרוּ ז״ל (יומא לט, א): „אָדָם מְקַדֵּשׁ עַצְמוֹ מְעַט, מְקַדְּשִׁים אוֹתוֹ הַרְבֵּה.

Holiness is twofold. It begins with labor and ends with reward. It begins with exertion and ends with a gift. I.e., it begins with one's own efforts at becoming sanctified and ends with his being sanctified by G-d, as the Talmud says, "If a person sanctifies himself a little, G-d sanctifies him a lot" (Yoma 39a).

Earlier we cited the Baal Shem Tov's explanation to a disciple as to why the struggle for spirituality may be frustrating. The Baal Shem Tov compared it to a father who wishes to teach his infant child how to walk, and with each step the child takes, the father retreats a bit further and beckons the child to come to him. The child may indeed be frustrated that the harder he tries to reach the father, the more distant the latter becomes. The father's goal is not for the child to reach him, but rather to teach the child to ambulate independently. So it is with the struggle for spirituality. The more one tries to reach G-d, the farther G-d retreats, in order to stimulate a person to make ever-increasing efforts in spiritual growth.

But the father loves the child, and as much as the child wishes to reach the father, even more so is the father's desire to embrace the child. It is just that to do so prematurely would undermine the lessons in walking. However, there comes a point where the child has walked well enough that the father embraces the child, kisses him, and holds him close to himself. This latter closeness and embrace is effected by the father, but only after the child has made sufficient progress in walking.

Ramchal says that the same is true of Holiness. A person can proceed in his efforts to attain spirituality and Holiness, and when G-d is satisfied that he has made a maximum effort, G-d embraces the person and brings him close to Himself.

הַהִשְׁתַּדְּלוּת הוּא שֶׁיִּהְיֶה הָאָדָם נִבְדָּל וְנֶעְתָּק מִן הַחָמְרִיּוּת לְגַמְרֵי, וּמִתְדַּבֵּק תָּמִיד בְּכָל־עֵת וּבְכָל־שָׁעָה בֵּאלֹהָיו . . . וַאֲפִלּוּ בִּשְׁעַת הִתְעַסְּקוֹ בַּמַּעֲשִׂים הַגַּשְׁמִיִּים הַמֻּכְרָחִים לוֹ מִפְּאַת גּוּפוֹ, הִנֵּה לֹא תָזוּז נַפְשׁוֹ מִדְּבֵקוּתָהּ הָעֶלְיוֹן . . . וְאָמְנָם לְפִי שֶׁאִי־אֶפְשָׁר לָאָדָם שֶׁיָּשִׂים הוּא אֶת עַצְמוֹ בַּמַּצָּב הַזֶּה כִּי כָּבֵד הוּא מִמֶּנּוּ כִּי סוֹף־סוֹף חָמְרִי הוּא וּבָשָׂר־וָדָם, עַל־כֵּן אָמַרְתִּי שֶׁסּוֹף הַקְּדֻשָּׁה מַתָּנָה. כִּי מַה שֶּׁיּוּכַל־הָאָדָם לַעֲשׂוֹת, הוּא הַהִשְׁתַּדְּלוּת בִּרְדִיפַת הַיְדִיעָה הָאֲמִתִּית וְהַתְמָדַת הַהַשְׂכָּלָה בִּקְדֻשַּׁת הַמַּעֲשֶׂה. אַךְ הַסּוֹף הוּא שֶׁהַקָּדוֹשׁ־בָּרוּךְ־הוּא יַדְרִיכֵהוּ בַּדֶּרֶךְ הַזֶּה שֶׁהוּא חָפֵץ לָלֶכֶת בָּהּ וְיַשְׁרֶה עָלָיו קְדֻשָּׁתוֹ וִיקַדְּשֵׁהוּ, וְאָז יִצְלַח בְּיָדוֹ זֶה הַדָּבָר, שֶׁיּוּכַל לִהְיוֹת בַּדְּבֵקוּת הַזֶּה עִמּוֹ יִתְבָּרֵךְ בִּתְמִידוּת. כִּי מַה־שֶּׁהַטֶּבַע מוֹנֵעַ מִמֶּנּוּ, יַעְזְרֵהוּ יִתְבָּרֵךְ וְסִיּוּעוֹ יִתֵּן לוֹ.

The effort component refers to detaching oneself from earthliness and the endeavor to remain in constant contact with G-d . . . not only when one is doing mitzvos, but in all one's daily activities. Inasmuch as the human being is limited in this respect, G-d rewards him by making his effort successful in reaching the goal of Holiness. G-d only asks of man to do whatever is within his capacity. Once a person has done so, G-d completes the task for him.

The Midrash says that Moses studied the Torah diligently but kept forgetting it, until G-d gave it to him as a gift, which made it his permanent possession.

This is not at all a difficult concept to understand. There have been numerous instances where wealthy parents withheld their fortune from their children, urging them to go out and earn a living on their own.

When the children demonstrated their willingness to work, their diligence, industriousness, responsibility, and sound judgment, their parents then turned over substantial wealth to them. To have done so earlier would have resulted in the child's failure to develop constructive living habits, in which case he might have dissipated the wealth.

Torah and even Holiness, like wealth, can be foolishly dissipated. Some people who have acquired Torah knowledge without having developed spiritual traits have distorted Torah to destructive ends. Torah is intended to elevate a person spiritually and raise him above physical indulgences. Those who have distorted Torah to try and eliminate many *halachic* restrictions so that people can be more indulgent in pleasures have used Torah knowledge destructively, in an antispiritual manner. Similarly, with Holiness, as exemplified by the prophet Bilaam, who was granted prophetic foresight, yet used his powers for evil (*Numbers* 22-24). Bilaam was a moral degenerate, and without spirituality, Divine-given powers can be used destructively.

G-d therefore does not give the gift of Holiness except to those who have worked for and earned it. The Midrash states that Bilaam was an exception, to placate other nations who might have claimed, "You gave the Israelites Moses as a prophet. Had you given us a prophet, we could have become as spiritual as Israel." G-d therefore gave them a prophet in the person of Bilaam. With that exception, the Divine gift of Holiness is given only to those who have earned it by achieving spirituality through hard work.

וְהִנֵּה הָאִישׁ הַמִּתְקַדֵּשׁ בִּקְדֻשַּׁת בּוֹרְאוֹ, אֲפִלּוּ מַעֲשָׂיו הַגַּשְׁמִיִּים חוֹזְרִים לִהְיוֹת עִנְיָנֵי קְדֻשָּׁה מַמָּשׁ. וְסִימָנָךְ אֲכִילַת־קָדָשִׁים שֶׁהִיא עַצְמָהּ מִצְוַת־עֲשֵׂה, וְאָמְרוּ ז״ל (פסחים נט, ב): „כֹּהֲנִים אוֹכְלִים וּבְעָלִים מִתְכַּפְּרִים.״

וְתִרְאֶה עַתָּה הַהֶפְרֵשׁ שֶׁבֵּין הַטָּהוֹר לַקָּדוֹשׁ: הַטָּהוֹר, מַעֲשָׂיו הַחָמְרִיִּים אֵינָם לוֹ אֶלָּא עַל צַד הַהֶכְרֵחַ, וְנִמְצָא שֶׁעַל־יְדֵי זֶה יוֹצְאִים מִסּוּג הָרָע שֶׁבַּחָמְרִיּוּת וְנֶשְׁאָרִים טְהוֹרִים . . . אַךְ הַקָּדוֹשׁ הַדָּבֵק תָּמִיד לֵאלֹהָיו וְנַפְשׁוֹ מִתְהַלֶּכֶת בֵּין הַמֻּשְׂכָּלוֹת הָאֲמִתִּיּוֹת בְּאַהֲבַת בּוֹרְאוֹ וְיִרְאָתוֹ . . . הוּא עַצְמוֹ נֶחְשָׁב כְּמִשְׁכָּן . . . כֵּן הַמַּאֲכָל וְהַמִּשְׁתֶּה שֶׁהָאִישׁ הַקָּדוֹשׁ אוֹכֵל, עִלּוּי הוּא לַמַּאֲכָל הַהוּא וְלַמִּשְׁתֶּה הַהוּא, כְּאִלּוּ נִקְרַב עַל־גַּבֵּי הַמִּזְבֵּחַ מַמָּשׁ . . . הֵם מַמָּשׁ כְּמִקְדָּשׁ וּכְמִזְבֵּחַ, מִפְּנֵי שֶׁהַשְּׁכִינָה שׁוֹרָה עֲלֵיהֶם כְּמוֹ שֶׁהָיְתָה שׁוֹרָה בַּמִּקְדָּשׁ מַמָּשׁ.

Once a person achieves Holiness, all his actions become holy, similar to the kohanim (priests) who ate of the offerings in the Sanctuary, where their partaking of the offering served as an atonement (Pesachim 59b).

This, then, is the difference between the level of Nekiyus and the level of Holiness. One who has achieved Nekiyus partakes of earthly behaviors only as an essential for life, so that he can exist to serve G-d. His earthly actions are thus elevated to being a means to the Divine service . . . But for one who has achieved Holiness, earthly activities themselves are converted into mitzvos . . . The person himself becomes a Sanctuary, and his food and drink are equivalent to the offerings and libations on the Altar . . . Similarly, every action becomes part of the Divine service. The tzaddik becomes a dwelling place for the Divine presence, which resides within him as it did in the Sanctuary.

If we have difficulty in understanding this latter concept, as most of us probably do, it is because this level of spirituality is beyond anything we have experienced. It may be difficult enough to eat a meal and detach oneself totally from the pleasant taste of the food and from the feeling of satiety as one's hunger is abated and concentrate only on the fact that one is providing nutrition for the body so that it can function as a vehicle for the *neshamah* to fulfill its mission on earth. Even if we may not have personally reached that level, we can at least conceptualize such a possibility for those who have achieved total self-effacement and have dedicated their entire being to the Divine service. But how can eating and sleeping and all other mundane activities actually comprise and *be* the Divine service?

Ramchal cites the Talmud, that the eating of the offerings in the Sanctuary was in itself a mitzvah, not merely a means to a mitzvah. We have at least a counterpart, when we eat the *matzah* at the *seder*. Yet the concept that all one's actions can be mitzvos may seem strange.

Strange, perhaps, but true nevertheless. There have been great *tzaddikim* who indeed reached this level of Holiness.

When Rabbi David of Lelov visited the chassidic master, the Maggid of Koznitz, the latter remarked to his students, "Pay attention to how that young man eats. Each bite is equivalent to the eating of the offerings by the *kohanim* in the Sanctuary."

It is related that the chassidic master of Rhizin once moved a salt shaker a few inches, and that he heard a voice declaring, "Woe unto a servant who rebels against his master." The moving of the salt shaker was an act done without any purpose in the Divine service, and for this *tzaddik*, to have used even the most minutest amount of G-d-given energy for anything but the Divine service was considered an act of rebellion against G-d! Can we conceptualize such absolute perfection in a human being? Is it realistic for a mortal to essentially be an angel?

Let us look at what the Talmud says in reference to the verse in *Malachi* (2:7): "For the lips of the *kohen* observe wisdom, and Torah may be sought from his mouth, because he is an angel of G-d." The Talmud comments, "If the teacher is like an angel of G-d, one should learn Torah from him" (*Moed Katan* 17a). It is thus considered possible that a human being can indeed achieve the status of an angel.

What is an angel? A spiritual being that has no personal needs, that does only the bidding of G-d. The Talmud thus tells us, and Ramchal states, that this is achieved when one reaches the level of Holiness. It may appear impossible, but it is in fact within the reach of man.

וְאָמְנָם זֶה בִּהְיוֹת שִׂכְלוֹ וְדַעְתּוֹ קְבוּעִים תָּמִיד בִּגְדֻלָּתוֹ יִתְבָּרֵךְ וְרוֹמְמוּתוֹ וּקְדֻשָּׁתוֹ, עַד שֶׁיִּמָּצֵא כְּאִלּוּ הוּא מִתְחַבֵּר לַמַּלְאָכִים הָעֶלְיוֹנִים מַמָּשׁ עוֹדֵהוּ בָּעוֹלָם־הַזֶּה. וּכְבָר אָמַרְתִּי שֶׁאֵין הָאָדָם יָכוֹל לַעֲשׂוֹת בָּזֶה מִצִּדּוֹ, אֶלָּא לְהִתְעוֹרֵר בַּדָּבָר וּלְהִשְׁתַּדֵּל עָלָיו . . . אַךְ אַחֲרֵי הֲכִינוֹ אֶת עַצְמוֹ בְּכָל הֲכָנוֹת אֵלֶּה, אִם יַרְבֶּה לִדָּבֵק בְּתֹקֶף־הָאַהֲבָה וְעֹצֶם־הַיִּרְאָה בְּהַשְׂכָּלַת גְּדֻלָּתוֹ יִתְבָּרֵךְ וְעֹצֶם רוֹמְמוּתוֹ, יַפְרִיד עַצְמוֹ מֵעִנְיָנֵי הַחֹמֶר מְעַט מְעַט, וּבְכָל פְּעֻלּוֹתָיו וּבְכָל תְּנוּעוֹתָיו יְכַוֵּן לְבָבוֹ אֶל מַצְפּוּנֵי הַהִתְדַּבְּקוּת הָאֲמִתִּי, עַד שֶׁיֵּעָרֶה עָלָיו רוּחַ מִמָּרוֹם וְיַשְׁכִּין הַבּוֹרֵא יִתְבָּרֵךְ אֶת שְׁמוֹ עָלָיו כְּמוֹ שֶׁעוֹשֶׂה לְכָל קְדוֹשָׁיו. וְאָז יִהְיֶה כְּמַלְאַךְ ה׳ מַמָּשׁ.

One who has achieved the level of Holiness has his intellect and thought constantly and firmly in the majesty of G-d, and it is as though he is a peer to the heavenly angels even while he resides in this world ... We have already indicated that this level cannot be achieved by man's efforts alone, but that if one has mastered all the previous levels of spirituality, G-d will bestow the trait of Holiness upon him, and he will indeed be akin to a heavenly angel.

This level of spirituality might appear to be far-fetched. We may think, perhaps the patriarchs, Moses, or the prophets could have achieved this, but they lived thousands of years ago. It is not realistic for us to consider reaching this level.

This is why learning about the lives of *tzaddikim* is enlightening. Only two hundred years ago the Gaon of Vilna was a mortal, like you and I. He was once visited by his beloved sister, whom he had not seen for several years. When she entered his study, he looked up from the volume of Talmud, stood up and recited the blessing *shehechianu* for happy events, then said to her, "My dear sister, in the eternal world we will have unlimited time to converse to our heart's content. Here we must utilize every precious moment for the Divine service," and he immediately returned to his study of Torah. Is it any wonder that his disciple, Rabbi Chaim of Volozhin, referred to the Gaon as a veritable angel?

At the very same time period another mortal lived, Rabbi Elimelech of Lizensk, who fasted and did *teshuvah* because, "When I was an infant and my mother nursed me, I beat with my hands upon her breasts. The Torah forbids striking one's parent."

The Talmud says, "If the earlier generations were angels, then we are people. If the earlier generations were people, then we must be donkeys" (*Shabbos* 112b). Yes, there were mortal angels here on earth.

But we need not go back two centuries. Pick up a book that describes the life of the Steipler Gaon, whom we were fortunate to have in our generation. Or one about Rabbi Avraham Mordecai of Gur, or the Chafetz Chaim, or the Chazon Ish, and you will realize the levels of spirituality which people in our own day and age had achieved. Nothing is impossible, just somewhat difficult. If one makes the proper effort to do that which is possible, G-d will make us a gift of what appears to us to be the impossible.

וְהִנֵּה מַה שֶּׁעוֹזֵר לְהַשָּׂגַת הַמִּדָּה הַזֹּאת הוּא הַהִתְבּוֹדְדוּת וְהַפְּרִישָׁה הָרַבָּה, כְּדֵי שֶׁבְּהֶעְדֵּר הַמַּטְרִידִים תּוּכַל נַפְשׁוֹ לְהִתְגַּבֵּר יוֹתֵר וּלְהִדָּבֵק בַּבּוֹרֵא.

מַפְסִידֵי הַמִּדָּה הֵם חֶסְרוֹן הַיְדִיעוֹת הָאֲמִתִּיּוֹת וְרוֹב הַחֶבְרָה עִם בְּנֵי־הָאָדָם, כִּי הַחָמְרִיּוּת מוֹצֵא אֶת מִינוֹ וְנֵעוֹר וּמִתְחַזֵּק וְנִשְׁאֶרֶת הַנֶּפֶשׁ לְכוּדָה בוֹ וְלֹא תֵצֵא מִמַּאֲסָרָהּ.

What assists one to acquisition of Holiness is solitude and abstinence, so that with eliminating distractions, a person can strengthen his union with G-d.

Deterrents to Holiness are lack of knowledge of truth and

excessive mingling with people, because earthiness finds its counterpart and can be aroused and reinforced.

There is a concept discussed in Tanya as the "absolute *tzaddik*," one who has completely eliminated the *yetzer hara* from within himself, and is essentially beyond the vulnerability to sin. Such individuals are few and far between, and it is of these that the Talmud says, "G-d saw that there were few (such) *tzaddikim*, and He planted them throughout each generation." The Talmud goes on to indicate that there may be only one such *tzaddik* in a generation (*Yoma* 38b).

With the exception of these isolated instances of such unique individuals, even the most spiritual person has at least a remnant of the *yetzer hara* within him, although it is totally subdued and completely inactive. However, since it is there it is capable of being aroused, just as a harmless spark can be fanned into a large flame by the wind of a bellows. It is for this reason that Ramchal cautions about excessive association with people, because there was always the danger of a harmful influence from an improper companion resurrecting the dormant fragment of the *yetzer hara*.

Let us recall, however, that although Ramchal recommends solitude for attaining the highest level of spirituality, he had earlier voiced a sharp criticism of a monastic lifestyle. Solitude does not mean isolating oneself from people. Solitude is an attitude rather than a physical state of detachment from people, which is isolation.

Those of us who have spanned several decades may have a way to grasp this. We may recall sitting in the dentist's chair, in a doctor's office, or in a laboratory for tests, where no one wore masks or gloves. Today, with the prevalence of dreaded diseases that can be communicated by infected persons, and since no one has a guarantee of immunity, great precautions are taken to protect oneself from possible infection; hence the widespread use of masks, gloves, and disinfectants. I know of health providers who were so fearful of being infected that they gave up their practice, which is analogous to isolation. Those who remain in practice to provide needed services and take precautions against infection are practicing the equivalent of solitude.

וּבְעֵזֶר הָאֱלֹהִי אֲשֶׁר יִתֵּן לוֹ, תִּתְגַּבֵּר נַפְשׁוֹ בּוֹ וּתְנַצַּח אֶת הַגּוּפְנִיּוּת וְתִדְבַּק בִּקְדֻשָּׁתוֹ יִתְבָּרֵךְ וְתִשְׁלַם בּוֹ. וּמִשָּׁם יַעֲלֶה אֶל מַעֲלָה גְבוֹהָה יוֹתֵר וְהִיא הָרוּחַ־הַקֹּדֶשׁ, שֶׁכְּבָר תַּגִּיעַ הַשְׂכָּלָתוֹ לִהְיוֹת לְמַעְלָה מֵחֹק הָאֱנוֹשִׁי. וְיָכוֹל לְהַגִּיעַ דְּבֵקוּתוֹ אֶל מַעֲלָה

כָּל־כָּךְ גְּדוֹלָה, שֶׁכְּבָר יִמָּסֵר בְּיָדוֹ מַפְתֵּחַ שֶׁל תְּחִיַּת־הַמֵּתִים כְּמוֹ שֶׁנִּמְסַר לְאֵלִיָּהוּ וְלֶאֱלִישָׁע . . . הִנֵּה הַדָּבֵק בּוֹ יִתְבָּרֵךְ דְּבֵקוּת גָּמוּר, יוּכַל לִמְשׁוֹךְ מִמֶּנּוּ יִתְבָּרֵךְ אֲפִלּוּ מֶשֶׁךְ הַחַיִּים עַצְמָם . . . וְהוּא מַה־שֶּׁסִּיְּמָה הַבָּרַיְתָא: ,,וּקְדֻשָּׁה מְבִיאָה לִידֵי רוּחַ־הַקֹּדֶשׁ, וְרוּחַ־הַקֹּדֶשׁ מְבִיאָה לִידֵי תְּחִיַּת־הַמֵּתִים.''

One who has reached a level of Holiness may transcend the bounds of human nature in his understanding, and achieve a spirit of Holiness. It is even possible that he can merit G-d turning over to him the key to resurrection, as we find with the prophets Elijah and Elisha, who resurrected the dead . . . Since it is G-d who gives life to all living things, one who is totally united with G-d can draw from Him this life-giving power . . . which is why Rabbi Pinchas ben Yair concludes his spiritual ladder with "the spirit of Holiness can lead to resurrection."

While none of us anticipates rising to the level of Elijah and Elisha to resurrect the dead, what Rabbi Pinchas ben Yair is indicating by including this is that the ultimate of spirituality is a total union with G-d, whereby one can exert miraculous powers. For G-d, Who is Omnipotent, there are no miracles. It is as easy for G-d to resurrect the dead as it is for Him to sprout a plant. Indeed, one who closely studies the miraculous growth of a tree from a single seed and the development of a human being from a single cell is an observer of miracles. Because such things are commonplace, they are "natural." A miracle is but an unusual occurrence. Just a bit of analysis will show that the emergence of a human being who can see, hear, speak, touch, talk, smell, and think, whose liver does more complex chemical processes more rapidly than would a fully computerized five-story factory occupying three acres, that the development of such marvelous organs and their formation into an even more marvelous organism all from a single cell is a much greater miracle than dividing the waters of the sea. The latter was a miracle only because it is not a regular occurrence.

If we may not aspire to resurrecting the dead through achievement of spirituality, let us realize, however, that there is much within ourselves that could be resurrected. Most of us have capacities that have been dormant, both intellectual and spiritual.

In my work treating alcoholics and drug addicts, I have seen people turn their lives around in what is tantamount to resurrection. I have said in jest that getting an alcoholic/addict to recover is a far greater miracle than resurrecting the dead, because a dead person will not offer any resistance to being resurrected, whereas with the alcoholic/addict the resistance to recovery can be ferocious.

But even those of us who do not have frank addiction problems are often victims of self-defeating lifestyles, a subject with which I dealt in some length in *Life's Too Short*, and we would be wise to embark on a course of spiritual growth in order to resurrect much within ourselves that is lifeless.

וְאַתָּה קוֹרֵא נָעִים, יָדַעְתִּי שֶׁכָּמוֹנִי תֵּדַע אֲשֶׁר לֹא כִלֵּיתִי בְּסִפְרִי זֶה אֶת כָּל חֻקֵּי הַחֲסִידוּת וְלֹא אָמַרְתִּי כָּל־מַה־שֶּׁיֵּשׁ לוֹמַר בְּעִנְיָן זֶה, כִּי אֵין לַדָּבָר סוֹף וְאֵין לְהִתְבּוֹנֵן תַּכְלִית. אֲבָל אָמַרְתִּי קְצָת מִכָּל פְּרָט שֶׁבִּפְרָטֵי הַבָּרַיְתָא אֲשֶׁר עָלֶיהָ יִסַּדְתִּי חִבּוּרִי זֶה, וְהוּא מַה־שֶּׁיָּכוֹל לִהְיוֹת הַתְחָלָה וְרֵאשִׁית לְהַרְחִיב הָעִיּוּן בָּעִנְיָנִים הָהֵם, כֵּיוָן שֶׁנִּגְלָה דַּרְכָּם וְנִפְתַּח אָרְחָם לְעֵינֵינוּ לָלֶכֶת בָּם בְּדֶרֶךְ מִישׁוֹר. וְעַל כָּל כַּיּוֹצֵא בָזֶה נֶאֱמַר (משלי א, ה): „יִשְׁמַע חָכָם וְיוֹסֶף לֶקַח, וְנָבוֹן תַּחְבֻּלוֹת יִקְנֶה״ . . . וְזֶה פָּשׁוּט, כִּי כָּל־אָדָם לְפִי הָאֻמָּנוּת אֲשֶׁר בְּיָדוֹ וְהָעֵסֶק אֲשֶׁר הוּא עוֹסֵק, כָּךְ צָרִיךְ לוֹ הַיְשָׁרָה וְהַדְרָכָה. כִּי דֶרֶךְ הַחֲסִידוּת הָרָאוּי לְמִי שֶׁתּוֹרָתוֹ אֻמָּנוּתוֹ, אֵינוֹ דֶּרֶךְ הַחֲסִידוּת הָרָאוּי לְמִי שֶׁצָּרִיךְ לְהַשְׂכִּיר עַצְמוֹ לִמְלֶאכֶת חֲבֵרוֹ, וְלֹא זֶה וָזֶה דֶּרֶךְ הַחֲסִידוּת הָרָאוּי לְמִי שֶׁעוֹסֵק בִּסְחוֹרָתוֹ . . . לֹא לְפִי שֶׁהַחֲסִידוּת מִשְׁתַּנֶּה, כִּי הִנֵּה הוּא שָׁוֶה לְכָל נֶפֶשׁ הוֹאִיל וְאֵינֶנּוּ אֶלָּא לַעֲשׂוֹת מַה־שֶּׁיֵּשׁ נַחַת־רוּחַ לְיוֹצְרוֹ בּוֹ. אֲבָל הוֹאִיל וְהַנּוֹשְׂאִים מִשְׁתַּנִּים, אִי־אֶפְשָׁר שֶׁלֹּא יִשְׁתַּנּוּ גַּם הָאֶמְצָעִים הַמַּגִּיעִים אוֹתָם אֶל הַתַּכְלִית כָּל־אֶחָד לְפִי עִנְיָנוֹ. וּכְבָר יָכוֹל לִהְיוֹת חָסִיד גָּמוּר אִישׁ שֶׁמִּפְּנֵי צָרְכּוֹ הוּא בַּעַל־מְלָאכָה פְּחוּתָה, כְּמוֹ מִי אֲשֶׁר לֹא יִפְסוֹק מִפִּיו הַלִּמּוּד . . . הוּא יִתְבָּרֵךְ שְׁמוֹ בְּרַחֲמָיו יִפְקַח עֵינֵינוּ בְּתוֹרָתוֹ וְיוֹרֵנוּ דְרָכָיו וְיוֹלִיכֵנוּ בְאוֹרְחוֹתָיו וְנִזְכֶּה לָתֵת כָּבוֹד לִשְׁמוֹ וְלַעֲשׂוֹת נַחַת־רוּחַ לְפָנָיו.

יְהִי כְבוֹד ה׳ לְעוֹלָם, יִשְׂמַח ה׳ בְּמַעֲשָׂיו (תהלים קד, לא). יִשְׂמַח יִשְׂרָאֵל בְּעֹשָׂיו, בְּנֵי־צִיּוֹן יָגִילוּ בְמַלְכָּם (שם קמט, ב).

אָמֵן אָמֵן אָמֵן.

My dear reader, you know as well as I that I have not exhausted all there is to say about Chassidus, because it is virtually endless. I have only said a little about each of the steps of Rabbi Pinchas ben Yair on which I have based this book, to serve as a beginning. Solomon says, "A wise person will listen and add to his wisdom (Proverbs 1:5), and it is upon the individual to make a broader study of the subject . . .

It is clear that every person must guide himself according to the activities in which he is engaged. The paths may vary for someone who is a full-time Torah scholar, for one who does hired labor, and for a merchant . . . It is not that Chassidus varies, since the goal of doing what pleases G-d is equal for all. But the means of achieving this goal may vary. A person with a humble trade may be as complete a Chassid as one who is constantly studying the Torah.

May G-d open our eyes in His Torah and direct and guide us in His paths, that we may merit bringing honor to His name. "The glory of G-d will endure forever. G-d will rejoice with His works" (Psalms 104:31).

"Let Israel exult in its Maker, let the Children of Zion rejoice in their King" (ibid. 149:2).

Amen, Amen, Amen

There is an amazing phenomenon in world history, in that several people, working independently and with no communication, come upon the same idea at just about the same time. There are numerous incidents in both science and philosophy where this has happened.

Ramchal (1707-1747) and the Baal Shem Tov (1698-1760) were contemporaries. Ramchal lived in Italy and later in Amsterdam, while the Baal Shem Tov was located in the Ukraine. There is no reason to assume that the two were ever in touch, yet they both came upon the same revolutionary concept. It is of interest that they shared other similarities, and that both had deep involvement in *kabballah,* and both were victims of persecution and condemnation by the established authorities.

The revolutionary idea is mentioned in the closing sentences of the book. "A person with a humble trade may be as complete a *Chassid* as one who is constantly studying the Torah."

Both Ramchal and the Baal Shem Tov glorify the common man. A person who did not have the opportunity to become a scholar, but who devotes himself sincerely to the Divine service, may reach a level of spirituality equivalent to that of a learned scholar.

Both Ramchal and the Baal Shem Tov emphasize the importance of the study of Torah. The question was, What is the value of someone who through no fault of his own did not become a scholar? In the poverty-stricken villages, where Jews lived under ruthless despots who controlled their lives and could decree their death, many young children grew up with no more than the ability to read Hebrew. If the value of a person depended on one's Torah knowledge, then these people were not only oppressed, but were left without a *raison d'etre.*

To these oppressed people, the message of Ramchal and the Baal Shem Tov was a breath of life. They gave meaning to everyone's life and made possible joy amidst suffering.

Since we know that G-d rejoices only when His children are happy, the first verse of *Psalms* that Ramchal chose wherewith to close his work is most significant: "The glory of G-d will endure forever. G-d will rejoice with His works."